The Model-Based Archaeology of Socionatural Systems

SAR Press gratefully acknowledges the support from the Santa Fe Institute, the National Science Foundation, the James S. McDonnell Foundation, and the School of Human Evolution and Social Change, Arizona State University, that made this publication possible.

School for Advanced Research
Resident Scholar Series

James F. Brooks
General Editor

The Model-Based Archaeology of Socionatural Systems

Contributors

Mark Altaweel
Decision and Information Sciences Division, Argonne National Laboratory, Argonne, Illinois

John M. Anderies
School of Human Evolution and Social Change and Global Institute of Sustainability, Arizona State University, Tempe

Jean-François Berger
Centre d'Études Préhistoire, Antiquité, Moyen Age, University of Nice, France

Oliver A. Chadwick
Department of Geography, University of California, Santa Barbara

Jung-Kyoo Choi
School of Economics and Trade, Kyungpook National University, Buk-gu Daegu, Korea

John H. Christiansen
Decision and Information Sciences Division, Argonne National Laboratory, Argonne, Illinois

Serge Cleuziou
Institut d'Histoire d'Art et Archéologie, University of Paris I (Panthéon-Sorbonne)

Jason Cowan
Department of Anthropology, Washington State University, Pullman

McGuire Gibson
Oriental Institute, University of Chicago

Michael Graves
Department of Anthropology, University of Hawaii, Honolulu

Sara Hotchkiss
Department of Botany, University of Wisconsin, Madison

Carrie Hritz
Department of Anthropology, Washington University, St. Louis, Missouri

Marco A. Janssen
School of Human Evolution and Social Change, Department of Computer Science and Engineering, Arizona State University, Tempe

C. David Johnson
Department of Anthropology, Washington State University, Pullman

Peter Jordan
Department of Archaeology, University of Sheffield; Arts and Humanities Research Council (AHRC) Centre for the Evolution of Cultural Diversity (CECD), Institute of Archaeology, University College London

Patrick V. Kirch
Department of Anthropology, University of California, Berkeley

Ziad Kobti
School of Computer Science, University of Windsor, Ontario, Canada

Timothy A. Kohler
Department of Anthropology, Washington State University, Pullman; Santa Fe Institute, Santa Fe, New Mexico; Crow Canyon Archaeological Center, Cortez, Colorado

Kenneth Kolm
Department of Anthropology, Washington State University, Pullman; BBL, Inc., Golden, Colorado

Nicholas Kouchoukos
Department of Anthropology, University of Chicago

Thegn Ladefoged
Department of Anthropology, University of Auckland, New Zealand

Jacob Lauinger
Department of Near Eastern Languages and Civilizations, University of Chicago

Laure Nuninger
Laboratoire de Chrono-Écologie et l'Institut des Sciences et Technologies de l'Information, Université de Franche-Comté, Besançon, France

Scott Ortman
Crow Canyon Archaeological Center, Cortez, Colorado

Tate Paulette
Department of Near Eastern Languages and Civilizations, University of Chicago

Robert Reynolds
Department of Computer Science, Wayne State University, Detroit, Michigan

John Sanders
Oriental Institute, University of Chicago

David Schloen
Oriental Institute, University of Chicago

Stephen Shennan
AHRC Centre for the Evolutionary Analysis of Cultural Behavior and Institute of Archaeology, London

Kathy-Lee Simunich
Decision and Information Sciences Division, Argonne National Laboratory, Argonne, Illinois

Eric Alden Smith
Department of Anthropology, University of Washington, Seattle

Schaun Smith
TSC Group, Arvada, Colorado

Jonathan Tenney
Department of Near Eastern Languages and Civilizations, University of Chicago

Shripad Tuljapurkar
Department of Biology, Stanford University, Palo Alto, California

Jason A. Ur
Department of Anthropology, Harvard University, Cambridge, Massachusetts

Sander E. van der Leeuw
School of Human Evolution and Social Change, Arizona State University, Tempe; Santa Fe Institute, Santa Fe, New Mexico

Mark Varien
Crow Canyon Archaeological Center, Cortez, Colorado

Peter Vitousek
Department of Biology, Stanford University, Palo Alto, California

Magnus Widell
Oriental Institute, University of Chicago

Tony J. Wilkinson
Department of Archaeology, Durham University, United Kingdom

Christopher Woods
Oriental Institute, University of Chicago

Henry T. Wright
Santa Fe Institute, Santa Fe, New Mexico; Museum of Anthropology, University of Michigan, Ann Arbor

Lorene Yap
Department of Anthropology, Washington State University, Pullman

The Model-Based Archaeology
of Socionatural Systems

Edited by Timothy A. Kohler and Sander E. van der Leeuw

A School for Advanced Research Resident Scholar Book

Santa Fe

School for Advanced Research Press
Post Office Box 2188
Santa Fe, New Mexico 87504-2188
www.sarpress.org

Co-Director and Executive Editor: Catherine Cocks
Manuscript Editor: Kate Whelan
Design and Production: Cynthia Dyer
Proofreader: Sarah Soliz
Indexer: Catherine Fox

Library of Congress Cataloging-in-Publication Data:
The model-based archaeology of socionatural systems / edited by Timothy
A. Kohler and Sander van der Leeuw.
    p. cm.
 "A School for Advanced Research resident scholar book."
 Includes bibliographical references and index.
 ISBN 1-930618-87-5 (pa : alk. paper)
 1. Social archaeology. 2. Ethnoarchaeology. 3. Human ecology—History. 4. Archaeology—Computer
simulation. 5. Archaeology—Methodology. I. Kohler, Timothy A. II. Leeuw, Sander Ernst van der.

CC72.4.M63 2007
930.1—dc22

Library of Congress Catalog Card Number
International Standard Book Number 978-1-930618-87-9 (paper). Fourth printing 2021.

Cover illustration © School for Advanced Research by Cynthia Dyer from Signature Series 47: Time &
Technology by Photodisc © Getty Images, and bitumen fragments from small storeroom at Ra's al-Jinz,
photograph courtesy Serge Cleuziou.

Contents

List of Figures

List of Tables

Plates

CHAPTER 1

Introduction
Historical Socionatural Systems and Models

Timothy A. Kohler and Sander E. van der Leeuw

How should archaeologists and other social scientists tackle the big and little questions of change in socionatural systems? Most nonpractitioners think that the answer is obvious—fieldwork! That is certainly the place to start, and we know very few archaeologists who were not first drawn to their profession because of a love of fieldwork and discovery.

Still, it does not take long before we realize that the things we discover, in and of themselves, are not immediately helpful in answering the questions that usually intrigue us most—those involving explanations for change. This realization might start with little questions: why is one raw material for making stone tools prevalent at this site, while right next door, another was more important? But before long, bigger questions surface: how and why do humans cooperate so successfully in large, unrelated groups, and how and why do human societies move from egalitarian to more hierarchical organizations?

Every time we ask one of these troublesome "how" or "why" questions, we build a model to try to answer it. This model may be very informal and even a little vague ("maybe the best source of stone was depleted, and later people had to settle for second best"). Thinking out loud about the possibilities shows that to understand anything, we make a mental model of it: a model here is just a candidate explanation. This is the first meaning of our title: in this volume are presented many models for how societies work and how they change. These models are partial, provisional, and subject to elaboration and revision.

Cognitive scientists have a view of models that explains their foundational character in our thought processes. We operate in the world, in their view, by constantly making representations of it. Cognitive scientists do not completely agree on the nature of those representations or on how they are constructed and retained; indeed, it seems likely that our minds use several methods to represent knowledge (Markman 1999:277–300). These mental representations, or models, are quite often incomplete, not infrequently wrong, and almost always qualitative (Markman 1999:248–76).

Beginning no later than the early Upper Paleolithic with artifacts such as the Blanchard Plaque (which seems to provide simultaneously a calendric calculator and a kind of topographic model for the placement on the horizon of the moon at sunset as it waxes and wanes through two-and-a-quarter months [Marshack 1985]), we humans have increasingly turned to tangible external models to supplement the operation of our cognition and to store and share the fruits of those cognitive labors. The creativity with which this can be done, even within the limited domain of graphic models, is wonderful (for example, Tufte 1990). This book is about new developments in applying dynamic models for understanding relatively small-scale human systems that are deeply embedded within, and studied as a part of, the environments they inhabit and alter.

Rethinking Archaeology as a Model-Based Science

But underlying this is a subtext. Taken together, the chapters in this volume constitute an argument for a new way of thinking about how archaeology is (and should be) conducted. Most archaeologists of a certain age will remember the call to re-create archaeology as a logical positivist or logical empiricist science (for example, Watson, LeBlanc, and Redman 1971), with its hope that generalizations, or "covering laws," could be found that would explain those phenomena that could be subsumed under them, with other trial explanations rejected in a Popperian fashion:

> If we agree that explanation means subsumption of the particular events and processes [to be explained] under appropriate general or covering laws, then we must agree on the source of these laws. Do the necessary confirmed laws already exist, or must we formulate and test them? If the former, what are they? If the latter, how do we go about it? Can we use the archaeological record to help us formulate and to test hypothetical laws about particular events in human prehistory and processual aspects of human behavior, and about major aspects of culture and cultural processes? Yes, of course, to the extent that archaeology is pursued as a science.... Logically speaking...scientific archaeology is a viable discipline whose practitioners are primarily con-

cerned with explanation of past events and processes, and also with the use of those particular events and processes to help formulate and test culture processual laws. (Watson, LeBlanc, and Redman 1971:171–72)

Progress in cumulating these laws, however, has been slow at best, as even advocates admit (for example, LaMotta and Schiffer 2001:47; for a demographer's perspective, see Burch 2006). Already in the 1970s this project seems to have been honored most frequently in the breach. Instead, we believe that archaeologists—especially those committed to explanation—have drifted *in practice* towards what philosophers of science call a "model-based" (Giere 1999) or "semantic" (Lloyd 1988; Suppe 1977b:221–30) approach to the task of explaining what happened, and why, in prehistory, and away from variants of either covering-law models or broader hypotheticodeductive, positivist approaches in the tradition advocated by many New Archaeologists.[1]

As described by Suppe for science more generally, when a new theory is undergoing development and is widely believed to be inadequate in some respects (which we take to be an accurate description of existing theory in archaeology), trying either to refute or confirm it is pointless:

> What *is* to the point is to use observation and experiment to discover shortcomings in the theory, to determine how to improve the theory, and to discover how to eliminate known artificialities, distortions, oversimplifications, and errors in the descriptions, explanations, and predictions of reality that theory affords.... Except in primitive sciences...one finds little concern with refutation or inductive confirmations of theories in actual scientific practice. Rather the focus is on the use of reason, observation, and experiment to develop a promising theory. (Suppe 1977a:706–07)

In what respects, then, does a model-based archaeology (we offer the uncapitalized acronym *mba* to emphasize the pluralism of this approach) differ from the scientific approaches to archaeology offered by the New Archaeologists? A critical difference is that, in mba, models are not true or false in the manner of hypotheses, though to be useful, they must be clear and internally consistent. A good model is not a universal scientific truth but fits some portion of the real world reasonably well, in certain respects and for some specific purpose (Burch 2006; Giere 1999:5–6, 73). Degree of fit is determined through empirical research, but a model that does not fit one case may be useful for another—as opposed to a candidate generalization or covering law that can be fully discredited by one contrary observation. The recognition that a model might be useful for one *purpose* but not for another recalls Hodder's (2001:5) observation that archaeological theories are always "of something" rather than completely general.

What is a model, in the approach we favor? It is an imaginary system, represented in language, mathematics, computer code, or some other symbolic medium, that has useful similarities to aspects of a target system in the real world. It is often highly simplified, omitting details that are thought to be noncritical to the aspects of the target system being explored. It might be viewed as an abstraction, a simplification, an idealization, or a conceptual device.

Why not try to understand a target system directly, without the use of models? Cognitive scientists would argue that this is impossible: we always interpose models between the real world and ourselves in any attempt to understand the world. Those who believe that they are following a nonmodel strategy have simply not made their models explicit.

If that is the case, then why not try to build an abstract model of a target system directly, rather than interpose some model possibly first constructed for some other use? The mba approach offers the possibility of making progress on two fronts simultaneously: the advancement of theory (How well and in what respects does this model fit this situation? How could the fit be improved?) and the application of theory (Is this target system a member of the class of systems described by this model? If not, why not?). It legitimizes development of toolkits of models that might be useful for different purposes (for example, to explain processes as viewed at various spatial and temporal scales). Model-based archaeology need not be limited to theories with measurable parameters, although it is true that theories with nonmeasurable parameters cannot be viewed as structures within phase spaces having configurations "imposed on them by the laws of the theory" (Suppe 1977b:227)—a foundational definition of theory in semantic approaches. Above all, the mba approach encourages a sense of flexibility in model choice and in joint exploration of the model and its target system, which is in contrast to the more rigid prescriptions of the covering-law model yet is more guided, disciplined, and theory-driven than simple exploratory data analysis.

This, then, is the second meaning of our title; we recognize what we are doing in this volume as a model-based approach to archaeology. Here, we use *model-based* to mean a way of doing science, which, in our case, involves use of specific, generally quantitative models that provide partial descriptions of socionatural systems of interest that are then examined against those systems.

Whether the reader agrees with us that this model-based view of science describes how archaeology *should be* conducted, within the past forty years models clearly have received much attention in archaeology. This is, in part, due to the fact that they promise to help us do things we have difficulty doing with our brains, for example, representing complex sets of interacting dynamics and "exercising" them by watching how they play out through time. This interest was triggered in the 1960s and 1970s by the introduction of computers that seemed able to extend our capacity to deal with such complex dynamics, coupled with a sense that the principles of general systems theory might be useful for understanding processes of change (for example, Flannery 1968). We soon found out, however, that these computers could not help us much in cases in which the dynamics are really complex. Moreover, many archaeologists (and commentators on archaeology, such as Salmon [1978:181]) began to suspect that the "systems" that archaeologists deal with are "too complex" to yield to these techniques.

Dealing with Complexity

After a lull, we now (since 1995) seem to have access to sufficiently powerful computers and to sufficiently sophisticated software to have another go at it. But more importantly, we have at our disposal a theoretical approach that differs in many ways from the relatively simplistic systems models of the 1970s. McGlade and van der Leeuw (1997) argue the relevance of these new ideas for archaeology. Contrary to earlier systems approaches, this "complex systems" approach acknowledges that all systems, including social ones, are in open interaction with their environment, exchanging matter and energy with it. Moreover, such system dynamics are now considered to be nonlinear, multiscalar, and irreversible, in the sense that they exhibit path dependence or history. The following chapters, we believe, show that the implications of this reconceptualization of systems dynamics are profound and far-reaching.

While definitions for complex systems, and for complexity itself, are elusive, we are satisfied to follow Boccara (2004), who suggests that such systems exhibit at least the following common characteristics:

1. They consist of large numbers of interacting agents.

2. They exhibit *emergence*; that is, a self-organizing, collective behavior difficult to anticipate from knowledge of the agents' behavior.

3. Their emergent behavior does not result from the existence of a central controller. (Boccara 2004:3)

We argue that the approach constructed on this basis does contribute significantly to a better understanding of (1) the dynamics responsible for long-term human (social and biological) evolution and (2) the ways human biological and social evolution have slowly transformed our environment and made it, in many cases, dependent on its interaction with society. We base this claim on the fact that the "complexity perspective" has shown itself to be capable of the following:

- Conceptualizing problems in both natural and social dynamics in a language independent of specific disciplines. Concepts used for genetic networks (Kauffman 1993), for example, have been shown to apply helpfully to networks of economic exchange in small-scale societies (Kohler, Van Pelt, and Yap 2000).

- Conceptualizing the interaction between phenomena at different spatiotemporal scales by viewing large, stable phenomena as the result of unstable interactions between smaller entities.

- Reformulating natural dynamics from an irreversible temporal perspective by introducing the notion that similar causes can have different results and different causes, similar results. A typical strategy is to characterize the various possible outcomes of a set of interacting processes in terms of their probabilities in the space of the parameters examined and in terms of their stability under perturbation (Skyrms 1996).

- Rethinking issues of cause and effect in the social sciences, in which a common research tactic has been the evaluation of causal hypotheses with statistical analysis of data on system behavior. In the nonlinear dynamics that are apparently so pervasive in nature, however, the effect of a change in a state variable depends to a very great extent on the state of the entire system at that moment (Wagner 1999).

- Describing in one approach both continuity and change, tradition and innovation, by relating the one to the other and thus moving away from our traditional emphasis on stability and our focus on investigating change. This is seen, for example, in the emphasis on the trajectories of systems in complexity approaches.

But theory alone is never enough. Keeping track of the actions of many agents, individually and simultaneously, who inhabit a spatially defined world and exhibit mostly local interactions was made immensely easier by the proliferation of object-oriented programming languages beginning in the 1990s and, following on those, various simulation platforms that built on those languages. Such approaches enable us to examine the possibility of the emergence of new structures (for example, institutions, alliances, and communities) out of the basal units and their interactions. But as we shall see, although these technical improvements have been important in making progress in studying some kinds of complexity, other kinds are more resistant.

Models can be characterized along a number of dimensions. The distinction among mental, verbal, physical (such as maps or three-dimensional models of buildings or landscapes), mathematical, and simulation models concentrates on the medium in which the representation is made; the last two together can be considered members of the class of "formal" models. Or we can focus on the degree of aggregation within the model, as in the distinction between systems (or systems-dynamic) models and agent-based (or individual-based) models. All the models collected here are, or are striving to become, formal models of some sets of processes that focus on explaining change in some human (usually prehistoric) system and involve both social and natural components in that explanation.

We suggest that, in developing multidisciplinary research of the kind in this volume, formal models offer advantages that might not be readily apparent (see also van der Leeuw 2004):

- Such models can be used to express phenomena and ideas in precise, unambiguous ways that typically involve economic logic and also can be understood by practitioners of all the disciplines involved in our kind of research.

- In theory, the domain of application of formal models is unlimited (but see below). They may be applied to all aspects of the social sciences, as well as the natural, earth, and life sciences, and are eminently suited to the study of the dynamics between society and the environment.

- Formal models are sufficiently abstract not to be confounded with reality and can be sufficiently detailed, rigorous, and "realistic" to force people with different backgrounds to focus on the same relational and behavioral issues.

- No less important in our context is the fact that formal models use a language (mathematics or computer algorithms) that differs from any natural language. This facilitates abstract thinking that links dynamic patterns in different domains.

- Certain kinds of formal models are able to describe changes occurring in complex sets of relationships. Hence, formal modeling is very suitable for constructing dynamic theories about complex phenomena (in the sense of Boccara, above), which can then be compared with the observations on which they are based. As Wilkinson and his colleagues argue in chapter 9, "if early state societies were truly complex, then it is necessary to tackle the full range of complexity that exists. If we are to do this with any degree of analytical rigor, we must build up large, complex models that incorporate a wide array of data sources and incorporate a range of interacting processes: social, economic, environmental, and political."

- Formal dynamic models may allow us to experiment relatively cheaply with different scenarios to explain certain sequences of cause and effect. This is particularly important in domains where real-life experiments are impossible.

- Certain classes of formal models enable us to study how interactions between individual, nonidentical entities at a lower level result in patterns at a higher level. This property is particularly relevant to the study of many collective phenomena that are the subject of the social sciences: the interactions between individuals create the society (and its culture), which, in turn, affect the behavior of the individuals or groups that constitute it.

A venerable but useful distinction that characterizes the focus of models was proposed by ecologist Richard Levins (1966). Levins argued that in models of complex systems it is, practically speaking, impossible to maximize the generality, realism, and precision of our models simultaneously: we can, at best, hope to maximize only two of these qualities (but see Sober and Orzack 1993). The most general of the models collected here, in the sense that the processes modeled might be applicable in a wide range of real-world systems, is certainly the contribution by Smith and Choi to understanding the emergence of social inequality (chapter 5). In part, this is due to the fact that it is also the least realistic, because there has been no effort to instantiate the model to fit a particular case. Most of the models here, in contrast, make an effort towards realism and precision that—inevitably, it seems—sacrifices generality to achieve goodness-of-fit to the situations at hand.

Models, then, enable us to explore concepts and theories either in relatively general (but perhaps never universal) contexts or in a specific context. Therefore, it is essential to consider the relationship among concepts, theories, and empirical research (for example, Dugatkin 2001:xii–vi). We understand concepts as deeper constructs that underlie theories in the way that the concepts of variation and differential proliferation (along with divergence or speciation) underlie Darwin's theory of evolution by natural selection. What is concept and what is theory, of course, is not always clear. Dugatkin (2001:xiii) considers Hamilton's "theory" of inclusive fitness (the notion that an individual's total fitness takes into account both her own offspring and, with discount determined by relatedness, those of her relatives) to be a fundamental conceptual advance stimulating much recent empirical research in behavioral ecology. Zahavi's (1975) "handicap principle" has been extremely fruitful in the same manner, leading in anthropology to the current widespread interest in costly signaling theory. In general, concepts give rise to theory that makes predictions about real-world phenomena. As theories (construed as classes of models) become more complicated, it becomes useful or even mandatory to have a computer derive the predictions of models derived from that theory: this is the process of simulation.

Do shared concepts underlie the chapters that follow? We suspect that there are several, though they are not articulated in most cases.

First, these researchers seem to share a view about the complexity of the world they are trying to understand. Auyang (1998:10) distinguishes three kinds of increasingly complex systems. First are systems regarded as being composed of many bodies but of only a few kinds and having only a few kinds of relations. Many physical systems, such as spin glasses and solar systems, fall into this category, and their complexity is fully described by Boccara's characterization, above.

Next in increasing complexity are organic systems, also composed of many bodies that, in this case, are highly specialized and integrated, as are the tissues and organs in an organism. The functional characteristics to which such organization gives rise complicate modeling considerably.

More complex still are what Auyang calls "cybernetic" systems, which, as in the case of people in societies, have all the complexity of the first two kinds of systems but add intentionality. Auyang suggests pessimistically, but realistically (in our view), that current theory can achieve a full understanding for only the first type of system and that we necessarily make radical simplifications when we study the second and third types of systems in order to try to understand them as many-body systems (often using concepts, such as optimization, developed for understanding physical systems). Modeling systems of these last two kinds thus requires considerable "coarse-graining" (a filtering out of insignificant details and an attendance to aggregate, large-scale behavior), successive approximations with models that apply only to specific regions (taken spatially, temporally, or with respect to a problem) of the phenomena of interest, and a willingness to move back and forth between models and historical narrative. This view of the way our target systems are organized and operate makes model-based archaeology attractive.

We suspect that the researchers assembled here would agree with this characterization but, at the same time, would push hard against these limitations, by trying to build theory that is appropriate to organic and cybernetic systems (see again chapter 5 by Smith and Choi) and by applying simulation methods that give us the possibility of creating specialized, variable, and tightly integrated agents whose behaviors can exhibit—if not intentionality—at least evolution through time (for example, see the use of cultural algorithms in chapter 4 by Kohler et al.). Also notable are the attempts by Jordan and Shennan to understand how the processes of culture change—though rooted in the processes of biological evolution—take on a life of their own, building on concepts pioneered by Cavalli-Sforza and Feldman (1981) and Boyd and Richerson (1985).

Beyond some shared notion of the complexities of the system they are dealing with, as well as the difficulties that this entails, several chapters rely on concepts such as trade-offs, or optimality, to give their argument structure and direction. This is most explicit in the case of chapter 8 by Janssen and Anderies and chapter 4 by Kohler and colleagues. Both chapters use these concepts as nonarbitrary points of entry into systems that, the authors realize, are affected by many forces in addition to possible tendencies towards optimization. These concepts are also implicit elsewhere, for example, in the arguments by Wilkinson and colleagues (chapter 9) that the differential costs of transport in southern and northern Mesopotamia structured many other differences realized in their divergent evolutionary trajectories.

In this volume, Cleuziou in chapter 10 and Berger and colleagues in chapter 3 seem the closest to developing concepts (or perhaps just theories) that are uniquely social in their referents. In part, this is a consequence of the fact that their questions are different from those asked in the other chapters. They study socioenvironmental change over very long time periods (millennia) in which different cultures and different societies have had different impacts on the environments concerned. They are therefore less interested in the detailed dynamics of human-environmental interaction than in the way in which such dynamics change over long-term time under the impact of *different* cultural regimes. Hence, they adopt the position that at the millennial-scale coarse-graining at which they are attempting to make sense of the available information, the societal dynamics are the drivers of change.

But, ultimately, that difference in focus is also a result of a difference in intellectual tradition. Both chapters are by archaeologists who have been trained in an inductivist tradition that finds its roots in the archaeology of historical periods, rather than in the anthropological archaeology prevalent in the United States. That approach owes much to history and, in particular, to the Annales school of economic and social history that was developed in France between the 1930s and the 1980s. It has therefore more of an eye for the societal dynamics but is also less willing to forego detail for the kinds of simplicity that accompany the more abstract types of models that find their origins in the natural and life sciences.

These French authors consequently have the opposite point of departure from that of authors such as Jordan (chapter 2), Shennan (chapter 7), and Janssen and Anderies (chapter 8). The latter begin their intellectual trajectory in the realm of concepts, often transposed (mutatis mutandis) from other disciplines (life sciences or economics, for example) and work from there towards the design of theories. The former are predominantly (but not completely) generalizing from observed data, building theories before they can reach the realm of concepts. In this they resemble more closely the work of those US and UK scholars trained in historical archaeology, who use both archaeological and historical data to design a very detailed and specific model of the socioeconomic systems operating over relatively short time spans. It might be said that the regional approach informed by training in geography that infuses the contribution by Wilkinson and his colleagues combines elements of both these approaches to very good effect.

No Apology for Neologisms

The editors of this volume are not enthusiastic about neologisms, but we acquiesce if an approach is significantly new and promises to grow to the point where a compact description is handy. This is the case for three words encountered throughout this volume, though they are not in common use in archaeology more generally.

The term *socionatural* is not entirely novel; the geographer Harold Miller used it, for example, to describe the complex of factors surrounding the founding of New Albany, Indiana, in a specific location and the resultant waxing and waning of its fortunes (Miller 1938). Reference to socionatural systems implies that neither social nor environmental factors are automatically accorded pride of place in explanation. Instead, emphasis is given to understanding how the dynamics of these two systems, traditionally considered from different perspectives, at different levels in a hierarchy, and analyzed by different means, might coincide to facilitate or inhibit change. Emphasis is also given to identifying the points of coupling between the systems (for more discussion, see McGlade [1995], van der Leeuw and Redman [2002], and Berger et al., chapter 3, this volume).

Ecodynamics is a term that, though in use earlier, was surely made famous by Kenneth Boulding in his 1978 book *Ecodynamics: A New Theory of Societal Evolution*. Boulding was a broad and provocative thinker whose work deserves to be remembered, but our specific use of this term owes more to McGlade (1995). He took up the term in archaeology to argue that "there is no 'environment,' there is no 'ecosystem,' there are only socio-natural systems." In particular, he reminded us that the concepts "environment" and "ecosystem" are objectified and reified cultural constructions embedded in contemporary attitudes and value systems. He called the study of the (essentially irreducible) natural and social phenomena and their interaction "human ecodynamics" and contrasted it with the then prevalent "human ecology," which in his view applies the more traditional perspective of societies as adapting to their environments.

Finally, this book owes much to the concept of "biocomplexity." Rita Colwell, director of the National Science Foundation (NSF) from 1998 to 2004, made biocomplexity a key initiative and was able to gain substantial funding increases for NSF, in part, to support increased biocomplexity-related research.

Biocomplexity research is designed to be both multidisciplinary and anti-reductionist, in that it is not supposed to study some parts of ecosystems in isolation from other parts. It is also designed from the outset to integrate social and behavioral sciences into studies of the ecosystem. In an interview with *Science* shortly after being named to NSF's top position, Colwell called biocomplexity research an attempt at understanding all the interrelationships between cells and organisms and between an organism and its environment.... We're taking all we know and utilizing it to build the type of models that we thought about 25 years ago that turned out to be so riddled with black boxes that we couldn't get the simulation we needed. But now, with the vastly increased power of computing and data mining, we can infuse a very strong science underpinning into environmental studies and make some dramatic gains in knowledge. (Mervis 1998)

To many anthropologists, the territory staked out by the juxtaposition of these three words should not seem alien—many elements of this approach can be found in our intellectual progenitors. From Julian Steward we can derive an interest in the great importance of the interface between societies and their environments that simultaneously acknowledges the importance of history, the "tools and knowledge" that people bring to bear on that interaction, and the "patterns of work necessary to bring the technology to bear upon the resources" (Murphy 1977:22). From Leslie White we can see an interest in what might be termed the "metabolic" basis of society—energy flows—which invites us to think about societies and ecosystems in terms of a common currency. Although one might object that Colwell's quotation asserts a greater role for modeling and simulation than has been traditional in anthropology, calls for this have been with us for some time now. Lewis Binford (1981:25–30) on numerous occasions emphasized that we must link our observations of the archaeological record to an understanding of systems dynamics to make reliable inferences about the past.

On with the Show

We invite you readers to view these chapters as exercises in coping with complexity in socionatural systems through successive approximations by models of various sorts. More specifically, we invite you to engage them on two levels: for what the application of these techniques can tell us about processes of change in some part of the world, or at some sociopolitical scale, and for what these authors have to say about the techniques themselves, as trial paths for approaching classes of problems. Here, the reader becomes an agent in the world of research:

In problems of complication, as decision makers...agents look for ways to frame the situation that faces them. They try to associate temporary internal models or patterns or hypotheses to frame the situation. And they work with these. They may single out one such pattern or model and carry out simplified deductions on it, if they seek guidance for action. As further evidence from the environment comes in, they may strengthen or weaken their beliefs in their current models or hypotheses. They may also discard some when they cease to perform, and replace them as needed with new ones. (Arthur 2005:296)

Use these models and learn from them, build on them, make them better, assess them against new data, and let this process assist you in making complexity a little more tractable.

Acknowledgments

The papers on which these chapters are based were presented at a workshop called "Modeling Long-Term Culture Change" held at the Santa Fe Institute in late October 2004. We thank NSF's Biocomplexity in the Environment Special Competition (through grant BCS-0119981 to Kohler), the James S. McDonnell Foundation (through a grant to Erica Jen), the Santa Fe Institute, and the School of Human Evolution and Social Change, Arizona State University, for their support of the conference and this volume. Finally, we thank David Johnson and Diane Curewitz, both of the Department of Anthropology, Washington State University, for their help in getting these papers ready for publication. Johnson was also instrumental in helping to organize the symposium on which this is based.

The chapters are arranged, more or less, according to the scale of the society under consideration (Bodley 2003), which has the happy effect of putting papers side by side that are quite different in approach. We hope that this emphasizes the range of possible approaches and gives some sense of the advantages of each. Given the funding by NSF's Biocomplexity competition, we have encouraged the three projects with Biocomplexity funding (Kirch et al., Kohler et al., and Wilkinson et al.) to give somewhat fuller accounts of their activities.

Note

1. The term *model-based science* can be associated with rather different programs (Godfrey-Smith 2003:186–89, 238). One earlier meaning employs a logician's concept of model and denotes an attempt to find general similarities of structure in all scientific theories. We are more interested in a second use, apparently more common now, that considers *model-based science* to denote a way of doing science that involves a two-step process of building an imaginary model system, for example, with a set of coupled differential equations, and then making arguments of resemblance between that model and aspects of a target system in the real world.

CHAPTER 2

Continuity and Change in Different Domains of Culture

An Emerging Approach to Understanding Diversity in Technological Traditions

Peter Jordan

In this contribution, I would like to examine the social mechanisms generating long-term patterns of cultural diversity, with a particular focus on how transmission processes work to promote continuity or change across different domains of technological tradition. I review "dual-inheritance" perspectives on cultural transmission and present a case study examining variability in languages, basketry, and housing styles among hunting, fishing, and gathering communities in northwest California. The chapter presents specific conclusions about the factors influencing local cultural evolution, and the broader methodology will have general utility for further "real world" and simulation-based studies of regional-scale cultural diversification.

Culture as a System of Social Inheritance

There are convincing grounds for attempting to understand culture as a self-replicating system of inherited information, grounded in complex networks of social learning, imitation, and interaction (Durham 1979; Cavalli-Sforza and Feldman 1981; Boyd and Richerson 1985; Shennan 2002). The core argument in this neo-Darwinian "descent with modification" approach to cultural inheritance is that social traditions are passed on—like genes and language transfer—via a similar, albeit more diverse, suite of mechanisms and processes that result in both continuity and change.

Anthropologists working within this field have suggested the existence of broad cultural analogues to the evolutionary biological processes of inheritance, mutation, selection, and drift (Cavalli-Sforza and Feldman 1981; Boyd and Richerson 1985):

- The transmission of genetic information takes place between a single set of parents and its biological offspring (that is, *vertically*, between generations). Complex cultural information also has an inherited component but is passed on through processes of social learning rather than through biological reproduction. In contrast to genetic transmission, social learning and the acquisition of the complex mesh of cultural skills may proceed in many ways and involve interaction among many groups and individuals (for example, teachers, parents, the wider community, and elite groups). The outcome is that cultural skills and knowledge are likely to be passed not only vertically, from biological parents to children (even from an older generation to a younger one), but also horizontally, between peers or nearest neighbors.

- In addition to the potential for horizontal transfer, the skills, traditions, and other sets of complex information are also likely to be affected by the cultural equivalent of biological "mutation." In cultural terms, some will be a random low-frequency process of imperfect replication: this is simple copying error. Other changes will result from deliberate experimentation. After an initial period of teaching, individuals may intentionally experiment and try out new variations (known as "guided variation"). As a result, new ways of doing or making things will constantly arise. However, neither of these "mutation" mechanisms will have a major short-term effect on the overall frequency of various cultural practices. For new ideas, beliefs, or novel ways of making implements to really "catch on," their popularity needs to be amplified through *deliberate* selection.

- Active selection of new, alternative, or existing traditions can have immense effects on which cultural traits or practices are passed on through time. As a result, some traits will spread; others will die out. "Directly biased" transmission takes place when individuals initially learn to do things one way, evaluate others by watching them do a similar task, and then (possibly) switch to whatever variant looks better or more efficient. In "indirectly biased" transmission, individuals watch and copy what certain other individuals do, often those thought to be prestigious or powerful in the local culture. However, they may not just copy a single set of behaviors from the prominent individual (for example, those directly related to making that person important); they may take up a wider set of behaviors and tastes from them. "Conformity bias" takes place when we initially do, for example, what our parents tell us to and then, in an attempt to conform, switch to doing what everyone else in the community does. Eventually, with all choosing to follow a local "norm," areas of cultural similarity arise and involve significant internal uniformity, perhaps reinforcing and reproducing a sense of cohesive group identity or ethnicity.

- Cultural drift is another important process and involves the random cumulative replacement of traits. This is the main process of culture change; the only transmission process operating is the random copying of traits from one generation to the next. Certain practices will achieve cumulative popularity even if there is no active selection for them. In other words, if there are equal chances of whom you learn from and there is no innovation, then eventually one trait will take over at random to the exclusion of others (Neiman 1995), and "rare or randomly performed variants may be lost entirely" (Boyd and Richerson 1985:9). Overall interacting population size is important here: small populations tend to have very rapid processes of drift, but in larger populations there are more chances for several traits to persist longer. Cultural "mutation" (innovation) rates are another crucial factor. With rapid innovation there will be a speeding up of the eventual "replacement" of traditions through cultural drift (Neiman 1995; Shennan 2002; Hahn and Bentley 2003; Bentley, Hahn, and Shennan 2004).

This dual-inheritance—or "descent with modification"—approach to long-term culture history directs attention to the ways in which these diverse processes are implicated in changing histories of variation in cultural traditions (Shennan 2002). Population dynamics are a further important factor influencing which traditions are passed on from one generation to the next. Attributes and traditions carried by biologically successful populations will be carried through to the present from deep history, while populations that die out will take many of their traditions with them. Even major reductions in populations through warfare or disease will generate profound "bottleneck" effects on subsequent patterns of diversity in cultural practices (see Shennan 2000).

The dual-inheritance approach has other attractions for archaeologists and anthropologists. Processes of biological evolution are much better understood than the factors affecting and encouraging long-term continuity and change in different domains of culture. Biologists and geneticists have developed a powerful suite of methods and theories for disentangling the processes of inheritance, selection, mutation, and drift—processes that have direct analogues in the cultural sphere (see Boyd et al. 1997). Further inspiration to adopt these methodologies from evolutionary biology and "translate" them for use in exploring long-term culture history stems from growing interest in correlating the histories of genetic, linguistic, and cultural diversity, part of a grand rewriting of world history—the "new synthesis" (for example, Bellwood and Renfrew 2003). With all three characterized by an underlying process of inheritance, dual-inheritance theory represents a common framework for tracing trajectories of genetic, linguistic, and cultural transmission through specific case studies.

Biological descent with modification is characterized by the gradual diversification of new species, and historical relationships among observed species can be plotted as a branching tree diagram. Long-term linguistic diversification has been shown to proceed in a similar manner, with slow rates of change in many core elements and the retention of deep historical signals that can be traced over centuries or millennia to reconstruct the historical relationships of "descent with modification." The processes by which new languages have "descended" from ancestral ones can also be plotted as branching tree diagrams (for example, the Indo-European language tree).

In contrast, both the patterns and processes of long-term cultural transmission are poorly understood. Does long-term culture change proceed through similar processes of branching diversification, and can culture histories be mapped in any straightforward way onto linguistic and genetic tree diagrams? Critics of dual-inheritance perspectives on long-term cultural transmission argue that culture change may simply be too rapid and chaotic to maintain any coherent historical signal, rendering any attempt to deploy biological models and methods a theoretically bankrupt exercise. As a result, much recent debate has therefore focused on evaluating the relative contribution of two processes, each argued to dominate long-term cultural transmission (Kirch and Green 1987; Terrell 1987, 1988; Durham 1992; Moore 1994, 2001; Guglielmino et al. 1995; Terrell, Hunt, and Gosden 1997).

According to the first hypothesis, "branching" processes of cultural descent predominate. Through time, communities expand, split, expand, and then split again, carrying genetic traits, languages, and assemblages of cultural attributes with them at each stage. These populations then become isolated from one another, either because of geographic factors or the emergence of a strong group identity, which together lead to the "speciation" of distinct but historically related languages and cultures. As all these groups will share ancestral features, branching tree diagrams can be used to map lines of descent and cultural and/or linguistic "speciation" or splitting events.

The fundamental criticism of this model is that it has clear utility for evolutionary biology but not for culture history. Clearly, reproduction between different biological species is generally impossible: dogs, humans, and horses have a shared evolutionary history but cannot exchange genes; once a split occurs, further gene flow is blocked and the integrity of divergent but historically related species is maintained. In contrast, human populations have always interacted, and there have always been opportunities for cultural borrowing and exchange, especially between geographically adjacent communities. As a result, a better analogy for culture history may well be the complex patterns of gene flow within a population of the same species. These cannot be reduced to simplistic tree diagrams but are better represented as a "tangled bank," thereby making simple correlations among languages, cultures, and genetic histories impossible.

It is important to stress that these starkly different perspectives on human cultural history are best understood as working hypotheses rather than final conclusions. As noted by Gray and Jordan (2000:1053), "these two models are not mutually exclusive, but are best characterized as two ends of a continuum of modes of human prehistory, with a pure tree at one end and a maximally connected network at the other...a microcosm of a general debate about whether human cultural evolution can be represented as a tree."

However, the debate about cultural evolution is slightly more complex than a simple tree-network opposition, because any community will have a diverse array of traditions and practices relating to different spheres of activity. If these are affected in different ways by various learning, innovation, and selection processes, then it is likely that each will have a separate descent history as a distinct "package" of cultural tradition. Conversely, if all are affected in similar ways, they may exhibit similar historical lines of descent, perhaps forming broadly defined "lineages."

Boyd and others (1997) outline a series of useful conceptual models for tracing out different kinds of descent history. On the one hand, the "culture as species" model explores how a full suite of traditions, isolated from outside influences, is passed down within different communities, enabling tree diagrams to closely represent actual descent histories. On the other hand, at the other end of the continuum, innovation may be so rapid that no historical depth or cultural coherence is identifiable; here culture is best conceived of as a "collection of ephemeral entities." Between these extreme models are two alternative scenarios. First, certain key traditions and traits may be passed on in tandem through history, thereby forming a unified cultural lineage or "core," whose descent can be mapped by tree diagrams. However, populations are not immune to outside influences, and ideas and the core may be surrounded by, and may co-exist with, other diffused, blended, and invented traits. Second, there may be no central cultural core, but many traditions or technologies will have deeper descent histories that can be mapped by tree diagrams. However, each of their descent histories is independent, and the trees cannot be mapped onto one another in any straightforward way.

These models move the debate away from simplistic arguments about trees *versus* networks and open up a more promising set of questions. Importantly, these four hypothetical culture-history scenarios also have direct analogues in evolutionary biology, and quantitative methods have been developed to test for different kinds of descent history. For example, cladistics can identify instances of branching descent in different domains of culture (see below). If several domains of culture have been transmitted in this way, then further tests, developed by biologists interested in the co-speciation of host and parasite lineages, can be deployed to identify the degree of "association by descent," that is, the degree to which various lineages have tracked one another with various degrees of fidelity through deep historical time (see Jordan and Mace 2006). A high degree of "co-speciation" between cultural trees and language trees could indicate a coherent accretion of lineages in the form of a culture core. A lack of evidence for cultural "co-speciation" would indicate that each domain of culture has been transmitted as a distinct and independent package, with its own descent history. In addition, network-based methods (for example, Bryant and Moulton 2002), specifically designed to examine more complex evolutionary relationships, such as recombination, hybridization, and lateral transfer, are well placed to examine instances of cultural blending around potential cultural lineages.

These models and methods enable us to move through particular case studies and test a range of hypotheses that can diffuse the heated debate between the relative and exclusive merits of branching versus blending models of cultural diversification. One challenge is that we do not fully understand the degree to which different kinds of learning, selection, and drift actually leave historical signals in particular cultural datasets. If conformist bias is strong in populations that have diverged and then become isolated (in either a social, symbolic, or geographic sense), then culture change may well be slow, perhaps proceeding at a pace similar to biological speciation, so that the cultural outcomes of these community diversification events (for example, in the form of pottery styles) are well recorded and can be modeled in the form of tree diagrams. Conversely, if innovation is more rapid, it will be very hard to reconstruct histories. If communities are well connected and prestige bias is present, then extensive diffusion could occur, perhaps at a global scale. In this latter scenario of rapid change and diffusion, very little original information is being transmitted *down* via successive generations compared with that being created *within* each single generation. Finally, another scenario can be explored: if most parents do things in similar ways and children receive their skills directly from their parents, changing these little in their lifetime and perhaps staying within an endogamous community, then descent will be vertical at both a parental and community scale. However, if offspring still get their skills vertically and then move between exogamous groups after marriage, they will take skills with them, leading to regional blending of traditions. Several more theoretical scenarios could be explored, but the key point is that the operation of cultural transmission, mutation, selection, and drift factors outlined above will have profound implications for the operation of either branching or blending descent, as well as the degree to which these processes might leave any recognizable historical "trace" in subsequent patterns of cultural diversity.

An important corollary to these general observations is that we need to be much more aware of the extent to which learning, interaction, and exchange are not devoid of real-world context but grounded in settlement, subsistence, and interaction systems, as well as being affected by kinship, taboos, and other beliefs. Much cultural transmission theory sets out series of mathematical models that still need empirical exploration, for example, ecology may not determine modes of transmission, but the dynamic way in which populations arrange themselves in relation to resources will have major implications for long-term transmission histories. Patterns and processes of diversification are likely to be significantly different in a highly mobile band society and in a sedentary, complex hunter-fisher-gathering community in which active boundary defense, and perhaps hostility to outsiders, may cause cultural practices to maintain a deeper historical coherence. Furthermore, colonization of new areas by an expanding ancestral population that branches out and occupies new niches, with subsequent local communities dropping out of regular contact with other "daughter" populations, may have very different outcomes for cultural diversification than, for example, long-term histories of regular interaction between adjacent populations in a densely settled valley floor. As a result, studies involving island chains have long been recognized as ideal for the investigation of cultural diversification, Polynesia being an obvious example. Nevertheless, much work needs to be done in continental settings, where descent histories may be much more intertwined. As Welsch comments,

> in most ordinary settings, human groups are constantly interacting with
> groups and communities that do not originate in the same ancestral units
> (either linguistically, culturally, or genetically)…this is just the sort of com-
> plex set of conditions that makes evolutionary questions interesting…. As a
> special case, Polynesia may offer some useful insights into evolutionary
> processes, but to understand cultural evolution requires methods and models of
> evolutionary processes that can be understood and applied in more typical situ-
> ations. (Welsch 1987:449)

It remains important to understand in more detail exactly why cultural diversification has proceeded in different ways in different world zones (see Kirch and Green
1987:443). The key research frontier for the future lies in our being able empirically
to identify exactly which kinds of real-world scenarios generate particular kinds of cultural descent with modification. With these challenges in mind, the following sections
examine a case study of cultural diversification in California, outlining a general quantitative approach to cultural descent with modification that will have wider utility in
other studies of "cultural transmission in action."

Modeling the Emergence of Cultural and Linguistic Diversity in Northwest California

At the end of the nineteenth century, the indigenous hunting, fishing, and gathering
communities of northern California had evolved a rich and distinct regional culture,
with some broad resemblances to the culture of the Northwest Coast groups farther to
the north and to the other Californian communities farther to the south (Kroeber
1925). The northwest California environment is diverse, with high rainfall, abundant
redwood and pine-fir timberland, and local concentrations of small game and acorn
groves (Baumhoff 1978:19). In particular, here were the richest fish stocks in
California, especially of anadromous species such as salmon. For successive human cultures, the exploitation of salmon was paramount in economic importance, especially
on the Klamath and its major tributaries, the Eel River drainage, and the Smith River
(Baumhoff 1978:16). Higher in the drainages, hunting was also important, as was
acorn processing, although these were generally secondary in importance here compared with many other areas of California. A major consequence of the varied ecology,
elevation, and drainage was the uneven distribution and degree of concentration of
resources over the landscape. Different local groups adjusted their subsistence regimes
and relative mobility accordingly. Many communities on the main rivers resided in
permanent villages, whereas others, often upstream, were much more mobile and
relied more heavily on hunting and gathering resources (Heizer 1978). Despite low
overall population density in the region, "extreme crowding" occurred along the best
fishing rivers (Baumhoff 1978:19).

Linguistic diversity was extremely high throughout northwest California. The languages spoken here belonged to several distinct stocks, some local and others brought into the region in recent centuries by some form of population movement. The most interesting examples of nonlocal languages are the Na-Dene (Athapaskan) languages, spoken in this region but also found in Oregon and the arid American Southwest, as well as in their original linguistic "homeland" to the north.

Interestingly, a number of researchers have explored links between the relative degree of biodiversity and the propensity for language diversity. Jorgensen argued that areas of concentrated, highly productive, and reliable resources would encourage localized procurement and ownership regimes. In turn, this would reduce long-distance population mobility and contribute to the maintenance of sharp language divisions among isolated communities (Jorgensen 1980:60). Smith (2001:106) has also noted high linguistic diversity in areas of high biodiversity, citing California as a prime example. He also has suggested that high biodiversity may encourage niche partitioning and, if those resources are stable, local self-reliant communities may emerge. Relative isolation due to reduced residential mobility may encourage the emergence of cultural and linguistic diversity through time, especially if ecological factors (environmental stability, localized and concentrated resources) are overlain by sociopolitical factors, including endogamy and the pursuit of strategies to undertake territorial defense (see Dyson-Hudson and Smith 1978). As Smith suggests, the salmon streams, shellfish beds, and acorn groves of California are "precisely where we would expect dense and localized populations to evolve considerable linguistic and perhaps cultural diversity" (Smith 2001:108).

While the degree of linguistic diversity is readily apparent, I would like to explore some of the methods, theories, and models outlined above to look for processes that may have encouraged, or prevented, northwest Californian cultural traditions to evolve a similar degree of diversity. Indeed, if boundary defense mechanisms were an important element in local forms of adaptation and social organization, then various forms of material culture may have played important implicit or explicit roles in marking out local and nonlocal identities.

Northwest California Basketry

Basketry represents an ideal craft tradition to explore long-term processes of cultural diversification. Broader Californian basketry traditions are well documented (for example, Elsasser 1978a), but, even with so much local diversity, the origins of this variability are poorly understood (Jordan and Shennan 2005). A general technical distinction is made between coiled and twined basketry weaves (figure 2.1), with both proceeding in either clockwise or anticlockwise directions (Elsasser 1978a). In northwest California all groups produced twined baskets, whereas some in the extreme south had also started to produce coiled types using a distinctive method that was probably spreading from the south. Coiling may be a recent technique, dating only

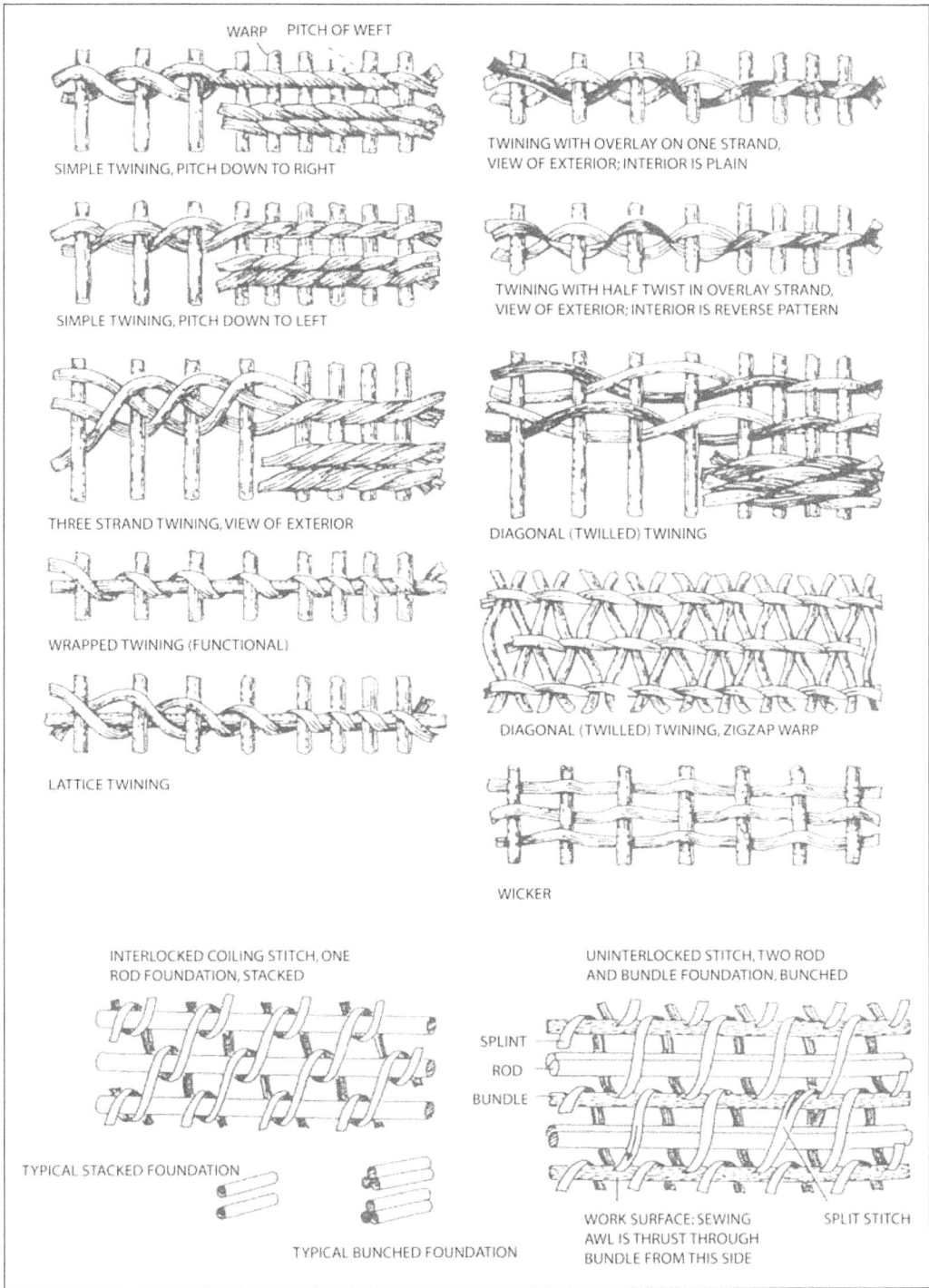

WARP   PITCH OF WEFT

SIMPLE TWINING, PITCH DOWN TO RIGHT

SIMPLE TWINING, PITCH DOWN TO LEFT

THREE STRAND TWINING, VIEW OF EXTERIOR

WRAPPED TWINING (FUNCTIONAL)

LATTICE TWINING

TWINING WITH OVERLAY ON ONE STRAND,
VIEW OF EXTERIOR; INTERIOR IS PLAIN

TWINING WITH HALF TWIST IN OVERLAY STRANDS,
VIEW OF EXTERIOR; INTERIOR IS REVERSE PATTERN

DIAGONAL (TWILLED) TWINING

DIAGONAL (TWILLED) TWINING, ZIGZAP WARP

WICKER

INTERLOCKED COILING STITCH, ONE
ROD FOUNDATION, STACKED

UNINTERLOCKED STITCH, TWO ROD
AND BUNDLE FOUNDATION, BUNCHED

SPLINT
ROD
BUNDLE

TYPICAL STACKED FOUNDATION

TYPICAL BUNCHED FOUNDATION

WORK SURFACE: SEWING   SPLIT STITCH
AWL IS THRUST THROUGH
BUNDLE FROM THIS SIDE

Figure 2.1. Diagram of northwest California basketry methods. (Adapted from Elsasser 1978a, with permission of the Smithsonian Institution)

from AD 1000, while twining is much older (Elsasser 1978a:634). For example, Kroeber, in discussing mainly the Yurok, Karok, and Hupa traditions, notes that "in regard to technique, the fundamental feature of the basketry of northwest California is that twining is the only method followed. Coiled weaves...are unknown.... [A]ll coiled baskets attributed to this region...are obtained from more southerly tribes" (Kroeber 1905:109).

Basketry also forms a coherent category of material culture because it formed an important technology for acorn processing, a key feature of the local subsistence adaptation: "Gathering, carrying, storing, milling and cooking of acorns, from north to south, [in California] were all performed in approximately the same way; and the similarity of procedures [is] reflected in the forms of the baskets that otherwise remotely related groups employed" (Elsasser 1978a:626).

Similar kinds of baskets are found among most Californian groups, including seed beaters, sifting baskets, trays, boiling baskets, burden baskets, storage baskets, and a range of other woven containers. At the same time, it is interesting to note that despite these broad similarities in basketry functions, many ethnographers have described "a high level of residual aesthetic sensibilities in an essentially functional medium" (Elsasser 1978a:641). Indeed, despite coherence in general modes of basketry usage, there were "numbers of remarkable variations in...form...technique...decoration ...sometimes among closely neighboring groups. While there is no ready explanation for these discrepancies...they may be looked upon as forming a simple corollary to the well-known cultural and linguistic separatism of California Indian groups" (Elsasser 1978a:626).

Finally, in behavioral terms, this category of material culture is coherent in that broadly similar skills are required to make each kind of basketry vessel. Production demanded high skill levels and was carried out at the household scale. Moreover, use of much basketry was related predominantly to female tasks, having close associations with domestic food preparation, serving, and storage (E. Wallace 1978). Moreover, E. Wallace (1978:683) stresses that throughout California "women wove the indispensable baskets.... It is noteworthy that the Californian Indians left this, the most advanced of their handicrafts, to females." In short, basketry traditions in the region represent a coherent yet complex craft skill, closely associated with female household labor.

Northwest California Housing

Northwest California groups built several types of residential structures, many located in the permanently occupied settlements at the river's edge. Sweat houses were also built by the groups and appear to follow the same local construction methods as houses, with a tendency for various plank-built rectangular buildings (figure 2.2) in the north, broadly similar to those of the Pacific Northwest Coast. Several methods were deployed in the buildings in the south, including a distinctive circular ground

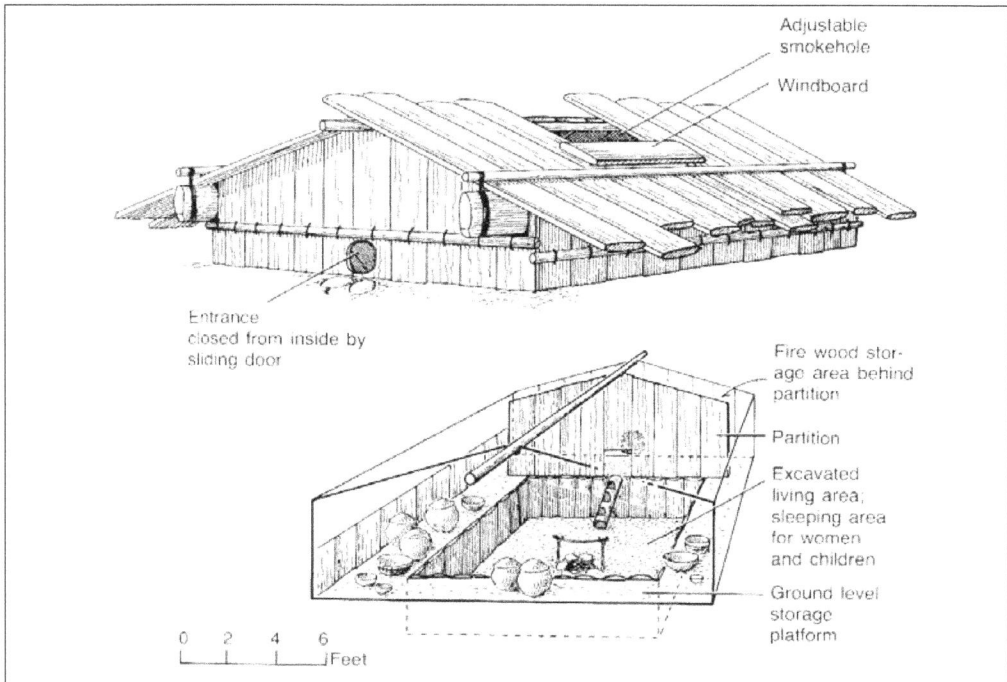

Figure 2.2. Tolowa house. (Adapted from Gould 1978, with permission of the Smithsonian Institution)

plan (Driver 1939). Overall, woodworking appears to have been more closely related to the male sphere of activities, with tasks of construction probably carried out by men as well (see Heizer 1978). In short, it would appear reasonable to argue that construction methods represent an interesting category of male-associated tasks that contrast well with basketry, with its strong female associations.

Northwest California Ethnic and Cultural Geography

As noted above, long-term patterns of interaction and exchange have important implications for cultural transmission. The physical geography of northwest California is characterized by drainage basins whose rivers run into the Pacific Ocean. From north to south, the most important rivers are the Smith, the Klamath, and the Eel (figure 2.3).

As Kroeber argued, the most distinctive ("climax") forms of local culture in northwest California were practiced by the Yurok, Hupa, and Karok ethnolinguistic communities, who inhabited different parts of the Klamath River drainage (Kroeber 1905:105). Although the Yurok had access to almost unlimited fish resources at the mouth of the Klamath River, they resisted exploiting these to the full, perhaps out of fear of reprisals from groups upstream (Baumhoff 1978:19). Nevertheless, the "superabundance" of fish enabled year-round sedentism (Pilling 1978:137), making them the most southerly exemplars of the village-based, Northwest Coast–type cultures.

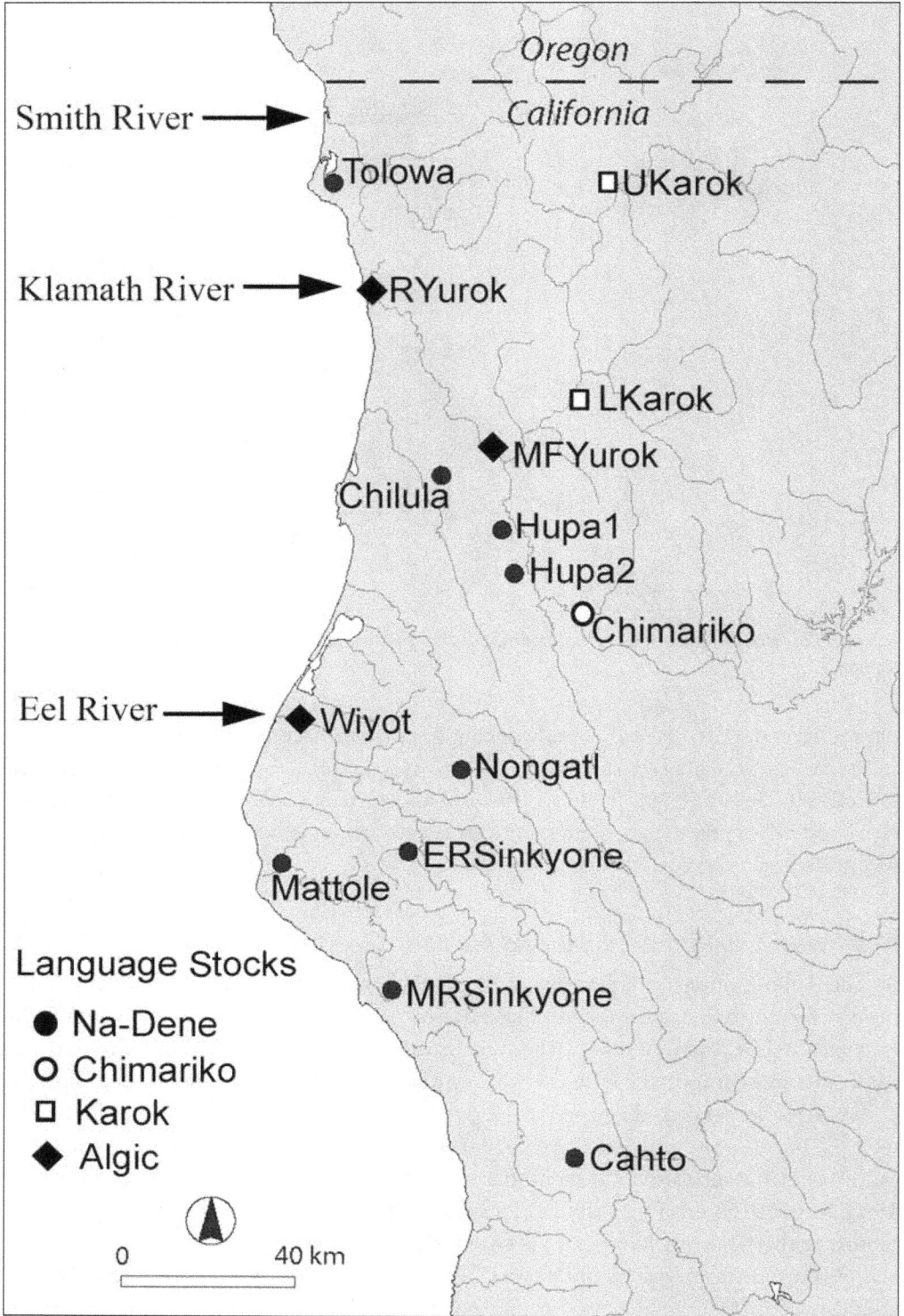

Figure 2.3. Location map (after Driver 1939).

Similarly, Yurok society was also heavily stratified. Members of the elite groups had named house sites and "relished travel and other language skills" (Pilling 1978:141). There are many accounts of the Yurok being driven by a fundamental desire for wealth acquisition. Kroeber (1925:2, 40) notes that everything had a price and that wealth played a "crucial role" in social relations. Property rights were based around the rights of the individual, and wealthy men were able to aggregate a group of followers often indebted to them. Postmarital residence was generally patrilocal, with extended discussions about bride price an important means for negotiating status. Females provided important labor contributions to the household, with more daughters bringing more wealth (via bride price) into the household. Rich men could afford to have several wives, and Kroeber notes that a "man usually marries outside" (1925:3) and that "they [Yurok] married whom and where they pleased" (1925:42). Indeed, one Yurok polygynist who died around 1859 had wives from Tolowa, Karok, Hupa, and Wiyot communities (Pilling 1978:137).

Upstream from the Yurok were the Karok, who dwelt in similar-style rectangular plank houses, sharing the same distinctive culture, and with whom the Yurok had strong marital ties (Bright 1978:180). The Tolowa and Wiyot (see below) were more distant and are less well-known (Bright 1978:180). As Kroeber detailed, the Karok were "a group so similar to the Yurok in everything but speech," indeed, this extends to their being "indistinguishable in appearance and customs, except for certain minutiae" (Kroeber 1925:97–8). As with the Yurok (Kroeber 1925:2), acquisition and the possession of property were crucial dimensions to life and social interaction (Bright 1978:180), making them "anxious about property, status, and the neighbor's opinion" (Bright 1978:181).

The Na-Dene-speaking (Athapaskan-speaking) Hupa also lived upriver from the Yurok; they were equals of both the Yurok and Karok. The Chilula were "close friends," but there was little contact with other groups in the area, including the Wiyot and Nongatl, although they met the Tolowa at "Yurok dances" (Kroeber 1925:132). The Hupa differed from other Na-Dene speakers (to the south) in having much higher population density along the banks of the (wider) Trinity River (a major tributary river to the Klamath), which was navigable most of the year (Kroeber 1925:128). Like many fishing cultures, the Hupa had permanent houses here of a rectangular three-pitch roof structure, including an internal plank-lined pit (W. J. Wallace 1978:167). Their main exchange partners were the Yurok, and they regularly traded acorns downriver. The family, inhabiting a dwelling house, was the main social unit, although several patrilineally related households sometimes formed a larger informal unit (W. J. Wallace 1978:168). Like members of neighboring groups along the broader Klamath River drainage, individuals were apparently obsessed with social position and the negotiation of bride price. As a general rule, the young married couple settled in the husband's village, but if not wealthy enough, then a half-marriage meant that he would reside in the wife's village. Rich men, in contrast, could have more than one wife (W. J. Wallace 1978).

The Tolowa also spoke a Na-Dene language (the most northerly in California) and resided on the Smith River and along the coast north of the Yurok (Kroeber 1925:121). Here, during the rainy winters, they occupied permanent plank-built houses along the coast, trekking inland for game and acorns (Gould 1978:128–30). Among the Tolowa, postmarital residence was patrilocal, although poorer men could engage in half-marriages, with residence at the wife's village upon an initial partial payment of bride price. Wealth and status also appear to have been major concerns. As Gould argues, "all anthropologists who have worked with the Tolowa agree that the principle of acquiring wealth to gain prestige was essential to the whole operation of Tolowa society" (Gould 1978:131).

This had unusual outcomes. By obtaining a bride from a more distant village, for example, "a wealthy man avoided paying bride-wealth to affinal kin within his own village. Since there were few wealthy men in any one village, such a man would almost certainly have to marry a woman from a family poorer than his own, thus narrowing the economic gulf between himself and his in-laws (which could undermine his prestige as a wealthy man in his own village)" (Gould 1978:132).

Prestige was accrued by the display of wealth—obsidian blades, red-headed woodpecker scalps, and dentalium beads, all of which could be used to purchase brides (Gould 1978:131–32). Women were economically important in that they made major labor inputs to the household economy, processing acorns and fish; also, they could produce daughters to be "traded" for bride price later. Wealthy men could have several wives (Gould 1978:132), thereby increasing their ability to generate further wealth. There was also intermarriage with the Yurok (Gould 1978:133).

Northwest California included a range of other groups. The Chilula were adjacent to the Hupa on the west, also spoke a Na-Dene language, and had, overall, very similar culture, despite some southerly cultural influences. The Chilula relied on the poorer fish resources of the Redwood Creek drainage, so hunting and gathering played a more important role in the local economy (W. J. Wallace 1978:177). The numerically small Chimariko were the "poor" upstream neighbors of the Hupa, occupying a narrow stretch of canyon on the Trinity River (a major tributary of the Klamath). Despite the presence of similar basketry traditions and some marriage contacts, there were recorded hostilities between these groups (Kroeber 1925:109–11). Here as well, social status arose from wealth acquisition (for example, dentalium beads), and bride price negotiation was an important means of forging social relations and acquiring prestige. However, after marriage, the newly wed couple could live with either set of parents. Along the shoreline to the east lived the shore-dwelling Wiyot (Kroeber 1925:117), who exploited the resources of the local marshes, lakes, and streams of the low-lying coastal strip.

To the south of the region was a large "enclave" of Na-Dene language speakers, including the Nongatl, Sinkyone, and Mattole (Elsasser 1978b). The Tolowa were also speakers of Na-Dene languages but were located farther to the north (see figure 2.3). Although often criticized as being "marginal" to the more elaborate "climax" cultures of northwest California farther to the north, these more southern Na-Dene groups exhibited distinct forms of local culture (Elsasser 1978b:191, 202–03). Society was organized into local "tribelets," which "acted as a homogenous unit in matters of land ownership, reaction to trespass, war and major ceremonies" (Elsasser 1978b:191). The Sinkyone and Mattole lived on the Mattole River; Sinkyone communities also lived along the upper Eel River. In these areas there was abundant grassland, with oak and pine-fir mountains and in some areas chaparral-type vegetation. Fishing was an important part of local subsistence activities. Mattole and Sinkyone were primarily reliant on fishing; the other groups integrated fishing with hunting and gathering.

Although settlements were located along major watercourses and the household was the basic social unit, there was not the same degree of emphasis on wealth acquisition as found among other northwest California groups like the Yurok and Hupa of the Klamath River, where there were fragmented villages and tight family organization (Elsasser 1978b). Moreover, bride price was also important (Elsasser 1978b:196), but there was more variability in postmarriage residence. The permanent winter dwellings of the southern Na-Dene language "enclave" were in stark contrast to the elaborate rectangular plank houses of the Klamath and Smith River peoples. Here, structures were round and conical in the form of a "central Californian type" (Kroeber 1925:146). However, "all basketry followed fairly closely that of Klamath River peoples" (Elsasser 1978b:200): the "basketry is…of a wholly northern kind: wholly twined" although the "technique is much less finished than among the Yurok and the ornamentation simpler" (Kroeber 1925:147).

Finally, in the far south of the northwest California region were the Cahto, who occupied the upper courses of the south fork of the Eel River. They were also speakers of a Na-Dene language (the most southerly Na-Dene speakers on the Pacific Coast), whom Kroeber (1925:154; see also Elsasser 1978c) argues are already representatives of another culture, that of north-central California, perhaps due to their being enclosed on three sides by speakers of Yukian languages (Myers 1978:244). Indeed, "Cahto baskets are scarcely distinguishable from those of Yuki manufacture" (Kroeber 1925:155). Residence appears to have been largely patrilocal (Myers 1978:245).

To summarize, this general ethnohistorical review of local settlement, interaction, and adaptation patterns points to the existence of several common practices running through the diverse cultures of the region. The first is a general tendency for relatively sedentary settlements, especially along the richest fishing rivers. Perhaps in association with this, postmarriage residence appears to be largely patrilocal, especially among the more northerly groups. In addition, the vital role played by the desire to acquire prestige through wealth accumulation shifts the emphasis in marriage contacts towards the negotiation of bride price. Moreover, a desire to avoid enriching the households of the local community may have encouraged an active quest to seek out brides from more distant communities, perhaps even from across linguistic frontiers. Furthermore, leading families in northern California created strategic alliances with distant groups through careful choice of partners: "marriage was an important mechanism in creating formal relations among competitive groups" (Jorgensen 1980:166), which otherwise had minimal political organization. At the same time, among most ethnolinguistic groups, the highest level of social organization (especially in the north) appeared to have consisted of powerful and wealthy individuals, with associated groups of followers and indebted people, instead of a formal tribe. Tribelets appear to have been more common in the south. There also appears to have been a high degree of bilingualism, especially in border areas.

To conclude, the region is characterized by high levels of intergroup social, trade, and marriage contacts despite the marked cultural and linguistic diversity. In behavioral terms, there were no borders impermeable to interaction and no record of explicitly endogamous social units. However, it appears that "people traveled only short distances: even people living on the navigable rivers did not travel far. People who were caught considerable distances from their home communities might be treated as poachers and repulsed. Even trade and ceremonial relations were maintained within and between neighboring communities in northern California" (Jorgensen 1980:168).

The implications of these behavioral factors in the generation of regional patterns of diversity in basketry and housing styles are examined in the following section.

Cultural Datasets

Datasets on buildings and basketry were drawn from Driver's (1939) Culture Element Distribution (CED) study of the ethnolinguistic groups in northwest California. The study—and others in the CED series—documents the cultural practices, social organization, and technology of different communities in presence-absence format, making them amenable to quantitative analysis. The data are derived from detailed informant recollections of "traditional" life in northwest California. The ethnohistoric "present" is the latter part of the nineteenth century; the earliest colonial contacts for this region are around 1850, much later than areas of southern California (Heizer 1978). In total, fifteen ethnolinguistic communities were selected for analysis (table 2.1 and figure 2.4). The cultural data element tables used in the present study appear in full in Appendix 1.

The languages spoken by these groups belong to different stocks, each with a distinct history (see Goddard 1996). It is clear that the Athapaskan languages arrived into the region most recently, probably via Oregon, from an original northern homeland. The presence of Na-Dene languages in northwest California must be linked to some form of recent population movement into the area, but the origins of the other languages and their links to earlier periods of human migration are much less clear (Shipley 1978:81–2).

It is important to note that the social "unit of analysis" in the current study is the "speech community." The analysis therefore focuses on community-level transmission processes, comprising cumulative actions by individuals or particular households within the wider ethnolinguistic group. There is widespread anecdotal evidence in the

Table 2.1 Groups Mentioned in the Text

Group Description*	Code (in Figure 2.3)	Language (in Figure 2.3)	Stock
Tolowa	Tolowa	Tolowa	Na-Dene
Chimariko	Chimariko	Chimariko	Isolate
Upper Karok	UKarok	Karok	Karok
Lower Karok	LKarok	Karok	Karok
Martin's Ferry Yurok	MFYurok	Yurok	Algic
Requa Yurok	RYurok	Yurok	Algic
Eel River Wiyot	Wiyot	Wiyot	Algic
Hupa	Hupa1	Hupa	Na-Dene
Hupa	Hupa2	Hupa	Na-Dene
Chilula	Chilula	Chilula	Na-Dene
Nongatl of van Deuzen River	Nongatl	Nongatl	Na-Dene
Mattole	Mattole	Mattole	Na-Dene
Sinkyone (of South Fork of Eel River)	ERSinkyone	Sinkyone	Na-Dene
Sinkyone (of Upper Mattole River)	MRSinkyone	Sinkyone	Na-Dene
Cahto	Cahto	Cahto	Na-Dene

* Kroeber (1939)

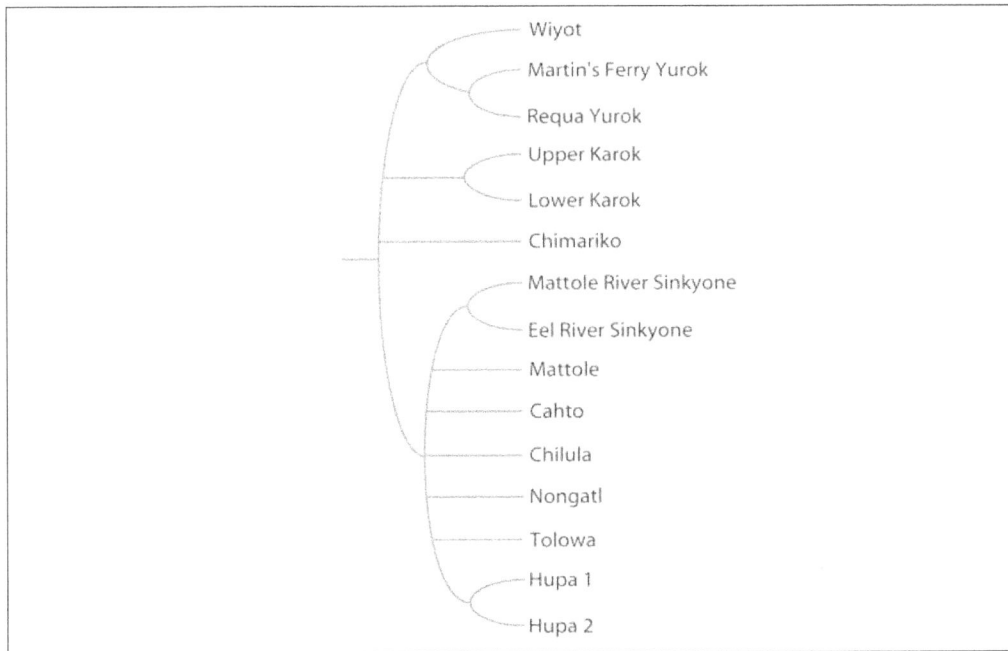

Figure 2.4. Northwest California language tree, based on current linguists' consensus (see Goddard 1996).

ethnographic literature that language did serve as an important marker of group identity. For example, "that something of an ethnic sense existed is shown by a gender in the Hupa language. One category included only adult persons speaking the tongue or readily intelligible…dialects. Babbling children, dignified aliens, and all other human beings and animals formed a second 'sex'" (Kroeber 1925:130).

The degree to which these patterns of linguistic diversity are linked to variability in material culture will be examined in relation to three core questions:

- What cumulative processes of cultural transmission were responsible for generating the observed diversity in basketry and house construction methods?

- Have individual traditions diffused across the mosaic of linguistic boundaries, or have these frontiers served to "channel" the transmission of diverse housing or basketry practices, so that distinct traditions have been passed down vertically between generations within each ethnolinguistic community?

- Can we identify the existence of more integrated "cultural lineages" (see Shennan 2000) in which distinct basketry *and* construction methods have been transmitted *together* within individual ethnolinguistic groups?

Basketry

Basketry elements were selected from the CED list and are presented in Appendix 1. It is worth noting that many of the descriptions in the data are relatively general, reflecting the basic modes of construction and the basketry types made and used locally rather than the kinds of raw materials used (Elsasser 1978a; Jordan and Shennan 2003) or the more subtle variations in decorative features or work quality that are often hinted at in the literature (for example, Kroeber 1905, 1925). Briefly, two basketry traditions of California are present, the ubiquitous twining and also the coiling methods practiced by the more southerly groups.

The basketry dataset of fifty-six elements was subjected to cladistic analysis. The method employs the null hypothesis that new cultural assemblages arise entirely through the successive bifurcation of ancestral ones, in the same way that new sets of biological species arise through processes of descent with modification (Hennig 1966; Forey et al. 1992; Kitching et al. 1998). The method involves determining which similarities result from shared ancestry (*homologies*) and which result from other processes, including borrowing (*homoplasies*). If variations in the data fit the tree model well, then it can be argued that branching processes of transmission have predominated. If the fit is poor, then other processes will have affected patterns of historical descent. While an initial parsimony analysis will generate insights into general patterns of similarity between "taxa" (the ethnolinguistic communities), the historical evolution of the character states that make up the cultural traditions can be deduced by using the outgroup method used to root the tree (Smith 1994:55–6; Kitching et al. 1998). In the present study, the Chimariko were selected as the outgroup on the grounds that they are located on the eastern edges of the study area and are linguistic "isolates," speaking a language with no known relatives either within or beyond the study area.

Initially, a general heuristic search was performed, with the Chimariko as an outgroup. The settings for the heuristic search were optimality criteria as parsimony, starting trees obtained via stepwise addition, and the branch-swapping algorithm tree-bisection-reconnection. The resulting trees were subjected to bootstrap analysis, a random sampling program that calculates levels of support for each branching section of the tree (for example, see Forey et al. 1992:76). Where there are few conflicting signals in the data, scores are low; where support for a tree diagram is good, these are higher. Here, a 70 percent confidence level was chosen and one thousand repetitions. Analyses were conducted in Paup 4.0b10 (Swofford 1998).

The results of the search were striking: five trees at length 59 were generated. Virtually no branches were well supported in the bootstrapping test; only Cahto and Sinkyone diverged on a clade that was 100 percent supported. This is best accounted for by the unique presence of coiled baskets that are absent from all other groups, and probably were adopted from the south. The phylogenetic signal in the data is therefore very weak—a clear indication that branching processes of descent with modification have not been operative at this analytical scale and that other hypotheses must be explored.

Recently, biologists have also shown increasing interest in the analytical challenges presented by more complex evolutionary processes such as hybridization, lateral transfer, and evolutionary patterns produced by more rapid rates of speciation. With social learning, imitation, and interaction at the core of cultural evolution, the cultural analogies to these processes are obvious, and this broader suite of tools developed by biologists would appear to have much to offer. As Bryant and Moulton note, "networks can provide a useful alternative to trees, for they allow the simultaneous representation of multiple trees, or at least give extra insight into the structure of the data set in question" (Bryant and Moulton 2002:1). Importantly, they also make clear that there is no model-free way of analyzing data and that if there is no well-established general model of evolution—as there is not with cultural data—then the testing of the data with the wrong models, with assumptions of tree-like data, can lead to inaccurate conclusions.

In the current study, NeighborNet (Bryant and Moulton 2002), incorporated into Splits Tree 4beta10 (Husan and Bryant 2006), was employed (for a wider review of the method, see Bryant et al. 2005). When the basketry assemblages are modeled using this method, the resulting plot (with boxes reflecting signals that conflict with a branching tree structure) represents a close approximation of a "tangled bank" (figure 2.5). This appears to be a classic example of cultural descent with modification, in which borrowing and blending of cultural traditions has led to a hybridization of regional basketry styles, despite the high linguistic diversity. Closer investigation of the plot reveals some more interesting details. Cahto and MRSinkyone have very different basketry assemblages and are pulled out a long way to the left, a pattern also picked out in the cladistic analysis. This cultural divergence can be accounted for by

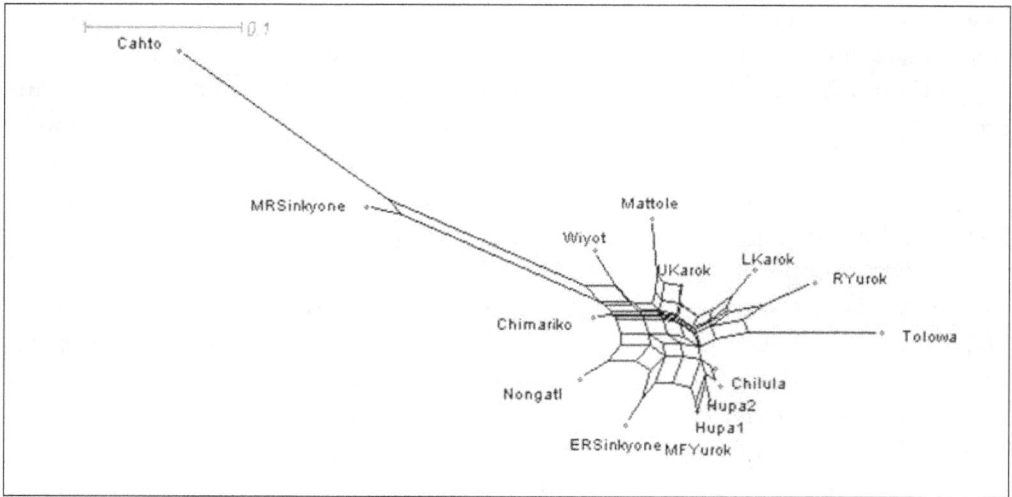

Figure 2.5. NeighborNet plot for northwest California basketry.

the presence of coiled basketry forms, which are absent from the basketry assemblages in the rest of the study area. MFYurok, Hupa 1, Hupa 2, and Chilula, that is, groups located in and around the Trinity River branch of the upper Klamath River drainage, do seem to be pulled out to the bottom right. The lack of a clear branch, however, suggests that much "conflicting signal" remains in the data. LKarok, RYurok, and Tolowa are also pulled out some way to the upper right. Tolowa and RYurok are nearest neighbors on the Pacific shoreline, but LKarok are located a long way upstream from the RYurok, beyond the MFYurok. Also puzzling is the fact that the UKarok are pulled out close to the Mattole, who are located at the other end of the study region. All other groups are pulled out in diverse directions, in an order that broadly reflects their relative geographic location. Adjacent groups along the coast (Mattole, Wiyot, Cahto, and MRSinkyone) are pulled out in a similar direction, whereas the inland groups of the south (ERSinkyone, Nongatl, and Chimariko) are pulled to the bottom edge of the diagram.

The geographic influence on the variation can be explored further by using Mantel Matrix tests, a useful method for exploring general correlations (Mantel 1967; for similar applications, see Barbujani 1995:776 and Jordan and Shennan 2003). The binary (presence/absence) datasets of basketry variation among the groups were converted into a similarity matrix, using the Jaccard measure. Linguistic variation among the groups can also be converted into a similarity matrix. The numerical values for linguistic similarity were calculated as follows: speaking the same language, 95 percent; the same family, only 50 percent; same stock, only 30 percent; and speaking a different stock, 5 percent. Finally, a geographic distance matrix was compiled recording point-to-point distances from Driver's (1939) informant base map. The three matrices were analyzed at the same time in order to obtain partial correlations, in this case, between basketry and language similarity controlling for distance (table 2.2).

Table 2.2 Mantel Matrix Partial Correlations: Basketry (y)/Language (x1)/Distance (x2)

Coefficient	Value
Correlation coefficient (rY1)	0.002744
Correlation coefficient (rY2)	−0.671529
Correlation coefficient (rY12)	−0.213668
Partial correlation (rY1_2)	−0.194428
Partial correlation (rY2_1)	−0.686806
Determination of Y by X1 (%)	−0.000405
Determination of Y by X2 (%)	0.472111
Total determination of Y (%)	0.471707
Unexplained variance of Y (%)	0.528293

Here, it is interesting to note that distance has a much stronger correlation with basketry variance than language. Indeed, 47 percent of basketry data—almost half the variance—correlated with the "crow flies" distances between groups. Conversely, linguistic affinity accounted for 0 percent of variation. Clearly, linguistic frontiers have not "channeled" or "confined" the transmission of distinct basketry traditions. Had they done so, the basketry of Na-Dene speakers (Tolowa in the far north and Cahto in the far south), for example, would have been pulled out together in the NeighborNet plot discussed above. Given these results, there is every indication that this dataset contains a high degree of "hybridization," which would fit the hypothesis that cultural diversification has proceeded through blending between adjacent groups irrespective of the languages spoken.

The final task is to interpret these results in the light of the ethnographic information outlined above. With basketry production (and use) a strictly female task and with insights into kinship practices suggesting that women are regularly married between different communities, as well as some suggestions that more distant brides are actually more desirable, there are grounds to suspect that in marrying and then entering new communities, women take their skills and practices with them. This leads to a gradual and cumulative "smudging" of basketry traditions across the region, driven perhaps by a steady trickle of females moving between groups.

Built Structures

The present dataset is also drawn from Driver (1939) and records construction methods deployed by the various ethnolinguistic communities. As noted above, different techniques are combined in different ways among the groups, and there is broad overlap between dwelling house styles and sweat houses. For this reason, the data were

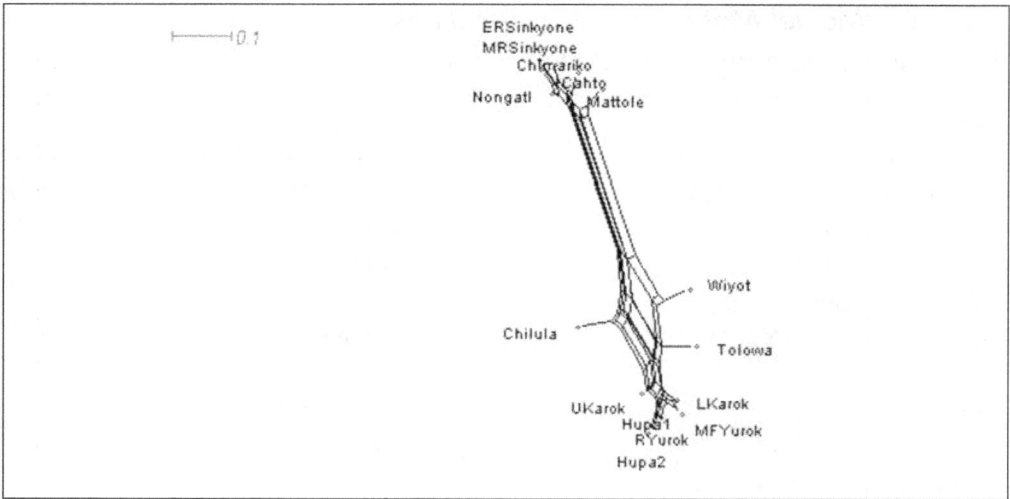

Figure 2.6. NeighborNet plots for northwest California construction methods.

recorded in the form of discrete elements—particular stages, tasks, skills, or arrangements—that could be combined in various ways according to the strategic decisions of local builders. For example, differing roof constructions allow both two- and three-pitch roofs; different materials are employed as roof coverings; in some houses, entire floors are excavated, and in others, just a central pit; some floors are planked, and others are flagged with stones. Overall, however, rectangular plank construction predominates in the north, and in the south there are conical dwellings with circular floor plans. Sixty-two elements were selected and are presented in Appendix 1.

Cladistic analyses revealed more branching structure in the housing styles data than in the basketry assemblages (figure 2.6). Analyses were conducted in Paup 4.0b10 (Swofford 1998), with similar heuristic search settings as for the basketry analysis. The search returned six trees of length 85. After bootstrapping, three clades were returned with more than 70 percent support, indicating that the data contained a signal for branching patterns of cultural transmission, which mapped out broad regional differences in construction styles.

As with basketry, further analysis of the data was conducted using NeighborNet, in order to explore these branching signals in more detail (see figure 2.6). The plot indicated a sharp regional divide between the construction styles employed by northern and southern groups, most specifically, between groups on the wider Klamath drainage (the Karok, Hupa, and Yurok), who had very similar construction styles, and the groups of the Na-Dene enclave in the south (the Cahto, Sinkyone, Nongatl, and Mattole). The Chilula, Wiyot, and Tolowa have more distinct styles of construction and are pulled out further along individual branches, but also form part of the wider northern grouping. Interestingly, the Chimariko form part of the southern cluster, despite being directly upstream from the Hupa groups. Clearly, some kind of stylistic frontier is running between these geographically adjacent groups, and Kroeber (1925:109) describes how relations among these ethnolinguistic communities were marked by "distrust and enmity" (Kroeber 1925:110). Silver also notes that "the Chimariko feared the Hupa and fought against them" (Silver 1978:205).

To summarize, both the NeighborNet plot and the cladistic analysis suggest the presence of two broadly defined traditions of house construction. However, *within* these two clusters appear to be two more localized "tangled banks" marked by intense exchange and borrowing, one northern, the other southern. In contrast, the evolution of basketry styles appears to have been characterized by multiple instances of borrowing and hybridization right across the region.

How do these variations in construction styles relate to linguistic diversity? Have languages and building techniques been "associated by descent"? This scenario can be explored further by using methods developed in evolutionary biology that can identify "co-speciation" in two independent datasets, the paradigm being that of the close association between host and parasite species (Page 2003). In biology, this relationship is not strictly parasitic, and many other factors may lead to co-speciation. Central to the process are factors that mean the parasite *speciates* along with the host. Generally, these are related to some degree of isolation, which means that it is difficult for the parasite to switch or disperse to other hosts. In short, parasite lineages are "forced" onto host phylogenies. The culture history analogy (see Jordan and Mace 2006) explored here would be whether northwest California languages, with their branching histories, had also "channeled" the transmission of construction techniques rather than enabled them to diffuse across linguistic frontiers. The most basic test for cultural co-speciation is whether the topologies of the language and construction methods of the phylogenies exhibit the exact same fit. If the fit is not perfect, further methods can be employed to distinguish significantly more similarity between trees than would be expected as a result of chance alone.

To test the stricter version of this hypothesis—perfect co-speciation—a Kishino-Hasegawa (1989) test was performed. This represents a means of testing explanatory hypotheses against a given best-fit tree (in this case, for house construction styles). In the version adapted for Paup 4.0b10, the tests employ parsimony as an optimality criterion to test the null hypothesis that no significant difference exists between the optimal tree and a tree constrained to fit a given hypothesis. The language tree (see figure 2.4) was translated into a "constraint" tree using MacClade 4.03. The subsequent structure of the language tree was then used to "constrain" the search for a new best-fit tree for house construction methods.

This exercise identifies two trees (or two sets of trees), which we can compare: (a) an unconstrained, best-fit, construction methods tree and (b) an "explanatory" tree constrained by language relations. If language and construction styles have been transmitted in tandem, then there will be no statistical difference between the two trees, and we can accept the hypothesis. The language tree was constructed in MacClade 4 (Maddison and Maddison 2000) for Californian languages, using Goddard's (1996)

Table 2.3 Mantel Matrix Partial Correlations: Construction Techniques (y)/Language (x1)/Distance (x2)

Coefficient	Value
Correlation coefficient (rY1)	0.132123
Correlation coefficient (rY2)	−0.516416
Correlation coefficient (rY12)	−0.213668
Partial correlation (rY1_2)	0.026038
Partial correlation (rY2_1)	−0.504145
Determination of Y by X1 (%)	0.003016
Determination of Y by X2 (%)	0.264167
Total determination of Y (%)	0.267182
Unexplained variance of Y (%)	0.732818

definition, which reflects current consensus among linguists. The Kishino-Hasegawa (1989) test modified to fit Paup 4.0b10 (Swofford 1998) uses parsimony as an optimality criterion. With languages constraining the search, four trees were returned at length 129. All were significantly different at $p < 0.05$, which indicates that there was no *exact* fit between the best-fit tree and trees constrained by the language tree. In short, there was no *perfect* association between the branching descent histories of language and construction methods.

To test for a *partial* association between lineages, the consensus tree for construction methods and the northwest California language tree were exported to COMPONENT 2.0, written by Page (1993). Unlike PAUP*, the software does not infer trees from data but rather requires that preexisting trees be entered into the program, after which comparison methods can be applied. Comparison of trees may employ a measure of similarity between two trees; the technique employed represents the two trees as sets of simpler structures and then uses a measure of similarity between sets. In the current study, the triplets measure was employed because this is the smallest possible informative subtree on a rooted tree. Again, the Chimariko were selected as the outgroup.

COMPONENT 2.0 also generates random trees for use in, and as the basis for, statistical tests. The program uses a uniform random number generator based on Schrage's (1979) FORTRAN implementation of the linear-congruence method. Measures of similarity between trees can then be compared with similarities between a set of random trees. If the similarity between two data trees—construction methods and language—is closer than between random trees, then we can assume that their similarity is greater than one would expect as a result of chance alone (the higher the figure, the more different the trees).

From the six best-fit trees outlined above, a strict consensus tree was generated in Paup 4.0b10 and imported into COMPONENT 2.0, along with the tree for northwest California languages (see figure 2.4). The distance between the two trees was recorded as *172 (resolved and different)*. However, when tested against triplets measures between one thousand randomly generated trees, it was readily apparent that the association between the topology of the language tree and that of the tree for built structures was no closer than one would expect by chance (triplets figures for structures is 172, well within the range of values from one thousand random trees [*min* 144; *max* 403; *mean* 302; *s.d.* 35]). To conclude, there is *no* identifiable association between languages and construction methods—they appear to have entirely separate histories of branching descent.

Finally, Mantel Matrix results were also performed and indicate a much higher level of unexplained variance in the data (table 2.3) than for the basketry assemblages. While proximity accounts for 27 percent, it is clear that the correlation with language is very low (less than 1 percent), as with basketry.

California: Summary

This study has employed a range of methods and models from evolutionary biology in order to reconstruct long-term processes of cultural diversification among hunting, fishing, and gathering communities of northwest California. Despite the region's high linguistic diversity, the evolution of basketry traditions appears to have been strongly influenced by the blending and borrowing of styles among the groups. With lines of river access and proximity measures providing the most convincing explanations underlying basketry variance, the conclusion is that face-to-face contacts and cumulative movements and exchanges of peoples and practices among the communities led to the observed patterns of basketry diversity.

Variability in construction styles shows more localized differentiation, with northern and southern traditions distinguishing themselves starkly from each other. To the north, the clusters (with much internal blending and hybridization) appear to map onto the broader Klamath drainage; the southern cluster is based on the broader Eel River area. Yet both these clusters contain diverse languages. Again, language is only weakly correlated with variability in this domain of culture, and there is a stronger association with proximity measures, suggesting that intercommunity contact and "nearest neighbor" interactions have generated much of the variation in construction styles. At the same time, stark boundaries in style run across the region, in particular, between the Chimariko and Hupa groups.

How can these findings be linked back to (a) the cultural transmission and social learning models and (b) the ethnography outlined above? Several general scenarios can be explored:

- *Kinship-Driven Basketry Diffusion:* Given that kinship details suggest that women were frequently married both within and between linguistic communities, it appears highly likely that the social mobility of basketry producers contributed to this pattern. It is easy to understand how initial production skills may well have been passed vertically, perhaps from biological mother to daughter, yet subsequently carried into new communities after marriage. If a girl learned skills from several teachers of the older generation, these, too, would be carried on into new communities, and vice versa. Conceivably, the only way in which basketry diversity could match branching linguistic diversity would be if kinship was more endogamous (within the speech community) or nonlocal brides were forced to adopt the local basketry styles of their husbands' communities after marriage.

- *Prestige-Driven Diffusion:* Kinship details also reveal that men tend to remain in their local communities and women move after marriage. If men are responsible for building structures (dwellings and sweat houses), then this might well lead to local "cultural lineages" forming. The results do indicate two distinct housing traditions in the northern and southern parts of the study region. However, at a local scale, there appears to have been much blending and borrowing across linguistic frontiers despite the general tendency for patrilocal residence. Obsession with prestige and the acquisition of household wealth does appear to be characteristic of regional culture, and it may be possible that housing innovations deemed to be "prestigious" would have been copied rapidly by neighboring households. Through time, this would have led to a more general conformity in housing styles across larger geographic areas inhabited by several distinct ethnolinguistic communities.

Finally, these working conclusions must be tempered by the realization that the colonial history of California was extremely traumatic for indigenous groups (see Castillo 1978), resulting in an estimated 90 percent demographic collapse between 1770 and 1900, as well as huge disruptions in their way of life. Overall, early impacts were more pronounced in the south of California, whereas contact with the tribes in northwest California came later, in the mid-nineteenth century, just before the postulated "ethnographic present" of the material presented here. The potential significance of this demographic bottleneck for the nature and extent of the linguistic and cultural variation recorded in the early twentieth century (albeit relating to the earlier "traditional" culture) should not be forgotten (Shennan 2000, 2001). Thus, even though enough traces of various northwest California languages may have survived long enough to be salvaged and recorded, increased dislocations and resettlements associated with colonialism may have thrown together isolated members of different communities, leading to a homogenization of diverse native cultures in ways that had not occurred during the pre-contact era.

To conclude, the current findings strongly support the blending or hybridization model of long-term cultural evolution, despite the region's high linguistic diversity and the fixed and predictable resources of northwest California. For further studies of cultural transmission, the strict phylogenetic model (for example, Boyd et al. 1997) remains a useful null hypothesis. In practice, this kind of transmission scenario may occur quite rarely and requires significant demic diffusion during early stages of colonization or expansion (for example, Gray and Jordan 2000; Holden 2002) and/or a strict endogamous kinship system, a strong mistrust of outsiders, and the use of material culture to actively signal group identity (see Collard and Tehrani 2005; Tehrani and Collard 2002). All these factors are absent from northwest California, and while the diverse languages spoken in the area do shed some light on "deeper" population histories, variability in material culture appears to be a product of more recent phases of regional interaction and local exchange.

Evolution of Cultural Diversity: General Outlook

Accounting for the emergence of spatial and temporal variations in material culture lies at the heart of the archaeological and anthropological endeavor. Cultural transmission theory represents a promising framework for combining regional scale studies of ecology, demography, and culture history with linguistic and genetic data, while retaining scope for integrating theories of human, face-to-face interaction and intent. Applying this broader body of theory to appropriate datasets will enable us to develop more integrated accounts of long-term human history in co-evolving cultural-ecological systems. The three regional-scale projects outlined in other chapters of this volume—covering the American Southwest, Hawai'i, and Mesopotamia—represent ideal bodies of material for taking this broader program of research to new levels. Further simulation studies might explore in more quantitative detail the kinds of general relationships among mobility, marriage practice, and material culture diversity that have been explored in the present "real world" case study.

Acknowledgments

I would like to thank Sander van der Leeuw and Tim Kohler for the invitation to take part in the lively meeting at the Santa Fe Institute in October 2004. Comments, suggestions, and feedback from other participants were gratefully received. I wrote this paper during my two-year Leverhulme Trust Special Research Fellowship at the Department of Archaeology, University of Sheffield. The first eighteen months of the fellowship were spent at University College London (UCL), and I would like to thank the Leverhulme Trust, UCL, and Sheffield University for jointly supporting this award. Work on the broader theme was initiated while I served as an Arts and Humanities Research Council (AHRC)–funded postdoctoral researcher at the Institute of Archaeology, University College London. In its continued support for the AHRC Center for the Evolution of Cultural Diversity (CECD), University College London, the broader contribution of the UK's AHRC is gratefully acknowledged. Finally, I would like to thank my friends and colleagues at CECD, UCL, and Sheffield University for providing an extremely stimulating intellectual atmosphere in which to work.

CHAPTER 3

Modeling the Role of Resilience in Socioenvironmental Co-evolution
The Middle Rhône Valley between
1000 BC and AD 1000

Jean-François Berger, Laure Nuninger,

and Sander van der Leeuw

This chapter discusses part of a research project investigating the spatiotemporal aspects of resilience in complex social systems.[1] That project aims to develop a conceptual model of the dynamics that drive the trajectories of regional socioenvironmental systems by looking at three case studies. We report here on one of those case studies.

The conceptual model combines elements of four research domains. The natural sciences have contributed to the set of ideas that is sometimes called "the science (or theory) of complex systems" (for example, Bak 1996; Kauffman 1993; Levin 1999; Nicolis and Prigogine 1977). The sciences of organization and information have contributed to our understanding of the dynamics of social organization (for example, Bateson 1973; Beer 1959; Simon 1973, 1981). Some of their ideas on the hierarchical nature of organizations have been taken up and adapted by ecologists (for example, Allen and Hoekstra 1992; Allen and Starr 1982; Allen, Tainter, and Hoekstra 2003; O'Neill et al. 1986; Pattee 1973). Other ecologists (for example, Carpenter et al. 2001; Gunderson 2000; Holling 1973, 1986) have contributed an approach called "resilience theory" to describe the internal dynamics of ecosystems. Finally, some social anthropologists (de Vries, Thompson, and Wirtz 2002; Thompson, Ellis, and Wildavsky 1989) have developed a very similar approach to societal dynamics, which they term "culture theory." The first attempt at a synthesis of these various ideas comes from a collaborative effort of ecologists and social scientists (Gunderson and Holling 2002).

McGlade and van der Leeuw (1997), and more recently Redman and Kinzig (2002), have attempted to show the relevance of some of these ideas to archaeology.

The dynamics of socioenvironmental systems oscillate between chance and necessity. In very general terms, one could say that the continued existence of socioenvironmental systems depends on the adequacy of the interaction between their societal and environmental dynamics. This adequacy varies through time with the development of both these domains. At certain times, they are impervious or indifferent to perturbations because their internal dynamics are sufficiently coherent and dominant to be able to ignore them. In such a "robust" state, a system necessarily follows its own trajectory. At other times, such socioenvironmental systems are so vulnerable that any perturbation, large or small, can cause an irreparable loss of coherence. In such a "window of vulnerability," the system will survive only if, by chance, no perturbations occur. The intermediate ("resilient") state, in which the socioenvironmental system survives by adapting, seems to us the most interesting. We will explore it further in order to understand the processes and parameters that impact on the sustainability of socioenvironmental systems.

First, the resilience varies with the connectivity between the system's societal and environmental dynamics. In many areas, the progressive appropriation of nature by society has, little by little, increased that connectivity, so that in the past few centuries, the slightest climatic or anthropogenic perturbation triggered an oscillation of crisis proportions.

Second is the speed with which the various dynamics that constitute the system can adapt to one another. This depends on the character of the regional environmental dynamics, the constraints inherent in the system, and the rates of change of its temporalities. Also, this depends on the speed at which the society's participants identified and analyzed new circumstances and devised ways to deal with them.

Third, the history of the socioenvironmental system is important. Participants in an evolving social system necessarily use extant elements previously constructed. These elements may be material, such as a road network, but may also be institutional, or sociocultural, as in the case of a society's values or worldview. Often, these are closely integrated, as in the case of technology. The material legacies are usually easier to change than the social or cultural ones, because they are more tangible.

To investigate the interaction between the successive social formations in a region and their environments, we must first understand the following:

- The periodicities of the climate dynamics over the very long term
- The natural dynamics of the landscape in the area
- The societal dynamics involved
- The technologies enabling the interaction between the societies and their environments

Once these are understood, we may hope to identify the respective societal and environmental dynamics by looking at the long-term co-evolution and interaction of both.

And that will finally put us in a position to model these dynamics formally, which is the aim of our project.

Environmental Characteristics of the Middle Rhône Valley

The Mediterranean constitutes a transitional bioclimatic zone between the temperate and tropical zones and between humid and arid zones. It is characterized by a "staged" vegetation (Ozenda 1964) adapted to summer drought and cool winters. This location makes the Rhône Valley vegetation highly reactive to climatic changes and human pressure. The middle Rhône Valley, between the Drôme Valley in the north and the Aygues Valley in the south, is located on the northern edge of the Mediterranean morpho- and bioclimatic systems (plate 1b), just south of Alpine climatic influences. Its average annual rainfall ranges between 700 and 1,200 mm. Precipitation is concentrated mainly in spring and autumn; during the two summer months, the area is affected by typical Mediterranean dryness. The river Rhône flows continuously because it is fed by the alpine climate, but the flow in its tributaries in the calcareous southern pre-Alps diminishes considerably in summer.

The two regions dealt with in this study, Valdaine and Tricastin, are juxtaposed but present different geographic contexts (plate 1a, c). The Valdaine Basin is characterized by the close proximity of the pre-Alps, and its relief is steeper than that of the Tricastin plain. The former consists primarily of large detritic fans and numerous hills and has a higher average elevation. The Tricastin consists of the Holocene floodplain and fans deposited by the Rhône and its tributaries, surrounded by lower alluvial terraces. Its relief varies between 1 and 3 m.

Global Climate Change...and a Regional Anomaly!

The main environmental events have been summarized in Berger (2003b) and Berger and others (2003). The beginning of the Holocene is marked by diffuse erosion under an expanding vegetation cover, dominated by bioclimatic parameters (9000–6500 cal. BC). Wildfires and erosion cycles are then strictly correlated. During the Atlantic and the "climatic optimum" (6500–3200 cal. BC), we observe biostasis and the first human-induced crises of the landscape in the Neolithic period. Later prehistory (3200–120 cal. BC) is characterized by strong contrasts between the human and the climate dynamics. The end of the Iron Age and the Roman period (100 BC–AD 100) shows an important and extensive weakening of the soil systems, with different morphological consequences. Late Antiquity (AD 100–600) appears more stable until the Early Middle Ages (AD 600–1000), which witness the return of landscape instability. The High Middle Ages (AD 1000–1500) are marked by a relative stability of the landscape, followed by delayed morphogenetic activity due to earlier human pressure on the vegetation. Finally, the modern and contemporaneous periods (AD 1500 to present) see the conjunction of a multisecular climatic deterioration (the "Little Ice Age") and the Holocene maximum in human pressure on the environment.

To summarize, in the early Holocene, major climate and anthropogenic factors have to act in conjunction to have effects on the landscape. But from the end of the protohistoric period (which saw an increasing intensification of societal impact on the environment), the slightest oscillation in either climatic or societal dynamics had major effects on the landscape. In ten thousand years, the combined system has become hypercoherent, and its tolerance highly compromised.

Overall, the correlation is excellent between these regional data and the global climate change data provided by ocean circulation patterns, glaciers, and lakes, as well as the residual ^{14}C in the atmosphere provided by the Arctic and Antarctic ice cores (plate 2). Both globally and locally, two kinds of climatic periodicity may be observed, of 2,500–2,300 and 1,500–1,000 years, respectively (Berger et al. 2003). The geosystems of the northern Mediterranean thus seem to register these millenary oscillations, which are closely related to oceanic and solar fluctuations.

That being so, recent geoarchaeological studies (Berger et al. 2003) show that no global climate signal indicates a major climatic "crisis" in the Roman period! Nevertheless, the pedosedimentary sequences observed in southern France seem to indicate that the landscape at this time was highly unstable. This period witnesses an important deterioration of the drainage systems of the lower Rhône Basin. Its impact seems almost equivalent to that of the Early Iron Age (the beginnings of the Sub-Atlantic, 800–600 BC) or the Little Ice Age (AD 1500–1900). This deterioration in Roman times seems principally due to human activity, in particular, to the very widespread and rapid transformation of the countryside from predominantly forest and grassland to intensively cultivated agricultural land.

Identifying the Component Processes of Landscape Change

We have chosen a wide range of indicators to identify the major fluctuations of the geosystems of the region. Among them are the following:

- The fluctuations between meandering and braided river systems that are associated with the relative proportions of solids and liquids in the river system

- The progress of the deltalike formations on the coast and upstream from the detrital cones of the piedmont

- The average accretion rate in the alluvial plains

- The variation in particle sizes of the high water deposits of the rivers

- The origin of the sediment flows (petrography of the detrital sediments)

- The fluctuation of the water level in the aquifers (as identified by analyses of the soils and microalgae, as well as malacological analyses)

- The micromorphological study of the structural stability of the soils (the state of their surface, the degree of destruction of their structural stability, their conductivity to water)

- The form and intensity of runoff on the slopes

- The structure and composition of the vegetation

- The fire regime and the intensity of wildfires

- The ways in which the soils were exploited by the inhabitants (Berger et al. 2003)

The torrential and sometimes excessive nature of the indicators observed in our area of study is due to its mountainous topography, its lithology (mainly soft rocks), and, above all, its subhumid climate, known to be one of the most erosive in the world. Soil micromorphological studies across the area enabled us to characterize its pedoclimatic features, to determine the spatial extent of all stages of soil degradation, erosion, and regeneration, and therefore to understand the combined effect of people and climate over the long term.

A recent regional chronostratigraphic synthesis of six river basins in the middle Rhône Valley, based on 300 soundings and cores and 250 ^{14}C dates, distinguished a hundred archaeological levels, combining into twenty-four hydrological and pedological phases between 1000 BC and AD 1000 (Berger 2003a; Berger and Brochier 2006). Three main states of the landscape dynamics were observed (plate 3). The first is associated with a stable optimum (see plate 3a): the soils are well drained, in and of themselves, with good agricultural potential; frequent wildfires occur, both natural and anthropogenic in origin. Many Neolithic to Bronze Age sites in the plains are associated with this kind of environment.

The second corresponds to maximum instability of the landscape, with a dominance of North Atlantic air currents (plate 3b). The annual and multiyear water balance is often positive. This leads to high instability of the river systems (braided styles) and rising water tables. Before people knew how to drain the landscape, these phases strongly limited subsistence in the lower plains and humid areas—only herding was possible. As a result, from the Neolithic to the Gaulish period there are very few settlements on the plains in these phases.

The third configuration is associated with short periods of high instability, dominated by tropical air currents (plate 3c). Flash floods and fires were common in these situations, but the alluvial plains do not show much evidence that these conditions imposed serious constraints on the prehistoric and early historic economies.

The Overall Evolution of Settlement Systems from the Late Bronze Age to the Middle Ages

Settlements reflect ancient choices about the landscape. In the Tricastin and Valdaine, intensive field walking, soundings, and rescue excavations have identified eight hundred sites, dating from the Late Bronze Age to the beginning of the Middle Ages (see plate 1a, d; figure 3.1). Because surface surveys are more representative of ancient settlement densities in certain periods or regions than in others, we corrected for the biases of the surface surveys with respect to certain cultural horizons by taking into account subsequent soil erosion and deposition. Next, the total probable number of sites in any one landscape unit was determined statistically (see Verhagen and Berger

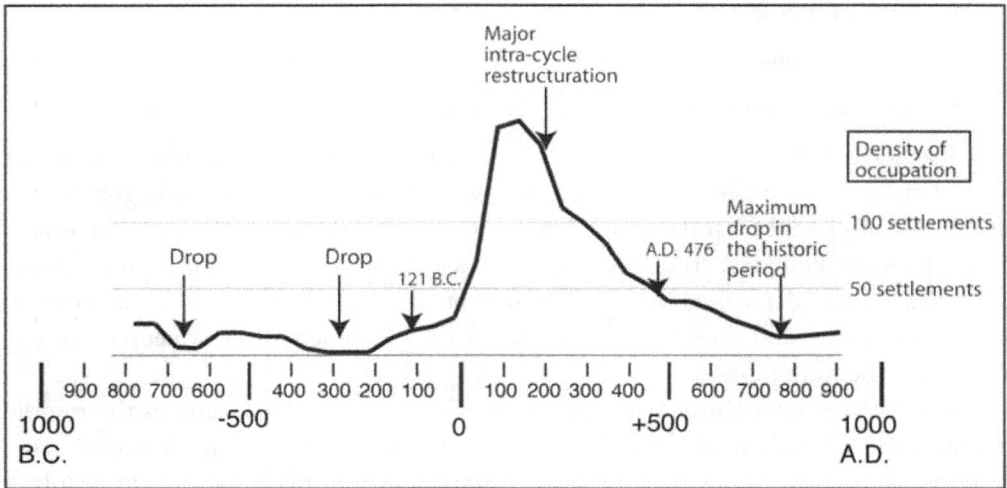

Figure 3.1. The evolution of settlement density between 800 BC and AD 800. Note that the Roman Empire constitutes only part of the cycle because it is riding on the back of a longer-term socioenvironmental expansion.

2001). The results indicate variation in settlement density between 800 BC and AD 800, marked by a first maximum at the end of the Bronze Age (ca. 800 BC), a first abrupt decrease during the seventh century BC, followed by another peak between 600 and 400 BC and a second drop in numbers during the fourth and third centuries BC. The third and most important peak in occupation density begins around 200 BC and culminates during the first century AD. It thus begins before the arrival of the Romans in *Gallia Narbonensis* (ca. 120 BC). A major intracycle restructuration occurs in the course of the second century AD. More than a third of the settlements are then abandoned in less than a century. This decrease continues during the following centuries, but more slowly. A brief respite in this trend can be observed in the fifth and sixth centuries AD, but it continues throughout the seventh century. Finally, a minimum settlement density is reached in the eighth and ninth centuries AD. The Roman Empire constitutes only part of the cycle, riding on the back of a socioenvironmental expansion.

But the number of settlements per period does not assess the real impact of settlements on the landscape. We have therefore calculated the total surface occupied by all establishments occupied in any century (figure 3.2a). For the Iron Age, the occupied total surface in the Valdaine and Tricastin is relatively variable, pointing to an unstable settlement system.[2] Moreover, there are considerable differences between the two areas. First, the total surface of the settlements occupied in the Tricastin during the first Iron Age is proportionally large, whereas that of the settlements in the Valdaine is almost negligible. Because the number of establishments in the Tricastin is almost zero in the seventh century BC and relatively low in the sixth and fifth centuries BC, settlement must have been agglomerated. In the Valdaine, the situation is clearly dif-

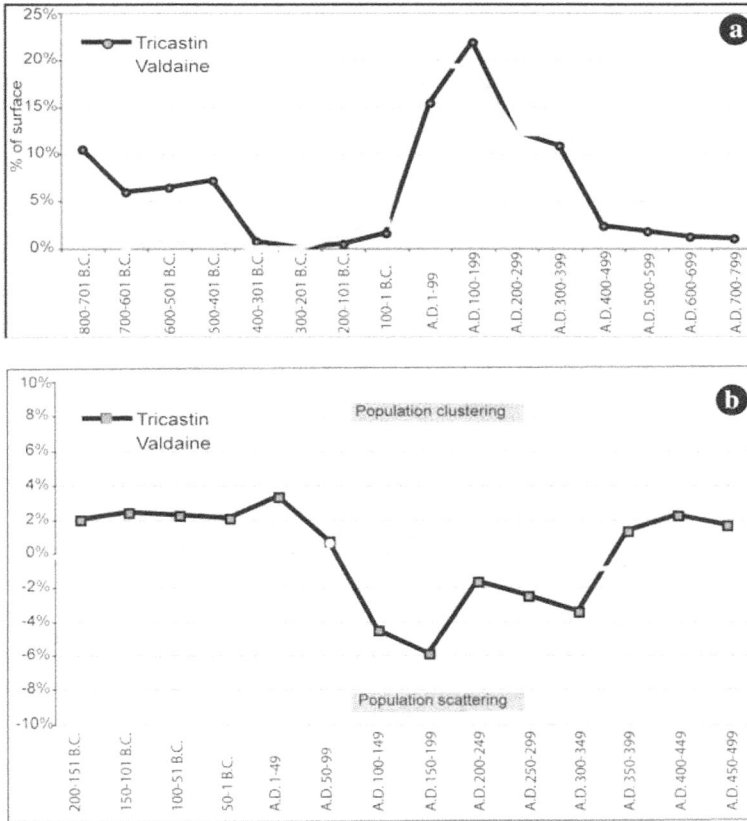

Figure 3.2. Aggregation and disaggregation of settlement: (a) graph of the total surface occupied per century in the Tricastin and Valdaine between 800 BC and AD 800 and (b) evolution of clustered/scattered systems of settlement in the Tricastin plain and the Valdaine Basin from 200 BC to AD 500.

ferent. There, in the sixth century BC, the number of establishments is relatively significant, but their total surface is not. Most individual settlements must have been very small.

Both the number and the surface of settlements in the third century BC is relatively low, as is the case in the nearby lower Ardèche (Durand 2002) or in the east Languedoc where big *oppida* (large hilltop forts) were still dynamic (Bertoncello and Nuninger in press; Nuninger 2002). The area seems to be almost depopulated. Many oppida are temporarily abandoned, and few smaller settlements are found. At the scale of the northwest Mediterranean region, an apparent decline in trade in the fourth and third centuries BC is also observed. But we observe a marked progression in the number of settlements during the second and first centuries BC, even though the total settlement surface increases very little. Roman colonization begins in small, relatively dispersed settlements.

At the height of the Roman Empire, the total settlement surface and the number of settlements increase hand-in-hand in both areas. But in Late Antiquity and at the beginning of the Middle Ages (fifth to eighth centuries AD), in spite of a general reduction in the number and surface of settlements, the Valdaine Basin seems to be doing a little better than the Tricastin. In the Tricastin, the major reduction in total settlement surface that accompanies a much less marked decrease in the number of settlements suggests settlement dispersal.

An Example of Analysis at High Chronological Resolution

To understand the dynamics behind these oscillations, we shall now focus on a shorter period (200 BC–AD 500), for which better documentation exists. Figure 3.2b shows the difference between the change in the surface occupied and that of the number of establishments. A positive difference indicates a clustered settlement system (fewer, larger sites), and a negative difference indicates a scattered system (more, smaller sites) (Nuninger 2002). The graph clearly contrasts the relative stability of the settlement pattern in the Valdaine (with fluctuations of less than 2 percent) with the more dynamic development in the Tricastin. But even in the Tricastin case, the greatest oscillation (which occurs over one century) does not exceed 10 percent. It clearly indicates the passage from a clustered settlement pattern to a dispersed one at the beginning of the second century AD (see figure 3.2b). This change accompanies the peak in new creations of agricultural establishments in the Rhône Valley during the first century AD (see figure 3.1). The return of the settlement system to a form close to that of its early days occurs in two stages, the first in the first half of the third century AD and the second in the second half of the fourth century AD. In Late Antiquity, the settlement pattern is clustered again, and that tendency continues into the Middle Ages, until the creation of the typical villages of the High Middle Ages (tenth to twelfth centuries AD) (see Favory et al. 1999).

We explain these differences in the development of settlement systems between these two nearby areas with reference to their geoeconomic history. The Tricastin plain is nearer to the regional capital (*Augusta Tricastinorum*) and to the major communication routes of the Rhône Valley (the *via Agrippina* and the river). Its soils are favorable for the establishment of vineyards (on the vast alluvial terraces), and viticulture led to large financial investments (wine-growing *villae*) during the first century AD (Jung et al. 2001). The area thus felt the full force of a crisis in viticulture that hit most of *Gallia Narbonensis* at the end of the second century AD (Buffat and Pellecuer 2001; Jung et al. 2001). The Valdaine, farther from the main economic networks and with more contrasted landscapes, is less dependent on viticulture (except for the quaternary terraces of the Rhône in its western part). Its economic profile is polycultural and less sensitive to economic fluctuations. Hence, during the Roman period it maintains stable settlements networks.

The Main Landscape Units and Their Relation to the Settlement Pattern

In order to define the main landscape units, we included in a geographic information system (GIS) a range of information on the middle Rhône Valley landscapes, including their lithology, soils, geomorphology, and pedosedimentary data (Verhagen and Berger 2001). Nine landscape units were defined and mapped by automated reclassification. We then positioned the settlements in their landscape and calculated their relation to the surrounding soils, the hydrology, and the lithological, morphostructural, and topographical parameters of their environment. That enabled us to identify the most probable vegetation surrounding them.

Calculating for each century the distribution of the settlements within the nine landscape units enabled us to compile regional diagrams (plate 4a) showing the principal tendencies in soil exploitation. The diagrams show a clear preference for fluvial soils and wetlands during the Late Bronze Age (800–700 BC). The total exploited surface in these rich alluvial plains and the wet basins of the piedmont is markedly reduced during the Early Iron Age (700–500 BC). An expansion of settlement begins again in the Late Iron Age (ca. 200 BC), in the same areas as before.[3] Settlement expansion reaches its maximum in Roman Antiquity (AD 1–500). At that time, a wider range of soils is exploited than ever before. In the third and fourth centuries AD, a restructuring of the settlement system occurs, which manifests itself in a brief period of increase in the number of hilltop settlements. It is followed by two centuries of partial recolonization of settlements in lower areas that had been abandoned a few centuries earlier. Finally, in the sixth century AD, Roman society (and its settlement system) begins to disintegrate. Hence, at the analytical scale of the physiographic unit (plate 4b), the tendencies observed above, including the abrupt rupture of the Early Iron Age, are confirmed. We observe the same dynamics in the eastern Languedoc (Favory et al. 1999; Nuninger 2002; Tourneux 2000).

The cumulative diagrams (see plate 4a, b) show a complete settlement cycle of fifteen centuries. They clearly highlight an abrupt break in the organization of the settlement of Valdaine and Tricastin around 700 BC, that is, during the Bronze/Iron Age transition.[4] The eighth century BC undoubtedly corresponds to the end of a settlement cycle that began at the end of the Middle Bronze Age (Berger and Vital, study in progress). The new cycle is marked by a progressive descent of settlements from the tops of the hills to the fluvial soils of the lower plains. The largest number of sites, the largest total settlement surface, and the widest range of exploited environments are reached in the middle of this cycle (first and second centuries AD); at the beginning of the Middle Ages, people move back to hilltops and similar locations. But the new settlement pattern is different: rather than scattered, it is now nucleated.

The second major rupture observed occurs in a much more progressive way during the second part of Classical Antiquity. It begins in the second century AD with a slow but constant reduction in the settlement of alluvial plains and humid areas and with a corresponding increase in the number of settlements on Pleistocene terraces and alluvial fans, as well as at the base of hillslopes. From the fourth century AD, the settlements are mainly distributed on hills and plateaus. This tendency culminates during the eighth century AD, marking the end of this cycle of settlement.

The Evolution of Settlement Systems

To monitor, insofar as possible, the main tendencies in territorial management over the period concerned, we carried out a correspondence analysis (AFC).[5] In the resulting plot (plate 5a), axis 1 separates the relief associated with sedimentary rocks from the other forms of relief, and axis 2 opposes the highlands and the lowlands. The projection of the archaeological settlements on these two dimensions reveals an almost perfect relation between their position in space (landscape units) and their chronology (plate 5b). The two periods characterized by a tendency to settle on, and exploit, heights (700–500 BC and AD 400–800) show clearly on axis 2, but they occur on opposite ends of axis 1, which distinguishes between different lithologies. The dynamics of the soil occupation, even when occupied geographical space contracts, is in perpetual movement on a secular scale (plate 5c).

The period 700–600 BC is characterized by exploitation of resistant limestones, karstic relief and hydrology, and not very thick Mediterranean red soils. Settlements are predominantly located on the hills and plateaus. Defensive concerns seem to take precedence over agropastoral production. In effect, this period sees important socioeconomic and political disturbances associated with migrations in both the Rhône Basin and in Switzerland (Vital 1990). But the possible contribution of simultaneous, abrupt climate change, on the scale of the Rhône Valley (or even the northern hemisphere; see plate 2), cannot be ruled out. From the end of the ninth century BC, we also see a strong and sudden increase in levels of the circum-alpine lakes and the lakes in the Jura (Van Geel and Magny 2002).

The second period of occupation of the high points in the landscape (Late Antiquity to the Early Middle Ages) is particularly interesting because it indicates a different choice of soils at the lithological level (with consequences at the level of landscape morphology, hydrology, and agricultural potential). At the end of Antiquity (fifth century AD), the settlements are concentrated at the base of the slopes, where thick colluvial soils dominate, and higher up on soft rocks, mainly marls and molassic substrates. During the sixth and seventh centuries, settlements are preferentially found on soft rocks and somewhat later on intermediate rocks. This concentration of sites in the highlands is due to the same processes that occurred during the first Iron Age (climate change and sociopolitical constraints), but the human communities responded in different ways. They chose soils that were easier to exploit and more productive (milder slopes; thicker soils; not very stony, lighter soils that are easier to work; better water availability). The eighth century AD sees a more marked retraction of agropastoral territories and their concentration on intermediate geological substrates (marno-limestones and sandstone). This period therefore resembles the seventh century BC in many respects, but concern with defense may be more marked in the Early Middle Ages, following the emergence of feudal society (see plate 5c).

The correspondence analysis shows that in the periods between these two extremes of the cycle, the sites located on the fluvial soils are of primary importance, and a maximum is reached in the diversification of the exploited landscape units.

Land Management Strategies and the Evolution of Agriculture

Although historical information about Roman agriculture and land management strategies exists, such information does not take the specifics of this region into account. Hence, we base our arguments in this section on both on-site and off-site paleoenvironmental data.

The data concerning the morphosedimentary and pedological evolution of the area have been published, and they are summarized above. The chronostratigraphical context is still being refined (Berger and Brochier 2006). For the moment, we can conclude that the period we are covering here has witnessed three major periods of climatic degradation, around 700–650 BC, around the beginning of our era, and around AD 550. Other, shorter or more localized phases of degradation appear around 350–300 BC, AD 200–250, and AD 750. Stable phases—in which soils regenerated, streams cut deeper into sediments, and fluvial plains were exploited—appear around 900–800 BC, 200–150 BC, AD 350–450, and after AD 900 (see plate 3a). The Gaulish-Roman expansion cycle is then coinciding with the middle of a stable hydroclimatic phase (figure 3.3).

Our information about agriculture comes from various sources: paleosols, ancient river courses and ditches in the landscape, and storage structures and hearths in archaeological excavations. The history of hydraulic technology and of the fluctuations in hydraulic regimes has been reconstructed by analyzing approximately one hundred fossil canals and ditches (Berger 2001; Berger and Jung 1999) and a score of ditches in a marsh near the villa of Vernai (upper Rhône Valley; Berger et al. 2003). Two kinds of interacting dynamics affect the costs and benefits of the region's water infrastructure for agriculture: (1) the form of the rivers, which determine both the level of the aquifers (and the need to extend the drainage systems) and the frequency of inundations (affecting the speed with which irrigation canals fill up with sediment) and (2) the maintenance of drainage ditches by the agrarian communities, which depends on the availability of manpower, the constraints imposed on agriculture by local, provincial, or imperial authorities, and the occurrence of sociopolitical unrest (see Berger 2001).

Paleobotanical data have been obtained from the sieving residues obtained from about thirty off-site geoarchaeological soundings and twenty recent excavations (Delhon 2005). The fill of agrarian structures has also been used. Charcoal and phytolith analysis of these residues has provided the bulk of the information, because pollen is poorly preserved in the region (Berger and Jung 1999). The vegetation dynamics and the pressure of agriculture on the Rhône landscapes are exemplified in a diagram (see figure 3.3) obtained in the southern part of the Tricastin plain (Delhon 2005). Several agropastoral cycles appear in the course of the sixteen centuries studied here. Human impact is in evidence in the development of vineyards and orchards, the exploitation of gallery forests, the increase in (mainly *garrigue*) species associated with the degradation of the climactic oak forest, changes in the relative proportions of Gramineae and dicotyledons in the phytolith spectra, fluctuations in the numbers of light-seeking plants in preforest vegetation associations, and, finally, fluctuations in frequency of pubescent oak and its undergrowth varieties (Delhon 2005).

The Long Term

From a long-term perspective, the various kinds of information obtained from independent sources point to a coherent picture that reinforces the hypotheses discussed here and enables us to understand landscape change in terms of human impact, climate impact, and/or the combined impact of climate and human population. These are the kinds of information concerned:

- Fluctuations in the extent of total plant cover and in the crops harvested (vine, olive, and other tree crops)

- Oscillations in the composition of oak forests between deciduous oak forest, evergreen oak forest, and boxwood

- Indications of soil erosion and sediment deposition in the streambeds

- Fluctuations and reorganizations in land use in the Rhône Valley

- Changes in the periodicities of use, maintenance, and cleaning of the drainage and irrigation networks

The spatial reorganization of the settlement pattern in the seventh century BC is accompanied by a decrease in the agricultural exploitation of riverine and marshy environments during a phase of high hydrosedimentary activity associated with braided river systems. These probably are transformed into pastures. But other landscape units continue to be cultivated (Berger 2003a; Delhon 2005). Never is there a total retreat from the exploitation of the landscape. Activities shift to those parts of the landscape that are better protected from fluctuations in the hydrosedimentary equilibrium, or they change in nature (reduction of cultivation and increase in herding) in periods of major restructuring, such as the seventh century BC and the eighth–ninth centuries AD.

All paleoenvironmental and hydraulic data confirm the expansion of agriculture and its impact on the vegetation, particularly in the very low areas of the region where we see the development of drainage systems from the fifth century BC onwards. From the beginning of the second century BC (cf. infra), the area witnesses the colonization of the fluvial domain, as is evident from the impact of agriculture on the riverine forests (figure 3.3). This phenomenon finds an equivalent in the eastern Languedoc (Lunellois, Vaunage), where intensive colonization of lower areas is documented (Nuninger 2002) and well correlated to an attack on the riverine forest (Chabal 1997). This leads to changes in the rhythm of agriculture, causing an increase in the pressure it exerts on the landscape from the second century BC onwards. Pressure is heaviest from the first century BC to the third century AD.

These new data, which are still subject to interdisciplinary discussions (Berger and Brochier n.d.), confirm in a remarkable way the tendencies observed in the simultaneous and independent analyses of the settlement pressure and the changes in hydrology. In fact, studies in the upper Rhône Valley (Berger and Royet 2003) and the Limagne

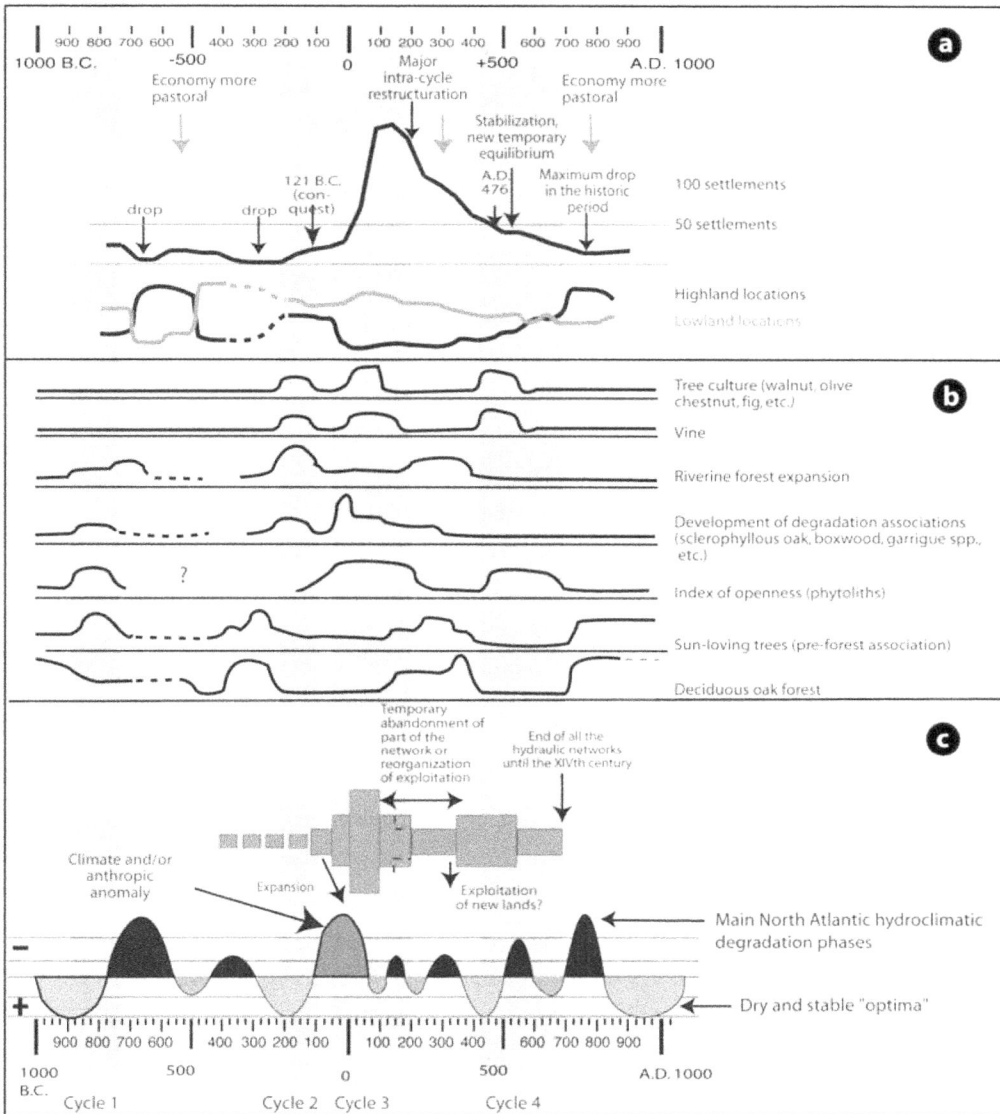

Figure 3.3. Correlation among the evolution of the vegetation in the southern Tricastin (adapted from Delhon 2005), the antique hydraulic system in the Tricastin-Valdaine region (adapted from Berger 2001), and the settlement patterns between 1000 BC and AD 1000. On the basis of these data, we propose a series of agropastoral cycles.

(Guichard 2000; Trément et al. 2004) indicate that the Romans conquered only lands that had been "prepared" by autonomous structuring.

The crisis of the landscape in the Late Republican period and the Early Empire (100 BC–AD 100) (see plate 2 and figure 3.3) was initially interpreted by many, including Berger (1996; Bravard, Verrot-Bourrely, and Salvador 1992; Bruneton et al. 2001; Provansal et al. 1999), as a phase of climatic degradation. But that hypothesis needs to be reconsidered in view of two observations. First, there is no sign of any major global climatic deterioration during Classical Antiquity (see plate 2). Second, the study area witnessed the installation and development of a kind of preindustrial, very intensive agriculture that heavily impacted the environment and fundamentally changed the behavior of the hydrological system. This caused the geosystems to become extremely fragile and increased water activity and erosion, all associated with the cumulative effects of the Roman agricultural system coupled with an irregular pluviometry (Berger 2003b; Berger et al. 2003). This protoindustrial, intensive kind of agriculture is characterized by

- The maximum spread of rural settlement and landscape exploitation in the first century AD (see below).

- The occupation and exploitation of all landscape units of the middle Rhône Valley (see below).

- The appropriation of the landscape by the imposition of Centuriations (land registers) associated with rectangular road and drainage systems (Berger and Jung 1999; Chouquer 1995).

- A significant reduction of the vegetation cover that serves to protect the soils coupled with the spread of regressive plant communities (evergreen oak and boxwood scrub) at the expense of those based on deciduous oak (see figure 3.3). The frequency of wildfires increases, and the proportion of tree pollen regularly dips below 20 percent (Berger 1995; Berger and Jung 1999; Delhon 2005).

- A significant increase of cereal cultivation (Berger and Jung 1999; Leveau 1998) and of the cultivation of crops that do not cover the soil very densely, such as vine and tree crops (Delhon 2005; Jung et al. 2001) (see figure 3.3).

- The progressive eradication of riverine gallery forests beginning in the Late Iron Age (figure 3.3), which removes an important element of protection against inundations from the landscape. Currents increase in speed, and riverbanks are undermined (Berger 2003b; Delhon 2005).

- The increased human control of the hydraulic system, which becomes artificial (Berger 2001; Berger and Jung 1996; Chouquer 1995) (see figure 3.3 and plate 6).

- The systematic drainage and drying out of humid zones (Berger and Jung 1996; Leveau 1998) (see figure 3.3 and plate 6).

- The destruction of structural stability of the soils and acceleration of rill formation, due to intensive agriculture (Berger 2003a; figure 3.4).

The fundamental change in the distribution of the settlements that occurs at the height of the Roman Empire (reorganization of land holdings, new ways to manage water, changes in agropastoral management) (Berger 2001, 2003b; Berger and Jung 1999; Delhon 2005; Jung et al. 2001) has an impact on the environment. The increased emphasis on pastoralism and polyculture, to the detriment of large-scale agriculture,

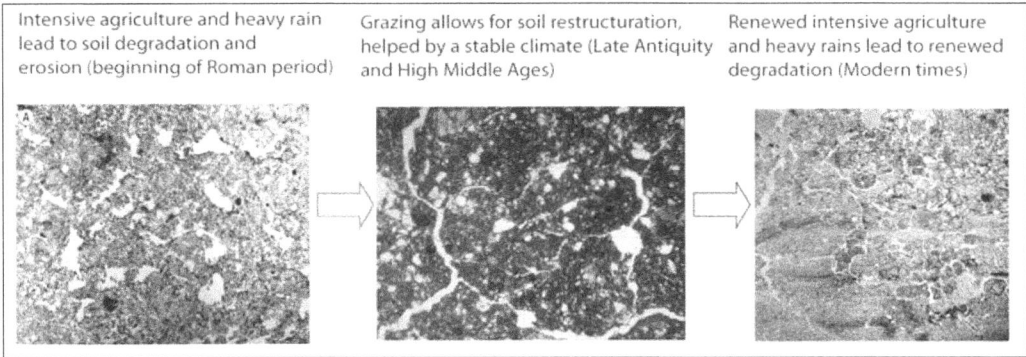

Intensive agriculture and heavy rain lead to soil degradation and erosion (beginning of Roman period)

Grazing allows for soil restructuration, helped by a stable climate (Late Antiquity and High Middle Ages)

Renewed intensive agriculture and heavy rains lead to renewed degradation (Modern times)

Figure 3.4. Resilience is based on the regenerative capacity of certain kinds of geological substrates. Soil micromorphology allows us to spatialize all stages of soil degradation, erosion, and regeneration and thus to spatialize the combined effect of people and climate.

engendered more stable landscapes and led to the recurrence of brownish paleosols until the end of the fifth century AD (Berger 2003a; see plate 3a and figure 3.4). This restructuring of agriculture led to the *agri deserti* described by the classical authors. Such temporarily fallow lands were probably grazed by herds, but in no way should this be seen as a major reduction in agricultural activity, such as occurs in the Late Roman Empire.

The vegetation history of this area registers this reduced human pressure on the countryside (see figure 3.3), but the reduction seems less important than during the first part of the Iron Age or the second part of the Early Middle Ages. A critical analysis of texts by Jaillette (1996) has shown that this process is part of a strategy of dissimulation adopted by the farmers in the face of increasing fiscal pressures. This phase of soil regeneration could explain the development of one last agrarian cycle from AD 400 to 700 (see figure 3.3), because it led to good natural drainage in the lower plains (initially at least) and optimal agrological conditions of the soil cover (requiring less investment and yielding high profits). A small number of ditches dating between the end of the fourth century and the sixth century AD (see figure 3.3c) could represent a new occupation of the landscape, which corresponds to the brief respite in the diminution in settlement observed around the fifth to sixth centuries AD (see figure 3.1). Quantitative data on the evolution of total settlement surface suggests that, at this time, settlement was dispersed in the countryside.

Although this is less easy to document, the end of Antiquity and the beginning of the Middle Ages do not correspond to a total disintegration of agrarian society and a return of the forest after AD 476. Rather, recent paleoenvironmental and hydrological data point to the continuity of the Roman exploitation system and its control over the vegetation until the end of the sixth or the middle of the seventh century AD (see above). And that is the case not only in the middle Rhône Valley. A similar process is documented by advanced palynological, sedimentological, and spatial analyses in the upper Rhône Valley (in the so-called Isle Crémieu between Lyons and Geneva) (Berger et al. in press; Salvador et al. 2005), as well as in the Paris Basin and the lower Loire

Basin in northwestern France (Barbier 1999; Leroyer 1997). The Merovingian tribes that merge with the Gallo-Romans at the end of the fifth century maintain the Roman agricultural system for almost two centuries, while in the Mediterranean Basin and the Rhône Valley an important erosive crisis sets in (see plate 3c and figure 3.3).

We are inclined to ascribe this Mediterranean landscape crisis to tropical rather than oceanic phenomena. It is associated with an increase in the frequency of wildfires and a developed evapotranspiration (concentration of $CaCO_3$ nodules in the soil) (Berger and Brochier 2006). These short-lived geomorphological phenomena may have an impressive impact locally, but they do not durably limit exploitation (see above and plate 3). The last humid hydrosedimentary fluctuation identified in the soils of the Rhône during the eighth century AD corresponds to the lowest human pressure on the landscape (see figure 3.3). Archaeological and paleoeconomic data are still so few during this time in the Rhône Valley that it is difficult to determine whether this retraction should be interpreted as due solely to a major North Atlantic influence on the northern Mediterranean Basin or whether the sociopolitical dynamics of the "Dark Ages" played an important role. It is possible that the settlement system shows centers or microareas of economic development and demographic concentration during this period at the scale of southern France, as happens along the eastern coast of the Languedoc (Raynaud 1990).

Paleoenvironmental data for the "Dark Ages" show a humid phase in which numerous lowlands in temperate and Mediterranean Europe became marshy (Berger and Brochier 2006; Provansal et al. 1999). But human pressure was relatively weak and limited the effect of this climatic deterioration on slopes and river systems (Berger 2003a; Berger and Brochier 2006). Erosion was limited, and the episode is mainly in evidence through the positive water balance in the aquifers, as well as an extension of hydromorphous soils (gley or peat).

Perception and Reaction of the Roman Actors in the Drama

It appears that the Romans did not measure the secondary effects of their agriculture on the soil cover, on erosion, and on the dynamics of the water system. The environmental transformations observed in the course of the Early Roman Empire are due, in part, to choices made by politicians and administrators, farmers, and engineers. Their perception of the landscapes of *Gallia Narbonensis* and their dynamics at the time of Roman conquest (the late second and first centuries BC) determined the spatial organization, the agricultural techniques, and the infrastructure (roads and drainage systems) that we still encounter. These people were not aware of the long-term hydrological dynamics and the effect that the drainage systems they installed had on these. Indeed, they were unaware of the need to maintain the long-term resilience of the geoecosystems involved until their system proved unable to deal with new environmental dynamics, for which they were to a great extent responsible.

The Gallo-Romans nevertheless attempted to respond appropriately to these transformations. They tried to protect themselves against the risk of inundation: in the towns, by regularly topping up the surfaces on which they lived with thick layers of debris, and in the countryside, by improving water management (see plate 6). But these measures often were insufficient in the face of the ever-higher water levels (plate 8).

This belated awareness of environmental changes—in part, due to secondary economic effects of the environmental transformations, which are difficult to monitor archaeologically—may explain the cadastral and fiscal reforms undertaken by the Emperor Vespasian in the second half of the first century AD, as well as Domitian's measures to protect Italian vineyards a few years later. And the rapid changes in the organization of rural settlement in *Gallia Narbonensis* at the beginning of the second century AD undoubtedly reflect local responses to the risks inherent in extensive monoculture (see Favory and van der Leeuw 1998). In fact, the climatoanthropogenic phenomena and problems with which Romans were confronted, and their solutions, appear highly similar to our own.

Summary

The 10,000 years of the Holocene, and, in particular, the period since the Neolithic, have seen major transformations of the northern Mediterranean landscapes. One observes climate cycles of 2,300 to 2,500 years and settlement cycles of shorter duration (two to five centuries), corresponding to phases of increasing and decreasing impact of society on its environment.

Interdisciplinary studies show that the prehistoric and protohistoric societies were heavily dependent on climatic conditions, which determined the size of exploitable soil surfaces, as well as annual agricultural productivity (Arbogast, Magny, and Pétrequin 1995; Berger et al. in press; Tinner et al. 2003). During climatic deteriorations (which were mainly of North Atlantic origin), suitable agricultural and pastoral soils were found only in the plains. Up to the Gaulish period, agricultural societies cultivating cereals are thus not very resilient and depend strongly on the state of the climate. Pastoral societies appear better armed to resist climatic changes, as in the case of the middle Neolithic "Chasséen" (Berger 2003a; Delhon 2005).

The new data presented here for the middle Rhône Valley show a significant rupture in the resilience of the agrosystems in the Middle Iron Age (600–400 BC) (figure 3.5). This crash leads to major transformations in all aspects of social organization. In the following centuries, we see the development of protourbanism, the intensification of economic exchanges (Py 1993), the extension of tree cultivation, and the introduction of Roman water-management technology in southernmost Gaul. As a result, the Roman socioenvironmental system is for some time impervious or indifferent to perturbations because its internal dynamics are sufficiently coherent and dominant to be able to ignore them. And even when it is not, the next two transitions are much more gradual (ca. 200–50 BC) and (AD 300–700). In both these later cases, the system does not crash, but reorganizes the structure shaped during the period 400–200 BC.

These reorganizations allow it to exhibit resilient behavior in the face of environ-

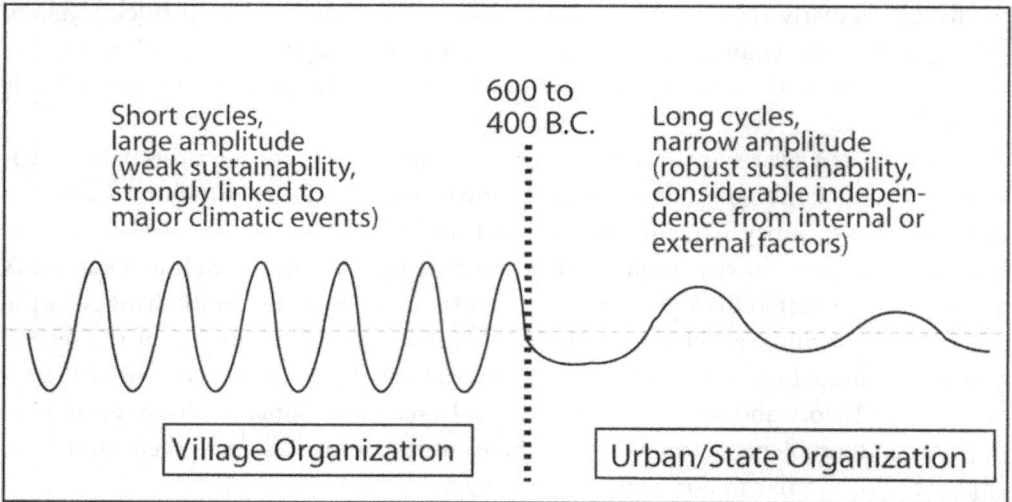

Figure 3.5. Rhythms of change in a sequence of settlement cycles in the middle Rhône Valley, from the Neolithic (village organization) to the Roman period (urban/state organization).

mental perturbations (that is, several hydrosedimentary crises, in part generated or amplified by agrarian exploitation of the landscape), as well as societal ones (that is, the political, military, or socioeconomic changes that characterize the second part of Antiquity). Its resilience may be due to the buffer effect inherent in the particular form of organization of Roman society (relatively loose, horizontal couplings between regions and vertical ones between the regions and the Empire's administration, diversification of agrarian exploitation during Late Antiquity, and so forth), as well as to the Romans' technical and management skills in the area of agricultural exploitation (mastery of hydraulic management, manuring, adaptation of soils to cultivation) (see figure 3.3).

The new balance achieved after these reorganizations resists the severe sociopolitical crises that characterize the last centuries of the Roman Empire. The barbarian invasions do not seem to disturb the system at all. Either the newcomers adapted rapidly by amalgamating with the Gallo-Roman substrate of the countryside, or they quickly adopted the Roman technology. Altogether, the agropastoral and economic system is thus even more resilient than the political system (which collapses at the end of the fifth century AD). It does not disappear until the beginning of the Middle Ages (towards AD 700), more than two centuries after the official fall of the Western Roman Empire.

A cycle of between nine and twelve centuries can therefore be defined (depending on whether one sees its beginnings around 200 or 500 BC). It appears much longer than earlier cycles and can be compared to the cycle that starts in the Early Middle Ages (tenth century AD) and continues until the beginning of the twentieth century, resisting one period of major climatic degradation (the Little Ice Age).

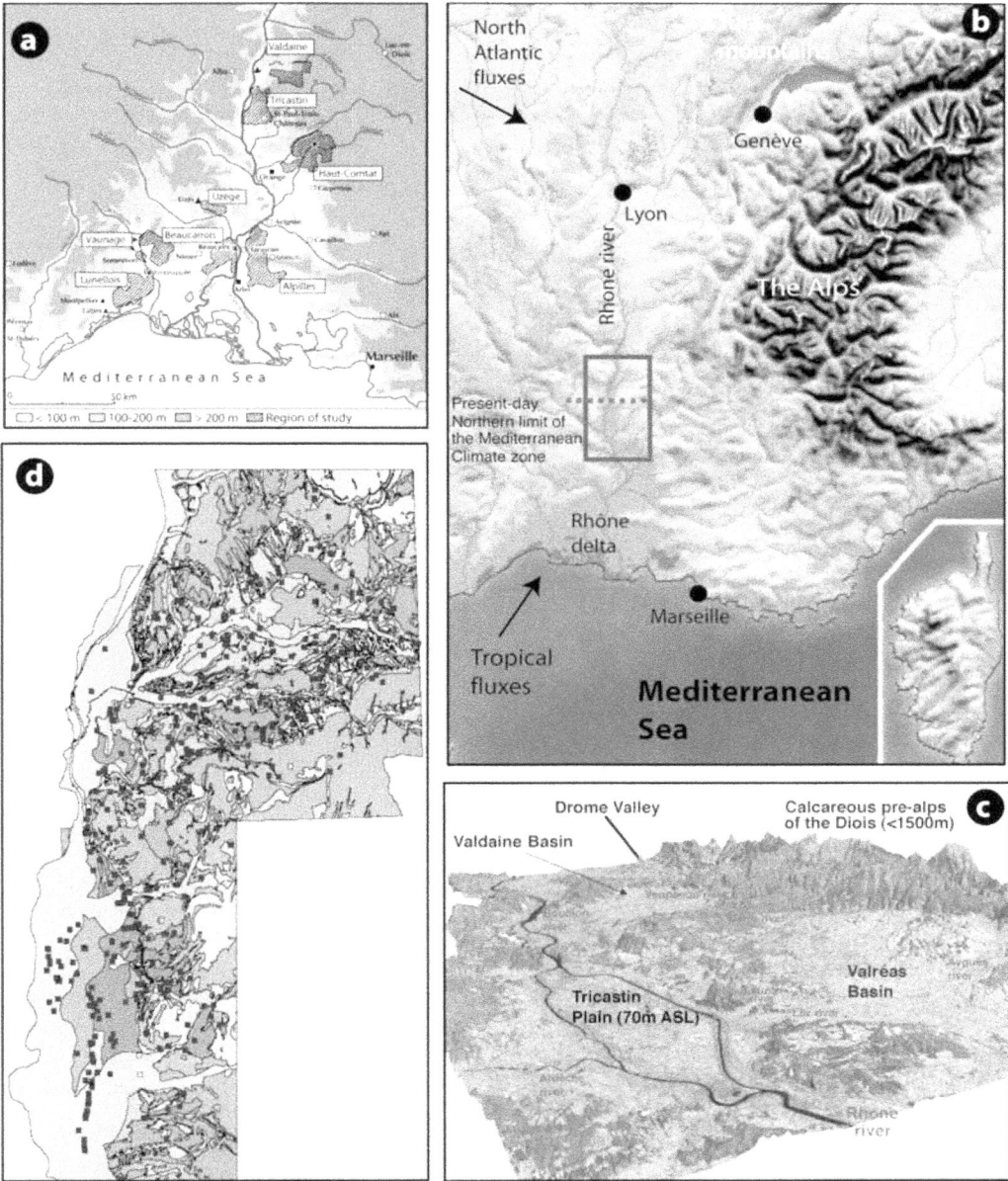

Plate 1. The middle and lower Rhône Valley: (a) location of the study areas in the Archaeomedes project; (b) location of the areas studied and the main bioclimatic characteristics; (c) three-dimensional view of the middle Rhône Valley from the southwest (SPOT satellite image over DEM)—in dark green, the spread of the forest cover since the beginning of the twentieth century (which is strictly located on plateaus, hills around the Rhône River, and more distant mountains); and (d) map of the sites in the Tricastin and Valdaine projected on the nine landscape units we distinguished.

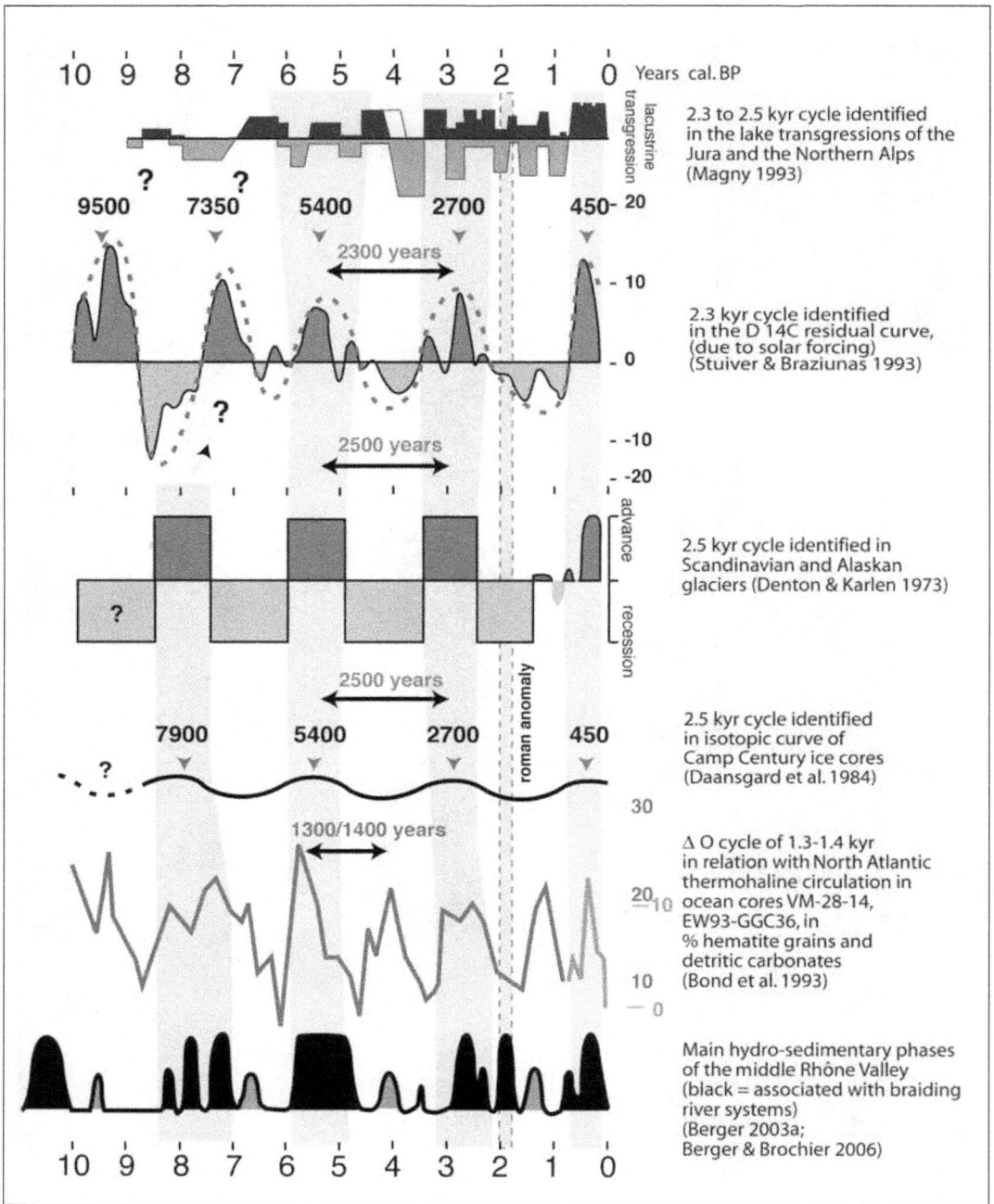

Plate 2. Global climate change curves at the global and regional scale. At the global scale, during the Holocene, two kinds of periodicities dominate, of 2,500–2,300 and 1,500–1,000 years, respectively. But at the regional scale, we find anomalies in the Bronze Age and the Roman Imperial period.

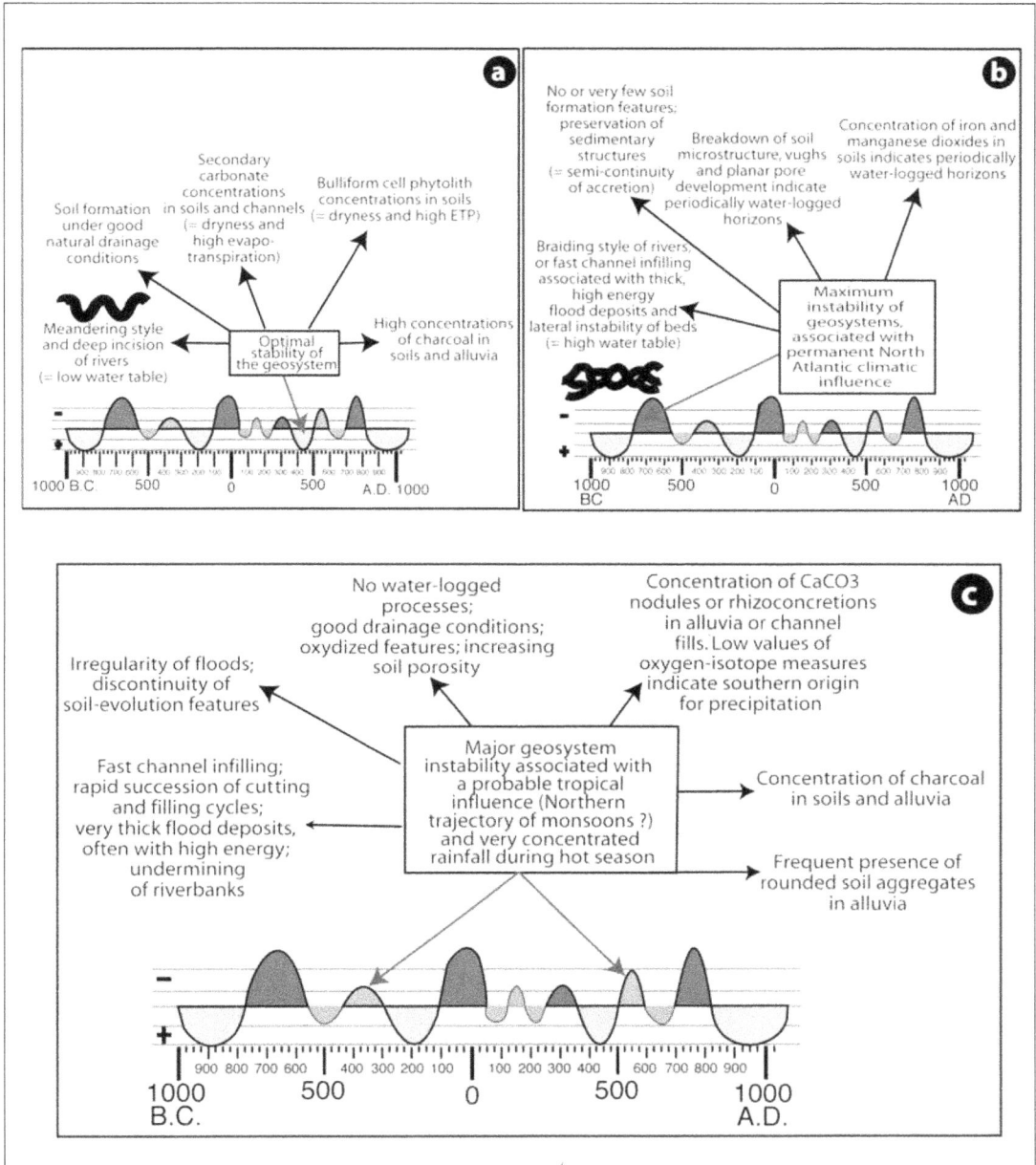

Plate 3. Different configurations of landscape-climate dynamics in the middle Rhône Valley: (a) optimal stability of the geosystems; (b) optimal instability of the geosystems, associated with a permanent North Atlantic climatic influence; and (c) major instability of the geosystems, associated with a probable tropical influence.

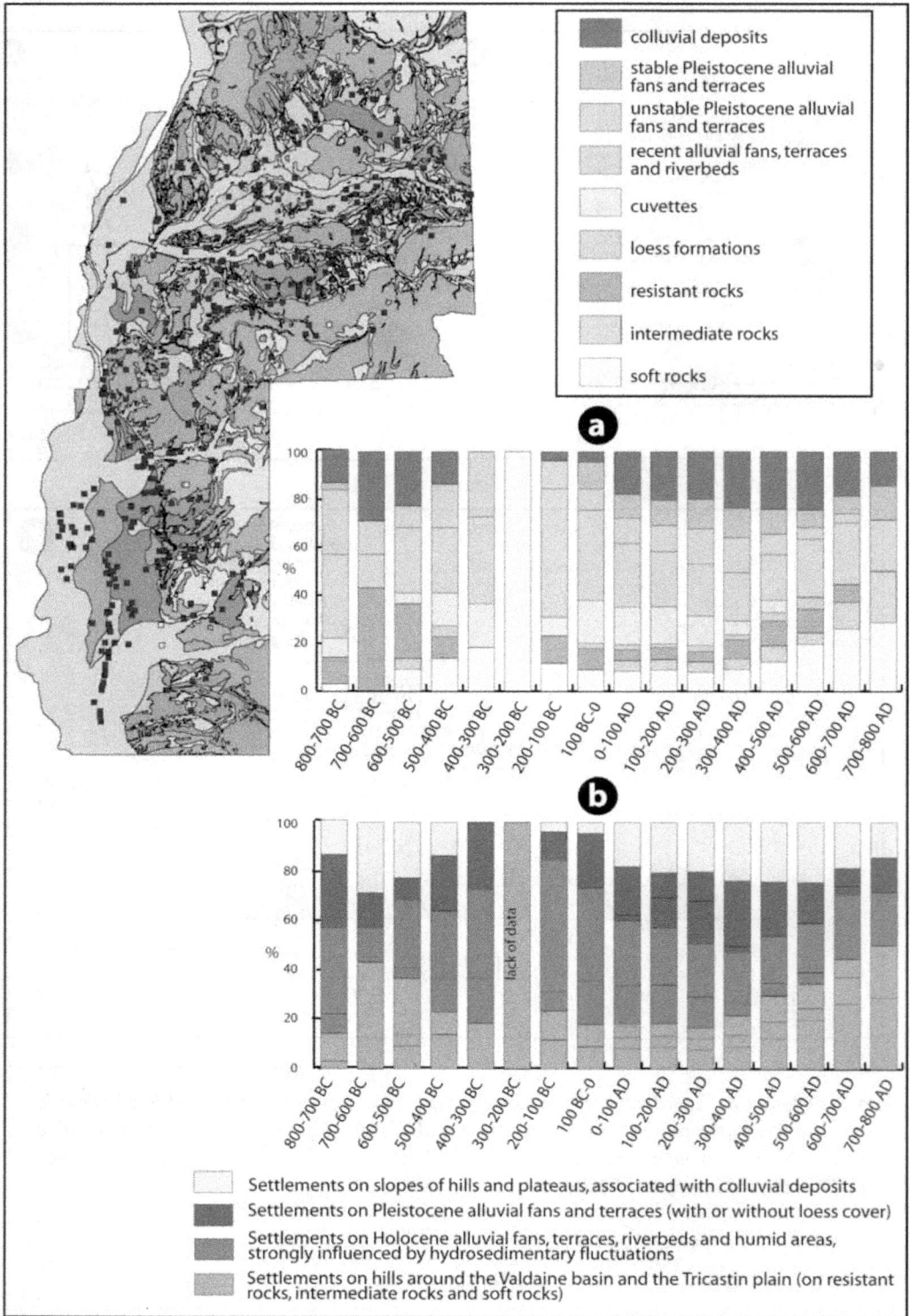

Plate 4. Landscape and site distribution: (a) calculation (per century) of the site distribution over the nine landscape units of the Tricastin and Valdaine, from 800 BC to AD 800, and (b) reclassification of settlement locations in the main physiographic units of the region.

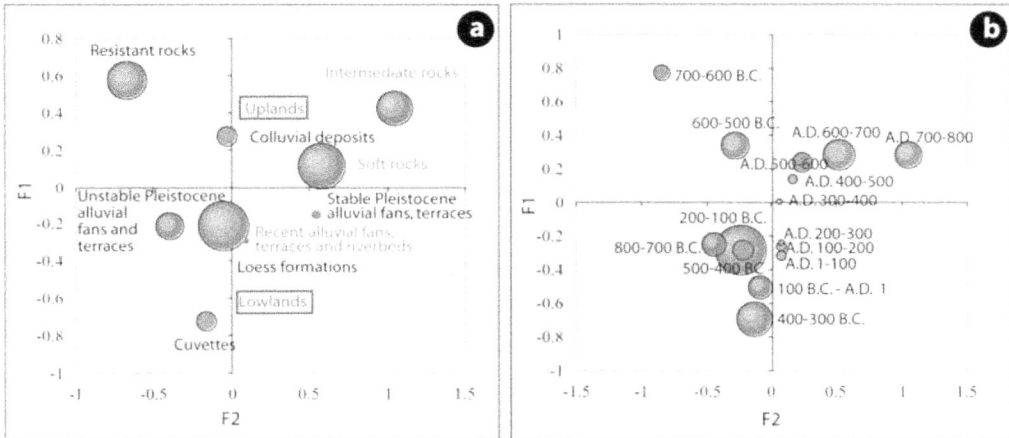

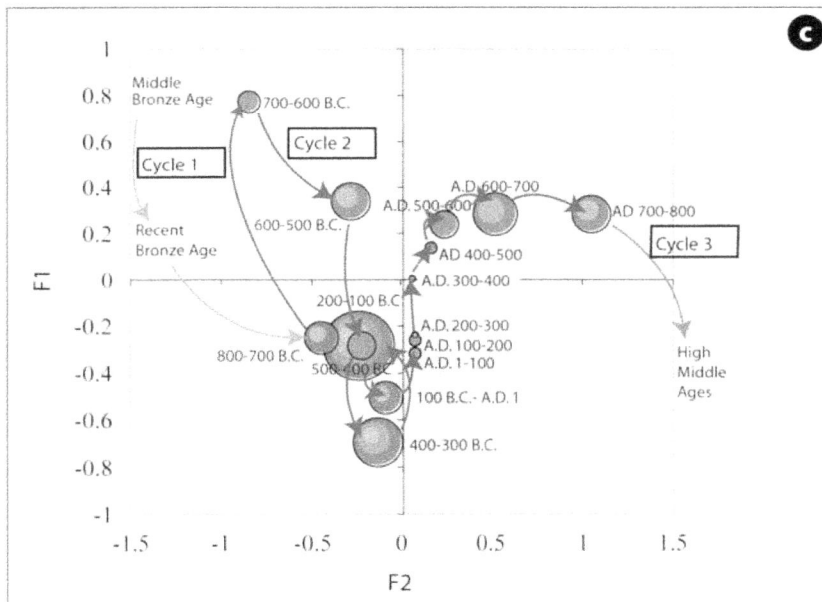

Plate 5. Choosing settlement location: (a) correspondence analysis showing the respective importance of various landscape units in choosing settlement location (800 BC–AD 800) (the principal contributing units are in blue); (b) correspondence analysis of the relative weight of each century in the total settlement load, relative to the location of settlements in the landscape. The Guttman effect is distorted, but the chronological factor is dominant and exceeds the current cycle (Braudel's "très longue durée"); and (c) the same graph, but with an indication of the potential trajectory of a settlement cycle.

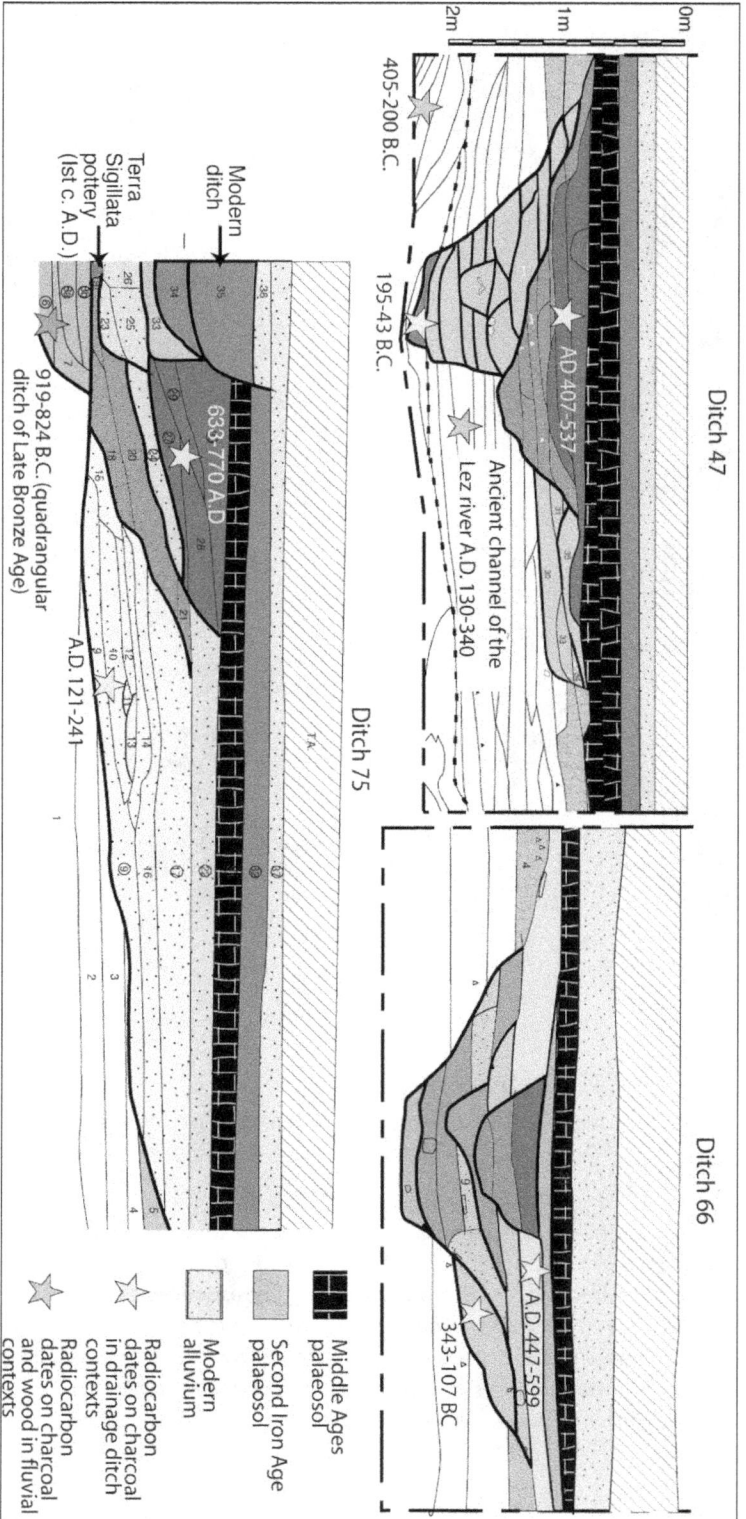

Plate 6. An example of drainage ditches that were used from the end of the Iron Age to the beginning of the Middle Ages at the site of Brassiere, in the southern Tricastin plain.

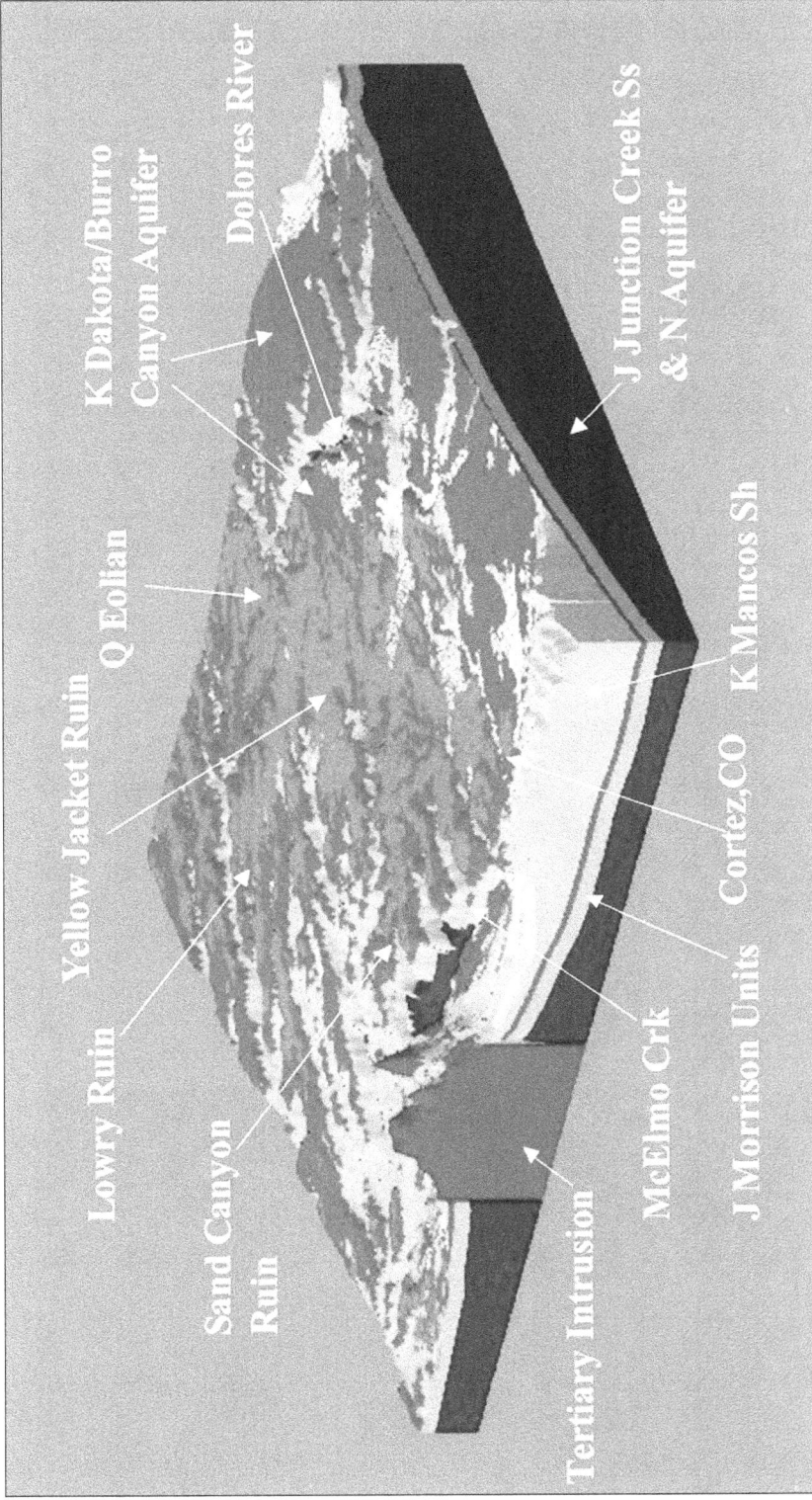

Plate 7. A 3D hydrogeologic block model of the study area at 200 m resolution.

First case: Bridges built during fluvial stability associated with entrenchment and a declining water level

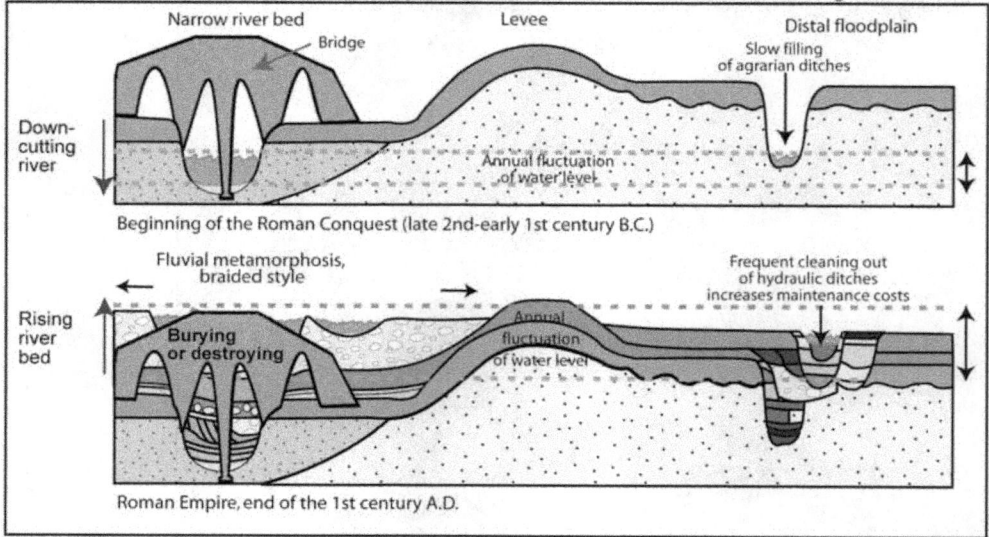

Narrow river bed

Bridge

Levee

Distal floodplain
Slow filling
of agrarian ditches

Down-
cutting
river

Annual fluctuation
of water level

Beginning of the Roman Conquest (late 2nd-early 1st century B.C.)

Fluvial metamorphosis,
braided style

Frequent cleaning out
of hydraulic ditches
increases maintenance costs

Rising
river
bed

Burying
or destroying

Annual
fluctuation
of water level

Roman Empire, end of the 1st century A.D.

Second case: Bridges built during fluvial crises with large active floodplain and rising water level

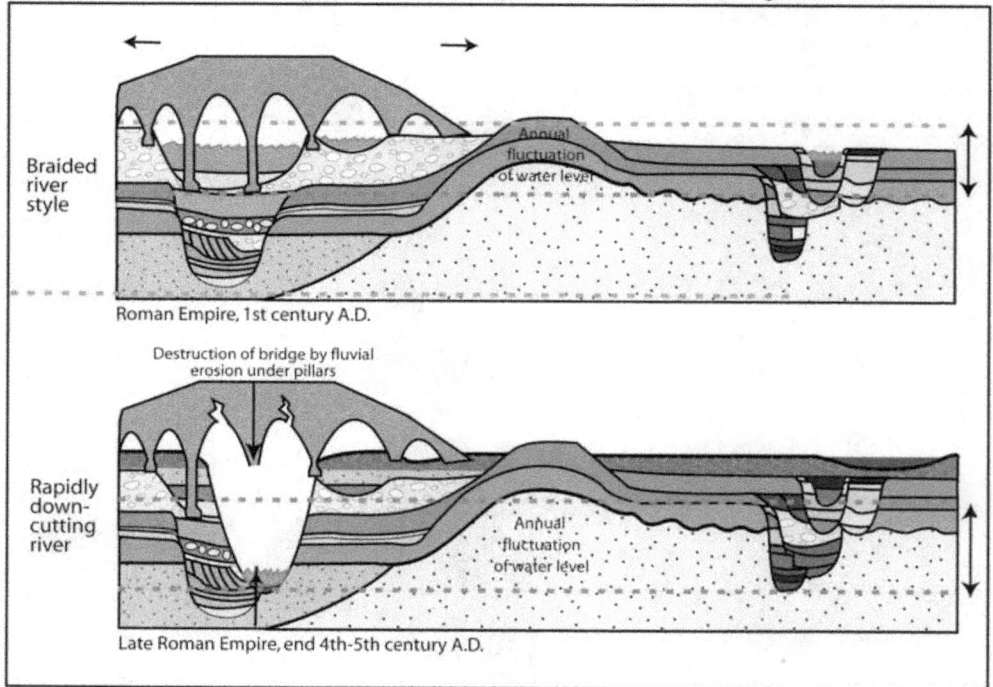

Braided
river
style

Annual
fluctuation
of water level

Roman Empire, 1st century A.D.

Destruction of bridge by fluvial
erosion under pillars

Rapidly
down-
cutting
river

Annual
fluctuation
of water level

Late Roman Empire, end 4th-5th century A.D.

Plate 8. The influence of fluctuations in fluvial dynamics on infrastructure such as bridges and
aqueducts.

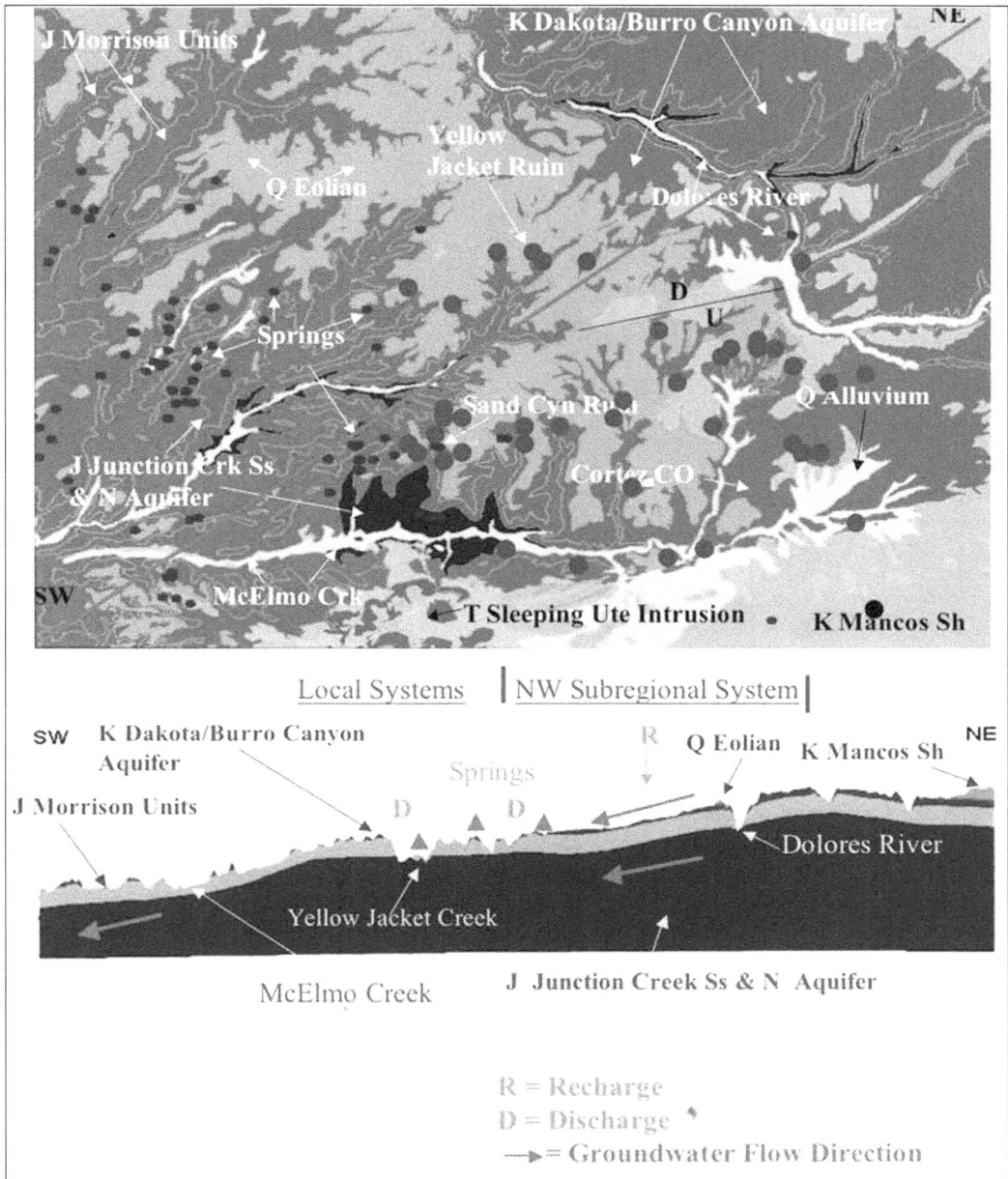

Plate 9. Top: *Distribution of hydrogeologic units and springs.* Bottom: *Subregional hydrologic cross-section showing groundwater flow paths with subregional and local systems.*

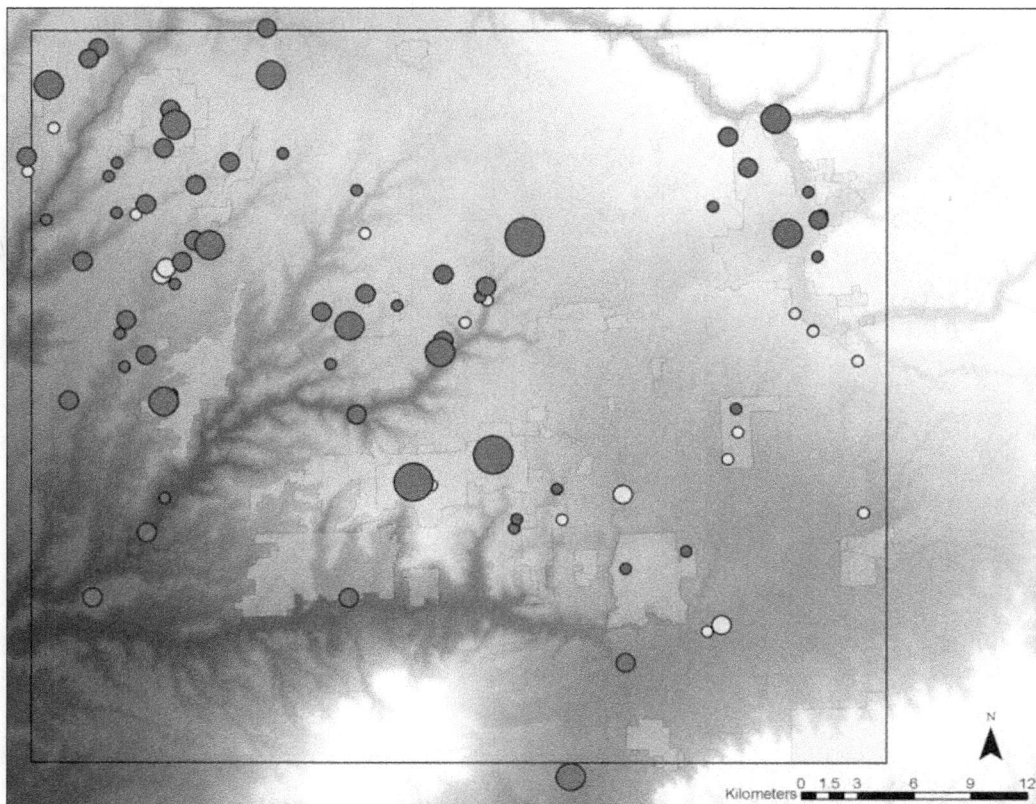

Plate 10. Distribution of community centers in the project area by size, class, and time period of peak population: blue, Pueblo I (AD 725–920); yellow, Pueblo II (AD 920–1140); and red, Pueblo III (AD 1140–1280). Lighter background shading indicates increasing elevation; block survey areas are shaded.

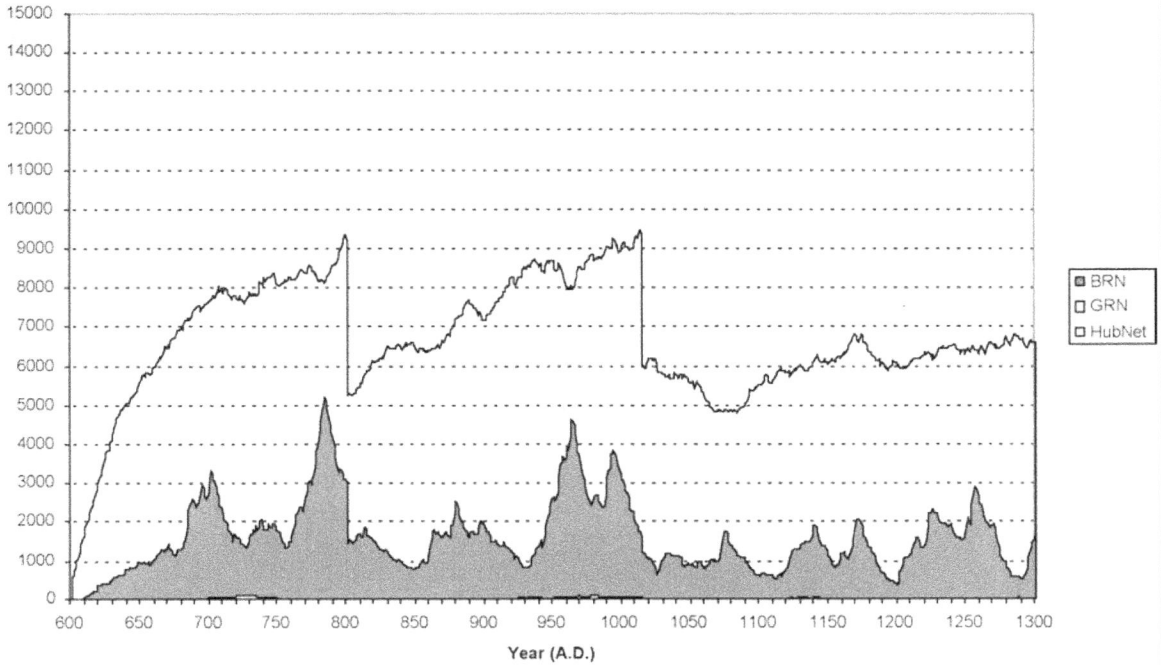

Volume of Social Networks through Time

Legend: BRN, GRN, HubNet

X-axis: Year (A.D.)

Plate 11. The volume of each of the three networks, GRN, BRN, and hub (coop 6). The volume of a graph is the product of the out-degrees of each of its nodes. The out-degree is the number of individuals to which it is connected in that graph. The volume of the GRN is the same as that for the entire system.

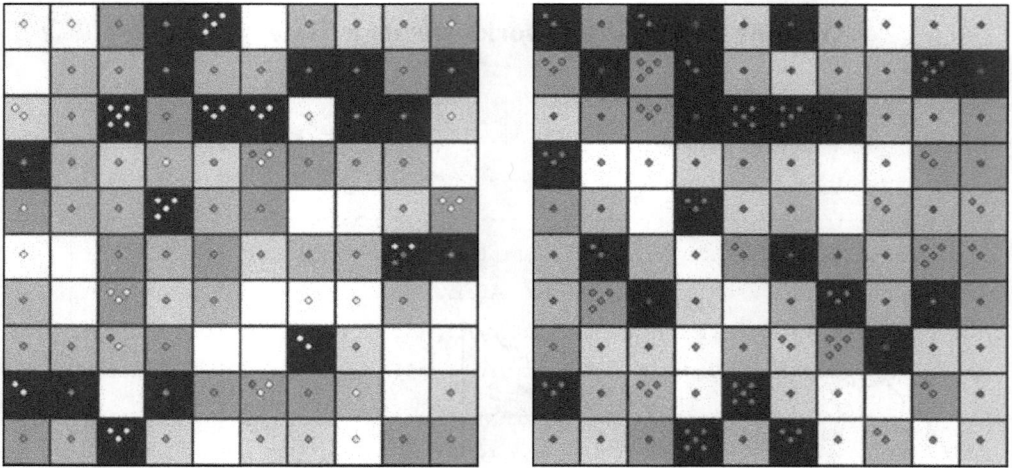

Plate 12. Patron-Client lattice at end of two runs (default parameter settings, 2,000 periods per run). (a) Run 1: Dove = 46.0 percent, Solo = 48.7 percent, Client = 5.2 percent, and Patron = 0 percent. (b) Run 2 (Patron-Client equilibrium): Dove = 0 percent, Solo = .7 percent, Client = 64.5 percent, and Patron = 34.9 percent. Note: Yellow diamonds = Dove; red = Solo; green = Patron. Shading of squares indicates patch richness, from one (white) to five (black).

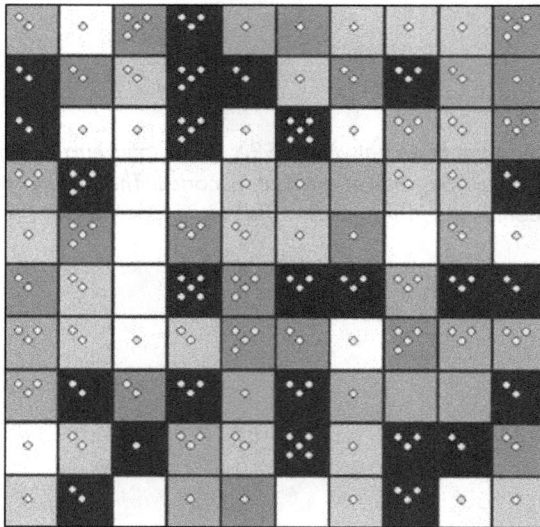

Plate 13. Patron-Client lattice shortly after initial all-Dove seeding. (See plate 12 caption for color key.)

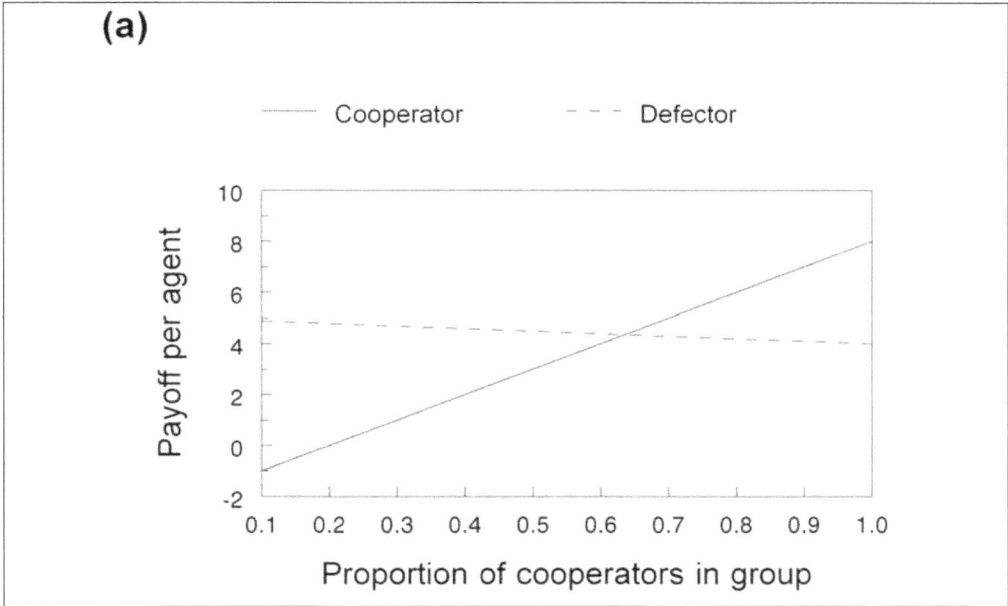

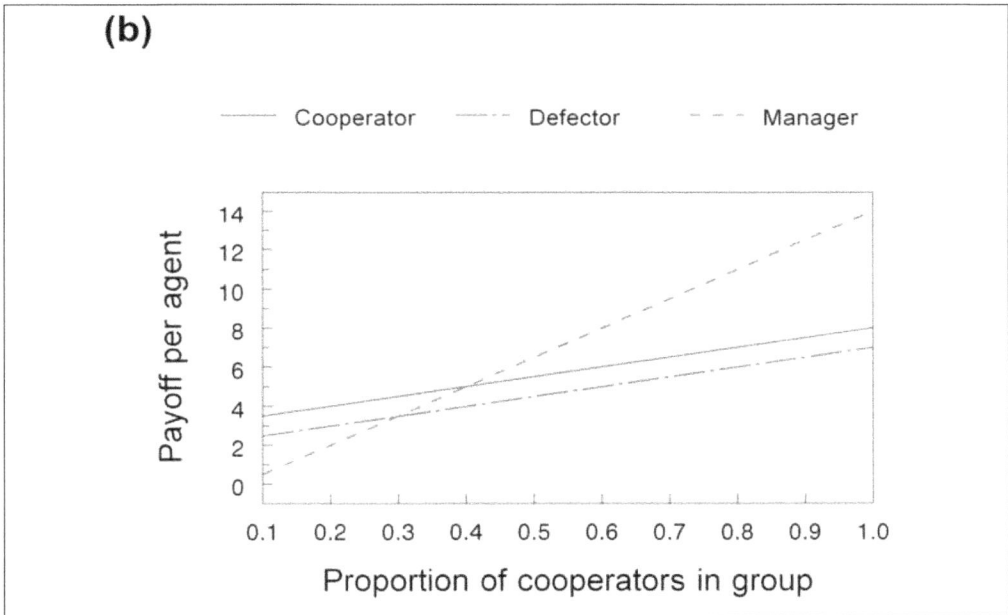

Plate 14. Managerial Mutualism model, showing agent payoffs with and without a Manager present (given default parameter values). (a) In groups without a Manager, Defectors outcompete Cooperators unless the latter are very common. (b) With a Manager present, Cooperators always do better than Defectors, but the Manager is at a disadvantage until Defectors are in the minority.

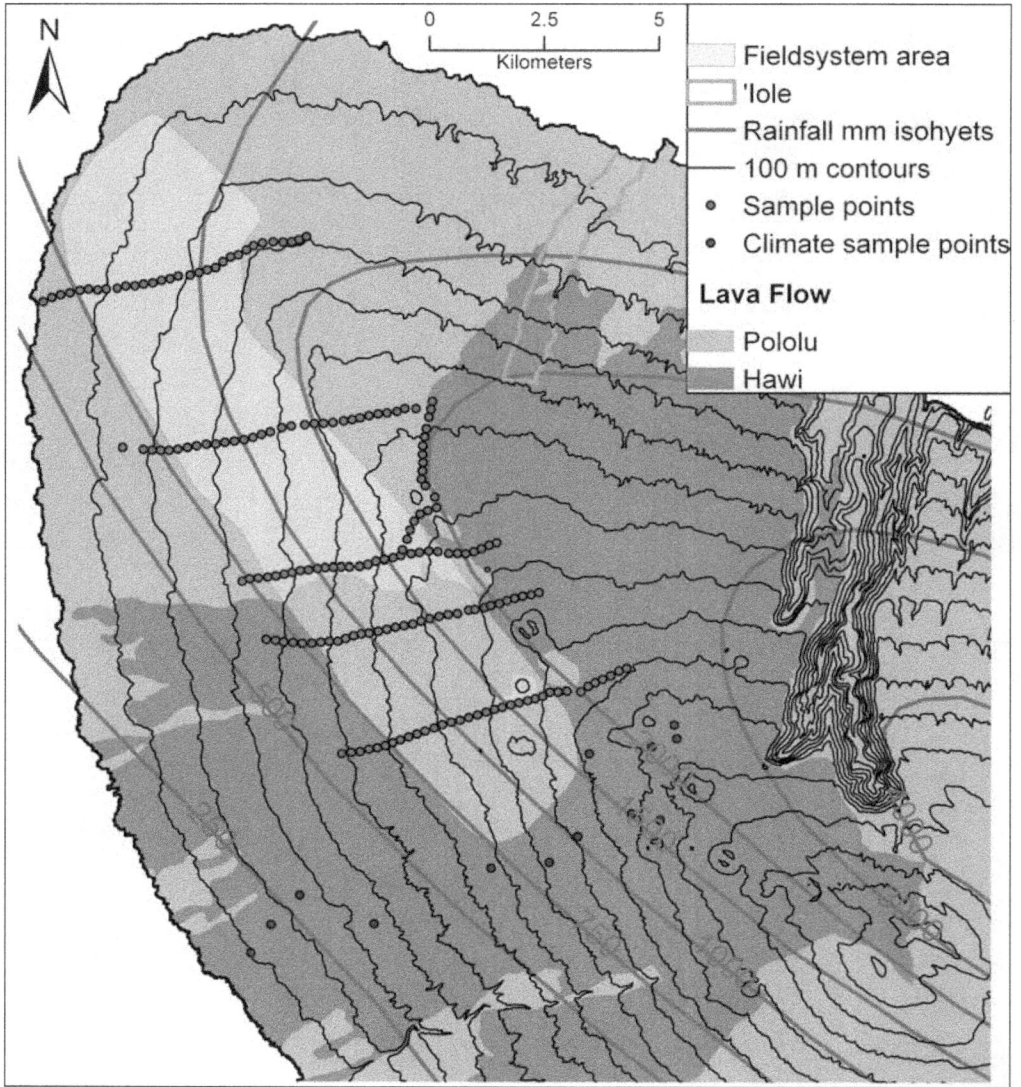

Plate 15. Map of Kohala showing the dryland field system in relation to rainfall and elevation, as well as the locations of soil sampling transects (Vitousek et al. 2004).

156°20' 156°17'30" 156°15' 156°12'30"
20°42'30"

Area of Figure 3

PRINCIPAL HAWAIIAN ISLANDS

2000 m

2000 m

20°40'

hkmole

Pu`u Pane

1000 m

1000 m

Manukani

hpane

Luala`ilua Hills

20°37'30"

hkah

hnaw hnaw

hkah

Pacific Ocean

hkah

Kipapa-Nakaohu

0   2   4 km

Old Hawaiian datum

Base from Lualailua Hills quadrangle, 1983
Contour interval 1000 m

20°35'

EXPLANATION

Hana Volcanics (Holocene and Pleistocene)

Lava flows 3-5 ky. Kamole Gulch unit labeled hkmole

Lava flows 5-10 ky

Lava flows 10-30 ky. Stipple indicates extent of Nawini ankaramite (hnaw)

Lava flows 30-130 ky. Stipple indicates extent of Kahikinui basanite (hkah)

Hana and Kula Volcanics (Holocene and Pleistocene)

Cinder cone deposits

Kula Volcanics (Pleistocene)

Lava flows 130-780 ky. Stipple indicates Manawainui land surface (kman)

Soil pits

Radiometric age sampling sites

14C

K-Ar

40Ar/39Ar

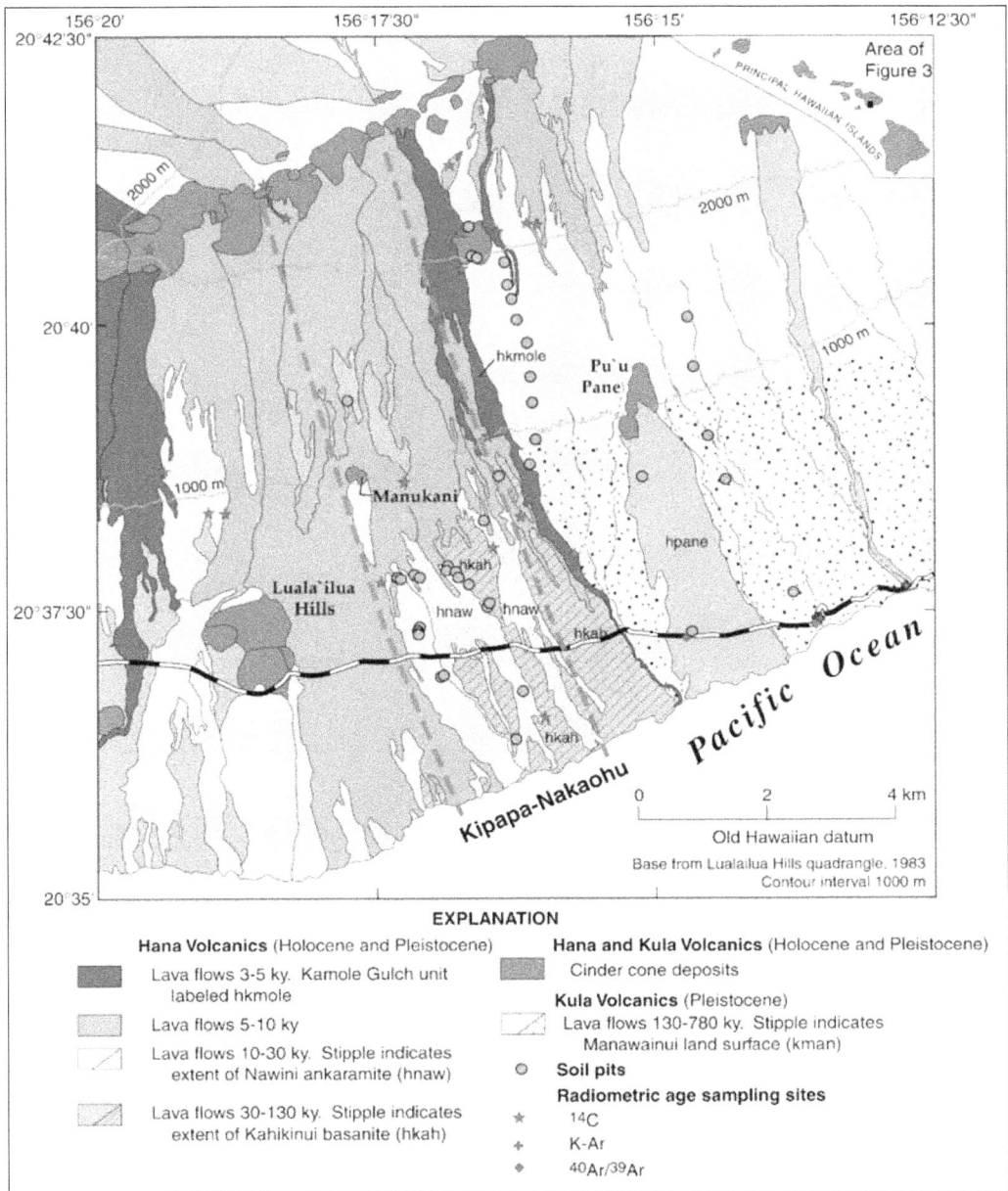

Plate 16. Map of the Kahikinui study area showing the geological mosaic of different substrate ages and soil sampling transects (Kirch et al. 2004).

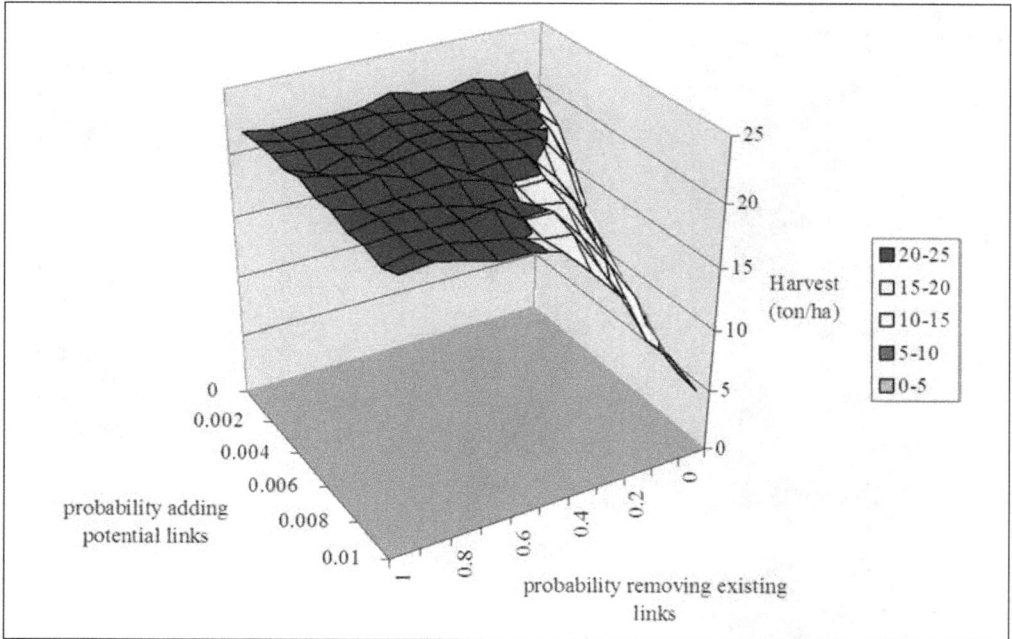

Plate 17. Average harvest per subak (per hectare) for various degrees of perturbation of links among subaks that disperse pests and are conditional imitators.

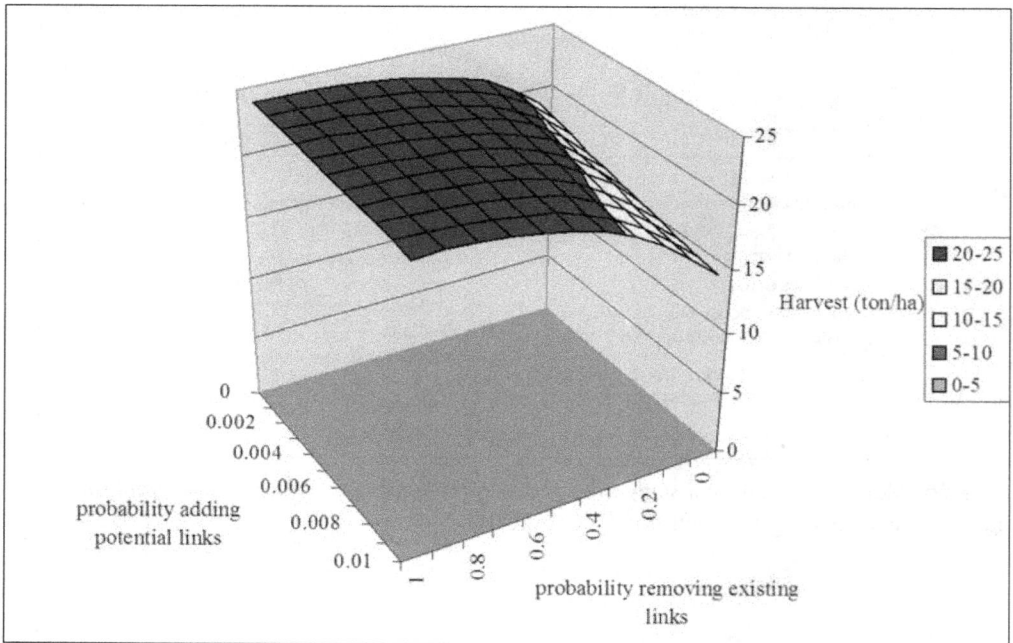

Plate 18. Average harvest per subak (per hectare) for various degrees of perturbation of links among subaks that disperse pests and are conditionally adaptive.

Conclusion

As this example illustrates, the crossing of interdisciplinary information does not simplify our vision of the co-evolution of social formations and their environments over the long term. On the contrary, it shows us the complexity of the natural phenomena and their close connection with the socioenvironmental processes that guide the evolution of the landscape.

How can we improve our theoretical understanding of these complex dynamics? One way would be to conceptualize different successions of robustness, resilience, and vulnerability in a framework that is applicable to all kinds of interactive socioenvironmental dynamics, at different spatial and temporal scales. It is argued here that the collective effort of the resilience alliance, as represented in works by Holling, Folke, Perrings, Gunderson, and others (see http://www.resalliance.org), has laid the basis for such a framework. But even though it does take the dynamics of interaction between social formations and their environments into account, it does not provide a model to conceptualize societal change itself. In part, this seems due to the fact that the time frame of the case studies used in this context is too short (at most, a century or two), so the (slow) evolution of the societies involved, and of their perspective on their environment, is not sufficiently in evidence. That gap is, to some extent, filled by the work of Thompson on "culture theory." The two approaches are very closely related, both historically and substantively (de Vries, Thompson, and Wirtz 2002). Our next step will be to link the two approaches and model the Rhône data in that light.

Notes

1. The project was funded by the McDonnell Foundation of the United States at the request of principal investigators A. Kinzig, C. Redman, and S. E. van der Leeuw (all at Arizona State University). Much of the work on which this chapter is based has been funded in the context of several other research projects, among which are the ARCHAEOMEDES Project (funded by DG Research of the European Union) and the French high-speed railways' (TGV) archaeological rescue operation between Lyon and Marseille. The authors wish to express their gratitude to Thierry Odiot, who initiated research in the Tricastin and coordinated the TGV project.

2. The area differs in this respect from others, such as the Eastern Languedoc (Nuninger 2002).

3. Our data relativize, but do not contradict, the traditional emphasis on fortified hilltop sites (oppida) in this period, at least for this area.

4. This cannot be ascribed to a taphonomic bias of the archaeological sample used, because the major surveys revealed the concentration of the majority of Late Bronze Age settlements to be near the rivers, which drain the two areas. They are identified today under 1 to 3 m of alluvium.

5. The analysis that was carried out, according to a method developed by Benzecri (1979), combines elements of correspondence analysis and factor analysis and is called in French "Analyse factorielle des correspondences" (literally, factor analysis of the correspondences). It is mostly unknown in the Anglo-Saxon world but, in our opinion, more effective than the statistical methods commonly used in Anglo-Saxon archaeology.

CHAPTER 4

Settlement Ecodynamics in the Prehispanic Central Mesa Verde Region

Timothy A. Kohler, C. David Johnson, Mark Varien,
Scott Ortman, Robert Reynolds, Ziad Kobti,
Jason Cowan, Kenneth Kolm, Schaun Smith,
and Lorene Yap

Many claims have been made about the influence of environment on society, settlement, and their changes through time. Environmental determinism, for example, assumes a simple one-way causation that, for extreme cases, is inarguable: "You cannot grow maize in the arctic or build igloos in the jungle" (Evans 2003:94)—at least without sophisticated technological inputs. This flow of causality is, of course, similar to that of standard evolutionary theory, in which variable organisms reproduce differentially according to their success in a given environment, which, in turn, increases their fit to that environment over time.

One problem with this perspective is obvious to social scientists, who, by training, are especially attuned to the ways in which humans modify their technology, work through their societies, and change their culture (or sometimes fail to change it) to achieve fit to an environment. But technologies, social arrangements, and cultural practices also modify the environment through a process that has recently been formalized as "niche construction" by Odling-Smee, Laland, and Feldman (2003). Therefore, humans, to an even greater extent than other animals, do not adapt to some environment given to them but are, instead, always modifying their technologies and practices to adapt to the environment they have helped create.

This chapter summarizes an on-going project that seeks to understand the given environment in southwestern Colorado between AD 600 and 1300, the niche constructed by its resident maize farmers, and the co-evolution of their societies and their environments over seven hundred years of regionally continuous occupation. The terse descriptions of our methods and results presented here are expanded in other publications now underway (for example, Ortman, Varien, and Gripp 2007; Varien et al. 2007). In contrast to other publications on this project, which report some particular aspect of our approach (Cowan et al. n.d.; Johnson, Kohler, and Cowan 2005; Reynolds, Kohler, and Kobti 2003) or discuss a much earlier version of the investigation (Kohler et al. 2000), here we try to give a current sense for the whole project and discuss some of our preliminary conclusions.

Two major efforts define our research. In the first, we build an agent-based model in which agents representing households are loosed on a landscape that represents, with reasonable fidelity, the landscape of prehispanic southwestern Colorado. In some of our models, households are embedded within a cultural algorithm framework that allows them to learn at both an individual level and a cultural level. Each household has a plan for procuring agricultural and animal resources, as well as plans for exchanging food with other households. These plans can be adapted over time in order to adjust to changes in the environment.

Spatially, our study area is represented as 45,400 cells (pixels) that are 200 m on a side; temporally, we represent time in the model at the same annual granularity with which the tree-ring records resolve climate. Households can grow corn on this landscape, and the amounts they produce are a function of the soils in which they plant, how many 1-acre plots they plant, the weather that year, and whether those plots have been farmed long enough that their production has begun to decline. Households consume water for drinking, food preparation, and personal hygiene; we do not differentiate among these uses in our model. We can control whether they may use all known water sources or are restricted to the highest-quality, perennial sources. We present here for the first time our ongoing efforts to build a paleohydrological model for the springs in our study area, which modulates the flows for modeled springs according to a lagged relationship with reconstructed precipitation.

Our households also use wood for heating and cooking. The amount of wood available depends on the native vegetation community supported by the dominant soil in that pixel, the size of the standing crop, the weather, the amount removed by grazing or browsing by native herbivores, and whether portions of that 4-ha cell have been cleared for farming.

Finally, unfarmed portions of the landscape produce jackrabbits, cottontails, and deer, the three species of greatest importance in hunting. For the first time, we report here on how that is done and on our efforts to include hunting among our resource-use activities.

Although implementation of the model is complicated, the underlying conceptual organization is simple. We have attempted to construct agents that will locate themselves to use this rich environment in a way that maximizes their net caloric gains to the extent practical, while also meeting requirements for protein, water, and fuel.

Adapting this perspective does not mean that we believe that societies actually achieve this goal or that human agents have this goal in mind as they determine their courses of action. Rather, it is just a null hypothesis (albeit one with a special status in behavioral and evolutionary ecology) in which it is assumed that organisms behaving this way will maximize their future reproductive success (Cuthill and Houston 1997:98). This we can subtract from what we actually see to isolate those behaviors for which more complicated and subtle explanations will be found in the domains of history, political and social processes, as well as perhaps underlying cognitive metaphors or systems of meaning. Our purpose in this chapter is to demonstrate the model that will eventually enable us to attain this goal.

The second major effort in this project is to understand, as best we can, the farming societies as they are represented in the archaeological record. We are particularly interested in the very basic questions: How many people lived in our study area? Where in this area did they live? When? It has required intensive work to organize what is known about the chronology, functions, and sizes of the thousands of recorded sites in the study area, as well as a new survey to expand that knowledge for the particularly critical class of large residential sites we call "community centers."

These archaeological data present us with two problems that provide the most important motivations for this work. First, what drives the two cycles of colonization, growth, and depopulation that we reconstruct? Second, how can we explain the general movement of people from hamlets into increasingly large community centers over the course of each cycle?

This chapter begins with three sections that discuss the major resource-availability models. Kohler first shows how we estimate maize paleoproductivity spatially and temporally. Then Kolm and Smith discuss procedures for estimating how much water was available and where it was available in our study area through time. Johnson then discusses how the model grows game and wood.

In the next major section, Varien and Ortman show how they were able to turn thousands of site forms into a high-quality database in which they divide 700 years of occupation into fourteen periods ranging from 20 to 125 years in length. We use this same database to reconstruct demographic trends for our area and determine the changing importance and size of the community centers through time.

The third major section focuses on the simulation model. Cowan, Johnson, and Kohler first discuss how the households in the model use resources. Then, they briefly report on certain dynamics that result from using resources whose availability changes both in response to use and as a result of changing climate. We are just beginning to make systematic comparisons between the output of these models and the archaeological record, so we defer most of that discussion to later publications.

Then Reynolds and Kobti discuss their efforts to introduce a mechanism allowing culture change to take place as the model is running, enabling households to select those behaviors that serve them best as conditions change. The activities that can be adapted in the version of the model presented here affect only those with whom the agents exchange maize or meat. We are just beginning to determine the effects of those exchange practices on the sizes, permanence, and locations of residences. Reynolds, Kobti, Kohler, and Yap report the state of those investigations in the section "A Sample Run of the Agent-Based Model."

Eventually in this project, we want to determine as rigorously as we can how much of the variability in the prehispanic Pueblo settlement pattern is due to attempts by individual households to minimize costs and maximize success in an environment that changes through time because of exogenous shocks due to climate change and because of slower internal processes such as population growth, decline, or environmental depletion of various sorts. We recognize that much else of interest is going on in these societies; we also believe that no one has a good measure of how much variability can, in fact, be explained by the processes we model. The tendency in contemporary archaeology is simply to *assume* that most variability will be due to other factors. The unique datasets at hand will enable us to begin to evaluate assertions such as the impressively precise (yet curiously undocumented) claim by Shanks and Tilley (1992:56) that "99% of [human] action has no direct survival value in terms of conveying any definitive selective advantage. The archaeological record is, primarily, a record of style."

Resource-Availability Models

We now discuss the resources produced by the model—maize, water, game, and fuelwood—before turning to a discussion of the local archaeological record itself.

Maize

Macrobotanical and stable isotope data strongly suggest that, with the possible exception of some marginal areas, maize (corn) seems to have been the single most important subsistence resource in the northern Southwest from at least AD 600, if not earlier (see Kantner 2004:60–7; Matson and Chisolm 1991). In fact, in its first incarnation the simulation model being developed here achieved some success using only the predicted potential productivity of maize under dry farming to predict settlement location (Kohler et al. 1996).

Van West's (1994) well-known estimates for maize production in our area provided our starting point in this project and still define the size and location of our study area (figure 4.1). Following Van West, we use the Palmer Drought Severity Index (PDSI) as a basis for our maize productivity calculations. The PDSI is a relative measure of soil moisture developed by Palmer (1965). We use PDSI values calculated from historic weather records for various soil categories in our study area to see how well they predict production for maize and beans from Montezuma County from 1931 to 1960. The utility of this unique series of crop records for archaeology was first noted by Burns (1983). We modified several aspects of Van West's approach to include portions of the study area for which soils maps did not exist when she did her work, to give temperature variability a more explicit role in production estimates, to modulate these estimates to represent harvest rates more similar to those of maize grown prehispanically in our area, to restrict growth on soils reported to be unsuitable for hand planting, and to extend the reconstructions back to AD 600. The major steps we took to produce our current estimates (which we will elaborate and defend in a separate publication) were as follows:

1. We determined the most appropriate proxies for local cold or short summers from the available tree-ring data. After much work, we settled on two high-elevation bristlecone pine sequences: one from Almagre Mountain about 350 km ENE of the project area and one from San Francisco Peaks about 335 km SW of the project area. Here, we use the scores on the first principal component extracted from both sequences, which are positively correlated to recent mean monthly temperatures of most summer months measured at the Mesa Verde, Cortez, and Yellow Jacket weather stations, with particularly strong correlations to the mean September temperatures (Mesa Verde: $r^2 = 0.49$; $p > F < 0.0001$; Yellow Jacket: $r^2 = 0.54$; $p > F = 0.01$; Cortez: $r^2 = 0.31$; $p > F = 0.02$).

2. We defined fourteen groups of soils within the study area that are similar in their productivity.

3. We produced PDSI reconstructions for the years 1931 to 1960, using instrumented data for these fourteen groups of soils and four weather stations, each representing one of four elevation bands represented in the study area.

4. We then determined whether each of these fifty-six (4×14) PDSI sequences has a significant relationship with the Mesa Verde Douglas-fir indexed series, allowing it to be retrodicted back to AD 600. All sequences, in fact, have a significant relationship with the Mesa Verde series, with values of r^2 ranging from .32 to .67 (most > .5).

5. We retrodicted PDSI values to AD 600 for the fifty-six sequences, using the Mesa Verde series as the independent variable.

6. We produced weighted, pooled PDSI values for those soils likely to have been producing maize and beans between 1930 and 1960 in Montezuma County.

7. We regressed those values against the historic maize and bean production in Montezuma County and against the two temperature proxies, holding "technology trend" (year) constant, with the following results for the first principal component (PC1) of the Almagre and San Francisco series: maize in bushels = 11.18 + 1.78 (year) + 1.33 (bean soil PDSI) + 1.28 (PC1 score) yielding an adjusted R^2 of 0.58 ($p > F < .0001$). All independent variables were standardized before regression.

8. Because these maize production estimates apply to the average productivity of the "bean soils," we next adjusted the productivity for each soil class in the study area by the ratio of the average productivity for soils in that class to the average productivity for the bean soils, gleaned from the normal-year, total dry-weight production published in the Cortez-area soil survey.

9. We took into account that the yields we are reconstructing are based on historic seed

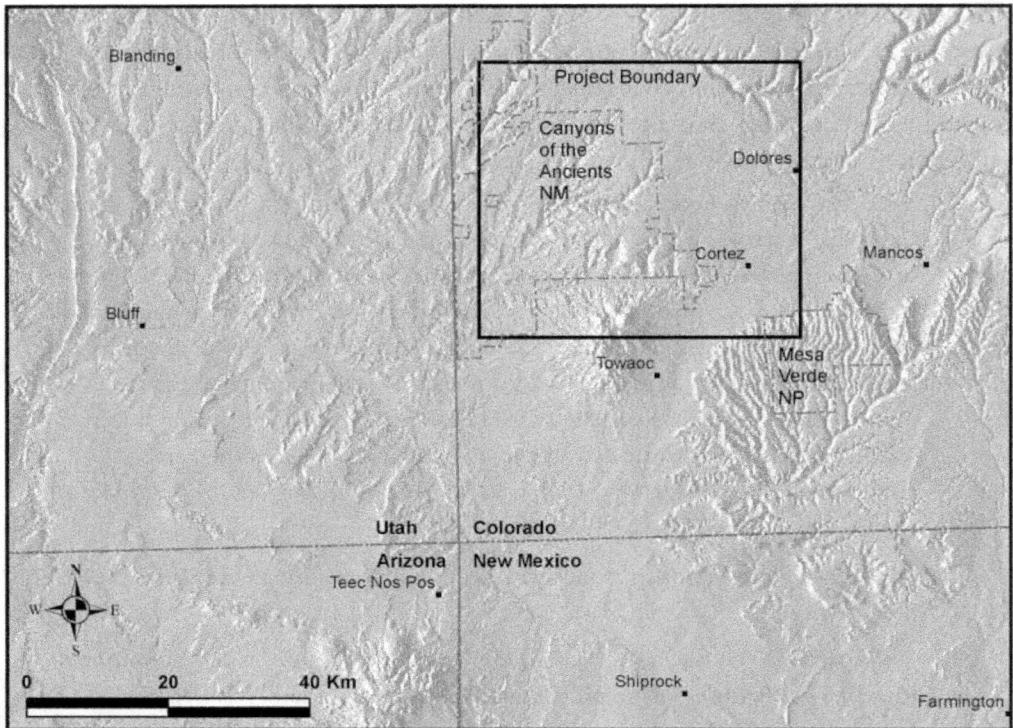

Figure 4.1. Village Ecodynamics Project study area in southwestern Colorado.

varieties and planting practices. Based on historical data from Zuni and Hopi and on ethnoagricultural experiments by Muenchrath and others (2002), Adams and others (1999), and other sources, we deemed a mean yield of 500 kg/ha in our better soils (the "bean soils") to be appropriate (though perhaps still generous). We therefore renormed the production so that the mean production in the bean-field soils is 500 kg/ha, by multiplying the yields from step 8 by a factor of .68.

10. We further reduced maize production on soils reported as unsuited for hand planting. The detailed soil descriptions in the soil surveys provide "Major Management Factors," indicating the suitability of each soil complex for a variety of uses. In addition, and somewhat independently of these general land-suitability classes, the surveys report hand-planting suitability restriction codes ranging from 0 to 1.0 for each soil. (A value of 0 means "no restrictions.") For those soils in our study area reported as "unsuitable" as to "Cropland Suitability," we multiplied the yields from step 9 by the inverse of the hand-planting restriction value. This further reduced the yields for sixty soil complexes in our study area. These sixty soils represent 53.2 percent (by area) of the total 1,816 km² encompassed by the study area.

11. We applied a "cold correction" by disallowing any maize production above 7,900 ft elevation and by progressively discounting production in colder-than-average years in the elevation band between 7,054 ft and 7,900 ft according to a linear function that

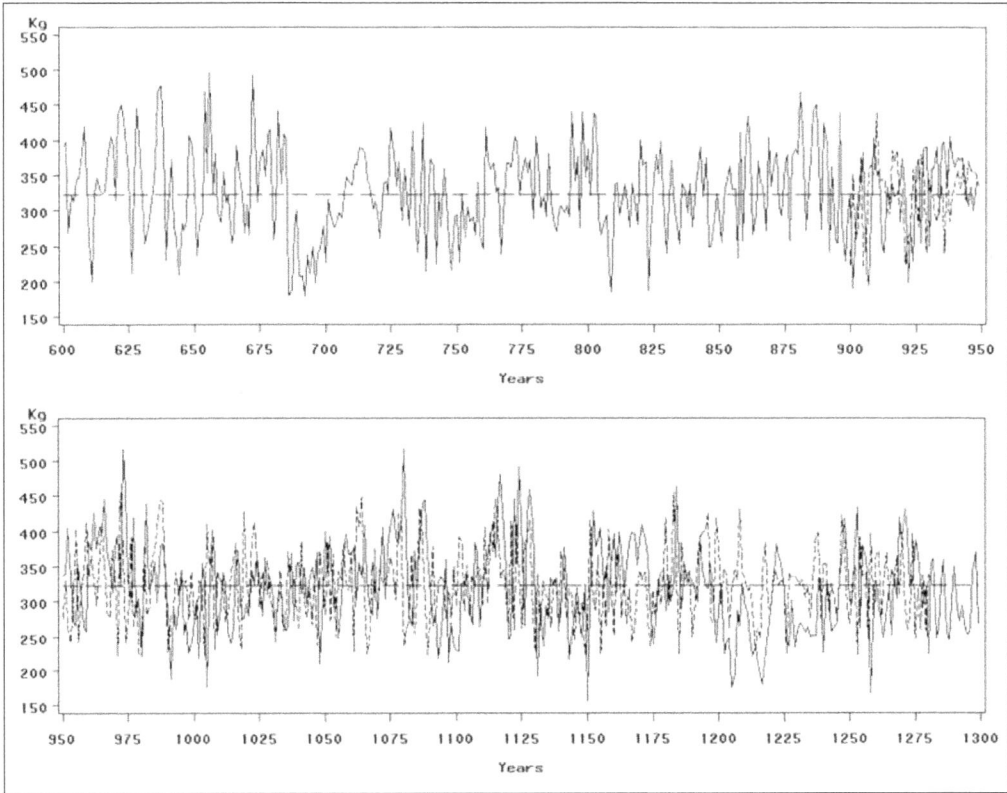

Figure 4.2. Potential annual maize yields in kg/ha, averaged across the study area. Current (PC1) reconstruction is graphed in solid line; Van West yields for AD 900–1300, graphed in dashed line. For this figure, the Van West series has been renormed to the same mean as the PC1 series by multiplying by .516.

takes into account both the elevation and how cold it was, using the tree-ring-based cold proxy.

12. Finally, we applied a fallow factor that dictates whether and how long a field that is "in production" is allowed to rest. This fallow factor is a tunable parameter in our simulation.

The average potential yields per year in our study area resulting from this process appear in figure 4.2. (These yields are not reduced by any fallow factor.) Noteworthy periods of low potential production appear in the late 600s, the mid 700s, the late 800s and early 900s, around 1000, around 1100, from about 1130 to 1150, and in the early and late 1200s. Our reconstruction differs from Van West's most dramatically in the late 1160s and early 1170s, when we estimate relatively higher potential production, and in the early 1200s, a very cold period, when we estimate lower potential production. Van West's estimates are higher throughout than our new estimates, though, and are renormed in figure 4.2 to illustrate their relative differences with the new estimates.

Water

The main problem we examine here is whether potable water was regionally limiting and whether changes in its availability contributed to the episodes of aggregation or depopulation outlined below. This is not a straightforward problem because ground-water quantities are controlled by complex hydrogeologic responses, in addition to direct climatic changes. The paleohydrologic model also contributes to examining community-scale dynamics because the model ultimately results in prediction of specifically located groundwater discharges directly related to the size of the local recharge areas for groundwater subsystems and to the hydrogeologic properties of Dakota and Burro Canyon sandstone. These relationships dictate that local water supply will not correlate directly to the magnitude and frequency of climate variability.

We conceptualize and characterize the modern central Mesa Verde hydrologic system using a multidisciplinary hierarchical systems analysis (HSA) approach applicable to the US Colorado plateau region, which integrates climate, surface water, groundwater, and geomorphological systems (for example, Kolm 1993, 1996). This required us to

1. Locate all groundwater discharge zones, including present springs and seeps in the study area and those possibly available from AD 600 to 1300 (a project that certainly remains incomplete, although we believe that we have now included all independently documented springs).

2. Develop a solid hydrogeologic block model to visualize and analyze the 3D framework of the groundwater flow system.

3. Develop and test mathematical models to simulate the flow paths and quantify the amount of water throughout the modern hydrologic system on a watershed–groundwater basin scale and on selected site-specific areas.

4. Develop scenarios of the paleohydrologic system based on tree-ring data, for identifying the relative roles of climate stresses on the system.

5. Compare the dynamics of this system's variations and fluctuations with the settlement dynamics of the project area. This was accomplished by incorporating the results from the dynamic paleohydrologic mathematical model into the agent-based model.

The methods and results for 2–4 are discussed below; our investigations of point 5 are now under way.

Characterization of Hydrogeology.

We first developed a 3D solid block model (plate 7) that incorporates interpretation of geologic and hydrogeologic data from Ekren and Houser (1965), Freethey (1988a, b), Hunt (1956), Thomas (1986, 1988), Weigel (1987), Whitfield and others (1983), and Witkind (1964), as well as USGS bedrock geology maps (Haynes, Vogel, and Wyant 1972). This model was developed using the Geologic Modeling System (GMS) software distributed by Environmental Modeling Systems, Inc. This shows the distribution of the main hydrogeologic units in our study area. On top lies an Eolian/Dakota/Burro Canyon (D) aquifer. This is underlain and isolated by a Morrison Formation confining unit. Below that lie a Morrison Formation sandstone, Junction Creek/Bluff sandstone, and the Navajo (N) aquifer unit. The block model illustrates that the D aquifer is topographically and hydrogeologically dissected. It is continuous in the northern and eastern parts of the study area, bounded by the Dolores River, and discontinuous in the southern and western parts of the study area, where numerous canyons and streams dissect it. The N aquifer, by contrast, is continuous throughout most of the study area but is rarely exposed for use as a water source by the prehispanic people.

Other than its relative lack of continuity, the two parameters of the Eolian/Dakota/Burro Canyon (D) aquifer that are significant for our modeling effort are its hydraulic conductivity (K) and its specific yield (Sy). Hydraulic conductivity integrates the complex effects of climate and recharge on the groundwater flow system in the aquifer, resulting in the observed spring discharges through time. Specific yield controls the quantity of water in storage that acts as the long-term reservoir of the aquifer.

Characterization of Hydrologic System.

The study area has regional, subregional, and local hydrologic systems. The N aquifer and lower Morrison Formation sandstones are regional and are exposed in canyon bottoms and in regional uplifts (plate 9a, b). These aquifers have limited use for prehispanic drinking water because of their locations and limited surface exposure. The spring discharge rates associated with these aquifers will not fluctuate greatly, however, because the recharge areas are located in regions far outside the study area, and groundwater travel velocities are expected to result in lags (from precipitation to discharge) on the order of hundreds to thousands of years.

By comparison, the Eolian/Dakota/Burro Canyon (D) aquifer is both subregional and local, based on topographic continuity (see plate 9a, b). Most of the dynamic groundwater discharge zones observed in the field (as springs, seeps, and phreatophyte distributions) are associated with this unit. Pueblo people utilized this dynamic D aquifer system as their primary drinking water supply.

The third type of aquifer system, stream alluvium (for example, the Dolores River and McElmo Creek alluvium; see plate 7), will respond to daily and yearly fluctuations of hydrologic stresses, both climatic and stream variations. In areas where the stream alluvium overlies impermeable geologic materials, such as shale, the stream-to-alluvial groundwater interaction is local, and the upstream variations in flow and chemistry will directly affect the alluvial aquifer at the site. In these locations, the underlying bedrock provides no new water and usually affects the water quality greatly by adding salts. In some areas, the underlying bedrock may be an aquifer (for example, the N aquifer) that provides additional water to the alluvium from below while the stream provides the alluvium with water from the surface. This can sometimes enhance the alluvial aquifer and stream flow considerably, and water quality may vary with bedrock groundwater input. In general, even though the streams in our area may have been used for drinking water in various places, their use was likely limited by water quality, including high total dissolved solids.

The Eolian/Dakota/Burro Canyon aquifer system (D aquifer) was chosen for dynamic modeling, then, because it was apparently heavily used as a drinking-water source prehistorically and will respond dynamically to climatic stresses. The D aquifer is conceptualized as containing two major subsystems divided by the House Creek fault, whose location is approximated by the location of Yellow Jacket Creek: (1) a southeast subregional system that recharges northeast and north of the city of Cortez and either discharges to McElmo Creek at Cortez or flows into the San Juan Basin regional system (see plate 9a and figure 4.2) and (2) a northwest subregional system that recharges in the northern and northwestern part of the study area and discharges in springs, seeps, and phreatophyte locations along the western and southwestern parts of the study area (see plate 9a, b).

Local or community-scale systems are conceptualized within the regional and subregional systems, using the same hydrogeologic framework and hydrologic system parameters. Prehispanic settlements are frequently located on the mesa tops and in canyon-rim settings near where groundwater recharge and discharge are occurring in the D aquifer. Recharge by infiltration of precipitation occurs in these mesa-top environments, where much of the farming is assumed to have occurred. Groundwater flow paths are from these mesa tops to the springs observed at or below canyon rims.

Mathematical Model of Hydrologic System—Steady-State Simulation.

Steady-state and transient mathematical simulations of the hydrologic system were conducted using the block-centered, finite-difference MODFLOW model (McDonald and Harbaugh 1988) built upon the 3D block model and using the conceptual model outlined above. This mathematical model simulates, dynamically, the groundwater flow in the primary hydrogeologic layer, the Eolian/Dakota/Burro Canyon aquifer. A hydraulic conductivity of 0.2 m per day was applied uniformly across the layer. A constant grid cell size of 200 m by 200 m was chosen to match the spatial resolution of the agent-based settlement model.

Naturally occurring hydrogeologic and hydrologic system features such as cliff edges or rivers define boundary conditions in most places. The MODFLOW model utilizes no-flow, head-dependent flux, constant heads, and cell input/output boundary conditions. Specifically, recharge is a cell input/output flux that is regionally distributed in four zones, based on precipitation and topographic elevation across the model domain. The ranges of recharge are from 1.5×10^{-5} to 5.0×10^{-5} m³ per day. This model incorporates seventy springs as discharge drains (head-dependent flux) within specified nodes where the springs occur. The drain discharge is allowed to vary during transient simulations, and ranges from 0 to greater than 100 cubic m per day. The output of each drain, then, is the simulated drinking-water availability at that point on the landscape.

Calibration is based on water levels (heads) within the aquifer and discharge at known spring discharge sites. Our database contains fifteen springs that can be used for calibration. Calibration sensitivity is based on recharge ranges from <2 to >4 percent of precipitation. These recharge rates are equivalent to the driest and wettest five-year periods in the climate data, allowing the hydrologic model to simulate transient stresses imposed on the system by climatic (precipitation) fluctuations.

The model is designed to be highly sensitive to changes in recharge from precipitation and resulting groundwater discharge. The lag time in spring response to recharge change is minimal. However, because of the hydrogeologic characteristics (K and Sy) of the Eolian/Dakota/Burro Canyon aquifer, the actual changes in spring discharge amounts at each location are the result of a complex response to hydrogeology and hydrologic system parameters.

The potentiometric surface calculated during the steady-state model simulation indicates that three hydrologic systems can be identified in the D aquifer: (1) the SE subregional system, from the House Creek Fault to McElmo Creek at Cortez; (2) the NW subregional system, from the Dolores River Divide to the canyons in the southwest, where concentrations of sites such as Lowry Ruin and Yellow Jacket Pueblo are high; and (3) various more local systems, such as in the Sand Canyon Pueblo area. The springs, for example, in the Sand Canyon area, and streams, for example, McElmo Creek near the city of Cortez, lower the water table locally.

Two transient models that simulated stress periods of fifty- and five-year intervals were run. The calibrated steady-state simulation was the starting point for the fifty- and five-year transient simulations. Dataset results are available for each period for these two models, and the spring output, including mass balance, is available for each time interval. The drains are available as a dataset per spring (simulated in zones as a drain) per interval (figure 4.3). The annual precipitation signal used for estimating recharge is derived from the same dataset graphed by Dean and Van West (2002: 85–7). It was developed by regressing precipitation data from the National Climatic Data Center's New Mexico Division 1 (Northwestern Plateau) on the Mesa Verde Douglas-fir ring width index series—the same series we use as a proxy for precipitation in our paleoproductivity reconstructions.

The results of the transient simulations indicate that spring discharge fluctuations may be small (Sand Canyon Pueblo) or large (Lowry Ruin) with respect to annual precipitation changes. During the fifty-year simulation, the aquifer did not show dominant drought patterns because most droughts were short (in the one-to-three-year range) and followed by wet years. The wet years that immediately followed the dry years appear to have effectively recharged the aquifer. By comparison, the five-year-interval transient simulations did show effects of drought- and wet-year variations. However, corresponding drinking water supplies, as suggested by modeled transient drain discharge results, remained generally reliable, though variable, for most locations.

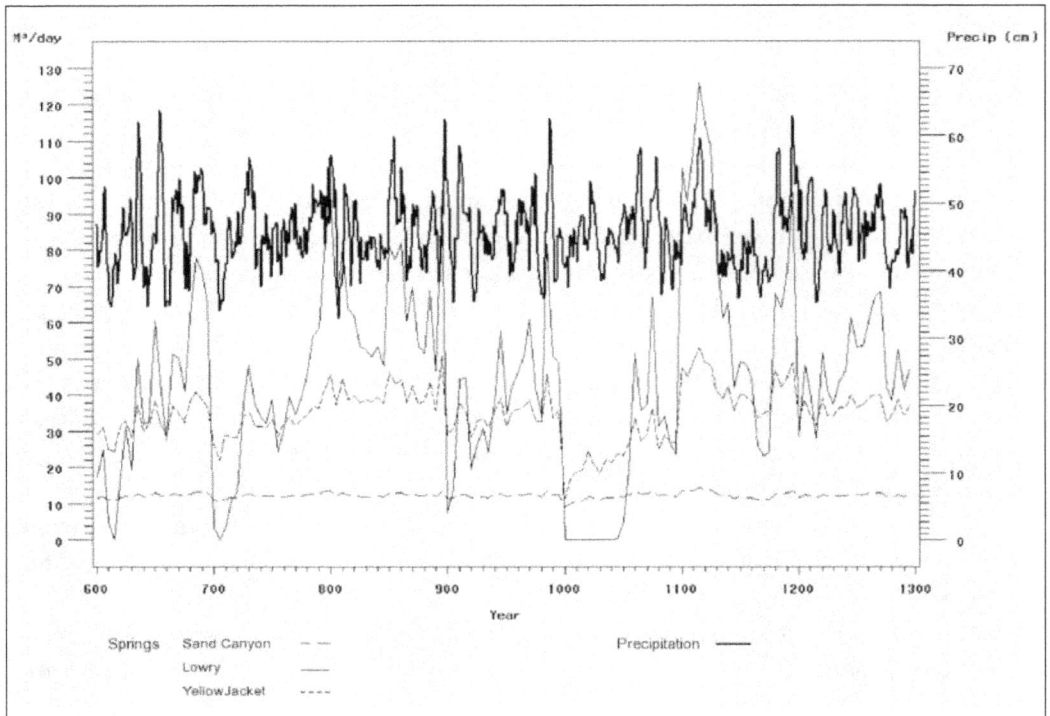

Figure 4.3. Annual variation in spring flow and average precipitation.

Figure 4.3 compares two springs developing out of large subregional systems (near Yellow Jacket Pueblo and Lowry Ruin), with one in a small local system (at Sand Canyon Pueblo). The Lowry spring showed the most variation, with discharge values ranging from approximately 0 to 125 cubic m per day. The Yellow Jacket spring varied from about 11 to 49 cubic m per day, whereas the Sand Canyon spring varied only slightly, between about 9 and 13 cubic m per day. It is notable, though surprising, that springs supported by the two large recharge areas can vary more than the spring supported by the smaller Sand Canyon recharge area. Also interesting is the retrodiction that the Lowry spring periodically went dry, for example, in the early AD 1000s. Archaeological evidence suggests that Lowry was inhabited during this period. This may have been possible because of reliance on other springs, or it may be that further calibration of the model is needed, perhaps including some consideration of the relationship between population locations and springs in various periods. Such considerations have not been used for calibration here, and, of course, we recognize the possible dangers of circular reasoning in use of such data.

The graphs of spring discharge fluctuations (see figure 4.3) indicate a pattern of similarity in timing, but not in amplitude. For example, the Sand Canyon spring varied around 4 cubic m per day, whereas the Lowry and Yellow Jacket springs varied on a much greater scale, at approximately 125 and 38 cubic m per day, respectively. Sand Canyon has a smaller recharge catchment area compared with the Lowry and Yellow Jacket springs. However, the Sand Canyon area has a slightly higher recharge rate because of greater precipitation associated with a higher elevation. The effect is to have a smaller magnitude of actual groundwater discharge, but also a smaller change in discharge over long-term climatic fluctuations. The Lowry and Yellow Jacket discharge zones are located towards the middle and end, respectively, of their subregional recharge areas. Apparently, the Lowry springs are more variable because they are located closer to the recharge and flow system water sources. The fluctuations of spring discharge compared with the precipitation (see figure 4.3, heavy line) illustrate the lag in the effect of precipitation, which is due to the hydraulic conductivity properties of the bedrock.

Conclusions.

Our results illustrate that time-lagged fluctuations of spring discharge did occur in response to long-term precipitation variation, based on the tree-ring climatic record. The results also indicate that the amplitude of spring-discharge variations over time is related to both the size of the groundwater recharge area and the landscape position of the spring within the groundwater flow system.

The five-year transient model results from this model serve as one input to the landscape in the agent-based simulation described below. That is, for the known springs that we modeled, as the simulation runs, flow rates are read in from an external database, with the values changing every five years. For known springs that were not modeled, primarily in the N aquifer, we used a constant estimate of flow averaged from springs in that aquifer for which flow rates were available. Households take as much water as they need from the nearest spring, up to its flow limits; if an isolated spring in a productive farming area declines significantly, this could provoke household relocation in the model.

In future work, we will try to expand our mapping of the known springs, conduct various sensitivity analyses for those we can model, and examine the possibility of refining our calibration of spring discharge, using human population distributions over time. At this point, we do not see any consistent signals across the project area that would attribute the episodes of aggregation or depopulation (which we review below) to changes in supply of potable water.

Game and Fuelwood

Any model that purports to study how prehispanic households in this area located themselves with respect to critical resources cannot consider only calories and water, although these were undeniably important. In our current models, households are also required to satisfy minimal protein requirements (Stillings 1973) by hunting rabbits, hare, and deer. In addition, households must obtain fuel for cooking and heating by harvesting woody plants (trees or shrubs). These resources were chosen—instead of, say, lithic materials—because of evidence that they place limits on the size and locations of human groups in certain times and places in the prehispanic Southwest (Kohler and Matthews 1988; Spielmann and Angstadt-Leto 1996).

Modeling the amounts of animals and fuelwood available in the project study area starts from the same point, so these are discussed together (and by Johnson 2006, in much more detail than is possible here). Both are attributes of each of the 45,400 cells in the model, and both are derived ultimately from tree-ring-recorded climatic variability acting on production capacities specific to particular soils. So we begin with the study-area soils.

The 148 productive soil complexes within the project boundary (Pannell n.d.; Ramsey 2003, 2006) are composed of one or more soil components. Each soil component supports a native vegetation community that, every year, produces new growth for each of its constituent plant species, according to the properties of the soil and the weather that year. Annual variation in the productivity of various plant species, in turn, determines the biomass available to support the three species of herbivores that people hunt in our model.

For each soil complex, we can determine the productivity for our native plant species in a normal year through calculations that begin with data in the published soil surveys. We apply these to our 4-ha cells after determining the dominant soil within each cell. The normal-year productivity values for project-area soil complexes range from 336 to 3,360 kg/ha. Table 4.1 gives some examples for the process by which we partition the total productivity in kg/ha among the plant species reported for each soil type. These values are multiplied by 4 to determine productivity for each model cell.

Annual variation in net primary productivity (NPP) for each soil, and therefore for each cell, is derived from step 7 in the process (described above) by which we produce the maize estimates (except that the output is re-expressed in different units to provide each model cell with its appropriate NPP of native vegetation in kg). The model also partitions that NPP among each of the native vegetation species in each cell.

Of the ninety-three plant species, fifty-two are reported as commonly consumed by one or more of the animal species whose populations we model as meat sources. Fuelwood is produced by ten species of trees and thirty-nine species of woody shrubs, as well as an "other" category of each. The NPPs of these specific plants contribute to the secondary productivity of these resources.

Modeling Game.

In modeling potential sources of animal protein for Pueblo households, we use the modern ecology of the three wild, herbivorous species most commonly recovered from archaeological contexts in the region. These are mule deer (*Odocoileus hemionus*), black-tailed jackrabbit (*Lepus californicus*), and desert cottontail (*Sylvilagus audobonii*). The production of these protein sources is modeled on the basis of populations of each species. Each of the three populations "grows" at rates dependent on its maximum reproductive rates (r_{max}), in conjunction with the availability of forage as produced by the NPP of standing crops of its preferred foods. Population growth is generated by the following equation:

$$N_{t+\Delta t} \;=\; \frac{KN_t}{N_t + \gamma\,(K - N_t)} \qquad\qquad \text{Eq. 1}$$

where $\gamma = e^{-r\Delta t}$ and the time step (t) is one year.

The r_{max} values for these animal species are based on the best available data from various sources; we use 0.4 for mule deer (McCullough 1997; Medin and Anderson 1979), 1.5 for jackrabbits (Wooster 1935), and 2.3 for cottontails (Myers 1964).

Of course, considerations of access and foraging efficiency preclude the total harvest of new growth from any given plant; each species is restricted to a percentage of the NPP of its preferred foods. For example, mule deer may browse up to 50 percent of the NPP of the trees and shrubs they target. Although deer browse consists mostly of new growth from shrubs, which is usually accessible, a significant portion comes from trees, much of which is inaccessible. Moreover, browsing more than 50 percent of the total new growth becomes increasingly inefficient (Wallmo et al. 1977). Black-tailed jackrabbits and cottontails are allowed to reap 70 percent of their preferred species, mainly because they obtain a much greater proportion of their diets from grass species, which are assumed to be fully accessible.

For the hare and rabbit populations, plant foods are produced by the various native plant communities supported by the dominant soil in each 4-ha model cell. In the various native vegetation communities supported by study area soils, rabbits target thirty-one species and hares, twenty six. Both species of leporid are subject to carrying capacities defined at the level of each 4-ha cell, based on the amounts of vegetation available for their consumption within each cell in each year.

We "grow" deer in a similar fashion, except that deer populations are modeled in a larger spatial frame, using 1-km cells superimposed on the original 4-ha grid of our model world. The 45,400 4-ha model cells, therefore, are contained within 1,816 deer cells. This is necessary because deer are much larger than either of the leporid species, consume much more of the NPP of their preferred browse species per individual, and have much larger home ranges. Optimal foraging theory predicts, and the archaeological record underwrites, the probability that these large-bodied mammals were the preferred prey of the prehispanic inhabitants of our study area to the extent that they were available (Ugan 2005). Whereas we restrict leporid populations to particular 4-ha model cells, deer populations are allowed to "diffuse" across deer cells. This is accomplished with an implicit diffusion algorithm based on the iterative "preconditioned conjugate gradient method" (Bulirsch and Stoer 1993:612–14) for solving large systems of linear equations. This algorithm transfers deer from deer cells that are at carrying capacity to adjacent deer cells that are below carrying capacity (because of depletion resulting from hunting or climatically induced changes in carrying capacities). Cowan and others (n.d.) describe this algorithm in detail.

Table 4.1 Normal-Year Productivity of Natural Resources for Selected Soils

Soil[1]	Area[2]	Prod[3]	Common Name[4]	% VC[5]	Kg/ba[6]	Trees[7]	Sbrubs[8]	Fuels[9]	Deer[10]	Hare[10]	Rabbit[10]	Protein[11]
105	5300.4	560.0	Galleta	21.1	118.4							
% Slope: 3 – 9	1297.0	469.1	Indian Ricegrass	18.1	101.4							
Rizno - .45		2.6	Utah Juniper	12.0	67.4							
Piñon-Juniper			Blue Grama	11.1	62.0							
Gapmesa - .35			Western Wheatgrass	11.1	62.0	89.9	34.0	25.5	2.8	4.2	1.4	2.7
Semidesert Loam			Needleandthread	9.1	51.0							
			Big Sagebrush	6.1	34.0							
			Bottlebrush Squirreltail	6.1	34.0							
			Twoneedle Piñon	4.0	22.5							
			Winterfat	1.2	6.8							
109	13175.0	392.0	Indian Ricegrass	16.7	65.3							
% Slope: 6 – 25	3302.0	339.2	Mountain Mahogany	16.7	65.3							
Romberg - .45		2.5	Galleta	11.1	43.5							
Crosscan - .4			Twoneedle Piñon	11.1	43.5							
Piñon-Juniper			Utah Juniper	11.1	43.5	87.0	108.8	146.9	5.4	1.3	0.6	2.2
			Western Wheatgrass	11.1	43.5							
			Common Snowberry	5.6	21.8							
			Muttongrass	5.6	21.8							
			Piñon Ricegrass	5.6	21.8							
			Utah Serviceberry	5.6	21.8							
142	1786.0	1008.0	Twoneedle Piñon	17.8	179.8							
% Slope: 25 – 80	451.0	601.1	Western Wheatgrass	11.9	119.9							
Wauquie - .4		3.0	Gambel's Oak	10.7	107.9							
Dolcan - .3			Indian Ricegrass	10.7	107.9							

Piñon-Juniper

Component	Col5	Col6					
Piñon-Juniper			239.8	371.7	458.6	13.9	2.9	1.1	5.5
Muttongrass	9.5	95.9					
True Mountain Mahogany	7.1	71.9					
Mountain Mahogany	7.1	71.9					
Utah Juniper	5.9	59.9					
Galleta	4.8	47.9					
Antelope Bitterbrush	3.6	36.0					
Big Sagebrush	3.6	36.0					
Common Snowberry	2.4	24.0					
Piñon Ricegrass	2.4	24.0					
Utah Serviceberry	2.4	24.0					

1. Village Project soil code; slope range; component name and proportion of complex; ecological setting

2. Number of hectares of soil complex within the study area; number of 4-ha cells represented by soil in study area

3. Normal-year NPP in kg/ha as reported for the primary component in soil surveys; mean annual productivity of model; sd

4. Components of native vegetation communities as listed in the soil surveys

5. Percent species contributes to native vegetation community, weighted by proportion component contributes to soil complex

6. Normal-year NPP per species in kg/ha

7. Total NPP of all tree species for normal year in kg/ha for soil complex

8. Total NPP of all shrub species for normal year in kg/ha for soil complex

9. Total woody biomass produced in kg/ha for soil complex, calculated as the sum of columns 7 and 8, less 25 percent for foliage lost/nor developing into wood

10. Kg/ha edible meat protein provided by the three herbivore species based on NPP of their preferred plant foods supported by soil complex and 65 percent of total body weight as edible meat

11. Total kg meat protein provided by the three herbivore species based on NPP of their preferred plant foods supported by soil complex and the average amount of protein per unit edible meat weight

Modeling Fuels.

The standing crop of fuelwood also depends, indirectly, on the NPP of the woody species. Annual new growth of woody species in piñon-juniper forest is reported as 1.3 percent of standing crop (Howell 1941). Because figures for standing crop are not available for most species, we estimate them by multiplying the mean annual production of each woody species (over the full model run) by the inverse of .013 (76.9). These values are seeded as standing crop into each model cell as appropriate to its soil type and associated native vegetation community. Annual deadwood production is modeled as 6.5 percent of tree standing crop (Howell 1941) and 3.35 percent of shrub standing crop (Chojnacky 1984). At model initialization, the total standing crop of woody species includes these percentages of deadwood. In procuring fuels, households first target nearby deadwood, and then, if deadwood becomes scarce, they cut the living forest (which is calorically more costly). "Nearby" can be defined when the model is run. After harvesting has taken place within a model cell, the standing crops of the live woody species and the deadwood are replenished at a rate appropriate to the soil type and climate during each model step.

In the rulesets for household behavior that we are currently exploring, model households attempt to obtain required resources in an efficient manner. Although each resource is replenished to some degree in every model step, local overharvesting of resources is possible and is often seen during simulation, as we discuss below.

The Archaeological Record

One goal of the Village Ecodynamics Project is to compare archaeological knowledge of the settlement patterns in our project area with virtual settlement patterns created through agent-based simulation. To document the archaeological settlement patterns, we assembled a database with information on all recorded sites. Our task was to use explicit and repeatable criteria to determine site location, site function, the period or periods of occupation, and population estimates for each residential site. Creating this database forced us to devise solutions to a number of common archaeological problems; we believe that these solutions will be of use to archaeologists working in many areas. In this section, we very briefly describe the methods used to compile and analyze the database. We then apply these methods to reconstruct the demographic history of the project area and examine the appearance, use, and decline of those large sites that we interpret as community centers.

Please consult Ortman, Varien, and Gripp (2007) for details on these methods and Varien and colleagues (2007) for details on the interpretations of these data. Our methods incorporate many assumptions that influence the results. We continue to evaluate the plausibility of these assumptions, and future analyses of these data could use different assumptions and therefore produce slightly different results. The analyses that follow use what we currently believe to be the best assumptions and reflect our current understanding of these data.

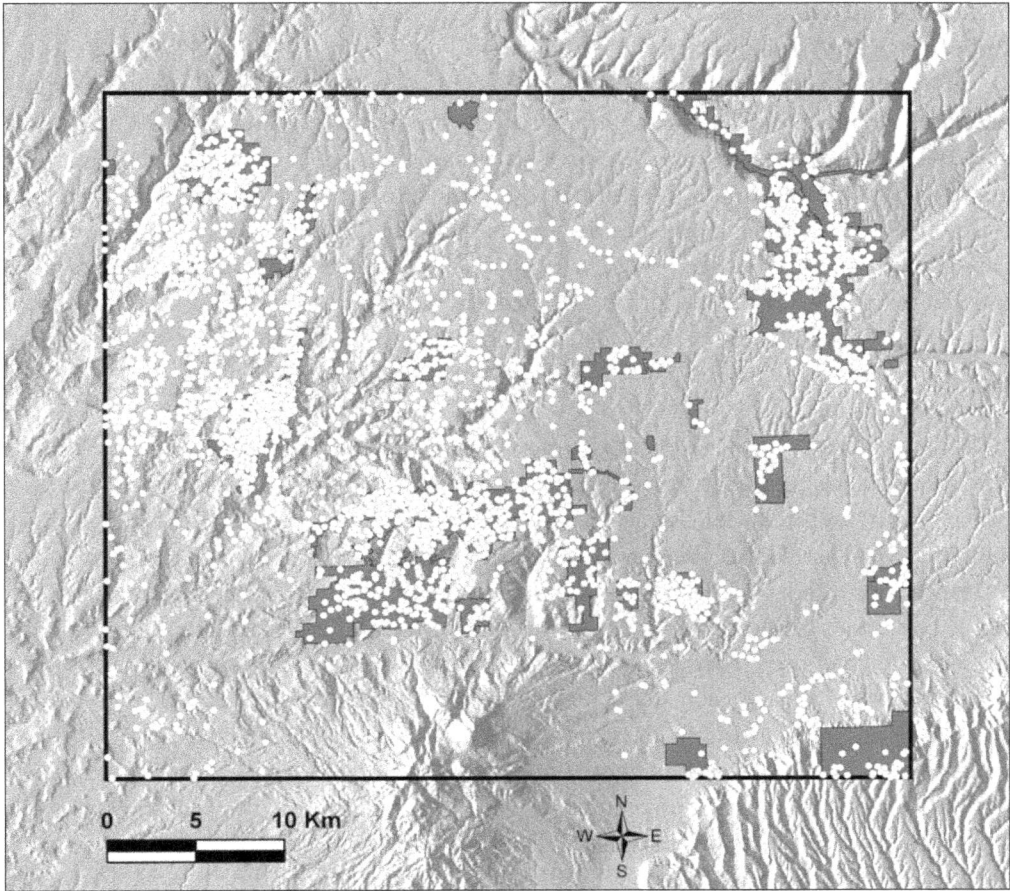

Figure 4.4. Village Ecodynamics study area, with all database sites and block survey locations.

The Database

The site database contains records for about nine thousand sites, most of which were recorded during one of the 336 surveys conducted in the project area (figure 4.4). Approximately 15 percent of the project area has been surveyed, including block and transect surveys. In our analysis of the database, we first assigned sites to various functional categories: isolated public architecture, single habitations, multiple habitations, field houses, and a variety of limited activity site types. Most residential sites are single habitations, and the primary features at these sites include a pitstructure, a roomblock, and a trash midden.

Determining the period of occupation was a challenge because the way sites are recorded has changed dramatically over the past fifty years. We needed a method that could be applied consistently despite differences in the type and quality of data, and we needed to detect even subtle evidence of multiple occupations. Ortman designed a

Bayesian statistical analysis (Buck, Cavanaugh, and Litton 1996; Iversen 1984; Robertson 1999) to address these issues.

We started with a calibration dataset of eighty excavated and well-dated site components, which we used to estimate the frequencies of eighteen architectural attributes and twenty-four pottery types in sites dating to each of fourteen separate periods between AD 600 and 1300. We defined these modeling periods to be as short as possible, given our current understanding of the local archaeological record. The periods vary from 20 to 125 years in length, but most span 40 years. The calibration data were used to specify the probability that each pottery type and architectural attribute dated to each of these fourteen periods. These probability distributions were scaled so that the area under the curve equals one and the probability for each period is a value between zero and one.

These probability distributions were combined with the sample data from each site to calculate composite probability density distributions for three categories of observations: architectural characteristics, undecorated pottery, and decorated pottery. A probability distribution was also created to reflect the surveyor's assessment of when a site was occupied. Finally, we weighted and combined probability density distributions, based on samples of eleven or more sherds for all sites within 7 km of each habitation site; we used this information to specify the occupational history of the "neighborhood" around each site. These neighborhood distributions are critical for our analysis because the available data for about half the sites in our database were insufficient for us to determine their most probable period of occupation. The use of neighborhood distributions to interpret when these poorly documented habitations were occupied is justified because ancestral Pueblo habitations of a given period tend to occur in spatial clusters (Adler 1990; Adler and Varien 1994; Fetterman and Honeycutt 1987; Lipe 1970; Rohn 1977).

After calculating these six probability density distributions—for architecture, plain pottery, decorated pottery, the surveyor's estimate, absolute dates, and the neighborhood—we averaged the available lines of evidence for each site (the neighborhood contributed to this average only for sites with fewer than eleven sherds) to produce a mean probability density distribution for each site.

In this project, we measure archaeological and agent populations in terms of households. Several lines of evidence indicate that each household used a single pitstructure throughout our sequence (Cater and Chenault 1988; Lightfoot 1994; Ortman 1998; Varien 1999). We therefore estimated the peak populations of habitation sites, using a two-step process. First, we estimated the total number of pitstructures present at each site, based on the number of depressions on the modern ground surface, the size of the surface roomblock, and the total site area. Then we used multiple regression trained on data from excavated sites where the peak populations were known to predict the peak populations of unexcavated sites, based on their total pitstructure estimates and various characteristics of their mean probability density distributions.

Finally, we integrated the peak population estimate with the posterior probability distribution for each site. We know from excavation that sites with one pitstructure were typically occupied during only one period (Varien, ed. 1999). For sites of this size, we simply assigned one household to the period for which the probability of occupation was highest; an additional household was also assigned to periods corresponding to secondary modes in the mean probability density distribution at these small sites. We also know, however, that larger sites were typically occupied for multiple periods (Kohler and Blinman 1987; Ortman et al. 2000). To determine the periods of occupation at these larger sites, we conducted a second multiple regression, using a dataset of thirty-five well-dated, multicomponent sites. This enabled us to predict the minimum probability value that signifies occupation. At these sites we assigned households to each of the periods that exceeded this threshold, based on the ratio of the nonpeak probability values to the peak value.

Demographic Reconstruction

Our analysis reconstructed the occupation histories of about 3,300 residential sites that have a total of 7,122 distinct components. The vast majority of these habitation components consisted of single-household farmsteads. In this section, we use these results to reconstruct the history of Pueblo occupation in the project area overall. Figure 4.5 shows momentary population estimates for these sites. This was computed using the total number of households in each period and factoring in the occupation span of sites and the number of years in each modeling period. The changing occupation spans of habitation sites over time were taken from research that uses the accumulation of cooking pottery to estimate the length of occupation at habitation sites (Varien 1999, in press; Varien and Mills 1997; Varien and Ortman 2005). As Varien and colleagues (2007) describe in detail, we have used three methods to extrapolate from the surveyed portions of our project area and estimate a range of values for the population of the total project area (see figure 4.5). We believe that the middle estimate (based on method 3) is the most accurate, but all three show that occupation of the project area occurred in two cycles: an early cycle between AD 600 and 920, with relatively low population, and a late cycle between about AD 920 and 1280, with higher population. We discuss the "settlement efficiency" estimate on figure 4.5 in the "Summary and Conclusions."

The Development of Community Centers

The next step in our analysis examines population aggregation and the development of large sites over time. We define "large" as sites with nine or more pitstructures, fifty or more total structures, or sites with civic architecture. Ninety-two sites fit one or more of these criteria (plate 10). We call these sites "community centers" because a cluster of smaller sites typically surrounds them, they are the largest site in each cluster, and they often contain public architecture, such as a great kiva (Adler and Varien 1994; Lipe and Varien 1999:345; Varien et al. 1996). In addition, these centers have the longest occupation histories of any sites in the region (Varien 1999:202–07), and

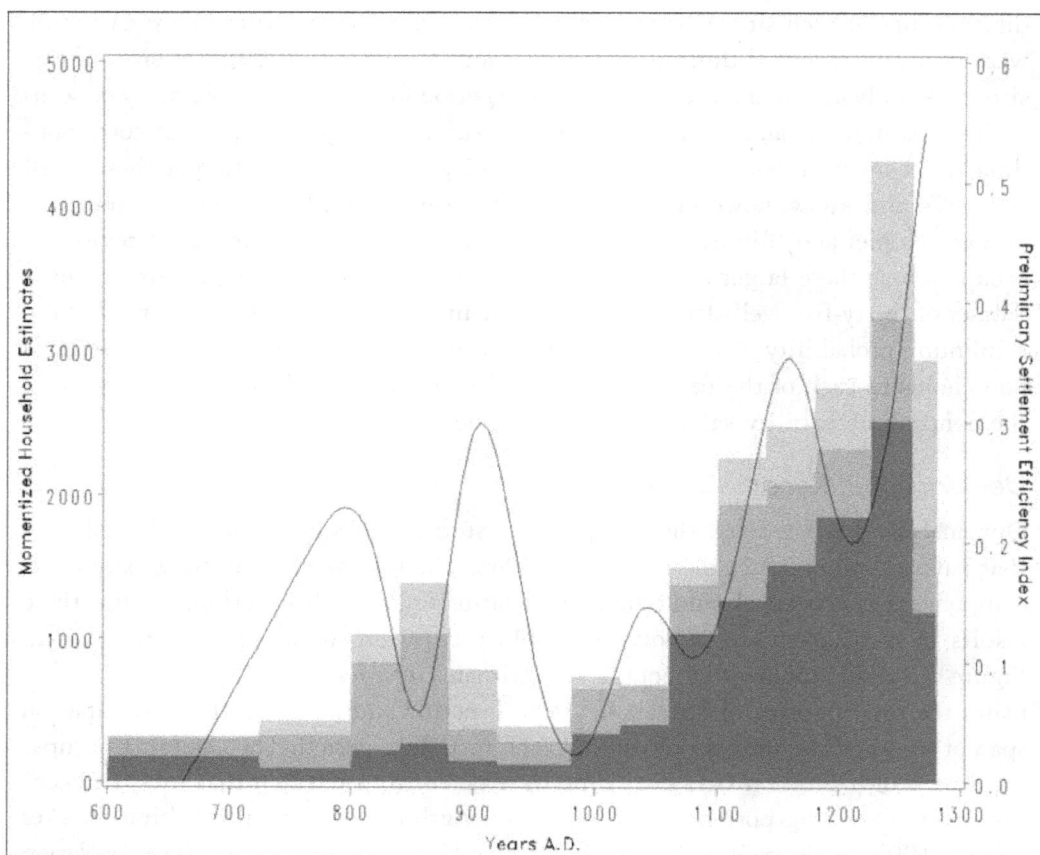

Figure 4.5. Momentary population (households) in the project area by modeling period, determined by three methods (in block histograms, after Varien et al. 2007). The middle estimate, produced by method 3, is preferred. The settlement efficiency index (shown in the spline-fit line) tracks the proportion of runs (reported in Cowan et al. n.d.) in which the distributions of simulated and actual households are positively correlated.

they were the location of social, economic, and political activities that did not occur at smaller habitation sites (Driver 1996; Lipe 2002). The existing records for these centers were evaluated, and new fieldwork was conducted at fifty-nine centers with relatively poor documentation. These sites were mapped to obtain better data on their size, including the number of visible pitstructure depressions, and samples of surface pottery were analyzed to yield chronological information.

The median population size of community centers is 14 households. Between AD 1225 and 1260, the range is 9–134 households at Yellow Jacket Pueblo, the largest center in the project area. The formation of centers appears to follow trends seen in the overall population: centers became increasingly common during each of the two population cycles and were most numerous at the end of the first cycle and the end of the second cycle. There were many more people, many more centers, and larger centers in the second cycle (Varien et al. in press). One of the most distinctive characteristics of the community centers is their long occupation spans (Ortman et al. 2000), but all were abandoned as a part of the migrations that emptied the region by the end of the thirteenth century.

Community Centers and Population Trends

In our project area, we have almost a 100 percent sample of the community centers but have identified only a small percentage of the small sites. Given this, we focus on data from the large block surveys to summarize settlement patterns over time, because these areas have a 100 percent sample of both centers and smaller sites. We use these data to examine the development of centers in the context of the overall demographic trends. Table 4.2 lists the momentary number of households living in small sites during each modeling period and the momentary households in community centers. It is apparent from these data that almost everyone lived in small sites during the initial period, but during the next four periods the total households in small sites decreased and the total households in centers increased. These trends peak at about AD 880, when the number of households living in centers actually surpassed the number of households in small sites. The number of households living in centers declined dramatically between AD 880 and the middle-to-late 1000s, when the number of households living in centers began to increase again. These two cycles of aggregation are seen even more clearly in the next column, which lists the percent of total momentary population of block-surveyed areas that lived in community centers during each period. These data clearly show how the proportion of households living in centers increased over the course of each settlement cycle.

To examine these demographic data and how they might be correlated with drought, we compiled a database of every tree-ring cutting date in the region—a total of about 4,600 cutting dates from 350 sites. Each cutting date tells us the year in which that timber was harvested, and table 4.2 summarizes the number of harvested trees in our dataset for each of the fourteen periods. We also tabulated the percent of years in each modeling period in which precipitation was more than one standard deviation below the long-term mean; we calculated the standardized mean precipitation for the years in each modeling period. These data suggest that, in general, tree harvesting tended to decline during periods with a high proportion of drought years and to increase during periods with fewer drought years. There appears, however, to be no consistent relationship between drought and population. These data suggest that tree harvesting and construction were curtailed during droughts but that drought did not always result in migration and depopulation, possibly because our study area had greater precipitation than many areas to the south and west and therefore served as a potential refugium during drought, particularly warm droughts.

Finally, it is instructive to compare the percent of population in community centers, the overall momentary population in the block surveys, and population growth

Table 4.2 Momentary Population, Community Center Characteristics, Aggregation, and Population Growth Rates through Time, Block Survey Areas

Modeling Period (AD)	Period Duration	Momentary Population (HH)	Percent of Households in Centers	Population Growth Rate (per 100 HH/year)	N Centers Occupied	Mean Center Size (HH)	Tree-Ring Cutting Dates*	Percent of Drought Years	Mean Precipitation (Z-Scores)
600–725	125	42	1.1	—	2	1.0	619	21.6	−0.06
725–800	75	64	39.7	0.56	10	7.1	248	14.7	0.09
800–840	40	145	28.4	2.05	12	5.8	214	25.0	−0.15
840–880	40	207	38.5	0.89	19	6.0	552	12.5	0.05
880–920	40	128	71.6	−1.20	23	5.4	85	17.5	0.18
920–980	60	45	24.0	−1.76	8	2.8	102	15.0	−0.07
980–1020	40	99	10.6	1.98	4	2.5	34	12.5	−0.06
1020–1060	40	95	8.4	−0.09	5	1.6	226	10.0	−0.02
1060–1100	40	208	25.0	1.95	14	3.7	196	17.5	0.05
1100–1140	40	283	22.6	0.77	14	5.0	265	15.0	0.16
1140–1180	40	304	26.0	0.18	17	4.6	137	20.0	−0.39
1180–1225	45	324	34.0	0.14	19	5.8	503	17.8	0.27
1225–1260	35	570	47.9	1.61	17	11.2	847	5.7	−0.01
1260–1280	20	490	64.1	−0.76	16	19.3	473	10.0	0.00

*Includes all dates from all sites in the study area

rates through time. Each peak in settlement aggregation corresponds to a period in which the proportion of drought years increased and emigration occurred. Apparently, community centers were especially important in the regional settlement system during these periods. We believe that this importance may be due to both ecological and social factors. For example, the centers appear to be associated with especially good soils and reliable springs. In addition, the larger populations at centers would have had more flexibility to organize labor and would have had more extensive exchange networks.

Perhaps even more important, the inhabitants in larger centers would have had more protection if conflict and warfare occurred during periods of drought and emigration. Based on recent research tabulating the local proportion of individuals with skeletal insults probably due to warfare (Cole 2006), warfare was most prevalent in our project area from the mid–late 1000s through the mid–late 1100s, and again in the late 1200s (Kuckelman 2000), both being periods when aggregation was pronounced. Aggregation in the late 1200s, though, is contrary to a microeconomic model proposed for our area by Kohler and Van West (1996), which suggested economic reasons why households should disaggregate in times of low average production accompanied by high spatial and temporal variability similar to those experienced here in the late 1200s. According to this model, households should be "risk seeking" under such conditions, taking a chance by going it alone rather than sharing with other households. One possible interpretation of our current results is that security concerns can trump any microeconomic "disaggregation signal"; risk seeking can become too risky.

Overall, our model of the settlement history of the project area suggests, first, a positive relationship between aggregation and overall population, in which aggregation appears as a continuous process during each occupational cycle. Although aggregation appears to be generally correlated with population growth, it does not clearly ebb and flow with changes in climatically induced changes in production. We suspect that the aggregation process is also related to social and historical factors, which we hope to clarify as we continue analyzing our data. Second, both periods of peak aggregation—during the late 800s and late 1200s—occurred when the local population had already begun to decline. This pattern suggests that aggregated settlements may have exerted a "gravitational pull" on their inhabitants. Perhaps aggregated settlements were more resistant to fission and abandonment than some previous models have proposed, or perhaps the probabilistic dynamics of emigration resulted in losing many more hamlets than centers during the initial phase of regional depopulation. By playing off the archaeological data against the agent-based model, we show below that interesting patterns in both depopulations are exposed.

Resource Use and Settlement Model

Having discussed resource availability and some of the things that the archaeological record can tell us about resource demand, we now turn back to the simulation and discuss its current structure. We begin by briefly defining how households use resources and relocate with respect to resources, and then we discuss how agents exchange resources.

How Resources Are Used

Each year, agents must find and collect resources to survive. Currently, agents are required to gather both fuel and water, grow and harvest corn, and hunt. To simplify this process, all resources in the model are converted into one of two currencies, calories or protein. An agent dies if its balance of calories or protein (but see below) ever becomes negative.

Maize.

Agents plant, weed, and harvest maize to create a positive net balance of calories, which are then used to collect the other resources. The number of fields planted and the productivity of those fields in a given year determine the amount of maize an agent can produce. The number of fields (1-acre plots) that can be planted by model households each year is limited to either one or two greater than the number of workers it has (we have experimented with both values; children under eight years old do not work). After maize is harvested, the model determines the number of calories produced. These calories are then available to perform other types of work, such as tending next year's crops and collecting other required resources.

Hunting.

We have developed two models for hunting. Here, we describe the first, developed by Kobti and Reynolds (2005); the second is described in a later publication (Cowan et al. n.d.). They differ in the granularity of their approach and in how knowledge and caloric costs are handled. In the Reynolds/Kobti model, agents store knowledge about the yields of each of the three animal populations (deer, rabbit, and hare) for visited cells. Cells with above-average performance are ordered in a best-first manner. Each of these lists constitutes a hunting plan, and each plan is processed using an approach based upon Charnov's (1976) Marginal Value Theorem. The idea is that when a cell on the list for an animal type falls below the hunter's average overall expectations, it is dropped from the list (figure 4.6) and replaced by a cell within a given distance from that cell. Figure 4.7 shows the process graphically. There, each of the cells currently visited according to the plan is shown. Each has an above-average expectation and is visited in order of its expectations. When one of the cells falls below the overall average for all cells, it is replaced by another within a limited radius. That radius can be set as a parameter in the model or learned by the agent.

Fuel and Water.

Water for domestic use and wood for fuel are also necessary for sustaining households. Each person in each household requires 1,130 kg fuelwood (Khan et al. 2001) and 3,650 liters water (Gleick 2000), although these parameters can be easily altered.

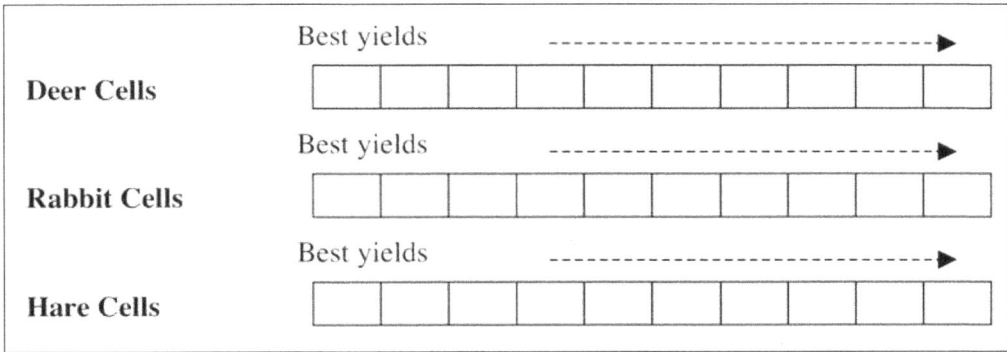

Figure 4.6. An agent maintains a dynamic list of hunting cells with above-average yields for each of the three protein resources; decreasing yields move to the right in each array.

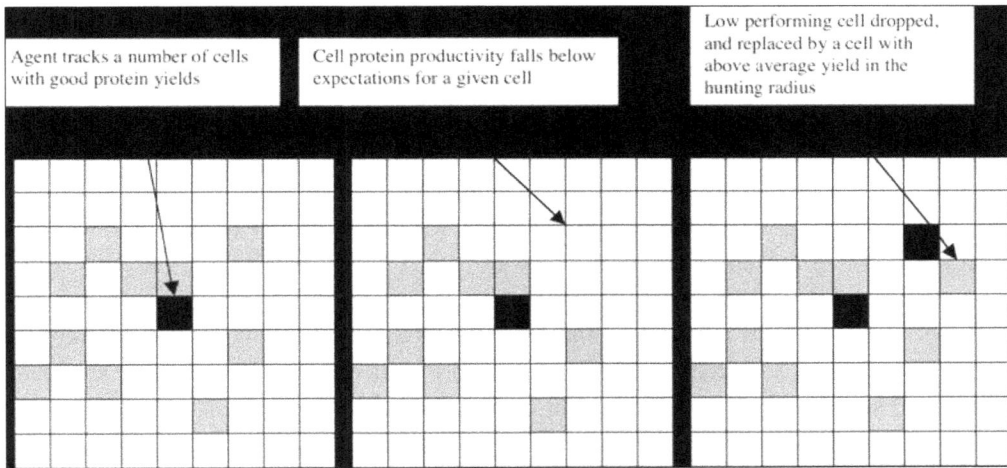

Figure 4.7. Illustration of the cell maintenance process, based on an adaptation of the Marginal Value Theorem.

When collecting water for the year, each household locates the source nearest to its present location and determines the number of trips required to fulfill its annual requirement by dividing the amount of water needed by the cargo capacity per trip. The default capacity for transporting water is 21 liters, determined by giving an individual the ability to transport 25 kg of weight and subtracting from that the average weight (4 kg) of a local Pueblo I *olla* (water jar) (Lightfoot 1994). When the distance between the agent and the water source is known and the number of trips are known, these are divided by the average travel speed of an agent (a tunable parameter in the model, to which residential location turns out to be quite sensitive) to determine how many hours of work are required. This is then multiplied by the caloric cost of one hour of work by the agent to yield the resource cost (equation 2):

$$R = \left(\left(\frac{2D * (N/C)}{S} \right) \right) * W \qquad \text{Eq. 2}$$

where R = resource cost; D = distance between resource and agent; N = amount of resource required; C = carrying capacity of individual; S = speed of agent; and W = caloric cost of one hour of work by an individual.

Fuel harvest is similar to water collection. For fuels, a person can carry the full 25 kg, however, because there is no container weight. When an individual reaches the resource collection location, an additional gathering cost is calculated, based on type of fuel being collected. For deadwood collection, one extra hour of work is added per trip; for standing crop harvest, two extra hours of work are added. Occasionally, the amount of resources required exceeds the amount found at a single location in the model. When this happens, the agent will collect all the available resources at that location, calculate the costs for harvesting those resources, recalculate its need, and then continue to look for resources at a new location. No fuelwood is available to agents where plots have been cleared for farming, and we assume that the plots are cleared wastefully, with none of the wood used for fuel. Although this assumption is questionable, we consider it to be approximately balanced by the fact that we do not require households to acquire wood for building or maintaining their houses or for equipment or site furniture. Moreover, we allow agents access to all woody biomass for fuel, even though some would be difficult or impossible to harvest because of limitations of stone axes.

Numerous model runs indicate that fuel harvesting by model agents often leads to local depletion (Johnson, Kohler, and Cowan 2005). In runs using various per capita fuel requirements, we typically observe the total removal of woody species from areas surrounding long-term concentrations of model households. Of course, the extent of such deforestation is linked to the size and stability of the local population, the level of demand simulated, and (less obviously) to the speed we attribute to workers traveling to obtain distant resources.

How Resources Affect Settlement

Settlement patterns seen in the model are a direct result of movement decisions made by the individual households. We have seen that households must keep a positive net balance of calories and protein to survive. To do this, households must maintain high maize production while keeping other resource costs low. Other than adding or subtracting local fields (plots), to the extent of their ability to do so, the only direct method that households have to keep these factors in this balance is to move their residences around the landscape.

When a Household Moves.

Each year, to determine how they are doing, households examine their maize production for the preceding few years, along with their rate of caloric expenditure. When this happens, a total of three states is possible. If a household is producing more calories than it needs and it has enough calories in storage to meet the next year's calorie requirements, then it is content and remains at its current location. If only one of these criteria is met, then the household determines whether planting additional plots in its current location is feasible. If neither of these criteria is met or if only one is but the household cannot add new plots locally, it attempts to move to a new location.

How a Household Moves.

When a household moves, it tries to find a location that will allow it to maximize caloric production while minimizing resource costs. It does this by first ranking every cell within its search radius, based on how many calories that cell would produce if the household were farming in that cell during that year. If a cell already has eight or more plots planted by other agents at this time, it is excluded from this ranking. (There are nine possible 1-ac plots in each 4-ha cell, with a small amount left over for habitation.) After this ranking is done, the household calculates the expected caloric costs for collecting other resources in the top one hundred calorie-producing cells. When these costs have been calculated, the one hundred cells are reordered, based on which would produce the most calories (after subtracting anticipated caloric costs for getting water, fuels, and sufficient protein) if the household were living in that location during that year. Finally, the household moves to the location with the best prospects, based on this ranking.

The result is a move that approximately maximizes household efficiency (defined as caloric benefit–caloric cost), but with a built-in bias to be close to productive agricultural areas that are not yet fully planted. This built-in bias may be more descriptive of household preferences in the first colonization cycle than in the second cycle. Overall, within just a few years of model initiation, agents approximate an ideal free distribution, but soon, as populations rise, the distribution begins to approximate an ideal despotic distribution (Fretwell and Lucas 1970; chapter 7, this volume).

Cultural Algorithms, Networks, and Exchange

We can now discuss our initial use of cultural algorithms in the context of implementing exchange among households, because these are layered on top of everything else we have described to this point. As shown in figure 4.8, cultural algorithms (CAs) assume a social population and a belief space (Reynolds 1979). "Cultural knowledge" resides in the belief space, where it is stored and updated based on household experiences and their successes or failures. In turn, the cultural knowledge controls the evolution of the population by means of an influence function. A cultural algorithm thereby provides a framework in which to accumulate and communicate knowledge, enabling adaptation in both the population and the belief space (Chung and Reynolds 1996; Cowan and Reynolds 2003; Reynolds 1994, 1999, 2005; Reynolds and Ostrowski 2003).

At least five basic categories of cultural knowledge are important in the belief space of any cultural evolution model: situational, normative, topographic, historical or temporal, and domain knowledge (Reynolds 2005). In our model, all these knowledge sources can be represented. For example, we currently assume that agents will

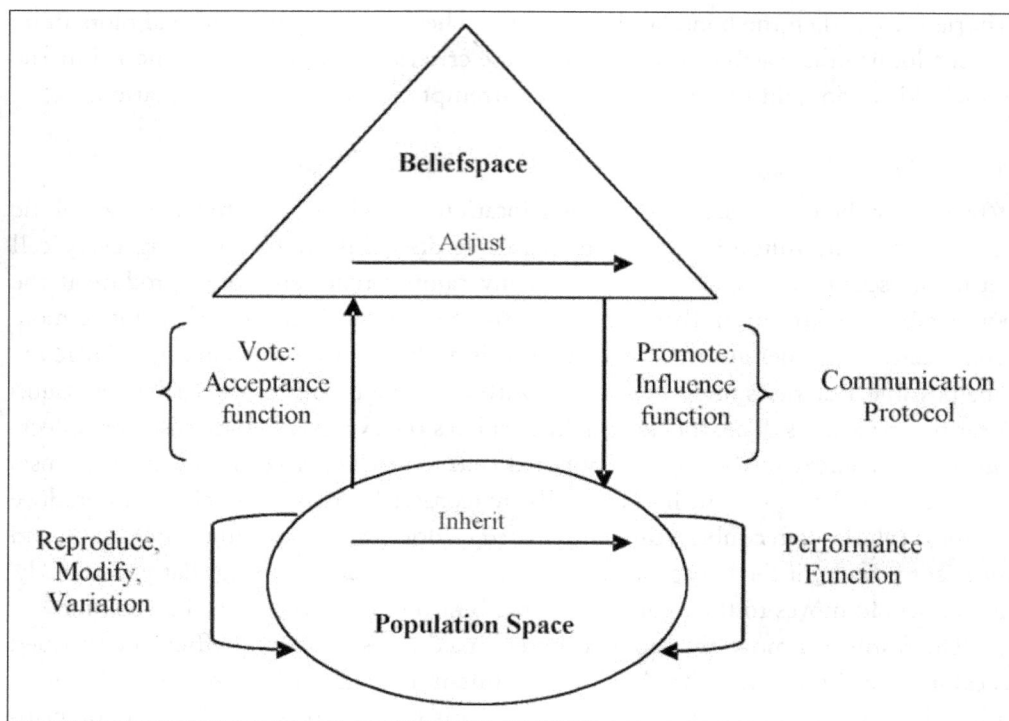

Figure 4.8. The cultural algorithm framework.

have access to knowledge about the distribution of current agricultural production and topography, the distribution of rainfall over the preceding few years to the extent that it affects agricultural production (historical or temporal knowledge), and agricultural planting and harvesting techniques (domain knowledge). These latter two knowledge sources are fixed at this time.

The comprehensive cultural framework shown in figure 4.9 is proposed as a guideline for the agent's learning strategies. The main components include the agent's maize storage status (based on resource needs), exchange, network relations, resource generation, and movement. As new data are added to the model, they can be accommodated within this framework. The current implementation includes agriculture and hunting, along with generalized and balanced reciprocal exchange of resources among agents. No production or exchange of artifacts has yet been implemented.

Social Networks

As noted in the introduction, in this phase of our project a key goal is to determine as rigorously as we can how much of the variability in the archaeological settlement pattern can be attributed to the responses of individual households as they attempt to minimize costs and maximize success in a changing environment. Our introduction of cultural algorithms coupled with exchange processes, in those simulations where we

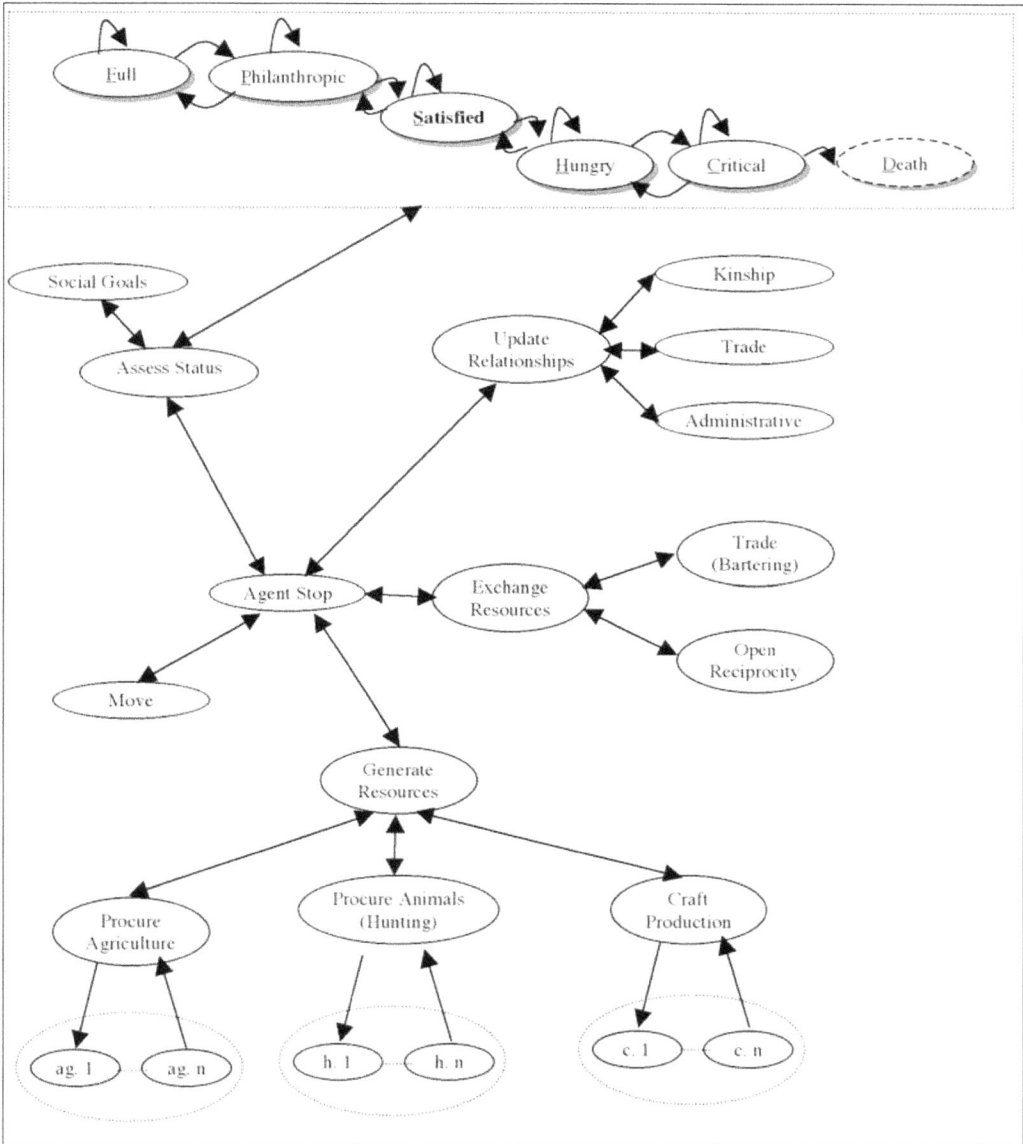

Figure 4.9. The comprehensive cultural framework.

enable exchange, departs slightly from this philosophy by allowing a sort of "primitive sociality" to arise. Here, we describe the three networks developed by Kobti, Reynolds, and Kohler (2004) across which exchanges may flow.

Kinship Network.

The emergent networks in the model are developed by households, the nodes in the network. Household members live together, share their production, and are affected

Table 4.3 Connected Nodes Identified by the Kinship Social Network

Name of Tag Enabling Link	Description
ParentHHTagA	A link to the parent from the mother's side
ParentHHTagB	A link to the parent from the father's side
ChildHHTag	One link to each child who moves away from this household and forms her or his own household
RelativeHHTag	One link to each extended family member

by the same environmental conditions. Children can grow up, marry, and move out to form their own households. Their connections to their parent households and siblings are maintained in our model. Similarly, the parents maintain ties to their children. When one of the parents in a household dies, the other can form a new household with an available single agent. If both parents die, we use the expedient process of promoting the oldest child remaining in the household (if there is one) to become the "parent," if that child is seven years old or older. If no child that old is available, the household dies. The structure of the social network supports the notions of parents, siblings, and grandparents on both sides of the family. The layout of the generalized reciprocal network (GRN) from the perspective of a household is described in table 4.3.

The original simulation model (Kohler et al. 2000) was based on households with no social or economic interactions. The first extension to that model in the current round of development introduced gender, marriage rules, and other localized enhancements enabling individuals to co-exist and reproduce within households. Reynolds, Kohler, and Kobti (2003) have described rules for marriage and kinship dynamics. Briefly, the kinship network links each living household to its parents, siblings, children, and other relatives. We implemented generalized reciprocal exchange (Sahlins's "generalized reciprocity" [1972:192–94]) over this network to enable agents to cooperate through resource exchange to improve their survival.

A small-world social network emerged. A small-world network is a "(large) graph with both local clustering and, on average, short distance between the nodes. Short distances promote accessibility, whereas local clustering and redundancy of edges promotes robustness to disconnection" (White and Houseman 2003:72). These distances can be measured in various ways (for example, in geographic space or kinship space). The farther away nodes are in the graph, the weaker the ties. Most nodes have many strong ties and support transitivity of exchange between nodes. Nodes with many weak ties and few strong ones are called "hub nodes." Transmission of matter, energy, and information in small-world networks shows signs of funneling through hubs (Travers and Milgram 1969). The presence of these hub nodes allows requestors to navigate through the network looking for resources.

In our first CA models, we used just the GRN, which is based on kinship distance. The resultant system was able to support a larger population than did the system in which no resources were exchanged among kin. The small-world network gives each agent multiple paths along which to search for resources. Within the network, agents can be reliable or unreliable donors. Thus, some paths will be fruitful and lead to agents that are reliable, and others will not (see Reynolds et al. 2005).

One of the key issues was how agents can learn to navigate the existing network effectively by avoiding unreliable agents and defectors, an important problem in the effective use of such networks (White and Houseman 2003). Motivated by household-level experience and population norms, households are able to learn and make more intelligent choices in cooperating over the kinship network through the CA. For instance, a household can learn to make a better choice when it decides whom to ask for food when in need. Over time, an individual can learn to select more cooperative kin, and, indirectly, a population identifies known exemplars and establishes its acceptable norms. As a result, established households can become good donors, and those in less productive locations can depend on the social network for survival. In our simulations, we can enable a "social move" in which households are allowed to relocate closer to the productive kin and, indirectly, to more productive farmlands (such moves are not implemented in the simulations reported here). Over time, individuals cluster closer together around productive lands weakly connected by hubs in a small-world social network. When we visually compare the simulated locations of these hubs with those community centers known archaeologically, a reasonably good fit is observed. In general, however, in work to date we have not rigorously evaluated the fit of our simulated distributions to the archaeologically known settlement system.

Economic Network.

A second, important baseline network, the economic network, is an implementation of what Sahlins (1972:194–95) called "balanced reciprocity" (a balanced reciprocal network, or BRN, in our model). The archaeological record for our region contains a large variety of ceramics, stone tools, and other artifacts that could have been exchanged among households. This suggests the potential for economically based exchange as a mechanism for distributing resources among the agents. In our implementation of balanced reciprocity, each household maintains a list of trading partners formed from nearby households. Requiring these exchanges to be relatively local reflects the constraints of increasing costs as travel distances increase. Each household maintains a set of trading partners that can be any household within a given radius from the focal household. (In the future, we may restrict this network to non-kin.) Households adopt a strategy to decide when, and with whom, to exchange. In contrast to the reciprocal exchange model, households in this network keep balances of the amounts owed and traded. The ability of agents to repay their debts reflects their reliability, generalized here as reputation. A well-reputed household is a good producer and lives without debt. This is typical of settlers of productive lands or those with strong social ties. Less reliable households reside on less productive lands and have weak social ties. A CA in the economic network guides the decisions that a household and the culture make in selecting reputable trading partners. The social networks produced by using both the GRN and BRN again fit a small-world pattern.

Hub Network.

Also new in our current implementation is the concept of a hub network, which emerges from both the GRN and BRN networks. Our implementation of the two base networks allows households to promote themselves to the next network: the hub network. Hubs are households that are central because they have an unusual amount of connectivity in the network. Central hubs provide the network with its searchability properties and enable agents to navigate the web to locate potential partners for exchange. Here, they are operationally defined as those nodes that are of sufficient complexity in both the GRN and the BRN; we use an intersection criterion for identifying hub nodes (figure 4.10). That is, the total number of connections in the BRN and the GRN must exceed a certain constant for a node to be eligible for promotion to the hub-node network. Promotion to hub-node status is determined through a probabilistic discrete Poisson distribution, based on a household's number of links to other hub nodes. A hub node can demote itself and remove itself from the hub network if it loses its importance in either the GRN or BRN. Hubs have the ability to exchange with one another (under the ruleset we call "coop 6"; table 4.4) and to defect on their trades. However, defection is not dealt with in detail here (see Reynolds et al. 2005 for additional discussion).

All the exchange mechanisms are incremental, and each assumes the existence of the "more primitive" mechanism. Thus, the BRN emerges from the need to address deficiencies in the GRN, and the hub net emerges from the need to address navigability issues in the BRN. In a given simulation, if the GRN is sufficient to distribute resources among agents, there is no need for the BRN to emerge. Likewise, if the GRN and BRN together can efficiently support the exchange of resources, there is no need for the hub net to emerge. The number of levels in the emergent network is, then, a function of the predictability in space and time of the resources involved.

Using Social Networks to Support Exchange

In this section, we describe how the GRN and BRN are integrated, using the example of our implementation of protein exchange. Exchange of maize takes place in a similar fashion and is discussed by Kobti, Reynolds, and Kohler (2003, 2004). A key idea is that exchange occurs when a household needs resources. After updating their networks, households try to satisfy their resource needs by calling in debts from their neighbors first, using the BRN for each needed resource. Currently, only exchange in kind is considered. If they are not successful, then they request aid from their relatives through the GRN. If they still are deficient in resources, they then go back to the economic network to initiate further exchange. The extent of an agent's search is a func-

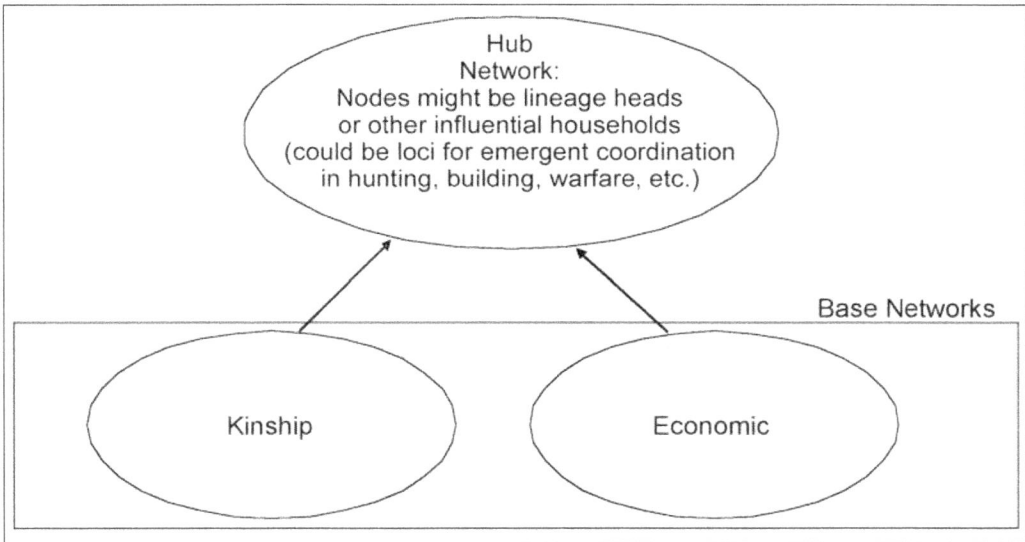

Figure 4.10. Overall social network structure, including the two base networks and the evolving communal (hub) network.

Table 4.4 Description of the Cooperation Methods at the Kinship Level

Coop Number	Action
0	When there is no cooperation, households do not exchange food.
1	When an agent requires food, it can select and request food from within its kinship network to survive.
2	When an agent has excess food, above a determined threshold amount, it can select one or more households from its kinship network and donate the excess.
3	Both methods 1 and 2 are enabled.
4	Full cooperation across the kinship and economic network (generalized and balanced reciprocal exchange simultaneously)
5	Hub network emergence based on the intersection of hubs from GRN and BRN networks, and accepted based on a discrete Poisson distribution
6	Hub nodes developed in coop 5 may exchange with other hubs

tion of the scarcity of the resource. If resources become scarce because of weather or soil depletion (in contrast to the case of northern Mesopotamia, described in chapter 9, we have no basis for inferring manuring of fields), dependency on all three network levels will increase. Table 4.5 shows how hunting and exchange are integrated, and table 4.6 describes the interaction of households with each of the three networks, assuming that hub-network exchange is enabled.

Table 4.5 Integration of Hunting and Exchange

Step	Action
1	Calculate protein need for the household for the year in order to survive, based on amounts set in the parameter file.
2	If the first hunt, then initialize the hunting location to the current cell.
3	If not the first hunt, then update the past hunting cell locations as follows: (1) Compute the average protein yield of the known cells by using the total protein yield from each cell (deer, rabbits, and hare). (2) If a known cell falls below the average, replace it with a nearby cell that has a better yield. This is done by searching within a hunting radius for the cell with the most yields.
4	Visit each known cell (most productive first), and hunt for deer, rabbits, and hares. (1) Continue hunting each cell until the household's needed protein yield is met. (2) If all the known cells are hunted without obtaining sufficient protein amounts, then search for additional hunting cells in the hunting radius, up to a defined maximum number of cells.
5	Consume the protein gathered from hunting activity.
6	If the household did not satisfy its protein requirements: (1) Then request the needed protein from relatives, using the CA to learn whom to ask, and update knowledge accordingly. (2) Then call in the debt by asking the trading partners to pay back their owed balance. Update the quality criteria with each partner accordingly. (3) If the household is still in need, request a protein trade from known partners on the BRN. Also, seek out new partners on the BRN, if needed. (Refer to the BRN for details.) (4) If the household is a hub and is still in need, then request protein from another hub.
7	If the household does not meet its protein requirements, then it may die, or its probability of having additional children may decrease and probability of death for members may increase, depending on settings elsewhere in the model.

A Sample Run of the Agent-Based Model

Here, we describe the results of a run of the simulation model, using all the resource models described above. Agents cultivate maize, hunt animals, and collect fuelwood and water. They can exchange animal and plant resources through both the GRN and BRN networks. The hub network can emerge from these networks if enabled by the simulation parameters and if needed by the population. These runs are not primarily designed to reference the archaeological record, so we do not expect a close fit between our results and the time series of local population size in figure 4.5. Here, we are interested primarily in various abstract properties of the simulated exchange systems.

Table 4.6 Exchange Actions

Step	Action
1	Update GRN.
2	Update BRN:
	(1) Remove dead partners (and non-active/out of region/expired).
	(2) Search each neighboring cell within a trade radius, get its settlers list, and add new ones to the trade list.
3	Update the hub network:
	(1) Promote or demote self to or from the hub network, based on current base status.
	(2) Remove dead partners, and search for new ones in range.
4	Request payback of debt from BRN and hub network partners.
5	If HUNGRY/CRITICAL (definitions for these states, in terms of amounts in storage relative to needs, can be changed in the parameter file), request food from GRN (no payback).
6	If still HUNGRY/CRITICAL, request food from BRN (with payback).
7	If still HUNGRY/CRITICAL, request food from hub network (with payback).
8	If CRITICAL, agent is dead and is removed.
9	If PHILANTHROPIC/FULL:
	(1) Donate surplus into GRN.
	(2) Pay back debt into BRN.
	(3) Pay back debt into hub net.

Figure 4.11 gives the population of agents produced by the model from AD 600 to 1300. We started with a small initial population of fewer than two hundred households. The system is closed; no agents arrive from elsewhere in these runs, nor can active households leave.

The system is able to survive several drought periods. The number of households in each of the three networks over time is given (all households correspond to the GRN because all households participate in the kinship network). Several drops in population correspond to periods of low potential production in the productivity data planes used. One result of a drought or another environmental stress is to reduce the total number of agents. This effect then ripples through the network, first to the BRN and then to the hub network, with a slight lag at each level. Although the hub network is the last to feel the ripples, it is the hardest hit and the last to recover.

Plate 11 presents volumes for each of the three networks. The network volume is the product of the out-degrees (number of connections) of each of the nodes in the network. This allows us to observe the impact of an environmental perturbation on the overall complexity of each of the three networks. Notice that after a drought around AD 800 the volume of the BRN is very close to that of the GRN. This means that most households are involved in each network to about the same degree. Later on,

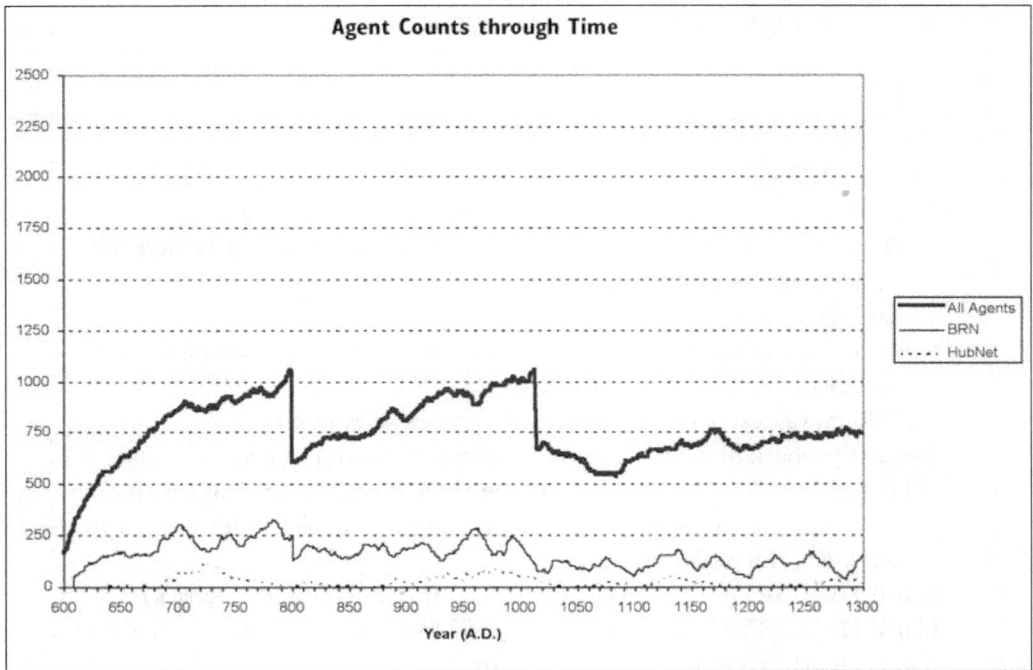

Figure 4.11. The number of agents (households) overall and participating in each of the three networks, GRN, BRN, and hub (coop 6). The total number of agents and the number participating in the GRN are the same because all agents have some kin connections to other agents. These experiments were conducted on paleoproductivity data planes different from those presented in figure 4.2 and represent a proof of principle for the exchange mechanisms.

the difference between the two becomes more pronounced after each environmental perturbation. This suggests the formation of more efficient but perhaps more isolated local groups.

Figure 4.12 gives a blowup of the hub network and its volume over time, from the same set of simulations used to produce plate 11. This network is the most cyclical of the three and disappears around AD 850, 1050, and 1200 as the result of low production in the data planes utilized here. It then re-emerges, gradually recovering after each episode of low production. But each time it recovers, the volume it reaches is less than the preceding peak. This drop in peak height may be due, in part, to the fact that the hub network is produced as a nonlinear combination of parts of the GRN and BRN. Losses in either the GRN or BRN make it harder to promote individuals back up into the hub network to replace lost nodes. In fact, hub-node volume is already descending around AD 1270, after reaching a peak that is far less than any previous one. In analogy to an automobile engine, each time there is a problem, the engine never quite reaches its former level of performance. After a recovery, the newly emergent hub network is never quite as effective as the former one; its peak volume exhibits a clear monotonic decrease through time.

This is a very interesting result in the sense that archaeological evidence supports

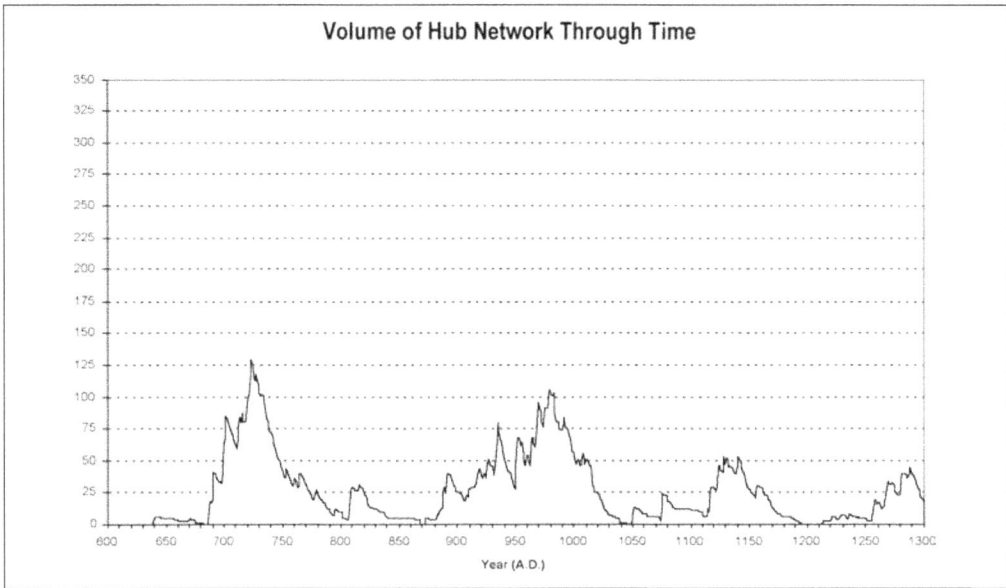

Figure 4.12. The volume of the hub network over time (coop 6). The volume of a network is the product of the out-degrees of each of its nodes. The out-degree is the number of individuals to which it is connected in that graph. After each collapse, this network achieves a new peak that is lower than its preceding peak.

increased populations until the mid-1200s. Because we have assumed that the system is closed and there are no incoming agents to replace the ones lost because of disruptions in the exchange network, this lack of fit with the archaeological data suggests that the system is far from closed and that, to understand the system fully, we need to understand the flow of humanity across the arbitrarily defined borders of our study region. In fact, it might be that the disruptions to our local social networks, though severe, were not as bad as those in other places. This may cause individuals from other regions to move into vacant "niches" in our system and firm up the network. (Varien et al. [2007], in fact, reconstruct four probable periods of immigration, following the initial colonization of our area by farmers.) If these immigrants were not related to current residents, they could overload the BRN because they would not be effectively integrated into the kinship structures (on which the GRN depends). Given that promotion to the hub network requires participation in both the GRN and the BRN, immigrants may not produce a resurgence in hub-net structure unless they can be integrated into the GRN. The integration of non-kin into social systems has been an important item for study in other cultures (Flannery, Marcus, and Reynolds 1989). Thus, it would be interesting in future work to model the effects of social integration on the system's overall stability. This could be done by opening the system, in a controlled way, to enable the immigration of new households into the region, along with the ability of resident households to abandon the region.

At the moment, this discussion is purely hypothetical (follow-up experiments are discussed in the next section), but it illustrates the power of simulation to show us alternative worlds, like so many "sandcastles," built and rebuilt. Although these worlds might not have existed, they may be able to tell us many things about the worlds that did. Simulation is truly a "sandbox for scholars."

Summary and Conclusions

As we write this chapter, we are beginning a series of runs in which we vary half-a-dozen model parameters (including type of exchange behavior, degree of soil degradation, whether households may move to protein-depleted areas, productivity of the landscape, amount of protein from hunting required per person, and which set of paleoproductivity dataplanes we use). We monitor the effects of each combination of parameters on population levels through time, location of population through time, degree and location of aggregations, the amount of time or calories spent in each major modeled activity (fuel and water collection, agriculture, and hunting) through time, and so forth. For some of these outputs (especially the locations and sizes of settlements through time and the total study area population through time), we have strong archaeological evidence that will help us determine which parameter combinations provide the best fit to the archaeological data. We expect to find that the best-fitting parameters will, in fact, change through time, giving us a sense of the directions in which household-level behaviors had to change through the seven hundred years we model.

For a century now, archaeologists have been developing approaches to examine the societies of the ancient Southwest within their environments (see partial reviews in Gumerman 1988; Kohler 2004). It might surprise us that aspects of these socioenvironmental relationships still remain to be appreciated. We have been surprised, in our preliminary results, to see how depletion of fuels—and especially of deer—becomes widespread in any simulation in which the model populations approach the levels actually achieved in this area, even when we keep per person protein requirements low. Population levels higher than those seen in the Pueblo I (PI; AD 750–900) period result in a severe depression of study-area deer populations even when protein requirements from hunting are on the order of only 15 g/person. For comparison, commonly cited protein requirements averaged for different ages and sexes are around .4 g/day/lb body weight. If our average individuals weighed 90 lbs, then they needed, by this calculation, about 36 g protein/person/day. An unknown but significant part of this would come from agriculture (corn, beans, squash, and cheno-ams) and another unknown proportion from gathering, trapping, and so forth. Spielmann and Angstadt-Leto (1996:82–3) conservatively estimate that southwestern agricultural populations needed 20 g/person/day of "high-quality" protein and permit half of that to come from small mammals and plants.

Because population levels in our area were considerably higher in the Pueblo II (PII; AD 900–1140) and Pueblo III (PIII; AD 1140–1280) periods than in PI times (see figure 4.5), we may find that post-PI populations as high as we see in our area were unlikely without the protein supplement provided by turkey domestication. Of course, long-distance hunting, beyond the area within which we model deer populations, could have alleviated local protein shortfalls to some extent (see the expansive range mapped by Ferguson and Hart [1985:Map 15] as the traditional Zuni hunting area). It is also possible that hunting of leporids was more efficient and larger in scale than we model. Nevertheless, the ease with which local deer populations could be depleted by these populations may help us understand the degree to which hunting was subject to strong ritual regulation in historic pueblos (for example, Ferguson and Hart 1985:43; White 1962:301–05).

In this light, it is interesting to contrast the settlement patterns of the deer-dependent PI and the turkey-dependent PIII populations. In the PI case, on one hand, settlement was concentrated in and around the valley of the Dolores River, in the high northeastern portion of our study area. Because of short growing seasons, farmers could not occupy the highlands northeast of that valley, an area predicted by our model to be very productive of deer. The PI populations might have located themselves to maximize joint access to agriculture and those productive hunting territories, even at the expense of living in areas that were high enough to be risky for agriculture. The PIII populations, on the other hand, were most numerous in the mid-elevation belt that runs diagonally from the northwestern corner of our study area down towards its southeastern corner. These locations maximized access to good farming land while avoiding higher elevations, where farming was sometimes excellent but subject to failure in cold years. If the PIII populations, in essence, obtained both their calories and protein through maize, which would be the case if turkeys were fed a substantial amount of maize, then the easy access to deer so coveted by PI populations may not have been worth the risk of poor maize production—especially if deer populations were considerably depleted. A possible alternative hypothesis—that PIII populations became attracted to the relatively large springs in this belt as other water sources in our study area failed—is not supported by our paleohydrological modeling results to date.

Our estimates of momentary population size through time in the project area (see figure 4.5) show the same rapid influx of population into our study area in the mid-AD 1200s that we reconstruct for just the block surveys (see table 4.2). This, too, is an unexpected result. Much recent thinking about population history in the larger northern San Juan region (for example, Duff and Wilshusen 2000)—of which our study area is only a small part—has tended to favor a relatively gradual decline throughout the 1200s. On the basis of our productivity reconstruction (see figure 4.2), we tentatively suggest that the generally cold and dry conditions from the late 1190s through about 1235 caused populations in less favorable areas to move into the refugium that our area provides, where they occupied many relatively small community centers concentrated in the western portions of our study area. Many of these people (or at least, many people) leave our area by 1260. This marks the beginning of the final depopulation, but the high population levels, to which these recent immigrants contributed, added to the generally hostile and resource-competitive conditions that seem to accompany the relocation of many community centers to canyon-head locations (or, on Mesa Verde itself, into alcoves) by the mid-1200s. These preliminary results lead us to suspect that the failures that cause the eventual, complete depopulation of our area began on the northern Pueblo periphery and cascaded into our study area—a possibility anticipated forty years ago (Davis 1965). It is a high priority to identify where these populations came from, to better understand their motives for leaving.

Although we have not begun a final assessment of the fit between our simulated settlement patterns and those in the archaeological record, we have generated some preliminary results relevant to the end of both population cycles, by assessing the goodness of fit through time for sixteen runs reported in detail by Cowan and colleagues (n.d.). Remembering that our agents approximate the efficient settlement pattern in each period, given the parameters under which they are operating and the patterns of productivity as they change in response to climatic variation, we can take measures of goodness of fit between the simulated and real records to assess the extent to which real populations were distributed efficiently with respect to resources. Johnson (2006:236–52) discusses how we correlate counts of real and simulated households across the landscape in each period, using unsmoothed and smoothed versions of the real household distributions, to arrive at a measure of goodness of fit.

Figure 4.5 recasts these measures of goodness of fit from those sixteen runs as a preliminary measure of settlement efficiency through time, superimposing it on our population estimates. Although we will have more to say about such measures in later publications, here we want simply to draw attention to the sharp increases in efficiency that occur at the beginning of each cycle of depopulation. At around 900 and around 1270, populations in our area were maximally aggregated, yet they were more efficiently distributed on the landscape than were populations at 860 and 1240, when population numbers in each cycle peaked. Clearly, each depopulation began with the departure or demise of those households that were least advantageously situated with respect to resources. Although households in the best locations were able to persist, they, too, ultimately left, at least at the end of the second cycle. These patterns strongly suggest that, at least in the periods of relatively high population and low production that terminate each population cycle, households risked being unable to meet their subsistence needs and their settlement decisions had direct survival ramifications and conveyed definitive selective advantages. Our preliminary measure of settlement efficiency reflects the fact that, as Robert Foley (1985:230) has noted, pressures towards optimality are always strongest when competition is most severe.

As we work more with exchange, we are beginning to understand its interactions with population size as well. Perhaps not surprisingly, agents practicing generalized reciprocity grow in number more than those with no exchange. Adding balanced reciprocity and then layering on exchange between hub nodes results in additional increases in simulated populations. (We conceptualize these hub nodes rather loosely as prosperous, influential households or lineages in community centers.) But this is a mixed blessing because exchange of all types tends to break up in periods of subsistence shortfall and these shortfalls then become more severe to the extent that the populations have come to rely on exchange. Similarly, interruption of exchange for other reasons, for example, between hub nodes during periods of intercommunity hostility, could also cause local subsistence shortfalls due to poor distribution. The breakup of exchange networks may prove to contribute importantly to the two depopulations of our area. Certainly, we will be examining these effects closely as we begin our final analyses.

Despite its relative complexity, the Village Ecodynamics world is vastly less complex than reality. The main virtues of "Village" are that it is simpler than reality in a very disciplined manner and that we know precisely the processes it uses to produce the patterns it generates (though sometimes it takes a little work to figure out how those processes interact to produce specific changes). It is simpler than reality in a *disciplined* manner because we did not just use a random sample of what we believe to be the full gamut of human behavior and its social phenomenology. Instead, we have systematically dispensed with any agent actions that cannot, in Bourdieu's (dismissive) phrase (1990:46), be reduced to a "mechanical reaction to mechanical determinations and…economic agents to indiscernible particles subjected to the laws of mechanical equilibrium." Moreover, except for what concerns the "primitive sociality" of exchange, our agents really are particles; they do not form or take action in groups. All households behave according to the same rules, although each household may still behave differently because of varying circumstances.

The advantages of this approach are that—assuming that we have done everything correctly—anything produced by the real world but not by the model has to be explicable by some thing or combination of things that the model leaves out: we project the pure transparency of our agents onto the opacity of the archaeological record. Although this "method of residuals" still leaves numerous explanatory possibilities, it also rules out important segments of traditional archaeological explanation. To what extent would villages form in our area if they were solely the result of households responding at a household level to local economic opportunities? Do we see villages bigger than those in the archaeological record, and in different times and places? If so, their formation must not be due to the "social physics" we model, leaving us free to investigate the remaining plausibilities by using any means at our disposal.

Another advantage of this approach is the strong linkage it makes to the present. Model results do not depend on any process we cannot see acting in our own world and, most particularly, do not depend on any murky subjectivity we may want to ascribe to the actors. We can, if we like, interact with the model and pose what-if questions of it. Certain aspects of it have present value for thinking about the future. The hydrological model, for example, can be used to forecast water futures under various climatic assumptions.

Less obviously, models such as this begin to train us to think about causality in a more subtle and sophisticated fashion because what happens in these models, though vastly simpler than life itself, is almost never a simple reaction to some specific cause. Rather, it is filtered through an interacting set of processes and circumstances. This suggests that we may never attain an explanation as completely simple as climatic deterioration for the general depopulation of the northern Southwest in the late 1200s. But this, in our view, is still preferable to abandoning the search for causal structure in human history.

Acknowledgments

This work is supported by the National Science Foundation (BCS-0119981). We thank many colleagues, including Kevin Cooper (Mathematics, Washington State University, Pullman), who contributed the implicit diffusion function we use for deer; Donna Glowacki (National Park Service, Mesa Verde, Colorado), who directed our Community Center Survey in 2002 and 2003; Carla Van West (SRI Foundation, Rio Rancho, New Mexico) and Jeff Dean (Laboratory of Tree-ring Research, University of Arizona, Tempe), who advised on the revisions to the maize paleoproductivity reconstructions we summarize here; Doug Ramsey (Natural Resource Conservation Service, Cortez, Colorado) for endless advice on updating soils data; Matt Salzer (Laboratory of Tree-ring Research, University of Arizona, Tempe), who allowed us to use his bristlecone pine ring-width index series from the San Francisco Peaks; Diane Curewitz, who helped with editing chores on this chapter and this volume; and William D. Lipe (Anthropology, Washington State University, Pullman), who has been a sounding board for all aspects of this project.

CHAPTER 5

The Emergence of Inequality in Small-Scale Societies
Simple Scenarios and Agent-Based Simulations

Eric Alden Smith and Jung-Kyoo Choi

Archaeological and ethnographic evidence indicates that human societies were egalitarian—that is, lacking institutionalized political and economic inequality—for most of our species' history. Nonegalitarian societies first emerged in certain settled hunter-gatherer groups in the late Paleolithic and Mesolithic (ten to fifteen thousand years ago) and began to proliferate with the spread of dense agricultural populations some six to eight thousand years ago. Autonomous egalitarian societies of foragers and agriculturalists persisted in some regions into the ethnographic era, and some merged into expanding state societies only in the past few decades. Egalitarian sociopolitical organization was remarkably stable in many areas for vast periods yet eventually yielded to more hierarchical forms of social organization. One of the perennial grand questions of comparative social science is, how and why did this happen?

The literature on the emergence of inequality is extensive but contains very little formal theory or quantitative modeling. The research reported here is meant to address this gap. The simulations are not based on any particular society but rather are designed to be general enough to apply to a wide range of possible cases. Drawing on game theory and evolutionary ecology, we use simple scenarios and agent-based simulation models to explore factors that might shape the emergence and stability of political-economic inequality in small-scale societies.

In the literature, such factors include population pressure; risk buffering and economic redistribution; information management; trade monopolies; spatially concentrated resources; military conflict; resource storage; control of production technology (for example, irrigation); scalar effects of increasing population density or community size; competitive feasting and gift giving; and manipulation of esoteric knowledge or ideology (Hayden 1995). Proposed causal variables therefore range from environmental to demographic to economic to social to ideological. We cannot hope at this stage to cover this expansive waterfront. Accordingly, we have concentrated on two distinct scenarios. One, which we term (after Boone 1992) the "Patron-Client" scenario, focuses on economic exchange driven by initial differences in resource endowment (land productivity). The second, termed "managerial mutualism," envisages a social division of labor, with the role of manager being to enforce adherence to collectively beneficial forms of production and distribution.

As with most theoretical efforts in evolutionary ecology, our primary aim is to construct models that reveal the outcomes that follow from a set of assumptions. Although our efforts here are exploratory and quite preliminary, we believe that they offer some initial insights. Our models are predicated on the assumption that a limited number of asymmetries, such as differential control over productive resources, can explain the emergence of institutionalized inequality. They also draw on contemporary evolutionary theory in order to avoid the pitfalls of naïve functionalism and teleology. Our approach is not to deny any possibility of collectively beneficial outcomes or directionality to sociopolitical evolution, but rather to show whether and how these might emerge from interaction of individual agency, social and demographic structure, and environmental constraints.

Basic Simulation Structure

Simulations were coded in C++ and run on Windows PCs. All results reported below involve runs of two thousand rounds for each stated combination of parameter settings. Unless indicated otherwise, outcomes are reported for the last ten periods averaged across a set of one hundred runs per parameter combination (see the appendix for a justification of parameter calibrations).

Environment

Agents inhabit patches arrayed in a square grid (for example, one hundred patches, ten on a side). Patches are endowed with varying amounts of a generic resource, and patch richness (P) is assigned at the start of the simulation (see tables 5.1 and 5.2 for lists of model parameters). Agents utilize this resource for survival and reproduction, as well as for economic activity (for example, trade), but do not augment or deplete patch productivity; the resource of each patch is renewed at the start of each period.

Demography

In most of our simulations, each agent continuously occupies a home patch and does not migrate. Agents reproduce at a rate proportional to their per period income (π),

Table 5.1 Parameters of the Patron-Client Scenario

Symbol	Definition	How Set	Default[a]	Min	Max
d	Territory defense cost	Exogenously fixed	.1	.01	.5
μ	Strategy mutation probability	Exogenously fixed	.01	.001	.05
n	Number of agents on patch j	Demographic	Variable	0	5
N	Total number of agents	Demographic	Variable	~80	~230
P_j	Productivity of the jth patch	Exogenously fixed	Random	1	5
π_i	Net income of the ith agent	Agent behavior	Variable	1	Variable
---	Reproductive rate	Function of π_i	.025	.01	.05
---	Mortality rate	Function of π_i	.01 to .05	.02[b]	.1[b]
τ	Patron's return from a Client's labor	Exogenously fixed	.3	.1	.5
λ	Client's labor cost	Exogenously fixed	.2	.1	.5
κ	Patron's payment for Client services	Function of κ and λ	$(\tau+\lambda)/2$	.15	.4

a. Initial value; all values are per period, unless otherwise noted.
b. Minimum and maximum of the upper end of the mortality range (see text).

which is a function of their home patch's productivity, modified by any costs and benefits they accrue from social interactions (see below). To avoid ever-growing populations, a carrying capacity ceiling ($K \leq P$) is imposed, and reproduction occurs only if there are undefended patches with sufficient untapped productivity to support additional agents. Offspring inherit the parents' strategy (subject to a probability [μ] per period of mutating to a randomly selected alternative) and populate available patches anywhere on the landscape (no population viscosity). Agents also face a mortality risk, with per period mortality averaging 1 to 5 percent per period, assigned randomly but in inverse proportion to each agent's income (π) in the preceding period.

Agent Interaction

Depending on assigned strategy and the goals of the simulation analysis, agents may interact in a number of ways (sharing or not sharing patches, exchanging services and goods, cooperating in production). Further specification of agent interactions and payoffs are given below, as these vary between scenarios.

Table 5.2 Parameters for the Managerial Mutualism Model

Symbol	Definition	How Set	Default[a]	Min	Max
μ	Strategy mutation rate	Exogenously fixed	.01	.001	.05
n	Maximum number of agents in local group	Exogenously fixed	10	5	15
	Reproductive rate	Exogenous range, $fn(\pi_i)$	.025	.02	.05
	Mortality rate	Exogenous range, $fn(\pi_i)$	.02	.01	.023
B	Base income per agent	Exogenously fixed	5	0	50
π^i	Net income of the ith agent	Agent behavior	---	---	---
G	Maximum aggregate gains from collective action	Realized value (pG) depends on local Cooperator frequency	50	10	75
c	Labor cost of producing collective good, per Cooperator	Exogenously fixed	1	.5	1.8
p	Proportion of Cooperators in local group	Demographic and evolutionary	.33	0	1
m	Cooperator's cost of monitoring	Exogenously fixed	.1	0	.25
M	Manager's cost of monitoring	Exogenously fixed ($M \leq m$)	.1	0	.25
e	Cooperator's cost of punishing Defectors	Exogenously fixed	.5	0	2
E	Manager's cost of punishing Defectors	Exogenously fixed ($E \leq e$)	.5	.25	1
s	Cost to Defector of being punished by a Cooperator	Exogenously fixed	.5	.1	1
S	Cost to Defector of being punished by a Manager	Exogenously fixed ($S \gg s$)	3	2	5
γ	Fee paid to Manager by each Cooperator	Exogenously fixed	1	.5	1.5

a. Initial mean value; all parameter values are per period, unless noted otherwise.

Patron-Client Scenario

Many scholars, from Rousseau and Voltaire to Marx and Engels, and beyond, have discussed the role that patron-client relations and private property (for example, land ownership) may play in the emergence of institutionalized inequality in a previously egalitarian society. The account in Boone (1992) has particularly influenced our discussion here.

In our model of the Patron-Client scenario, some agents (Patrons) control patches with greater per capita resource endowments and can trade access to these for services from less fortunate agents (Clients). Heterogeneity in environmental productivity, and therefore variation in property endowment, provides the initial opportunity for the emergence of inequality. Yet this is not sufficient, nor can this be glossed as "environmental determinism," because alternative strategies interacting with the same resource heterogeneity do not generate socioeconomic inequality. Some (Solo) agents simply defend richer patches for their exclusive use; others (Doves) share any resources on their patch with other nonterritorial agents (Doves or Clients). Thus, population density per patch (n) depends on both patch richness (P) and agent behavior. At the outset, all patches are seeded with a single occupant playing the Dove strategy; by making all-Dove the initial state, we examine when inequality can evolve from an egalitarian starting point.

Patch Defense

Resource control (via territorial patch defense) is critical to the Patron-Client scenario (Boone 1992). Territorial agents (Solo and Patron strategies) pay a cost (d) to defend sole occupancy of their patch, regardless of patch productivity (as long as $P \geq 1-d$). A territorial agent cannot colonize a poor patch ($P = 1$). Other strategies (Dove and Client) do not defend, so they will equally share the productivity of their patch (but not other income, that is, Client exchange earnings) with co-resident nonterritorial types. For patch-sharing types, P/n must be ≥ 1 (though a sufficient amount of exchange earnings for Client types could relax this constraint, a possibility we have not modeled). At equilibrium, we therefore expect that population density per patch (n) will match patch productivity (P) for nonterritorial types (that is, approach an ideal-free distribution) but be lower for territorial types (where $n \leq 1$ regardless of P). Thus, territoriality should lower total population (N) and social efficiency ($\Sigma\pi$).

Political Economy

Solo agents do not interact with others, and Doves simply coexist with other Doves or Clients in richer ($P > 1$) patches. The only economic exchanges are between Clients and Patrons. We assume that Patrons can have multiple Clients (but not vice versa); it might prove interesting to relax this assumption. Patrons maintain exclusive control of resources on their patch but are willing to exchange some share (κ) of P with Clients for any profitable return (τ). Clients are willing to expend labor costs (λ) in exchange for a profitable wage (κ) from the Patron offering the best deal. Thus, exchanges are

Table 5.3 Strategies and Payoffs in the Patron-Client Scenario

Strategy	Behavior	Payoff[a]
Dove	Shares any patch where $P/n > 1$ with other Doves or Clients	P_j/n
Client	Same as Dove, plus exchanges labor for resources with Patron	$P_j/n + \kappa - \lambda$
Patron	Defends exclusive control of patch and exchanges resources for services from Clients	$P_j - d + \Sigma(\tau - \kappa)$
Solo	Defends exclusive control of patch, no exchanges	$P_j - d$

a. See table 5.1 for definition of variables.

subject to the condition that $\tau > \kappa > \lambda$. In the initial simulation, the values of these exchange variables are set exogenously, and we assume that any Patron-Client exchange divides the surplus equally (that is, that $\kappa = (\tau+\lambda)/2$).[1] Strategies and pay-offs appear in table 5.3.

Simulation results.

Because of stochasticity in initial conditions, few if any parameter settings produce invariable outcomes (plate 12). In particular, given the initial seeding of all patches with a single Dove agent (plate 13), much depends on the chance that territorial (Patron or Solo) mutants will replace solitary Doves inhabiting richer patches relatively early in a simulation run and thus gain a substantial toehold in the population. This stochastic element aside, the basic dynamical behavior of this simulation is easily summarized. We concentrate here on factors that favor a stable Patron-Client system (that is, one in which Patrons and Clients are numerically dominant and resist replacement by other types).

Under default parameter values (see table 5.1), nonterritorial strategies dominate, split equally between Dove and Client types, and Solo and Patron types are about equally represented in the remaining patches. However, a stable Patron-Client regime emerges in about one-third of all runs and takes over the population about 10 percent of the time (table 5.4).

The hiring returns parameter (τ) has the strongest effect on emergence and stability of a Patron-Client regime. This is quite intuitive because the value of this parameter strongly affects the payoffs of both Patrons (who receive τ from each Client with whom they interact) and Clients (who receive a wage κ proportional to τ). When returns are high ($\tau = .6$, twice the default setting), virtually all patches are occupied by Clients and Patrons in about a 5:1 ratio; more than 90 percent of runs end with almost no other strategies present in the population (see table 5.4). Conversely, low returns ($\tau = .1$) are very unfavorable for Clients (who then cannot do as well as Doves and remain a tiny minority of the population). Intermediate hiring returns (τ = .4 or .5) are quite favorable for the Patron-Client regime, with the ratio of Patrons to Clients reaching about 3:1. Half to three-quarters of the runs end with these two strategies constituting more than 90 percent of the population (see table 5.4). The same results are attained with less favorable hiring returns but lower labor costs (see table 5.4).

Demographic parameters have a strong effect on the relative success of territorial and nonterritorial strategies. When mortality is high or reproductive rate low, the initial (all-Dove) population expands slowly so that Solo and Patron agents are able to spread and control rich patches, effectively keeping Dove and Client numbers low at equilibrium. Conversely, low mortality or high reproductive rate allows Doves to proliferate rapidly, and territorial agents are locked out (with Clients arising in modest numbers through mutation and drift). Increased mutation rates are favorable to the spread of Client and Patron strategies, but only because this retards the initial proliferation of Doves.

As anticipated by Boone (1992), environmental heterogeneity is critical because Patrons capitalize on their relatively rich patch endowments to participate in exchanges with Clients. Most of our simulations feature a random uniform distribution of patch richness (P varying from 1 to 5), with territorial agents (Solo or Patron) restricted to patches with $P \geq 2$. Because territorial agents do not proliferate within their patches, their average patch resources equal 3.4 (the mean of P = 2 to 5, minus defense cost). In contrast, nonterritorial agents proliferate to the point where average per capita patch resources approach 1. In simulations where patch richness is set uniformly high (P = 5), territorial strategies are very rare (presumably because of the rapid proliferation of nonterritorial agents); in uniformly poor environments (P = 2), the opposite results. In both cases, homogenous environments effectively prevent the emergence of a Patron-Client system (see table 5.4).

The remaining parameters have only modest effects on strategy success. As might be expected, low labor costs (λ = .1) are favorable to establishment of a Patron-Client regime; high labor costs (λ = .4) keep Client frequencies very low (see table 5.4). Territory defense costs, paid by all Solo and Patron agents, have surprisingly little effect on simulation outcomes; high costs (d = .4) hurt Solo more than Patron types, presumably because the latter can recoup some of these costs via exchanges with Clients. Because they have no direct effect on Clients, though, the net effect on emergence of Patron-Client regimes is insignificant.

Managerial Mutualism

Many scenarios regarding the origins of inequality posit that hierarchy emerges from mutualistic arrangements involving specialized socioeconomic roles (for example, Johnson 1982; Keeley 1988; Service 1975). These accounts envision a small number of managers (chiefs, priests, etc.) who provide benefits to the members of their social

Table 5.4 Patron-Client Simulation Outcomes under Different Parameter Settings (Means = Last 10 Periods over 100 Runs, 2,000 Periods per Run)

Parameter	Value	Mean Terminal Frequency: Dove	Solo	Client	Patron	PC > 90%[a]	Comments
All default values	(see Table 5.1)	.29	.19	.29	.23	.10	Stable PC regime emerges in about 1/3 of runs.
Mutation rate (m)	High (.05)	.16	.11	.46	.27	.10	PC regime dominates more often.
Defense cost (d)	High (.4)	.33	.12	.33	.23	.13	Little effect compared with default settings.
	None (0)	.31	.21	.29	.19	.09	Same.
Hiring returns (τ)	Low (.1)	.52	.21	.06	.22	0	Client strategy does very poorly.
	Moderate (.4)	.14	.09	.54	.23	.49	More favorable for PC regime than default.
	Higher (.5)	.07	.07	.66	.20	.76	Even more favorable.
	High (.6)	.02	.02	.81	.16	.94	Very stable and consistent PC regime.
Labor cost (λ)	High (.4)	.52	.21	.06	.22	0	Client strategy does very poorly.
	Low (.1)	.14	.09	.54	.23	.49	More favorable for PC regime than default.
Increased hiring returns + decreased labor costs	($\tau = .4, \lambda = .2$)	.07	.07	.66	.20	.76	PC regime usually dominates.
Mortality curve	Steep (max = .1)	.06	.42	.05	.47	.18	Highly variable outcomes; generally favors territorial strategies (Solo and Patron).
	Shallow (max = .02)	.89	0	.11	0	0	Doves spread rapidly, so no PC regime.
Reproductive rate	High (.05)	.75	0	.25	0	0	Territorial strategies cannot get established.
	Low (.01)	.00	.44	.00	.55	0	Territorial strategies completely dominate.
Lattice size	Larger (20x20)	.15	.18	.37	.30	.05	Slightly more favorable to PC regime.
Patch richness	Uniformly high ($P_j = 5$)	.51	.01	.46	.02	0	Territorial strategies very rare.
	Uniformly low ($P_j = 2$)	.04	.33	.05	.57	0	Territorial strategies dominate.

a. Proportion of runs in which >90 percent of agents are playing Patron or Client strategies by the last 10 periods

group by coordinating important aspects of production, distribution, or information flow. In light of established theory in evolutionary ecology and collective action, some of these scenarios are more plausible than others.

Our analysis of what we term "managerial mutualism" focuses on whether managers who help solve collective action problems within a social group can instigate institutionalized inequality in a previously egalitarian system. Specifically, we seek to address the factors that favor the emergence of such a system of managerial mutualism, as well as the conditions under which those who manage collective action accrue above-average gains.

Demography

Agents reside in social groups of size n, which can reach some local maximum size n'. A proportion p of the n agents play Cooperate and the remainder play Defect, except for groups that also have one agent playing the Manager strategy (see below for strategy specifications). Agents reproduce at a rate proportional to their per period income (π), which is a function of their base income augmented by any gains (or losses) from collective action and its related enforcement costs (as explained shortly). Offspring can colonize empty or partially saturated ($n < n'$) patches, with no viscosity or migration cost. Agents also face a mortality risk averaging 1 to 5 percent per period, assigned randomly but in direct proportion to each agent's income in the preceding period (see table 5.2 for a list of all parameters and their assigned values). Offspring inherit the parents' strategy (subject to a probability m of mutating to a randomly selected alternative). However, the Manager strategy is fixed at ≤1 per group and is thus not subject to within-group proliferation. Accordingly, offspring of Managers who cannot colonize another (no-Manager) group retain their Manager "genotype" but play the Cooperator strategy. If the resident Manager dies and any such "phenotypic Cooperators" are resident in a group, one is randomly selected to become next Manager.

Collective Action

Agents interact once per period in a public goods game, which we envision as a form of group production with gains to cooperation, such as running an irrigation system or collectively harvesting prey. Cooperators contribute to production of this public good at a personal cost (c); both Cooperators and Defectors (who do not contribute to group production) obtain an equal share (pG/n) of this production. To prevent free riders from completely unraveling this cooperation, agents must be monitored and punished if they fail to contribute. This enforcement is costly to the enforcers, creating a second-order collective action problem. We can envision various possible outcomes: (a) collective action fails, and agents obtain only their base income; (b) some level of collective action is achieved, and Cooperators pay the enforcement costs; or (c) one agent assumes the specialized role of Manager and pays all enforcement costs in return for a profitable managerial fee (paid by Cooperators). This last outcome is the one of primary interest here.

Payoffs

An agent's net income per period (π) is a function of that agent's strategy and interactions. We do not include environmental heterogeneity directly in this model, though variation in base income and collective production (see below) can be viewed as environmentally constrained. We assume that Defectors contribute neither to the costs of publicgood production nor to monitoring and punishing free riding. Each agent has a base income (B) that is independent of agent type and of shares from collective action. Because this just adds a constant to every payoff, it has no effect on relative payoffs, and we omit it from the equations below. If no Manager is present in a local group, then for each Cooperator, payoffs are

$$\pi_C = pG/n - c - nm - n(1-p)e$$

and for each Defector

$$\pi_D = pG/n - nps$$

where n is the number of agents in the local group (not counting the ≤ 1 agent who acts as Manager); p is the proportion of n agents who Cooperate, and $1-p$, the proportion who Defect; G is the maximum possible aggregate public-good production; c is the cost per Cooperator of producing G; m is the cost per Cooperator of monitoring all other agents; e is the cost per agent of punishing one Defector; and s is the cost of being punished by one Cooperator. If $G/n < s$, there is no incentive to defect from cooperative production, and $(1-p)e$ tends towards zero as Defectors become rare. However, this requires that the second-order problem of monitoring and enforcement has been solved, which is, in fact, the key problem on which the managerial mutualism scenario focuses.

If the local group includes a Manager, so the group size is $n + 1$, then payoffs are

$$\pi_C* = pG/n - c - \gamma$$
$$\pi_D* = pG/n - S$$
$$\pi_M = n\{p\gamma - M - (1-p)E\}$$

where γ is the "management fee" that each Cooperator pays the Manager; M is the cost the Manager pays to monitor cooperation; E is the cost the Manager pays to punish a Defector; and S is the cost a Defector suffers when punished by a Manager. We assume that Managers are at least as good as Cooperators at monitoring (that is, there can be gains to specialization), so $M \leq m$. We also assume that Managers can impose a larger punishment on any Defector, so $S \gg s$. Note that Managers are enforcement specialists and do not directly produce or consume the collective good; relaxing this last assumption would not alter the qualitative results but would significantly complicate the algebraic representation.

Effect of Parameter Values on Equilibria

Because we model this scenario in explicit game-theoretical form, some analytical conclusions (independent of simulation results) can be derived. Specifically, we deduce the following:

1. The collective action problem can be solved without a Manager if the proportion of Cooperators (p) is sufficiently high. With the default values of other parameters, the critical value of $p = .636$, which is the value at which the payoffs to Defector and Cooperator are equal (assuming that no Manager is present). This value of p defines an unstable equilibrium point: if the initial $p > .636$, then p goes to 1 (that is, the all-Cooperator equilibrium), and if the initial $p < .636$, then p goes to 0 (that is, the all-Defector equilibrium), as illustrated in plate 14a.

2. Managerial mutualism is a Nash equilibrium if $\pi_M > \pi_{C*}$ and $\pi_M > \pi_{D*}$ (see above for payoff abbreviations).

3. Under the right initial conditions, $\pi_{C*} > \pi_{D*}$ even when cooperation is relatively rare (plate 14b); thus, Cooperators can invade a group of Defectors as long as the Manager strategy arises simultaneously.

4. Group size (n) affects the relative payoffs of Cooperators and Managers and therefore prospects for managerial mutualism; specifically, n must be large enough to provide an adequate incentive to Manager but not so large that the value of the collective good is shared among too many Cooperators.

5. The aggregate value of the collective good G has no effect on relative payoffs to Cooperate or Defect. But if G is too large, then the payoff to Manager is lower than that to Cooperator, and the managerial equilibrium is less likely.

6. The labor cost of producing the collective good (c) cannot be too high, or Cooperators do worse than Defectors, even with a Manager present.

7. If the monitoring cost (M) or enforcement cost (E) experienced by a Manager becomes too large, the Manager strategy cannot persist.

8. Managerial mutualism requires a sufficiently high value for S, a Defector's cost of being punished; if S is too small, then Defectors outcompete Cooperators even when a Manager is present. We have adopted a default value for S that is six times the cost a Manager pays to punish a Defector, but with default values of other parameters, S can drop as low as 1 even if half the group is Defectors. However, the emergence of the managerial regime requires that S be not much less than the default value of 3.

9. The management fee (γ) must be in a relatively narrow range to maintain the managerial equilibrium. If it is too low, then Managers cannot prosper; if it is too high, Cooperators are better off without Managers.

Simulation Results

As shown in table 5.5, the simulation model closely matches the analytical results just described. A system of managerial mutualism emerges readily (nearly 90 percent of the time) under default parameter values and is even more likely if production costs for the collective good are lowered. The MM equilibrium is less likely to evolve if production costs are high, management fees are too high or too low, the value of the collective good strays too far from the default value, or costs to Managers of monitoring or punishing defectors are high. Demographic parameters (mortality, fertility, and group size) also have a predictable effect on the MM regime. The punishment cost borne by defectors is, of course, critical as well, as discussed above.

Our simulation results indicate that the present model is very sensitive to initial conditions. In particular, the Manager strategy must be present in sufficient numbers in the population (roughly one Manager per group) to allow the MM equilibrium to evolve. This, plus the narrow value ranges required on several parameters (see above), presents a more difficult route to the emergence of inequality than the Patron-Client model. This finding could be an artifact of model structures or assumed parameter values, but for various reasons, we suspect that it reflects a realistic difference between systems based on dyadic mutualism (as in the Patron-Client scenario) and those based on collective action (as in managerial mutualism).

Future Refinements

Our model assumes that Defect and Cooperate are fixed strategies. If we were to make Defect a conditional strategy, so that Defectors shirk only if the expected cost of being punished is lower than the cost of contributing to public good ($s < c$), then realized enforcement and punishment costs approach zero, and payoffs change accordingly. But in the long run, absence of defection will favor evolution of variants that do not bother to monitor and punish (Boyd et al. 2003). It is possible that the Manager strategy will suffice to prevent this subversion, but further modeling would be required to examine this.[2]

The fee that Cooperators pay to the Manager (γ) could be made proportional to group productivity (that is, $\gamma = \text{fn}[G]$), rather than a flat, per producer amount. Even more interesting would be to allow g to evolve (via random mutation) or to vary strategically in a population already consisting of stable groups with Managers. In such a context, we could expect the Managers to benefit from setting the management fee as high as producers would tolerate, right up to the point where the Cooperators would do better without a Manager.[3] This is precisely the type of dynamics envisioned in many models of "reproductive skew" (Reeve and Emlen 2000; Vehrencamp 1983). Cooperators would then have the choice of (a) staying in the group while paying the fee set by the Manager, (b) joining another group with a Manager offering better terms, or (c) joining a group without a Manager.

Modeling competition among Managers would also be instructive. This could happen either among groups (the Manager in one group trying to offer a better deal to draw producers in from other groups) or within groups (someone trying to usurp the existing Manager by offering a better deal).

Some of these options open the door to analyzing potentially interesting effects of population structure and migration, including multilevel selection. Of course, such enrichment would come at the cost of a corresponding increase in complexity of model design and interpretation.

Table 5.5 Managerial Mutualism (MM) Outcomes (Means for Last 10 Periods over 100 Runs, 2,000 Periods per Run)

Parameter	Value	Mean Terminal Proportion: Cooperators	Patches with a Manager	Comments
All default values	(See table 5.2.)	.88	1.00	Stable MM regime emerges in most runs.
Mutation rate (μ)	Low (.001)	.89	1.00	Little effect compared with default settings.
	High (.05)	.87	1.00	Little effect compared with default settings.
Value of collective good (G)	Low (10)	.53	.74	Much less favorable for MM regime than default.
	High (75)	.79	.88	Less favorable for MM regime than default.
Production cost (c)	Low (.5)	.89	1.00	Little effect compared with default settings.
	High (1.8)	.17	.21	Very unfavorable to MM regime.
Management fee (g)	Low (.5)	.39	.28	Very unfavorable to MM regime.
	High (1.5)	.44	.76	Very unfavorable to MM regime.
Cost of monitoring:				
For a Manager (M)	Low (0)	.86	.97	Little effect compared with default settings.
	High (.25)	.75	.84	Less favorable for MM regime than default.
For a Cooperator (m)	Low (0)	.88	1.00	No effect compared with default settings.
	High (.25)	.88	1.00	No effect compared with default settings.
Cost of enforcement:				
For a Manager (E)	Low (.25)	.88	1.00	No effect compared with default settings.
	High (1)	.01	.01	Very unfavorable to MM regime.
For a Cooperator (e)	Low (0)	.88	1.00	No effect compared with default settings.
	High (2)	.88	1.00	No effect compared with default settings.
Cost of being punished:				
By a Cooperator (s)	Low (.1)	.88	1.00	No effect compared with default settings.
	High (1)	.88	1.00	No effect compared with default settings.
By a Manager (S)	Low (2)	.00	.01	Much less favorable for MM regime than default.
	High (5)	.89	1.00	Little effect compared with default settings.
Mortality rate	Low (.01)	.90	1.00	More favorable for MM regime than default.
	High (.023)	.42	.14	Very unfavorable to MM regime.
Reproductive rate	Low (.02)	.17	.02	Very unfavorable to MM regime.
	High (.05)	.90	1.00	Same as low-mortality setting.
Maximum local group size (n)	Low ($n = 5$)	.13	.42	Very unfavorable to MM regime.
	High ($n = 15$)	.62	.82	Much less favorable for MM regime than default.

Conclusions and Prospects

In the history of social thought, accounts of the rise of inequality tend to sort into two categories: those that emphasize the benefits that hierarchy brings to all (what a biologist would call "mutualism") and those that emphasize exploitation or coercion by one segment of society (elites) against the interests of the remaining members (commoners, producers, slaves, etc.). Of course, many scenarios combine both elements, but this mutualism/exploitation contrast is a useful one, particularly if viewed as a continuum rather than as a dichotomy. Both scenarios analyzed in this chapter fall towards the mutualistic end of this continuum, although this is less true of the Patron-Client scenario.

Despite the mutualistic nature of the underlying interactions, both scenarios are capable of producing marked and stable inequality in income. This inequality averages about 2.2:1 for the Patron-Client model examined here and about 1.4:1 for the Manager-Cooperator model. The evolutionary dynamic translates income into enhanced survival and fertility and helps determine the equilibrium frequency of different strategies. But structural aspects of the strategies and their interactions are equally important and, in fact, mean that the wealthier agents in each scenario (Patrons and Managers, respectively) are actually less numerous than their poorer counterparts. In the case of Patrons, this is because of their territorial exclusivity, which gives them a richer resource base than Clients (and thus the wherewithal to exchange surplus resources for Client services) but also lowers their population density. In the case of Managers, role specialization limits Manager frequency to one per local group—somewhat artificial yet plausible in making producers more numerous than administrators—although our model allows Manager offspring to proliferate and phenotypically display the Cooperate strategy if no Manager openings are available.

As Clark and Blake (1994:17) have argued, "explanations of the origins of institutionalized social inequality and political privilege must resolve the central paradox of political life—why people cooperate with their own subordination and exploitation in non-coercive circumstances." We propose that a limited number of asymmetries can explain most cases of emergence of institutionalized inequality. These might include asymmetries in control over productive resources, control over external trade, differential military ability (and resultant booty and slaves), or control of socially significant information. As our models demonstrate, these asymmetries need not be employed coercively, as long as they are economically defensible (*sensu* Brown 1964) and can provide an advantage in bargaining power sufficient to allow the concentration of wealth and/or power in the hands of a segment of the social group or polity. Our modeling indicates that such asymmetries can be self-reinforcing and therefore quite stable to moderate perturbations over time. Because most of the social transactions based on them are mutualistic instead of coercive, we suggest that such systems are likely to be more stable than the stratified social systems (for example, nation states) that eventually succeed them.

Clearly, there are many directions for future work. Besides further elaboration of these two models, along lines suggested above, new scenarios that feature other determinants of the emergence of inequality could be developed using the same methods of evolutionary game theory and agent-based simulation we have utilized here. Plausible candidates for such additional determinants include intergroup trade (the germs of which are present in the Patron-Client model), warfare, and multiplayer alliances. In addition, current and future scenarios could explore the effects of adding more dynamism to agent-environment interactions (such as resource depletion and enhancement) and more population structure (which might create opportunities for multilevel selection). We nevertheless stress the value of starting with the simplest interesting models possible for any given scenario, in order to understand the results of simulations, as well as to articulate these with analytical insights such as those offered by game theory.

Finally, there is the matter of relating models to empirical data. Unlike most of the research reported in this volume, our goal was not to analyze a particular socioecological system found in a particular time and place; accordingly, we emphasized generality and simplicity of model structure and dynamics. Our ultimate goal, though, is to understand patterns found in the real world. This will require the generation of testable hypotheses from these or from similar models and empirical analyses to determine the extent to which they might help explain the emergence of inequality in actual transegalitarian societies.

Acknowledgments

Eric Alden Smith thanks Sam Bowles for hosting his 2004 stay at the Santa Fe Institute (SFI), where this work began; Jim Boone, for much inspiration and helpful discussion over the years; and the National Science Foundation (BCS-0314284) and SFI for support. Jung-Kyoo Choi thanks SFI for support. Many thanks to Rob Boyd, James Kitts, Fraser Neiman, and Lore Ruttan for comments on earlier versions of the chapter.

Notes

1. In later versions, we intend to let values of κ and τ vary, either by mutation or strategically. If Clients can search globally for the Patron offering the best deal, κ should assume a uniform value in the population. A more interesting variant would specify a diminishing marginal value of Clients for any Patron; this would entail a decline in τ as a Patron gains additional Clients and a corresponding decline in the value of κ that a Patron will offer existing or new Clients.

2. If Defectors are effectively eliminated, Manager variants who extract a managerial fee without providing enforcement benefits would be behaviorally indistinguishable from the original variant and could perhaps drift into the population (Rob Boyd, personal communication, September 21, 2005).

3. We are indebted to James Boone (personal communication, May 13, 2004) for making this point.

CHAPTER 6

Human Ecodynamics in the Hawaiian Ecosystem, from 1200 to 200 Yr BP

Patrick V. Kirch, Oliver A. Chadwick, Shripad Tuljapurkar, Thegn Ladefoged, Michael Graves, Sara Hotchkiss, and Peter Vitousek

In this chapter, we summarize key results from the first phase of an innovative collaboration among archaeologists, demographers, ecologists, soil scientists, and paleoecologists, focused on a centuries-long sequence of dynamically coupled cultural and natural systems in the Hawaiian Islands. Our project goal is to use Hawai`i as a "model system" to understand long-term co-evolutionary interactions between people and their environments ("human ecodynamics"; see McGlade 1995; van der Leeuw 1998; van der Leeuw and McGlade 1997; van der Leeuw and Redman 2002), including the emergence of social and cultural complexity. Our theoretical orientation is that of ecosystem-culture "co-evolution" (Butzer 1982, 1996; Durham 1991; Kirch 1980), putting to advantage the long-term historical data uniquely provided by archaeology and paleoecology (Kirch 2004; Redman 1999; Redman et al. 2004).

Why Study Hawai`i?

Oceanic islands, in general—and the Hawaiian Islands, in particular—offer unique opportunities for understanding fundamental mechanisms underlying evolutionary radiation and speciation (Baldwin and Sanderson 1998; Price and Clague 2002), ecosystem ecology and biogeochemistry (Chadwick et al. 1999; Vitousek 2002), and the evolution of human cultures (Kirch 1984, 1985, 2000; Kirch and Green 1987,

2001). Islands generally are simpler than continents in important ways, yet they are real, dynamic systems that embody essential features of more complex continental systems. As such, islands can be used as model systems for understanding both land and culture.

For understanding ecosystems, the extreme isolation and low species diversity, consistent geology and geomorphology, and wide and well-defined variation in climate and substrate age of the Hawaiian Islands allow us to focus on biogeochemical mechanisms with a precision that cannot be duplicated elsewhere. Environmental gradients in mean annual temperature (from <10 to 24 degrees C), in annual precipitation (from <200 to >5,000 mm), and in substrate age (from hot rock to >4 myr) are among the clearest, broadest, and most orthogonal on Earth. These gradients can be used to understand fundamental mechanisms through a combination of process measurements, integrations based on stable isotopes, ecosystem-level experiments, and simulation models. Chadwick and others (2003) and Vitousek (2004) recently synthesized results from many publications, based on rainfall and substrate age gradients, respectively, and our project builds on those syntheses.

The Hawaiian Archipelago also presents an ideal region for understanding complex interactions between human populations and their environments over a controlled, and relatively short, time scale. When first made known to the West on the third voyage of Captain James Cook in AD 1778–1779, Hawai`i was occupied by an isolated population of at least 450,000 indigenous Polynesians (Stannard 1989), with economies based on complex systems of irrigated and dryland farming, aquaculture, and animal husbandry that differed markedly across the archipelago (Allen 1991, 1992; Kirch 1985, 1990, 1994). Ancestral Polynesians arrived in Hawai`i accompanied by a suite of commensal and synanthropic taxa (crop plants, domestic animals, weeds, ectoparasites). Archaeological research suggests initial human incursion into the archipelago ~1200 ± 200 yr BP (Athens 1997; Athens and Ward 1993; Athens, Ward, and Wickler 1992; Kirch 1985, 2000). It can be inferred that the size of the colonizing human propagule was small, probably <200 persons (although periodically increased by additional voyagers). Over a period of approximately one thousand years, this population grew to high densities (~150–200/sq km in some areas) and extensively modified the biota and landscapes of lowland (<1,000 m asl) zones of all major islands (Athens 1997; Kirch 1982).

A Case of Emergent Cultural Complexity

Over this same approximately one-thousand-year time span, the Hawaiian culture underwent dramatic changes, including emergent complexity in economy, sociopolitical organization, and religious ideology. Reconstructions of Ancestral Polynesian society (Kirch and Green 2001) indicate that the colonizing group was structured as a house-based, fluid kin structure, with heterarchical competition among local groups, each associated with its land or estate (Kirch 2000). Between four hundred and six hundred years after colonization, Hawaiian social units underwent variable amalgamation and dramatic hierarchization (Abad 2000; Cordy 1974, 1981, 2000; Earle 1977, 1978, 1987, 1997; Hommon 1986; Kirch 1985, 1990; Sahlins 1958, 1972). Although Polynesian societies generally are regarded by anthropologists as classic representatives of chiefdoms, protohistoric Hawaiian society stands apart as qualitatively distinctive (Kirch 1984; Sahlins 1958) for five reasons: (1) a high degree and diversity of modes of agri- and aquacultural intensification and of craft specialization; (2) ritualized controls on production, manifested by a hierarchical system of temples (Valeri 1985); (3) the emergence of endogamous classes and the ideology of kingship; (4) replacement of a lineage-based system of land control with a territorial system in which land rights were held by elites; and (5) a formal system of corvée labor and surplus tribute extraction. Hawai`i thus offers a model system for exploring the initial formation and dynamics of archaic states (Feinman and Marcus 1998; Spencer 1990, 1993) during this late prehistoric time frame, within environmental and demographic parameters that can be closely constrained.

Contact-period Hawaiian society is noted for its complexity, indexed by economic specialization (Earle 1977, 1978, 1987; Kirch 1990), social stratification (Sahlins 1958), and specialized religious cults and ritual regulation of production (Valeri 1985). Anthropologists and archaeologists have characterized Hawai`i variously as a "ranked society" (Fried 1967), a "complex chiefdom" (Earle 1991; Kirch 1985), or an "archaic state" (Allen 1991; Flannery 1972, 1995; Hommon 1986; Kirch 2000; Marcus and Flannery 1996). We believe that the latter rubric is the most accurate. A variety of proximate or ultimate causal factors have been identified or proposed as having played some role in the rise of this complexity, which developed out of a less complex or specialized Ancestral Polynesian society. These include (a) demographic change, especially population increase (Clark 1988; Cordy 1981; Kirch 1984); (b) agricultural expansion and intensification, including "landesque capital" (irrigation) and "cropping cycle" (dryland) modes of intensification (Earle 1978; Kirch 1994); (c) warfare, especially territorial conquest (Kirch 1985; Kolb and Dixon 2002); (d) status competition among chiefly lineages (Goldman 1970); and (e) resource diversity coupled with a redistributive economy (Sahlins 1958).

Understanding of how these critical "state factors" interacted—with respect to characteristics of particular prehistoric landscapes and to connections among different landscapes—has largely remained at the level of metatheory, couched almost exclusively in qualitative terms (for example, Cordy 1981, 2000; Earle 1997, 1991; Friedman 1982; Kirch 1990, 2000; Sahlins 1972). A "complexity" perspective (Byrne 1998; Kohler and Gumerman 2000; van der Leeuw 1998) provides a powerful theoretical apparatus for modeling these state factor interactions in Hawai`i over approximately one thousand years. Such models need to be landscape-specific, as well as temporally dynamic, in order to link the state factors listed above with the spatial diversity of resources.

Archaeological models of Hawaiian sociopolitical development have emphasized the dichotomy between windward and leeward environments and the contrasting agricultural systems that these supported. In their simplest form, these models suggest that the productive windward valleys, with their irrigation systems, were the primary nexus for political development, with more marginal leeward regions being—at least initially—peripheral. In a reconfiguration of this basic dichotomy, Kirch (1994) noted that leeward areas of the younger Hawaiian Islands supported large, intensive, dryland agricultural systems and large populations but that the point of diminishing marginal returns in agricultural intensification was likely to have been reached at lower output levels in dry leeward areas than in wet windward environments. Also, he noted, yields in the dryland systems were more variable and more vulnerable to environmental perturbation, such as drought, than those in irrigated wetland systems. In Hawai`i and other Pacific islands (see Ladefoged 1995), reaching this critical inflection point could have provided a stimulus for warfare, territorial expansion, and the emergence of greater hierarchy. Wetland systems, however, were constrained by the limited areas (valleys and slopes with water supplies) suitable for irrigation. Earle (1997) also recognizes the importance of environmental heterogeneity and suggests that, given high population densities in circumscribed environments, individuals can engage in warfare, ideological manipulation, and the control of subsistence resources to develop and maintain social inequalities.

At European contact (AD 1778–1779), the Hawaiian Islands were divided into four competing, incipient archaic states centered on the major islands of Hawai`i, Maui, O`ahu, and Kaua`i. Although each polity exhibited the social, economic, and political characteristics noted above, these took different forms on the younger islands (Maui and Hawai`i), where rain-fed dryland agriculture predominated, than on O`ahu and Kaua`i, where food production was concentrated on irrigated wetland systems (figure 6.1). Those polities based on intensified dryland agriculture were particularly aggressive and expansionist (Allen 1991; Earle 1997; Kirch 1984, 1994). Shortly after European contact, the Hawai`i Island polity conquered and absorbed the formerly independent Maui and O`ahu kingdoms, creating a greatly enlarged archaic state incorporating more than 15,000 sq km of territory and more than 300,000 subjects.

In short, Hawai`i offers exquisite possibilities for constraining analyses of both ecosystems and human societies across space and time, allowing us to track dynamically coupled interactions over a time frame of approximately one thousand years, a period sufficient to have witnessed the emergence of significant complexity. Our project seeks to analyze this model system through an interdisciplinary analysis of coupled human-natural systems in leeward contexts (Kirch et al. 2004; Vitousek et al. 2004), bringing together archaeological, pedological, ecological, and demographic approaches to evaluate the distribution, history, dynamics, biophysical constraints, and implications of rain-fed dryland agricultural systems and societies in two study areas on Maui and Hawai`i. The active integration of theoretical perspectives and methods from several disciplines that we have pioneered in this project has enabled us to move beyond a descriptive, qualitative "historical ecology" towards testable, dynamic, quan-

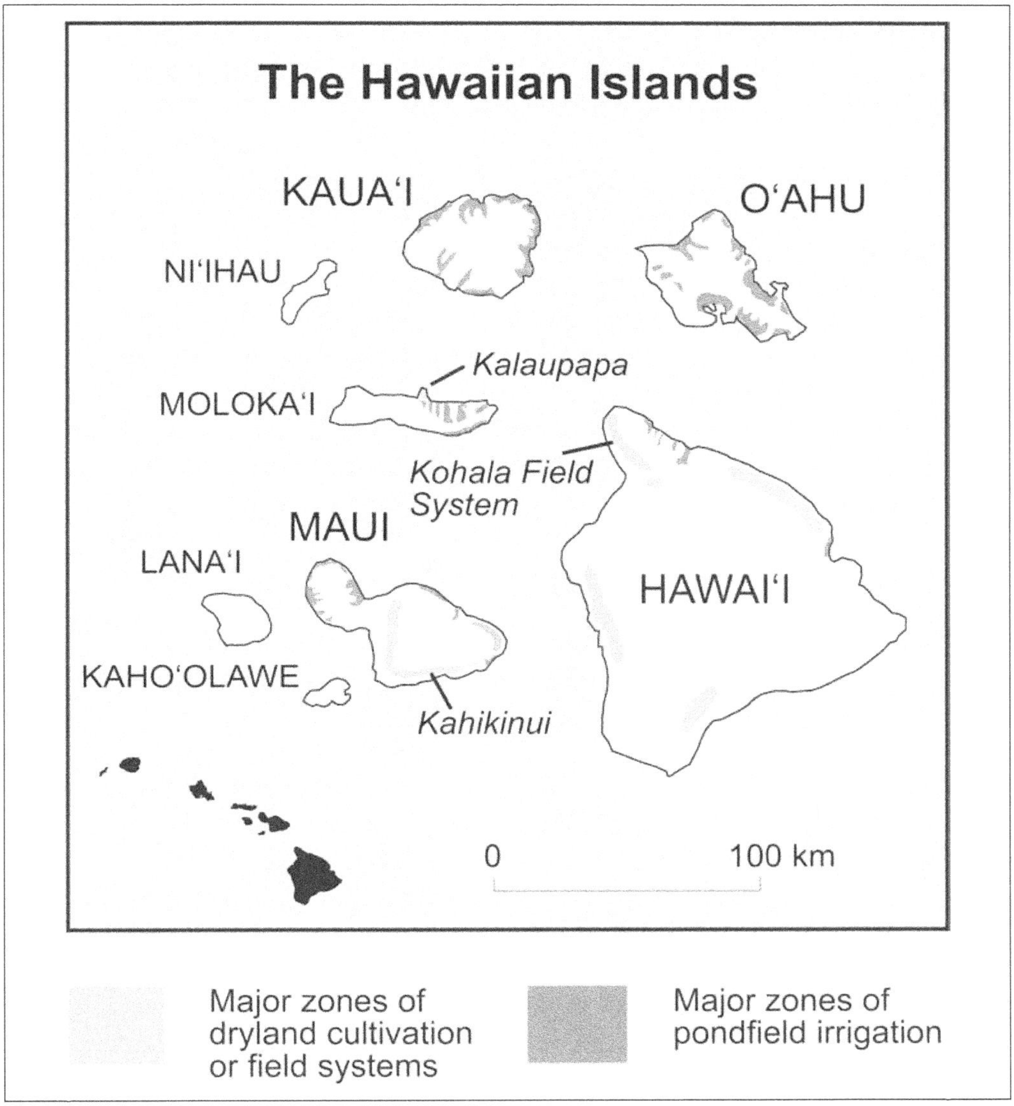

Figure 6.1. Map of the Hawaiian Islands (not in actual geographic relationships) showing the distribution of major zones of dryland field systems (light gray) and of wetland pondfield irrigation (dark gray). Also shown are the locations of major study areas (after Vitousek et al. 2004).

titative models that incorporate feedback processes; thresholds and nonlinearities; and selection, risk, uncertainty, and vulnerability.

The Hawai`i Biocomplexity Study

In the first three-year phase of our project, our research has been organized around five explicitly interdisciplinary modules and focused on two leeward study areas: Kahikinui District on Maui Island and Kohala District on Hawai`i Island. Both study areas supported extensive dryland agricultural systems, although Kahikinui is more arid and lacks a formal field system. Here we describe the study areas and then proceed to a summary of our key results, organized around five major topics.

The Study Areas

In *The Anthropology of History*, Kirch and Sahlins (1992) argued that peripheral or marginal regions—those most susceptible to risk and uncertainty—are often the best localities in which to study periods of rapid cultural and ecological change. Our project has focused on two such study areas on the geologically younger islands of Maui and Hawai`i, whose human settlement histories have been fairly well resolved through long-term archaeological investigation (see figure 6.1). Both areas began to be exploited and occupied by small groups of Hawaiians during the Expansion Period (AD 1100–1650) of the Hawaiian cultural sequence (Kirch 1985, 1990, 2000). This phase was characterized by an archipelago-wide population increase at an exponential growth rate (Clark 1988; Dye and Komori 1992a, 1992b; Kirch 1994). By the time of initial European contact (AD 1778–1779), both regions were densely settled, with local variations corresponding to the spatial environmental mosaic.

The Kahikinui study area (Maui Island) encompasses the ancient political district (*moku*) of Kahikinui, on the southern slope of Haleakala Volcano. Haleakala rises from sea level to 3,055 m asl, representing a magnificent altitudinal gradient crosscut by substrates of varied geological age. Kahikinui typifies a leeward climatic zone with pronounced seasonality (winter kona rains predominate) and a total annual precipitation ranging from <500 to >1,000 mm, depending on elevation. This puts it on the margin for dryland cultivation of Polynesian crop plants, especially in drought periods (Stock, Coil, and Kirch 2003). The vegetation of this leeward slope exemplifies the high taxonomic diversity characteristic of Hawaiian dryland forests (Rock 1915). The eastern half of the district has older substrates of the Kula Volcanic Series (226 kyr), with deeply weathered soil profiles and considerable hydrologic incision (Kirch et al. 2004). In stark contrast, the western part of the district consists of young lava flows of the Hana Volcanic Series (0–96 kyr), a rejuvenation phase of Haleakala, with rugged, unweathered or barely weathered surfaces lacking significant stream incision. The differential weathering times of the Kula and Hana surfaces correlate with significant differences in critical soil nutrients such as phosphorus (P), influencing patterns of human land use and tenure, especially after local populations became densely concentrated. A further resource restriction in Kahikinui is imposed by the coastal geomorphology, largely one of low sea cliffs and an absence of coral reefs—and therefore relatively low biotic diversity and biomass—rendering marine protein exploitation marginal.

Since 1994 Kahikinui has been archaeologically investigated by three coordinated teams of archaeologists from the University of California at Berkeley, Northern Illinois University, and the State of Hawai`i (Coil 2004; Coil and Kirch 2005; Dixon et al. 1997, 1999; Kirch 1997; Kirch and Millerstrom 2004; Kirch and O'Day 2002).

Several large zones with a total area of 19 sq km in central Kahikinui have been intensively surveyed archaeologically, from the coast up to 1,200 m above sea level (where site density becomes very sparse), resulting in a database including more than 3,300 archaeological features incorporated into a GIS database. Additionally, extensive excavations in a series of habitation, agricultural, and ritual sites have provided the basis for a detailed, local-level history of land use, local environmental modifications, resource use, microdemographic distributions, group organization and interactions, and iconic (ritual) marking of the landscape with monumental architecture. Using multiple lines of evidence, including zooarchaeological faunal materials (Kirch and O'Day 2002), charcoal, opal phytoliths, and other plant microfossils (Coil 2004), pulmonate gastropods, and other sources, we have begun to develop a temporally and spatially fine-grained reconstruction of biotic resources and their distributions over the period of Polynesian occupation. A suite of 160 ^{14}C age determinations, recently augmented by U/Th dating of coral offerings from ritual sites (Kirch and Sharp 2005), anchors this cultural history firmly in time, at a resolution of ±75 years (in the case of the coral dates, ±10 years). Frequency distributions of dated habitation sites further provide the basis for a proxy estimate of the rate of population growth, beginning with initial human incursion into the region up to abandonment, roughly AD 1870.

The Kohala study area (Hawai`i Island) encompasses the oldest volcano on the Island of Hawai`i. The edifice of Kohala Volcano was formed by volcanic eruptions between 400 and 600 kyr (Pololu series); substantial areas of its surface were covered by postshield eruptions between approximately 150 and 200 kyr (Hawi series). The volcano's wet windward slope is divided by deeply incised valleys, the largest of which (Waipi'o Valley) was the major locus of irrigated taro agriculture and (probably not coincidentally) an important seat of the island's paramount chiefs (Abad 2000; Cordy 2000). The undissected leeward slope supports one of the most spectacular rainfall gradients on Earth, reaching from <200 to >3,500 mm annual precipitation in a distance of 15 km (Chadwick et al. 2003; Giambelluca and Schroeder 1998). Leeward Kohala also supported one of the most extensive dryland farming systems in the archipelago, covering roughly 19 km by 4 km (~60 sq km) (Kirch 1984, 1985, 1994; Rosendahl 1972, 1994). The Kohala field system is characterized by a reticulate grid of earth and stacked-stone field boundaries; it incorporates thousands of smaller, free-standing, stone architectural features, including habitation sites and ritual structures.

The Kohala study region has been the focus of extensive archaeological, pedological, and ecological investigations. Archaeological research has traced the temporal development of both the field system and associated coastal and inland residential patterns, beginning as early as AD 1000 and continuing into the first decades after European contact (for example, Cordy and Kaschko 1980; Newman 1970; Pearson 1968; Rosendahl 1972, 1994; Tuggle and Griffin 1973). Most recently, Ladefoged and Graves have been applying a GIS approach to model the spatiotemporal development of the leeward field system (Ladefoged and Graves 2000; Ladefoged, Graves, and Jennings 1996; Ladefoged, Graves, and McCoy 2003; Ladefoged et al. 1998). Their spatial analyses and associated radiocarbon dates document the development of this system through expansion and increasing cropping-cycle intensification between AD 1400 and 1800.

Soils, Biogeochemical Gradients, and Agricultural Systems

The biogeochemical template upon which agriculture developed is well characterized in Hawai`i. Weathering of basaltic rock supplies most elements except nitrogen (N) to sites with young substrates and/or dry climates (Chadwick et al. 2003; Vitousek 2004), but over time—less time in wet sites, more in dry—almost all the calcium, magnesium, and potassium are lost. Thereafter, marine aerosol in rainfall and cloud-water provides the only significant source of these elements (Chadwick et al. 1999). The dominance of marine sources can be demonstrated unambiguously, using strontium (Sr), which has isotopically distinct (and unusually consistent) sources in Hawaiian basalt versus marine aerosol (Kennedy et al. 1998). Phosphorus is less mobile than most elements, and rock-derived P remains in circulation within ecosystems for more than one million years (Vitousek 2004). Eventually, however, even P from the rock is depleted, and several mineralogic and geochemical tracers demonstrate that continental dust from central Asia, more than 6,000 km away, thereafter constitutes the most important source of P (Chadwick et al. 1999; Kurtz, Derry, and Chadwick 2001).

We have carried out research on soils and biogeochemistry in relation to Polynesian agriculture at local, landscape, and archipelago-wide scales; local-scale results are described below. On the landscape scale, we have focused on understanding limits to the distribution of rain-fed intensive agricultural systems, sampling across rainfall gradients from dry areas below agricultural systems, through lands that were cultivated until the early 1800s, and into wetter areas above. Kohala supported a large and well-developed field system, covering at least 55 sq km with a dense network of field walls and paved trails (Ladefoged, Graves, and McCoy 2003); here we sampled soil properties on multiple transects across both 150-kyr and 400-kyr substrates (plate 15 and figure 6.2). At Kahikinui, we sampled a substrate matrix of lava flows ranging in age from 11 ky to >226 ky, within which the agricultural system was embedded (plate 16 and figure 6.3).

These landscape-scale soil analyses demonstrate that soil fertility peaked within the agricultural system in both areas, with base saturation and available P lower in drier sites and much lower in wetter sites, compared with sites within the agricultural area (Kirch et al. 2004; Vitousek et al. 2004). High levels of available P within the field system reflect both a greater fraction of total P in available form and a larger pool of total P in these soils. Using niobium (Nb) as an immobile index element, we determined that many formerly agricultural soils are absolutely enriched in P, relative to parent material—an enrichment that pre-dated the development of the field system, as demonstrated by analyses of soils from under field walls and from sites with similar rainfall outside the agricultural system (Vitousek et al. 2004). In addition, we

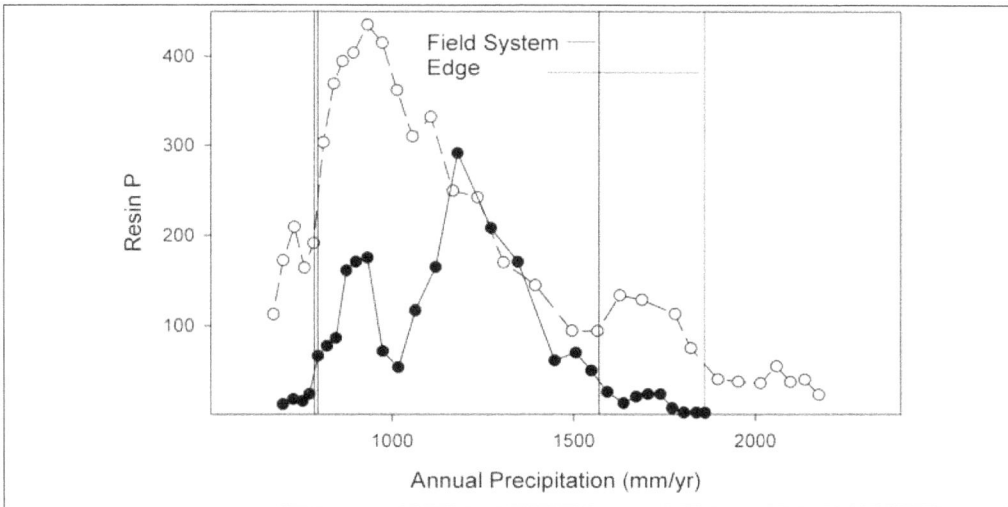

Figure 6.2. Analytical results for P and base saturation as measured along transects across the Kohala field system (after Vitousek et al. 2004).

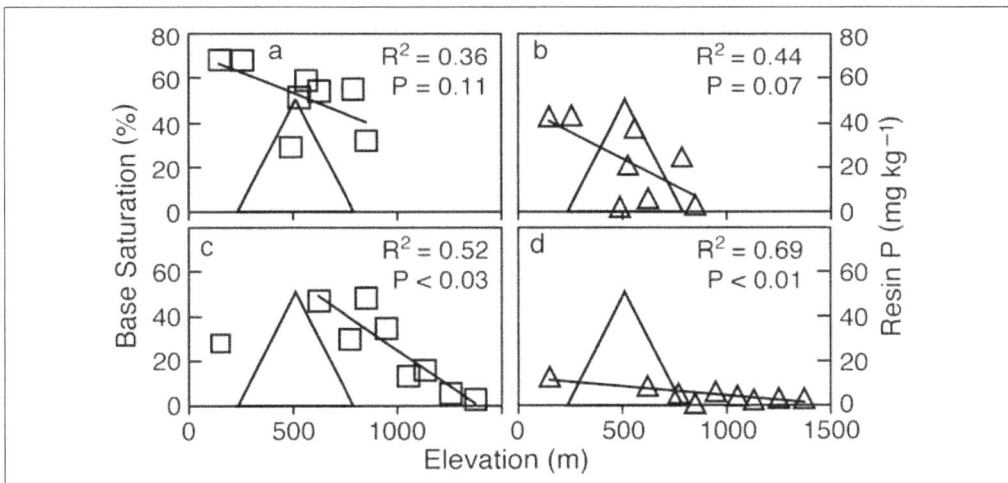

Figure 6.3. Soil properties in relation to the distribution of archaeological sites in Kahikinui (after Kirch et al. 2004). Soil properties are integrated to 30 cm depth and plotted against the distribution of household/agricultural complexes (large triangles) along the 53-ky climate gradients: (a) base saturation (%); (b) resin P (mg kg −1 and 226-ky); and along the 226-ky gradient: (c) base saturation (%); (d) resin P (mg kg −1). We used linear regression to assess changes in soil properties with elevation, transforming variables to meet assumptions of normality and homoscedasticity of error terms.

observed lower soil fertility on older substrates within both Kohala and Kahikinui (Kirch et al. 2004). Analyses of rainfall gradients on older substrates across the Hawaiian archipelago extend this pattern (Chadwick et al. 2003), demonstrating that the spectrum of sites with both fertile soils and adequate rainfall for intensive dryland agriculture progressively narrows and eventually disappears on substrates much older than 400 ky.

Overall, we conclude that within Kohala and Kahikinui, Hawaiian cultivators found, farmed, and intensified production on lands that were poised between being too wet and too dry. The distribution of intensive rain-fed agricultural systems was constrained on its lower end by conditions that were too arid to support intensive agriculture reliably (Ladefoged and Graves 2000). At the upper margin, many millennia of leaching had depleted soil fertility, so intensive rain-fed agriculture was infeasible (Vitousek et al. 2004). In essence, Hawaiian cultivators in intensive dryland agricultural systems were "farming the rock"; their field systems extended to the wettest point that still supplied nutrients via basalt weathering. This pattern makes sense: long-fallow shifting cultivation can make use of nutrients accumulated from the atmosphere over a period of time, but intensive dryland agriculture requires relatively rapid renewal of nutrient supply (from weathering or cultural inputs) if productivity is to be sustainable. On an archipelago-wide scale, substrates young enough to support sufficiently fertile soils were confined to the younger volcanoes, primarily on the Island of Hawai`i and Haleakala Volcano on Maui (see figure 6.1). Our findings suggest that before European contact, Hawaiians had expanded dryland agriculture to cover all the sites in which intensification was feasible, thereby reaching at least the geographic limits to such dryland intensification, if not absolute limits of productivity. We believe that this agricultural context relates directly to the highly aggressive, territorially expansionist strategies of the Hawai`i and Maui island polities in the centuries immediately preceding European contact (Kirch 1984; Vitousek et al. 2004).

Agricultural Systems and Intensification

Processes that drive sequences of agricultural intensification have long engaged anthropologists, archaeologists, and geographers (for example, Boserup 1981; Brookfield 1972, 1984; Geertz 1963; Johnston 2003; Kirch 1994; Morrison 1994; Sahlins 1972). Several modes of "intensification" have been differentiated (for example, expansion and innovation, cropping cycle and "landesque" capital modes of intensification; Kirch 1994), and critical linkages to both demographic and sociopolitical inputs and outputs have been qualitatively defined (Brookfield 1972, 1984). Intensification, however, occurs across and in relation to environmental mosaics, which in Hawai`i include some of the most dramatic environmental gradients on Earth.

For both of our dryland study sites, we used a combination of archaeological, biogeochemical, and quantitative modeling approaches to reconstruct details of agricultural practice and sequences of intensification over time. In Kohala, 398 ha were intensively surveyed, and 6,500 archaeological features were precisely located by GPS; all archaeological data have been integrated into a GIS incorporating excavation data from fifty-five residential features, as well as environmental information. In addition, eighty-eight geoarchaeological trenches provided soil samples for nutrient and archaeobotanical analysis. Relative chronologies of agricultural infrastructure construction in three intensively surveyed areas have been established (Ladefoged and Graves 2000; Ladefoged, Graves, and McCoy 2003), and one of these has been independently evaluated with a suite of eighteen AMS ^{14}C dates. Additional sections of the field system will be AMS dated. Geoarchaeological and nutrient analysis of soil samples from the trenches bisecting agricultural walls, fields, and trails demonstrates spatial and temporal variability in planting techniques. These analyses demonstrate variability in the level of intensification and timing of development throughout the field system. In aggregate, we can now refine a model of agricultural intensification in leeward Kohala as one of "cropping cycle intensification" (Kirch 1994), a sequence that moves along a pathway from long to short fallow over time, requiring increased labor inputs into defining and maintaining smaller and smaller individual plots. This sequence most closely approximates the classic Boserup (1965, 1981) model of agricultural intensification (see also Johnston 2003; Morrison 1994).

The younger, drier, and more mosaiclike landscape of Kahikinui required a more localized and varied adaptation of Hawaiian planting practices. Archaeological evidence of intensive cultivation of sweet potato and other dryland crops is extensive, including walls, terraces, mounds, and other features (Coil and Kirch 2005). Detailed investigations at several kinds of gardening sites included a large swale surrounded by residential complexes and an agricultural temple; excavations confirmed intensive gardening over three to four centuries, resulting in substantial geomorphological and pedological modifications. A ritual garden feature and shrine were also identified and excavated within the swale complex. A second swale site had a shorter cultivation sequence and higher anthropogenic nutrient inputs from the surrounding residential complexes. Open-field agricultural sites in Kahikinui lack walls and terraces, but excavations and stratigraphic trenches revealed abundant evidence of digging stick depressions, which had penetrated a tephra/cinder/tephra soil sequence. Comparisons of soil properties within and outside the features yield significant reductions of key plant nutrients (but not of elements not utilized by plants), confirming that the levels of harvesting in these dryland systems were sufficient to result in measurable nutrient depletion (Kirch et al. 2005).

These field observations and measurements are complemented by results from soil-agriculture models for the dryland system. We modified a version of the Century model (Parton et al. 1987; Parton, Stewart, and Cole 1988) as an analytical system to handle (a) soil hydrology in volcanic substrates (Chadwick et al. 2003), (b) more rapid analysis of stochastic inputs and outputs, and (c) sensitivity analysis. Our version is a system of differential equations relating carbon (C) and nitrogen (N) in plants, litter, and soils in terms of fluxes. The system contains nonlinear nitrogen fluxes and variable dynamics of C/N ratios for such crops as sweet potato. In addition, all kinetic factors (for example, growth and decomposition) are functions of rainfall, temperature, and plant-available mineral nitrogen. Our simulations of dryland systems yield complex dynamics (aperiodic or chaotic) with seasonal forcing (Lee, Tuljapurkar, and Vitousek 2006). Although previous studies have shown that temporal variation in

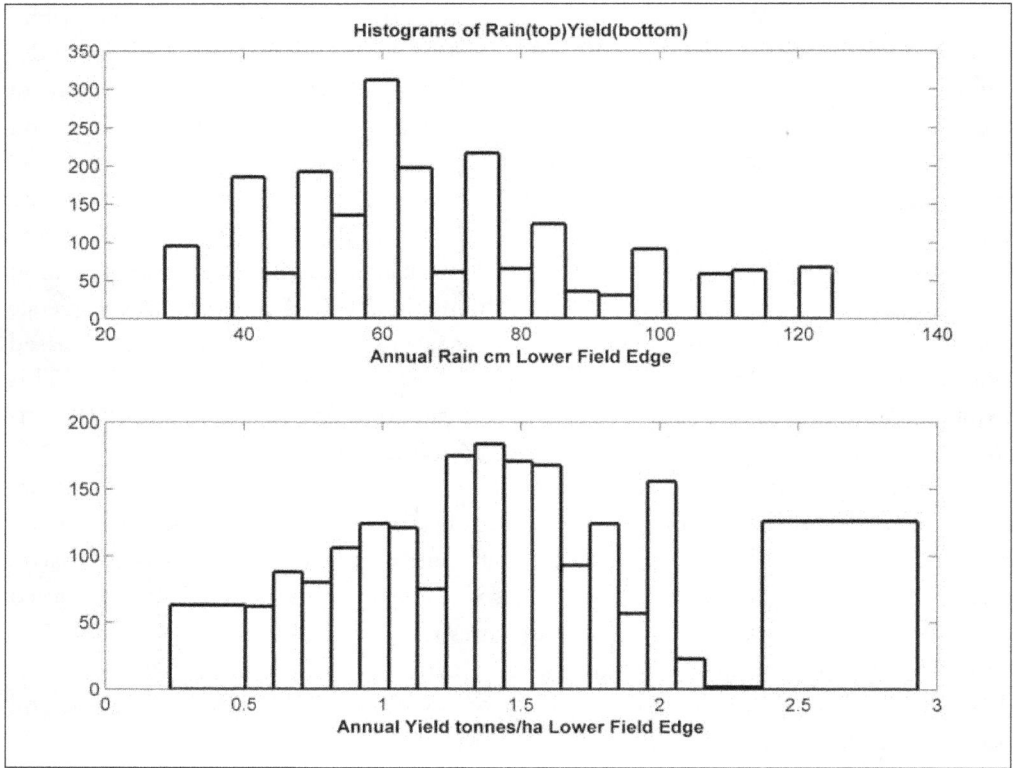

Figure 6.4. Amplification of rainfall variation by soil dynamics translated into yield variation.

rainfall may predict variation in plant production purely due to interactions with nutrient dynamics (Burke, Lauenroth, and Parton 1997; Oesterheld, Loreti, and Sala 2001), our results raise the possibility of a previously unrecognized dynamical mechanism for this phenomenon.

We then used rainfall and temperature data at or near the field sites to build stochastic models (time series Seasonal Autoregressive Integrated Moving Average models, Monte Carlo resampling) of weather across time and across the elevation gradient. We modeled sweet potato yields in dryland fields with only rain-derived nitrogen inputs. The mean and variability of rain change with elevation—as do nitrogen dynamics—so we expected the mean and variability of productivity to change as well (Burke, Lauenroth, and Parton 1997; Hooper and Johnson 1999). Figure 6.4 illustrates amplification of rainfall (cm/yr) variation by soil dynamics into yield variation (metric tons/ha/yr). We find that (a) variability of yield is as much as twice the variability of rainfall at low elevations and drops to below the variability of rainfall only at elevations above the upper boundary of the field systems; (b) the downside risk of low annual yield is larger at low elevations, but so is the potential benefit of high yield; and (c) the spatial correlation between yields at different elevations falls rapidly with distance, so elevations 270 m apart have correlation coefficients of only .5.

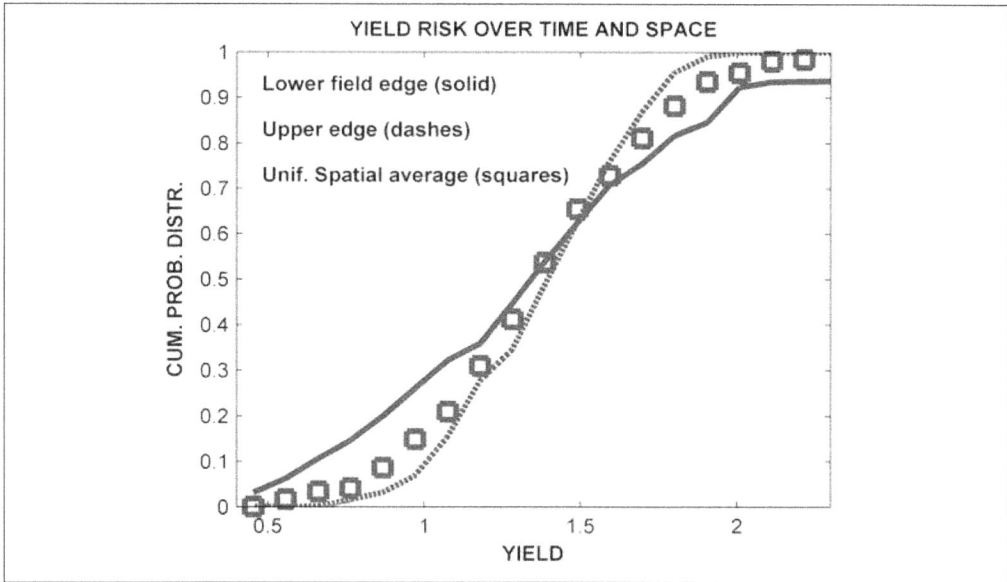

Figure 6.5. Yield risk over time and space for upper and lower portions of the Kohala field system.

Modeled yield is limited by interactions of N and precipitation at lower elevations, but observations suggest that available phosphorus (P) should be a limiting factor at high elevations—implying a localization of agriculture consistent with empirical findings (Lee, Tuljapurkar, and Vitousek 2006).

This model offers an important baseline from which to explore the intensity of agriculture across space, the effect of external nutrient inputs, and other questions. For example, consider the distribution of yields over time along an elevation gradient, as in figure 6.5. For each elevation, the stochastic model yields a steady state probability distribution of annual yields. The solid line to the right shows the cumulative probability of yields at the lower elevation boundary of the Kohala field system, and the dashed line indicates yield distributions at the upper boundary. Note that both the downside risks of low yield and the upside potential of high yield are higher at the lower elevation, even though our initial assumption of constant N inputs means that the average yield does not change significantly. Because spatial correlation falls fairly rapidly with distance up the slope, there is clearly potential to reduce overall yield variation by farming at several elevations. This pattern has, in fact, been documented in the earliest phase of agricultural development in Kohala (Ladefoged and Graves 2000). Indeed, a uniform spatial average across elevation leads to the probability distribution displayed by the square symbols. It is interesting that this average across elevation reduces the downside risk of low yield years without sacrificing much upside probability. To generalize from this example, any hypothesized spatial (or temporal) distribution of agricultural effort can be analyzed in the model as a spatial average across field locations, in which the level of effort is used to weight yields at different locations. Thus, allocations of agricultural effort across space, which are determined by social organization, can be translated into a distribution of means and variability of agricultural yields over time (Lee, Tuljapurkar, and Vitousek 2006). Moreover, the stochastic distribution of yields can be used as input to our demographic analysis of the effect of variable food supply on human vital rates, enabling us to generate testable hypotheses linking soils and agricultural practice to social and demographic change over time.

Anthropogenic Effects on Natural Vegetation

To monitor the cumulative impact of agricultural intensification on natural ecosystems, we systematically sampled macrobotanical and microbotanical materials from a peat core near the upper margin of the Kohala field system, from excavations in agricultural fields, from residential sites, and from soil test pits in both study areas. Pollen from the peat core indicates substantial upland vegetation change during the period of Hawaiian agriculture, with an overall decline in trees and episodic increases in shrubs and species of open areas. Microscopic charcoal influx indicates at least one local fire coincident with the final decline of tree pollen; analysis of earlier fire history is ongoing.

Within the Kohala field system, we evaluated the composition of the precultivation vegetation, insects, and land snails at a range of altitudes, the spatial and stratigraphic distributions of carbonized wood and seeds, the identity of fallow weeds, and crop plant distribution. We found an increase over time in carbonized seeds of the native weed *Chenopodium oahuense*, tentatively confirming fallowing as a component of agricultural strategy in the Kohala field system. Observations of wood charcoal suggest that burning of more substantial vegetation occurred sparingly throughout the field system and that natural fires pre-dating human settlement of Kohala were lacking.

In Kahikinui, we used wood charcoal, carbonized seeds, pollen, and phytoliths from dry contexts to reconstruct native vegetation and its compositional change over the time span of pre-contact settlement (Coil 2004). Shrub taxa increased and arboreal taxa declined over time, as vegetation around areas of settlement was increasingly altered by human activities. Phytolith assemblages from Kahikinui frequently contain abundant palm-type phytoliths. As in Kohala, natural fires in Kahikinui were limited, with no evidence of burning before the initial human use of the area.

Identification of wood charcoal before radiocarbon dating has enabled us to create a body of dates free from "old-wood" or "inbuilt age" bias. In Kohala, the relative chronologies of field expansion and intensification developed through analysis of surface architecture (Ladefoged, Graves, and McCoy 2003) can now be compared with radiocarbon dates from wood charcoal buried during field wall construction. For Kahikinui, a larger suite of 169 radiocarbon dates not only offers chronological control for the sequence of agricultural intensification but also enables us to estimate changing human population over a four-century period.

Population and Demographic Trends

For several island cases in Remote Oceania, archaeologists have confirmed the general applicability of a model of population growth that predicts a shift from early, colonizing populations marked by high population growth (r), low density, density-independent mortality, and limited cultural regulation, to populations in late prehistory characterized by low r, high density, and the application of varied cultural forms of regulation, including abortion, celibacy, warfare, infanticide, and even cannibalism (Kirch 1984, 2000; Kirch and Rallu in press). The Hawaiian case is of particular interest because a wealth of empirical data supports an archipelago-wide model in which a phase of exponential population growth followed initial colonization by a small founding propagule (Clark 1988; Cordy 1981; Dye and Komori 1992b; Hommon 1986; Kirch 1984). Significantly, this exponential growth phase appears to have peaked between AD 1400 and 1500, after which the archipelago's population stabilized or possibly oscillated. In wet valley regions, archaeological evidence documents major construction of irrigated agricultural complexes between roughly AD 1200 and 1600 (Allen 1991, 1992). It was just as the archipelago-wide population reached its peak in the fifteenth century that dryland agricultural zones such as Kohala and Kahikinui began to be permanently occupied. Therefore, the dryland systems represent a late phase of regional population growth on the younger islands. As our research has shown, these leeward landscapes underwent a sequence of cropping cycle intensification accompanied by significant increases in local population densities. Our hypothesis is that the apparent transition, from a phase of rapid exponential population growth to a phase of population stability that has tentatively been identified for the archipelago, can be decomposed into discrete regional population trajectories that differ between wet valley and indeed various dryland environments. These regional population trajectories were accompanied, we hypothesize, by contrastive trends in agricultural intensification and in the emergence of sociopolitical complexity.

For archipelago-wide modeling, prehistoric skeletal mortality data from four Hawaiian collections display low infant mortality and high adult mortality relative to other world populations. We developed a data-driven model for prehistoric mortality by using singular value decomposition to identify a two-parameter family of relational models, focusing on the levels of mortality of young (under fifteen years of age) and reproductive-age adults, as well as the total fertility rate. When held constant, age-specific mortality and fertility entrain a long-run growth rate. If age-specific mortality and fertility vary stochastically, the long-term growth rate results from the joint effect of average rates and variation in those rates. The right panel of figure 6.6 shows the range of possibilities with constant rates, suggesting that mortality must have been high for either young or adults. The left panel shows fertility and mortality varying stochastically over time; we suggest that the stochastic case is more plausible and that average mortality was low for young and adults. The high variability in this case, however, means that cohort survival was quite variable over time. Given the high levels of variability in food supply from our climate/soil models, as well as ethnohistorical

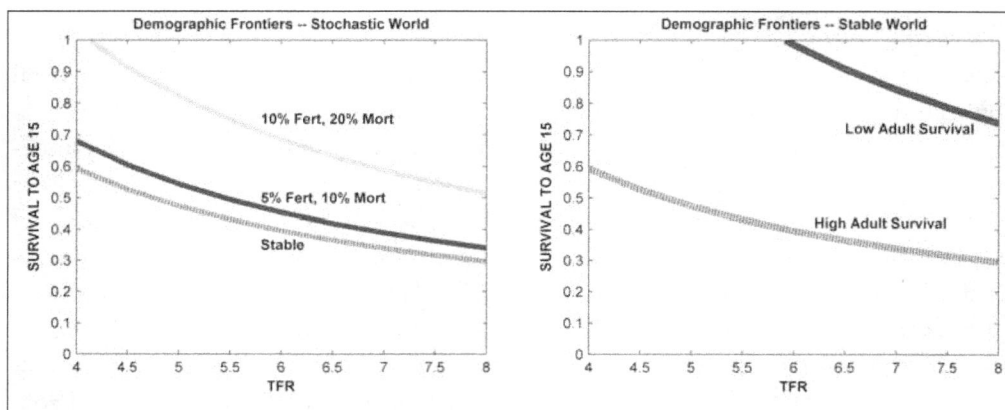

Figure 6.6. Sochastic (left) and deterministic (right) models of mortality and fertility.

evidence of warfare, the lower panel represents likely combinations of mortality and fertility.

With model mortality schedules and bounds on the possible combinations of mortality and fertility, we are now positioned to evaluate demography in particular landscapes—and to model explicitly the effects of variable food supplies on population dynamics. For Kahikinui, our sample of 169 ^{14}C dates reflects exponential growth from approximately AD 1400 (initial settlement of this arid landscape) until European contact, with no reduction in the number of dated sites for the later time intervals and therefore no basis for inferring a logistic process (Kirch and Rallu in press). This contrasts with prior evidence for the archipelago as a whole, indicating an exponential growth curve until approximately AD 1400–1500, after which the population numbers remain relatively constant. Significantly, people began to settle and utilize the Kahikinui lands *at the same time that the archipelago-wide population apparently reached its peak.* The occupation of Kahikinui was a population "overflow" from other regions, beginning only as the main period of "inland expansion" was coming to a close. This pattern presumably reflects the marginality of Kahikinui in terms of water, resources, and agricultural potential (Kirch et al. 2004). Kahikinui is a high-risk environment, one that people tackled only when other options became closed to them (Dixon et al. 1999). We also applied a "house count" method to estimate specific population sizes and densities for a representative sample area of approximately 6.75 sq km, containing 544 individual stone structures grouped into 117 residential complexes. We conclude that the maximum density achieved in the lowland zone was 43 to 57 persons/sq km, depending on average household size. The figures for the *ahupua`a* territory, as a whole, are approximately 19 to 25 persons/sq km—on the low end of ethnographically documented population densities in Polynesia (realistically so, in view of the environmental marginality of Kahikinui).

For Kohala, we based a demographic model on 195 residential features in a 1.3-sq-km detailed study area in the southern part of the field system (Ladefoged and

Graves 2005a, b). Our data suggest that this area might have been developed relatively late in relation to other portions of the field system (Ladefoged and Graves 2000; Ladefoged, Graves, and McCoy 2003). Within this area, we estimate that population grew from a density of 20 persons/sq km to 91 persons/sq km as the field system expanded and intensified. Extrapolating these figures to the entire Kohala field system, we calculate a peak population of approximately 5,025 within the system. These levels are much higher than Kahikinui, corresponding to the higher agricultural potential of Kohala and its formalized field system. Initial estimates of population growth along the Kohala coastline show expansion there as well.

Social Structure and Control Hierarchies

As the dryland agricultural economies of Hawai`i and Maui were undergoing the sequences of intensification and linked demographic change outlined above, their sociopolitical systems were becoming more complex. Hawai`i is especially suited for modeling the emergence of social complexity because Hawaiian culture materially indexed complexity in a number of ways that are archaeologically recoverable. These material indices can be spatially referenced by GIS and dated by AMS ^{14}C or U/Th methods. These include (a) an elaborate system of temples (*heiau*) operating on a hierarchy of levels (from "state temples" of war and agriculture, to territorial-level agricultural and fertility temples, to household and specialized economic shrines), constructed on stone architectural platforms and terraces (Dixon et al. 1997; Kirch 1985; Kolb 1992, 1994a, b; Kolb and Radewagen 1997); (b) attributes of residential or household sites reflecting rank or status, such as differential quantities of faunal and floral remains, high-grade stone tools, or architectural features (Kirch and O'Day 2002; Weisler and Kirch 1985); and (c) aspects of the agricultural landscapes themselves, including formal property boundaries and land division markers, such as permanent field boundaries, stone-lined trails, freestanding walls, mounds, and cairns.

We have made significant progress in tracking the development of a control hierarchy associated with the emergence of archaic states on these islands late in the precontact period. In Kahikinui, this control hierarchy is manifested materially in a system of temples, marked archaeologically by complex and varied stone foundations. As ethnohistorically documented (Valeri 1985), this temple system corresponded to a hierarchy of major gods, with two primary temple classes: those associated with food production (*heiau ho`ouluulu*) and those associated with war (*heiau kaua*). Prior efforts at dating Maui Island temples using [14]C (Kolb 1992, 1994a, b) suggested a quantitative increase in temple construction between roughly AD 1400 and 1650—but ^{14}C dating in the last five hundred years is confounded by ambiguous regions of the radiocarbon calibration curve, as well as other problems. We developed a chronology of temple construction in Kahikinui via [230]Th dating of branch corals used as dedicatory offerings (Kirch and Sharp 2005). This approach offers significant advantages over ^{14}C dating; uncertainties in [230]Th ages for approximately four-hundred-year-old corals are seven to twelve years at 95 percent confidence intervals.

Calculated dates for the coral offerings fall in a narrow range from 1568 ± 8 to 1635 ± 6—within an interval of less than seventy years—and as little as half that time when we account for coral growth rates (Kirch and Sharp 2005). Our sample includes small and mid-size temples, as well as the largest temple structure in the district. The timing of intensive temple dedication implies that fundamental change in the sociopolitical structure of the district occurred far more rapidly than previously documented. The Hawaiian ethnohistorical record of chiefly genealogies and oral traditions (Abad 2000) sheds light on the broader context in which this abrupt social restructuring took place. For Maui Island, two formerly independent chiefdoms were brought under the control of a single leader during the reign of Pi`ilani, approximately AD 1570–1600. His grandson Kamalalawalu (approximately AD 1610–1630) took over the nearby islands of Lana`i and Kaho`olawe, expanding the Maui polity from about 940 sq km to more than 2,360—just the kind of territorial expansion predicted with archaic state formation (Marcus 1992; Spencer 1990, 1993). A parallel process of sociopolitical change apparently occurred on Hawai`i Island at the same time (Abad 2000), although territorial consolidation in the seventeenth century was followed by a cycle of disintegration and reintegration. In the late eighteenth century, territorial expansion on Hawai`i Island eventually comprised the entire island, an area of nearly 10,500 sq km. Accordingly, the temples provide tangible archaeological evidence of the speed with which a fundamental sociopolitical transition occurred in protohistoric Hawai`i.

Recent analyses in the southernmost ahupua`a of the Kohala field system, however, suggest that this process might have occurred over a longer period of time in Kohala than in Kahikinui. Archaeological and ethnohistoric data indicate that the boundaries of community territories (ahupua`a) were subdivided through time, a process that would have facilitated the monitoring and management of agricultural production (Ladefoged and Graves 2000). A seriation of religious structures (heiau) in the field system reveals spatial and temporal patterning that coincides with the changes in territorial boundaries (Mulrooney and Ladefoged 2005). The eight heiau can be assigned to four classes, with heiau in the earliest class being distributed in the center of the earliest defined territories. Heiau assigned to subsequent temporal intervals are located in the center of later territories that were partitioned off from the earlier units. The final stage of heiau construction corresponds with infilling of the already established territories. The size and shape of agricultural plots in this area also display evidence of standardization over time (Ladefoged and Graves 2000; Ladefoged, Graves, and McCoy 2003). Although the imposition of chiefly hierarchy in Kahikinui occurred rapidly, the evidence from Kohala suggests that this was a longer process, which is not surprising, given the more marginal environment of Kahikinui in relation to Kohala.

Conclusions

The research we have outlined above is focused on the Hawaiian Islands, yet the issues we seek to address are global. The cultural and biological processes that developed and interacted in Hawai`i, from population growth and intensification of agriculture and resource extraction, to the increasing centralization of political power and economic control, have happened everywhere and indeed are taking place globally today. The Hawaiian Islands are unique in the precision with which we can define the arena in which these processes play out, from the biogeochemical matrix underlying agricultural development to the nature and isolation of the founding culture. The approaches, concepts, and models we are endeavoring to develop can contribute to basic understanding of how soils, ecosystems, agriculture, and sociopolitical structure interacted in a constrained, isolated world—and this understanding can illuminate issues of resource use and human societies in the world at large.

Within archaeology, research on sociopolitical development has tended to focus on qualitative descriptions of adaptations in specific environmental contexts, providing for a general understanding of evolutionary trajectories but not for empirically grounded comparisons and insights. Our research—like that described in other chapters in this volume—takes an explicitly quantitative approach to modeling human interactions over regional landscapes. Our work, to date, on the dryland agricultural systems of the younger Hawaiian Islands (Maui and Hawai`i) has provided a clearer understanding of how societies dependent on dryland agriculture evolved within dynamic environmental settings. In the future, we plan to extend our work to wetland systems (windward valleys with extensive pondfield irrigation) and to interactions between wetland and dryland areas. The modular approach we use integrates multiple disciplinary perspectives. Biogeochemical and hydrologic conditions, distribution of agricultural infrastructure and modes of intensification, population dynamics, and political control hierarchies are quantified across landscapes for a time series extending from approximately AD 800 to 1800. These quantitative reconstructions can be used to model both human demography and agricultural output under changing cultural and environmental conditions, as well as how these interacted in the emergence of complex archaic states out of chiefdoms.

CHAPTER 7

The Spread of Farming into Central Europe and Its Consequences
Evolutionary Models

Stephen Shennan

The use of Darwinian evolutionary models to understand patterns of social, economic, and cultural change in the prehistoric past is becoming increasingly well established (Dominguez 2002; Holden and Mace 2003; Lyman and O'Brien 2000; Nagaoka 2002; Neiman 1997; Shennan 2002; Stiner and Munro 2002). However, it remains the subject of many misconceptions (Kristiansen 2004), because of the erroneous assumptions that those unfamiliar with evolutionary theory bring to their reading of the evolutionary literature and because of the inherent complexity of the whole endeavor. The complexity is unsurprising in the light of the history of biology over the past 150 years, during which the substantive and philosophical implications of Darwinism have continued to ramify (for example, Jablonka and Lamb 2005). In applying these ideas to the study of human societies and their history, we are much closer to beginning the process of developing appropriate theory. The subject matter is more complex, although there are increasing suggestions that the complexity of inheritance in animal populations has been underestimated (Danchin et al. 2004; Jablonka and Lamb 2005; Laland, Odling-Smee, and Feldman 2000). Moreover, different topics call on different aspects of evolutionary theory.

In this chapter, I look at two different but interrelated topics that have long been of interest to archaeologists of virtually all theoretical persuasions and present a specific, concrete example of how evolutionary theory can be used to illuminate them.

The topics concern the history of human populations, the history of social institutions, and the link between them. Darwinian theory is equally illuminating for two other types of histories—histories of culturally transmitted norms, practices, and artifact attributes and the process of "niche construction" (Laland et al. 2000)—but they are not the main focus here.

Obviously, the basis for describing and explaining such histories from an evolutionary perspective is the establishment of a connection between them and relevant processes and entities in evolutionary theory. There must be an inheritance mechanism, a means of generating novelty, and processes that affect the frequency with which things are represented in future generations.

In the case of the cultural practices of interest to archaeologists, the inheritance mechanism is social learning, and novelty is produced by innovation. The latter can be mere copying error, but it can also arise from trial-and-error experimentation that leads individuals to give up what they were originally doing and do something else instead, in the belief that it will produce better results in some sense. This does not mean that problems always call into being their own solutions. Necessity may be the "mother of invention," but not necessarily *successful* invention. Success depends on a variety of processes, one of which is natural selection.

The operation of natural selection for humans needs some "unpacking." In the first place, it assumes that humans, like other animals, have evolved to have a propensity to maximize their reproductive success and to recognize and respond to variations in their environment relevant to achieving that success. This leads to the assumption that, in the day-to-day business of getting a living, the principles of optimal foraging should hold. Subject to these, if changed conditions alter the trade-offs involved in achieving reproductive success, people will respond accordingly, increasing fertility in good times and decreasing it when times are hard.

Natural selection can also act on people via their cultural traditions. In other words, particular inherited cultural beliefs and practices may lead to greater survival rates and reproductive success for some than for others. If these successful beliefs/practices are transmitted to the next generation, then their prevalence will increase and will, in turn, increase the reproductive success of that generation, and so on, for as long as these practices are advantageous.

A further cultural twist on natural selection also exists (Boyd and Richerson 1985; Richerson and Boyd 2004). A particular set of beliefs or practices may not lead an individual to greater reproductive success and associated transmission of the successful beliefs to children but, instead, to greater success as a model to be copied in various respects. If the beliefs/practices that make the individual a successful model to be copied are adopted, then the copiers, too, will be more likely to become models for the beliefs and practices of subsequent generations. In the former case, competition among cultural attributes affects who will be the biological parents of the next generation. In the latter case, the competition is about who will be the "cultural parents."

The frequencies of beliefs and practices through time are also affected by what

Boyd and Richerson (1985) have called "decision-making biases." These include the preferential copying of practices because they appear to give better results in some sense (directly biased transmission) and the preferential copying of practices simply because they are common (conformist transmission). There may be complex feedbacks among all these different processes. On one hand, a conformist bias may lead to greater replicative success for one particular belief/practice than for another. But it also might have deleterious effects on the reproductive success of members of a community if it means that they respond too slowly to changes in, for example, the natural environment. On the other hand, those who conform might tend, in general, to be more successful in obtaining a partner and bringing up children. Thus, a process of gene-culture co-evolution may develop if relevant aspects of human psychology are genetically influenced.

A special position in analyses of natural selection and culture is occupied by evolutionary game theory (for example, Skyrms 1996) focused on the competition among social interaction strategies in terms of the pay-offs these give to the interactors in different social situations. Here, what is changing through time as a result of differential pay-offs is the frequency of social strategies in a population. Obviously, this, too, may have survival/reproductive success consequences for the practitioners of the strategies, as well as for the replicative success of the norms associated with the favoring of particular strategies.

Of the evolutionary processes that affect the frequency of transmitted cultural practices over time, last but not least is drift: the effect of chance variation in the frequency with which practices are copied, unrelated to their properties. The idea that drift is relevant to understanding cultural change has a long history in anthropology and archaeology (Binford 1963; Rivers 1926), but its significance was most explicitly argued by Dunnell (1978) in his distinction between style and function in artifacts. The latter refers to all variation that is under selection, and the former, to that variation which is not (that is, which is neutral). For Dunnell, this was an absolute distinction—attributes either are under selection or are not. But, in fact, even when particular attributes are under selection, their representation in subsequent generations may be almost entirely the result of chance factors if population sizes are small.

By now, it should be apparent why the evolutionary understanding of histories of norms, populations, and social institutions is so complex. The histories are interconnected but certainly not reducible to one another. Processes affecting one can also have repercussions for the others, not to mention potential effects on the genetic constitution of populations. For prehistory, the situation is further complicated by the relative inaccessibility of some histories. Archaeologists have been tracing the histories of norms of artifact production with considerable success since the discipline began. As yet, however, we have very little direct information about the history of populations because we lack the means to establish who was the biological descendant of whom, except in very exceptional cases. Inferences on this subject depend on assumed links between people and their traditions. For decades, we have known these to be problematical, for reasons arising from the wide range of routes of cultural transmission. Tracing the history of social institutions is also difficult, although it is one of the main areas in which anthropological archaeologists have made progress in the past forty years.

Rather than despair about these complexities, we can use evolutionary models based on well-founded assumptions to address specific archaeological issues. Following this approach, the example here is the rise and decline of the first farming societies in central Europe, approximately 5600–4900 BC, in the context of a broader phenomenon—the spread of cereal-based agriculture from its Near Eastern origins to northwest Europe. The starting point is a demographic one.

Demographic Processes

If the history of human population in a given region were simply a very gradual rise over the long term, then, arguably, population processes could be discounted in our attempts to understand patterns of change and continuity in human history. In fact, it is increasingly clear that local populations have fluctuated very considerably in response to a variety of endogenous and exogenous factors (see Shennan 2000). Because human populations are the fundamental support for all cultural processes, documenting and explaining those fluctuations is essential.

The mechanism behind population processes is natural selection. Humans, like other animals, have evolved to maximize their reproductive success. The idea that children are a good, in themselves, instead of simply a means to an end—for example, to increase the pool of agricultural labor, although this may well be relevant to the specific costs and benefits of bringing up children—seems to be held in virtually all human cultures. Some people have been more successful than others at surviving, finding a mate, and bringing up their children and, as a result, have left more descendants (see Scriver 2001 and Zerjal et al. 2003 for striking examples).

In these circumstances, there are always trade-offs between the maximum number of children you can produce and the maximum you can bring to the stage of being successful parents. If changed conditions reduce the severity of those trade-offs, then people will take advantage of them and population will expand to new limits (see Wood 1998). Those changed conditions may be entirely exogenous, for example, climatic variations, or may stem from innovations leading to new adaptations. Thus, a regional population increase, unless it is a point on a curve of endogenous cyclical fluctuations, is likely to be an indicator of new conditions promoting increased reproductive success. Population stability indicates that a local ceiling has been reached, a process that will not take very long, given the rapid increases in numbers that even relatively low growth rates produce.

New adaptations will be especially successful if dispersal opportunities are available to the human populations practicing them (Voland 1998) so that expansion can continue elsewhere when a local population ceiling is reached. The spread of farming into Europe can be regarded as a classic example of a dispersal opportunity. In large parts of Europe, away from coastal and riverine areas with rich aquatic resources, Mesolithic hunter-gatherer population densities were very low. However, the areas with low population densities included zones that were very suitable for growing cereal crops and could thus sustain much higher densities of farmers than hunter-gatherers. Moreover, the combination of annual cereals and domestic animals, in addition to supporting higher population densities and therefore greater reproductive success before the new, higher ceiling was reached, was extremely portable, far more so than many other agricultural systems. The result was a process of demic diffusion, which would have subsumed the small hunter-gatherer populations existing in the areas initially occupied by early farmers (see Ammerman and Cavalli-Sforza 1973; Pinhasi, Fort, and Ammerman 2005). In other words, this is a classic example of natural selection acting on people through an inherited cultural tradition that gave a selective advantage to those who adopted it and passed it on to their children. In fact, not only was a tradition inherited, but also the actual descendants of the cereal crops and of the animals that had originally been domesticated.

The visible evidence of this process is seen in the greatly increased density of human settlement in those areas where farming arrived and also in the demographic profiles of cemeteries, as Bocquet-Appel (2002) has shown (figure 7.1). The zero point on the horizontal axis of figure 7.1 marks the arrival of cereal agriculture at a given place. To the left, time before the arrival of farming at that place increases; to the right, time after its initial arrival. The figure shows that before the arrival of farming, population growth rates inferred from cemetery populations were at or just below replacement level; afterwards, they were growing, albeit at varying rates.

On the basis of studies on the number, size, and density of settlements of the Linear Pottery Culture in central Europe, Petrasch (2001, 2005) has calculated population growth rates between 0.9 and 2.7 percent per year for the first farming societies in this area.[1]

In detail, the expansion process seems to have involved the colonization of patches favorable to the new economy, instead of uniform expansion (van Andel and Runnels 1995), hence the rapidity with which it occurred in many areas (see Zilhao 2001 for the north Mediterranean coast).

The Ideal Despotic Distribution

There has been a tendency to assume that demographic growth models of the spread of farming presuppose that spatial expansion would not have been triggered until local populations were coming close to an absolute local carrying capacity. That this cannot have been the case is suggested by the speed of the expansion into Europe. Also, in certain areas, we can see that new places were colonized before others reached any sort of carrying capacity (see below). The basis for understanding why further expansion does not necessarily presuppose demographic saturation is again provided by principles derived from thinking through the implications of natural selection, in this case, as

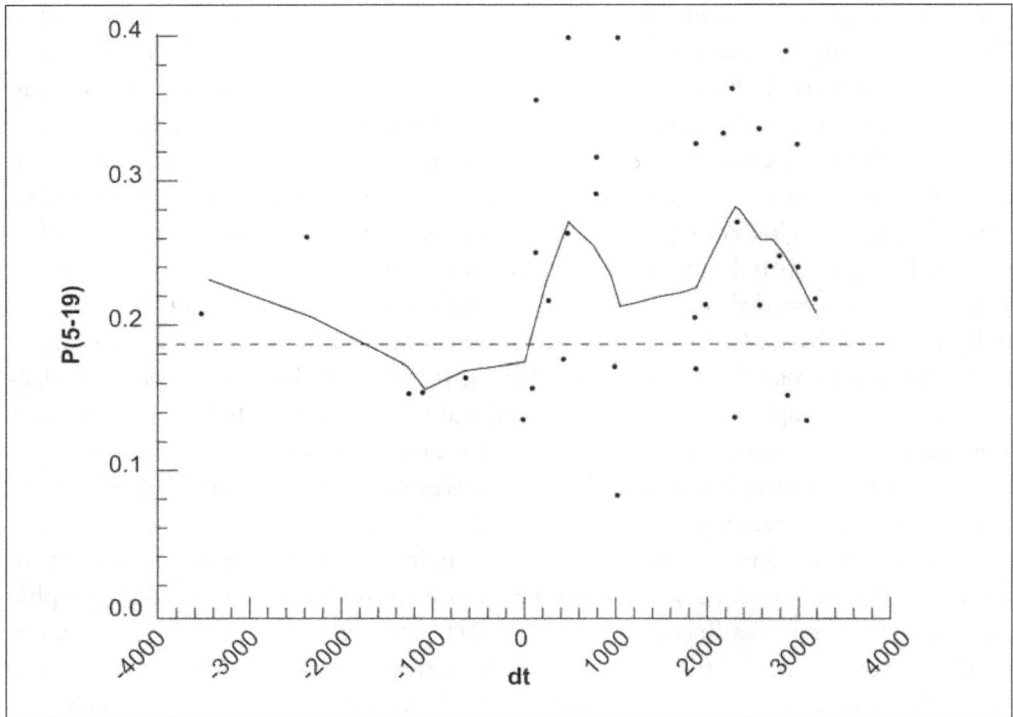

Figure 7.1. Estimated proportions of individuals in the age five–nineteen category from a series of Mesolithic and Neolithic cemeteries in Europe, with a best fit line produced by Loess fitting. The dashed line shows a value corresponding to a population growth rate of zero. The zero point on the horizontal axis marks the estimated time of arrival of cereal agriculture at a given place. To the left, time before the arrival of farming at that place increases; to the right, time after its initial arrival (from Bocquet-Appel 2002).

they relate to decision making concerning spatial behavior. Here the principle in question is the "ideal despotic distribution" from population ecology (Sutherland 1996). The "ideal free distribution" proposes that individuals occupy the resource patch that gives them the best returns. As more individuals occupy the patch, the returns to each individual decline, to the point that the returns to an individual from the best patch are no better than those from the next best patch, which has no occupants. Now the returns from both patches are equal, and they will be occupied indiscriminately until the population grows to the point that equal benefit is gained by occupying a still worse patch, and the process is repeated.

When territoriality occurs, however, the situation is different. Here the "ideal despotic distribution" applies (figure 7.2). The first individual occupying the area is able to select the best territory in the best patch. Subsequent individuals settling there do not affect the first arrival but have to take the next best territory, and so on, until the next settler will do just as well by taking the best territory in the next best patch. Subsequent individuals will then take territories in either patch where the territories are equally suitable. In the ideal free distribution, new settlers decrease the mean

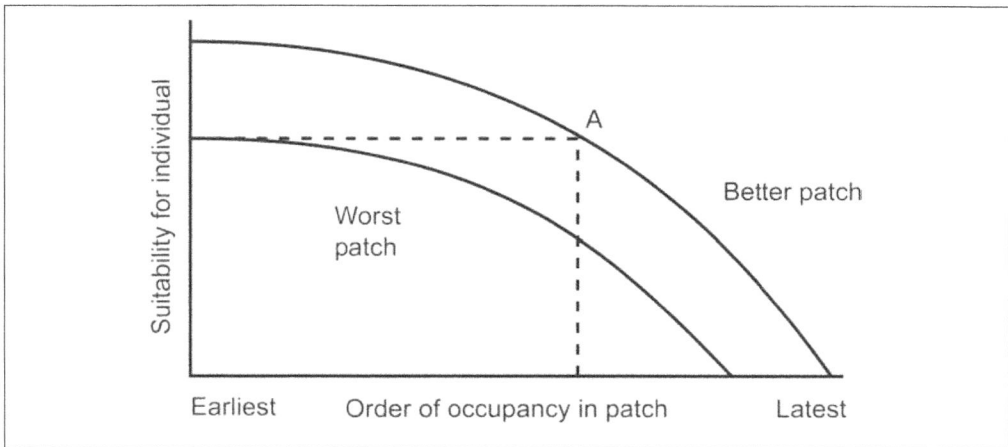

Figure 7.2. The ideal despotic distribution. Because of territoriality, the suitability of a patch for each individual decreases with the order of settling. Subsequent individuals do not affect the quality of the territories of those who settled first. Individuals settle in the better patch until point A, when a new arrival does equally well by taking the best position in the worse patch. Later, individuals settle equally in both patches. However, the average return differs between the patches (from Sutherland 1996).

return for everybody, including those who arrived first; in the ideal despotic distribution, the returns depend on the order of settlement. The initial settlers of the best territory in the patch will do best, that is, as long as they can defend the territory against anyone who might seek to take it from them.

I propose that during the spread of farming into Europe, the new households being formed as population expanded would have evaluated the costs and benefits of staying near their parents' household or finding some other place, following the principles of the ideal despotic distribution. All that would have been required for further spatial expansion is a shift in the balance of costs and benefits, between accepting the next best local territory available and taking the risk of finding and settling a new, top-quality patch some distance away.

The First Farmers in Central Europe

By the beginning of the sixth millennium cal. BC, groups with agricultural economies had spread through southeast Europe into the Carpathian Basin. The so-called Linear Pottery Culture (or *LBK*, after its German name) characterizes the first farming groups of central Europe and appears to have originated in western Hungary/eastern Austria approximately 5600–5500 cal. BC. The LBK spread extremely quickly westwards. The area covered by the earliest LBK (figure 7.3) seems to have been settled in less than 150 years (Petrasch 2001). The occupation was not spatially continuous, however, but restricted to particular patches. Across this broad area, the earliest pottery is extremely uniform (Cladders 2001). Subsequently, the area expanded still further, as figure 7.3

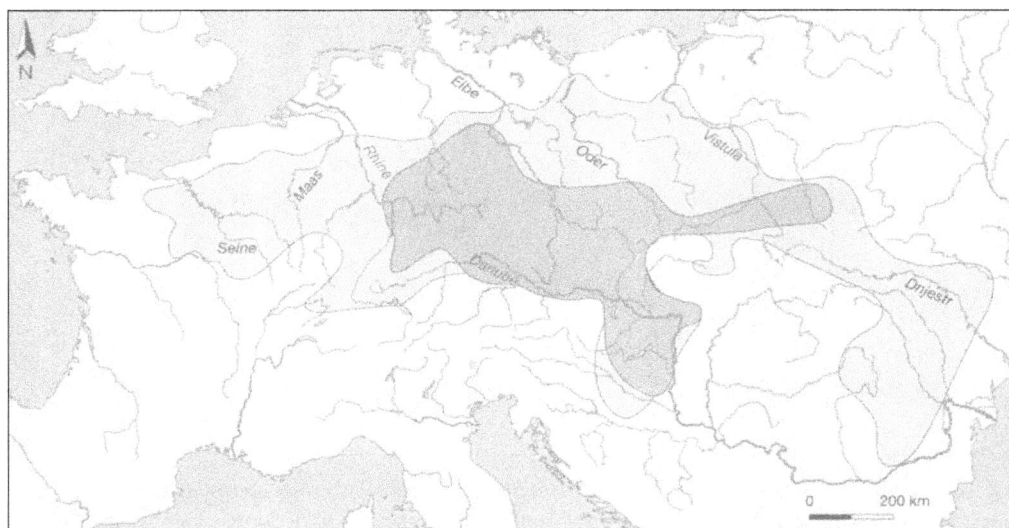

Figure 7.3. The distribution of the LBK. The dark shading represents the distribution of the earliest LBK; the light shading, the later LBK (from Zimmermann 2002).

shows. The LBK seems to have ended approximately 5000–4900 cal. BC, later in some areas than in others (Strien 2000).

Detailed fieldwork in Germany in the western Rhineland enables us to trace this process at a local scale (summarized in Zimmermann 2002). Figure 7.4 shows part of the sequence of occupation on the Aldenhovener Platte. Occupation began at the site of LW8 in phase 1 of the local LBK sequence (see figure 7.4a). LW8 subsequently expanded and new settlements were founded adjacent to it, but the local carrying capacity was not reached until later (figure 7.5; see below). In the meantime, however, in phase 2 (as figure 7.4b indicates) other favorable, local microareas were already being settled. The founding settlements in particular areas remained the dominant ones. LW8, for example, was occupied throughout the approximately four hundred years of the local LBK sequence and was always the largest. Apart from its presumptively best location (from the farming point of view), it also seems to have been a redistribution center for lithic resources. These were obtained from a major source of high-quality, raw material some distance to the west, as a result of controlling exchange relations with local foragers beyond the agricultural frontier or through direct access to the source (Jeunesse 1997; Zimmermann 2002). Moreover, it was at LW8 that a ditched enclosure of possible ritual significance was constructed in the latest local phases of LBK occupation.

Over time, these local LBK societies seem to have become more unequal. The evidence for this comes from settlements and cemeteries. For the settlement evidence, the case was made by van der Velde (1990) on the basis of sites in the southeastern Netherlands and the Aldenhovener Platte, discussed above. LBK houses seem to be made up of three modules—northwest, central, and southeastern—with different

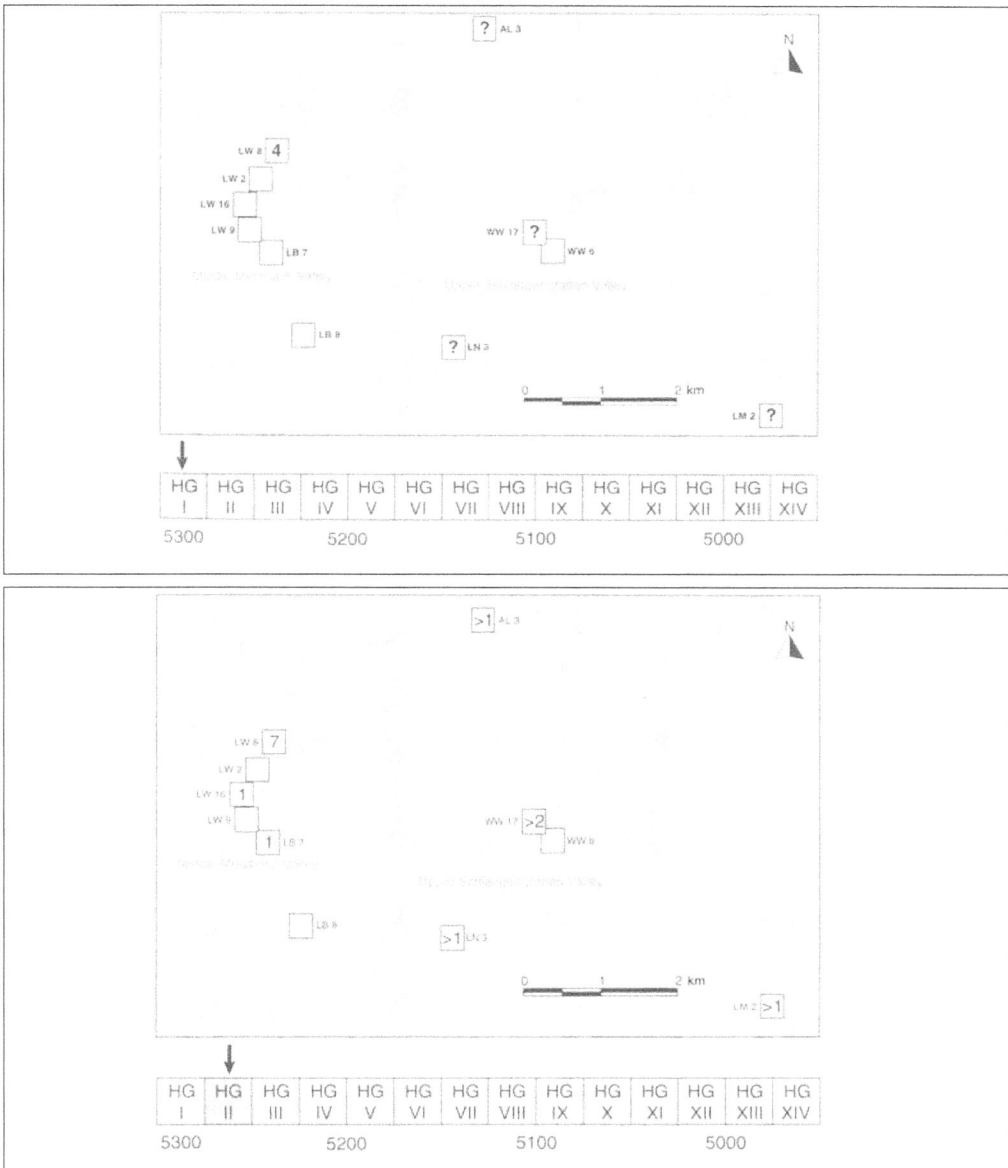

Figure 7.4. (top) Simplified soil map of the eastern Aldenhovener Platte, showing the first LBK house generation. At LW8, there are already four houses; the other major settlements perhaps begin a house generation earlier or later and are indicated by a question mark. The empty squares mark the location of later subsidiary settlements. (bottom) Same as 4a but showing the situation at house generation II. (Both from Zimmermann 2002)

functions. Some houses have only the central module; others, a central and northwest; and others still, all three modules. The southeastern, believed to be the front, is generally argued to have included a granary. Van der Velde (1990) proposes that the distinctions between houses with larger and smaller numbers of modules relate to the

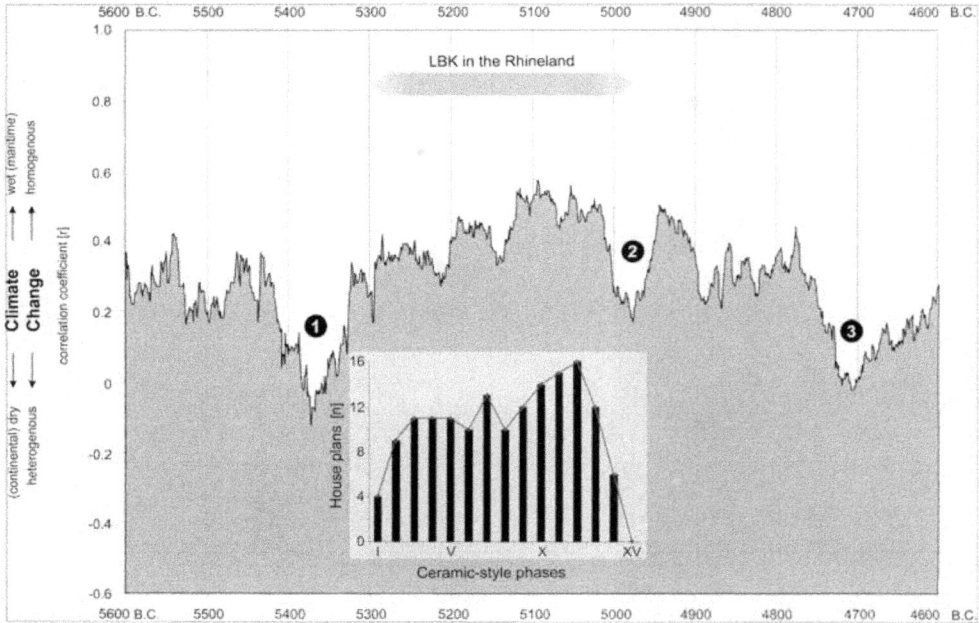

Figure 7.5. Reconstruction of variation in precipitation in western Europe between 5600 and 4600 cal. BC on the basis of an homogeneity analysis of oak tree-ring data. After a very dry phase at approximately 5360 BC (marked 1 on the figure), the following phases are wetter. After the third wet phase, there is another dry period (marked 2), which corresponds with the end of the LBK. There is another dry phase roughly 4700 BC. The histogram in the figure shows the chronological distribution of the LBK houses from the Merzbach Valley. The correspondence between the variations in precipitation and in the number of houses is striking (from Schmidt, Gruhle, and Rück 2004).

wealth and status of their associated households and cannot be explained by changing household composition arising from family life cycles or qualitatively different household compositions. At the Dutch sites, the houses with all three modules had more room than the others (the individual house elements were larger), and more stone adzes were associated with them. At the site of LW8, cereal-processing waste was preferentially associated with the large houses (Bogaard 2004). Elsewhere there is evidence of higher proportions of domestic animal bones associated with large houses and more remains of hunted animals associated with smaller ones (Hachem 2000).

On the basis of a spatial analysis of the settlements he studied, van der Velde (1990) also shows that the units of which the settlements were composed suggest the existence of long-term social patterns: particular households and groups of households seem to have continued through time, with continuing inheritance of status witnessed by the rebuilding of houses of the same type in the same places. Moreover, it seems that over time the proportional frequency of small houses increased, suggesting growing inequality. Coudart's (1998) analysis of LBK houses leads her to conclude that major rank or wealth differentiation did not exist, but she also points to some indications of status differences. She notes, for example (Coudart 1998), that granaries were never associated with small houses and that some buildings were more spacious than others. Interestingly, Coudart also suggests that perhaps the largest houses were associated with the groups that had first established the settlement.

Burial clearly displays complex patterns of spatial differentiation, because burials occur within settlements and also in separate cemeteries mainly of individual inhumations, which are very rare in the earliest LBK phases. Jeunesse (1997) concludes that the earliest ones present a picture of relatively egalitarian societies, with indications of achieved status for older men. The later ones tend to have a small group of graves, including child burials, clearly distinguished from the rest by the presence of markedly richer grave goods and possible symbols of power. This is the case, for example, in the cemetery of Niedermerz, which belonged to the settlements of the Merzbachtal on the Aldenhovener Platte.

The evidence for social differentiation, or the lack of it, has generally been discussed in terms of stage concepts from neo-evolutionary theory, for example, the existence of "big men" (Coudart 1998; van der Velde 1990). In my view, the key to understanding the patterns discerned in the settlements and cemeteries lies in the ideal despotic distribution discussed above. There it was invoked to account for the rapid spread of the LBK farming system and its bearers in a context of rapid population growth. It provided the basis for understanding why people would move on to new, unoccupied patches rather than accept inferior territories in areas that had already been occupied, even if those areas were not demographically "saturated." But the theory also explains the history of settlement within individual patches.

The first comers to favorable settlement microregions were able to settle in the best locations. Despite the high population-growth rate, competition did not exist among different groups because, as new households were formed, people were able to move to favorable locations elsewhere—indeed, this is what made the population growth possible. Relatively rapidly though, as the Merzbach evidence shows (see figure 7.5), the individual microregions began to fill up. This did not affect the suitability of the area for those who had already established themselves there, because success depended on having a territory and they controlled the best ones. Cemeteries would have come into existence for precisely the reasons proposed in the long-standing Saxe-Goldstein model: to represent an ancestral claim to territory in the face of increasing competition as local carrying capacities began to be reached. Indeed, just this argument has been used by van der Velde (1996) and Kneipp (1998; Zimmermann 2002) to account for the establishment of the Niedermerz 3 cemetery on the Aldenhovener Platte in the fifty-second century cal. BC.

What the limits on carrying capacity were is unclear. Zimmermann (2002) has argued that more than enough land would have been available for the small-scale, intensive garden agriculture that was most probably practiced (and likely implies some form of land ownership) (Bogaard 2004). But, Zimmermann points out, ensuring the availability of fodder for cattle would have required very large territories. As figure 7.5 shows, the evidence that a ceiling was reached is in the number of Merzbach houses. Supporting this is the recent suggestion (also shown in figure 7.5) that local climatic patterns affected the fluctuations in house totals after an initial ceiling had been reached (Schmidt, Gruhle, and Rück 2004). If confirmed, this would also point to the fragility of LBK subsistence at the limit.

Strontium isotope analyses (Bentley et al. 2002) suggest that in the early phases of the LBK there was fairly general mobility but that in the later phases mainly women moved. This would point to the emergence of patrilineal corporate groups. One can therefore postulate that, on one hand, over time the senior line of the lineage in a given microarea would have maintained control of the prime location and its territory, represented archaeologically by the larger houses in the settlements. The junior branches, on the other hand, would be in increasingly inferior positions and would have relatively little option to go elsewhere because the same process was going on everywhere around them, hence the increasing number of smaller houses noted by van der Velde (1990).

One can further speculate that after local microregions became full, contest competition among lineages would have become increasingly important, and members of the senior line would increasingly have had to assert their position in order to maintain it. The deposition of rich grave goods as a form of costly signaling (Bliege Bird and Smith 2005; Neiman 1997) would probably have played a role here. The number of rich burials would reflect not only the size of the senior lineage but also the competitive pressure it was under in particular places and times.

Whether the processes described above occurred throughout the LBK distribution is unclear, but they appear to have been prevalent in its western half, on the basis of the evidence and sources cited above. The reasons for their prevalence seem to be twofold. First, similar processes of demographic growth and local filling up would have been going on everywhere the LBK settled. Second, all these local societies ultimately had a common origin and therefore a very similar starting point in terms of social norms and institutions. This is very apparent in the material dimensions for which we have evidence. As noted already, the pottery of the earliest LBK is extremely uniform across a very large area, and the uniformity of the houses is equally striking. Subsequent to the initial colonization, however, LBK communities also had continual contact. This is evident not merely in lithic and other exchange networks (Zimmermann 1995) but also in innovations (for example, in pottery decoration) that are not entirely localized, but spread across large areas (for example, Strien 2000).

The Decline of the LBK

The emergence of local inequality in hereditary social and economic distinctions, based on priority of access to the best territories during the colonization process, is not the only widespread institutional trend observed in the course of the LBK. The appearance of an apparently ceremonial enclosure in the late phases of the founding settlement LW8, in the Merzbachtal, has already been mentioned, and it is not an isolated occurrence. The pattern of later occupation phases with ditched and/or palisade enclosures seems to characterize many settlements of the LBK farmers. The function of these late enclosures has inspired considerable discussion. In recent years, the finding of two massacre sites dated to local late LBK phases (Teschler-Nicola et al. 1999; Wahl and König 1987) has supported the idea of defense. But some enclosures certainly have ritual significance, an idea supported, for example, by evidence of special burial rituals (Orschiedt et al. 2003).

Kerig (2003) has suggested that the enclosures represent the emergence of a new type of social institution integrating larger numbers of people into a single social unit. Presumably, this would have been integrated with the patrilineal land-holding lineage system postulated above. The existence of institutions capable of bringing together large numbers of men for warfare, at least on a temporary basis, is suggested by the scale of both the Talheim and Asparn-Schletz massacres (Teschler-Nicola et al. 1999; Wahl and König 1987). In the former, the remains of thirty-four individuals were recovered, and in the latter, at least sixty-seven, even though not all the enclosure ditch was fully excavated. These figures imply very large numbers of attackers.

One possible analogy comes from Barth's description of the Faiwolmin group in New Guinea (Barth 1971; Soltis, Boyd, and Richerson 1995; see also Tuzin's [2001] description of an analogous situation with the New Guinea Abelam and Arapesh). Barth pointed out that the western Faiwolmin communities lived in nucleated villages centered on cult houses whereas populations in the east were dispersed. The centralized communities thus had a military advantage and, as a result, were able to expand towards the east, where the social system could not organize as many people for defense.

Whether the LBK enclosures were always defensive constructions is not really the point if one accepts that they represent a new kind of social institution involving larger-scale integration. In the light of the evidence for massacres, it can be suggested that with the emergence of institutions integrating larger numbers of people into a cooperating, competitively successful unit, other groups had little choice but to copy these if they wanted to avoid potentially disastrous consequences. The general context in which to see this is the reaching of local carrying capacities in many areas where LBK farmers had settled, as well as the apparent vulnerability of the farming system in these circumstances to climatic stresses such as those suggested by Schmidt, Gruhle, and Rück (2004). Everyone might have been better off, economically and reproductively, if this social innovation had not occurred, for it created a prisoner's dilemma situation in which the only viable response was to do the same. This probably led to the decline in overall regional population and carrying capacity seen in the archaeological record.

The emergence of enclosures is not the only indicator of change in the late LBK. Long-distance lithic exchange also declined. Through most of the LBK period, supplies of high-quality flint were obtained from special sources and exchanged very widely. In the latest phase, exchanged lithic raw material declined in frequency at settlement sites, and increasing proportions of the lithic assemblages were made of material from local sources of poorer quality. Relations between adjacent groups may have broken down so completely that long-distance exchanges, with material passing through many hands, became impossible. In other words, the decline was probably an unintended consequence of the new social institutions described above and the prisoner's dilemma that these produced.

Whatever the reasons, around 5000–4900 BC a widespread collapse of the LBK system clearly occurred, though not simultaneously in all areas. In at least some regions where the detailed work has been done, such as the Aldenhovener Platte, there was a general demographic collapse. This area was largely, if not entirely, abandoned for nearly one hundred years; when it was reoccupied, the settlement pattern was a much more nucleated one. New Middle Neolithic systems seem to have originated in limited areas of the existing LBK, and their spread seems to have involved, at least in part, recolonization processes and new demographic expansions, albeit on a much smaller scale than that which produced the LBK in the first place.

Conclusions

Complex evolutionary processes are at work in human populations, many of them with no parallel or little importance in nonhuman species. However, we can learn much about the mechanisms involved in the spread of farming into Europe, as well as their consequences, by starting from some very basic assumptions arising from the theory of natural selection. First, it is entirely predictable that people would take reproductive advantage of the opportunities for dispersal provided by the culturally (and physically) inherited cereals/pulses/domestic-animals package. In a subcontinent with favorable resource patches and very low existing population densities, these people would have absorbed existing populations as they went. In more detail, the ideal despotic distribution, a specific ecological implication of natural selection, provides a basis for understanding settlement and colonization decisions *and* for explaining their subsequent consequences in terms of the gradual emergence of social inequalities based on settlement priority and control of the best territories as population increased. In turn, costly signaling theory in a situation of contest competition for the best territories offers a framework for understanding the growing differentiation in grave goods and its apparently hereditary dimension, indicated by child graves with rich grave goods. Previous workers, such as van der Velde (1990), have made suggestions in a similar direction, from a neo-evolutionary perspective, but without placing these in the integrated theoretical framework offered by Darwinian theory. However, it seems unlikely that such widespread parallel development would have occurred in the LBK had it not been for the fact that the norms and institutions of local communities shared a recent common origin: the patterns identified here do not appear to be universal in the European early Neolithic.

The end is far less clear. It is still uncertain whether, and in which regions, the demise of the LBK and the beginning of the Middle Neolithic involved the collapse of local populations and subsequent recolonizations as opposed to the end of a cultural pattern and a set of institutions. In understanding these possible trajectories, we have yet to untangle, from an evolutionary perspective, the roles of entirely exogenous factors such as drought and of internal processes such as warfare, as well as their possible interactions, using the kinds of powerful concepts and models demonstrated in this chapter.

Acknowledgments

I would like to thank Tim Kohler and Sander van der Leeuw for the opportunity to attend the Santa Fe Institute workshop "Modeling Long-Term Culture Change," from which I learned a great deal; my colleagues and students at the AHRC Centre for the Evolutionary Analysis of Cultural Behavior for their continuing stimulus and the UK Arts and Humanities Research Council (AHRC) for making this possible; Stuart Brookes for doing the drawings at short notice; Andreas Zimmermann for the copy of his important 2002 paper; and Detlef Gronenborn and Joerg Petrasch for the opportunity to attend the conference "Die Neolithisierung Mitteleuropas."

Note

1. In the context of the extensive recent debates about the proportion of "Paleolithic" or "Neolithic" genes in present-day European populations, it is worth noting that recent simulations of the expansion of farming into Europe show that even very low rates of genetic interaction between hunter-gatherers and farmers, under the assumption of much higher population densities for farmers than hunter-gatherers, still produce a situation in which present-day European populations are largely characterized by genes of local Paleolithic ancestry (Currat and Excoffier 2005).

CHAPTER 8

Stylized Models to Analyze Robustness of Irrigation Systems

Marco A. Janssen and John M. Anderies

Irrigation systems are a prevalent feature in human history. They are archetypal examples of human efforts to control spatial and temporal environmental heterogeneity. In this chapter, we report on some preliminary results to understand the emergence, robustness, and collapse of irrigation systems, using a suite of stylized models. As a starting point, we perceive irrigation systems as similar to control systems in engineering. The "irrigation society" may usefully be thought of as a controller engineered to meet specific performance criteria defined by sustained, relatively constant food output, given both spatially and temporally variable water input. That is, the well-functioning irrigation society control system will get the right amount of water to the right place at the right time.

This, of course, is a nontrivial task. Flying a large jet on autopilot is a nontrivial task as well, yet modern feedback-control systems can do this quite well. Control engineers have devised highly effective control systems that perform well under a variety of conditions. Key issues faced by feedback control designers are noisy feedback from the system (either because the system has some random components or because the system's state cannot be perfectly known) and uncertainty about how the system actually works (model uncertainty). These conditions would certainly be characteristic of an irrigation system. How does one design a feedback (closed-loop) control system under such circumstances? This question is the subject of the field of robust control. It is in

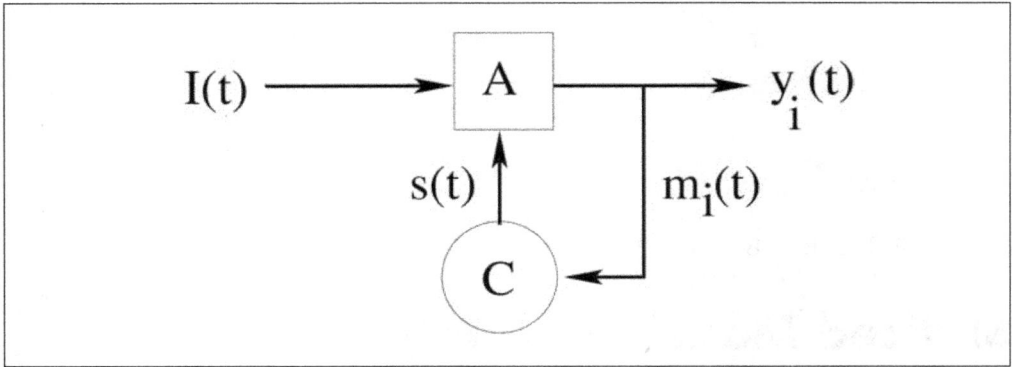

Figure 8.1. Schematic of a simple control system. Given outputs $y_i(t)$ at each location, i, and time, t, the controller, C, receives measurements, $m_i(t)$, and generates a signal, s(t), which it sends to the actuator, A, to adjust flows, given I(t).

this context that we are interested in the robustness of irrigation systems.

Although there is a nice analogy between irrigation societies and engineered control systems, they are different in several respects. These differences are what make the former so interesting.[1] To illustrate, consider the following task: given a known distribution of incoming water volume and an area of productive land, design the infrastructure to deliver water in a way that maximizes some performance index, most likely involving the amount of food produced, conditioned on some aspect of the cost of producing it. In the reasonably controlled environment characteristic of most engineering problems, this is a straightforward task. The infrastructure would comprise a series of pipes (perhaps open, as in canals), a series of valves (or head gates), and a set of flow monitors that are at key delivery points and feed back to the valves to control flow. The design problem is to produce the infrastructure that accomplishes the objective with the lowest capital cost (fewest values, minimal pipe size and length, and so forth) and lowest operation costs (least friction loss, simplest configuration, and so forth) and is not "too" sensitive to noise in measurement or in the water input data.

Two important issues for irrigation systems are not mentioned in the preceding paragraph. The first is the matter of scale. The description above assumes that the system to be controlled is small enough in scale that a single entity coordinates the signals arriving from flow monitors and controls the valves accordingly, as shown in figure 8.1.

Now consider that the scale of the problem is such that getting the measurements, $m_i(t)$, from each location, i, to the controller and subsequently propagating the signal, $s(t)$, to the actuators is difficult, simply because of the distances between entities. This is the problem faced by many irrigation systems. Next, consider the situation in which the controller, C, is not a single entity with control over the system, but rather a collection of individuals who must cooperate to generate accurate $m_i(t)$, agree on how to transform them into $s(t)$, and cooperate again to operate the actuator, based on the signals $s(t)$. This additional complexity emerges because the scale of the task at hand is too large for any single agent to achieve. So challenging is this task, it has been argued that its solution required the evolution of complex societies (Wittfogel 1957). That the "controller" of irrigation societies comprises a collection of independent agents who must coordinate their activities is what makes this problem so interesting.

When societies construct irrigation systems and become adapted to regular variability, based on past experience, this can lead to the development (or emergence of) specialized institutions. Such adaptations may generate highly optimized complex systems that are robust to a particular range of variability but may be fragile to changes of that variability (Carlson and Doyle 2002). We hypothesize that many long-term irrigation systems developed a highly optimized tolerance (HOT) to a particular set of conditions but then became vulnerable to qualitative shifts in those conditions (a regime change). A system becomes "robust yet fragile" because it can never be robust to each possible disturbance; Csete and Doyle (2002) refer to this as "conservation of fragility." As a result, whatever adaptation is made to the irrigation system, it will always be fragile to certain disturbances. Thus, becoming more robust to disturbances of type A might increase the fragility of the system to disturbances of type B.

In this chapter, we extend some ideas concerning robustness from control theory, based on systems like that in figure 8.1, to explore the robustness characteristics of irrigation systems. We do not apply results from control theory strictly but rather use them as a motivation to explore the robustness of systems, based on trading off one type of robustness for another. Certain characteristics of this trade-off can be characterized precisely (Bode 1945). For the systems we are interested in, we do not precisely characterize this trade-off but rather explore the vulnerability trade-offs between various types of organizational structures in irrigation systems. Compared with most other chapters in this volume, we use more stylized models for which we can more thoroughly explore the parameter space that characterizes the underlying assumptions on which the model is built. We think that the use of styled models complements more comprehensive models because the simpler models can be used to understand the consequences of specific assumptions and to identify the main drivers of observed phenomena.

Two areas in which vulnerabilities may enter the system shown in figure 8.1 are explored in this chapter. First is that the controller is composed of individual agents interacting in a social network to achieve a common, larger-scale goal. Differences in goals, information-processing abilities, and the usual problems associated with collective action can influence the ability of an artificial social-ecological network to function (in this case, generate accurate $m_i(t)$, produce $s(t)$, and enable A). We use a model based on the Bali irrigated rice agriculture and temple system to explore this question. The second area is related to the way in which the investment infrastructure required to generate the feedback controller pictured in figure 8.1 affects the range of options open to deal with external shocks. To explore this issue, we use a simple model motivated by the Hohokam experience in the American Southwest.

Network Density, Interacting Agents, and Irrigation Performance

In this section, we illustrate the consequences of various assumptions about decision rules for controllers—in our case, communities deciding when to plant rice—on the performance of a rice irrigation system. We show that different assumptions about decision making have different sensitivities to a change in the density of pest-related connections among the communities. We use the Lansing-Kremer model of a Bali irrigation system, reimplemented in Java (Janssen in press), as an arena for our analysis (Lansing and Kremer 1993). The Lansing-Kremer model describes water flows and rice terrace ecology along two rivers in south-central Bali (Lansing 1991; Lansing and Kremer 1993).[2] Rainfall and the water from the volcanic lake provide water, allocated by twelve dams, for 172 *subaks* (collections of farmers). The runoff between dams is formulated as the difference between supply (runoff of dams from higher elevation and rainfall) and demand from the subaks related to each dam. When subaks ask for more water than is available, all subaks receive the same reduction of water supply, and the fraction of demand that is met depends linearly on a measure of water stress on the crops in these subaks. The time step of the model is one month.

A subak's water demand depends on rice variety and area planted. Each rice variety has a maturation time after which it yields a harvest per hectare, calculated by multiplying the rice variety's specific potential yield by the accumulated water stress. If a rice variety takes three months to grow and had water shortages of 0, 10, and 50 percent during each month, respectively, then the water stress is

$$\left(\frac{1+9/10+5/10}{3}\right)$$

which is equal to .8. Therefore, the harvest is 20 percent lower than the maximum potential yield.

The harvest can also be reduced by pest outbreaks. Each subak has a pest density, p, that changes because of migration and local growth. The direction and magnitude of pest migration depend on the gradient in concentrations between a subak and each of its neighbors.

For diffusion of pests, up to four adjacent neighbors are defined for each of the 172 subaks. Furthermore, for each subak, the source dam that provides the water is given, as well as the return dam for water that is not used. The source dam and return dam can be the same. Finally, seasonal rainfall patterns are known for each subak.

Local Control and Macro-level Patterns

Lansing and Kremer (1993) performed exercises in which they allowed subaks to imitate the cropping pattern from the neighbor with the highest production. We looked at two alternative models of agent decision making and illustrate here the implications of various strategies and changes in network structure on system performance. We can analyze the decision-making process of subaks from a control perspective (figure 8.2).

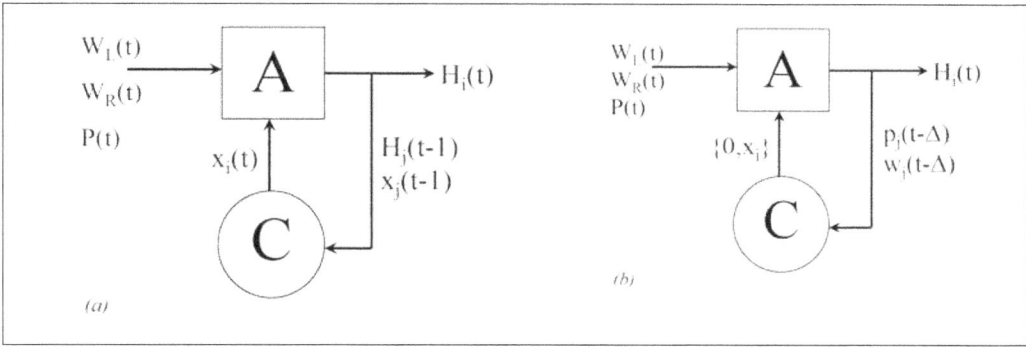

Figure 8.2. Schematic of subak decision making from a control system perspective: (a) the imitative subak and (b) the adaptive subak.

The input to the system, a subak, is water from the lake, $W_L(t)$; water from rainfall, $W_R(t)$; and pests from neighboring subaks, $P(t)$. An imitative subak derives information about cropping patterns, $x(t–1)$, and harvest, $H(t–1)$, of other neighboring subaks from the preceding year. The controller, C, makes a decision on the cropping pattern, x, for time, t. The adaptive subak updates each month and derives information on pests, p, and water availability, w, from the preceding month, $(t – \Delta t)$, of the neighboring subaks. In case a subak had no crop on its land, the controller decides whether to start planting rice, $\{0, x\}$. We describe the decision rules in more detail below.

Imitative Subaks.

The first type of agent is similar to the Lansing-Kremer model, but instead of defining a limited set of neighbors, we assume that subaks had access to the cropping patterns of all other subaks. We defined networks for water and pest dispersal and calculated the minimum number of connections it takes for each node to connect to the other nodes in the network. The network for water includes both dams and subaks as nodes. We assume that subaks that are more distant are less likely to be imitated. Differences of harvest between distant subaks are less influential on changing cropping patterns than differences between closely connected subaks. The harvest of a distant subak has to be significantly higher before that cropping pattern is imitated. This results in the decision rule of when to imitate a cropping pattern shown in equation 1. A cropping pattern in subak j will be considered for imitation by subak i if

$$H_i < \frac{Hj}{1 + MIN\{\gamma_p \cdot \chi_p^2, \gamma_w \cdot \chi_w^2\}} \qquad \text{Eq. 1}$$

with sensitivity parameters, γ_p and γ_w, and the number of connections separating two subaks via pest dispersal links, γ_p, and water flow links, γ_w. From all the subaks meeting this condition, the subak with the highest harvest per hectare will be imitated. If no subak meets this condition, then the existing cropping pattern of the subak itself is repeated.

Starting with randomly distributed cropping patterns, subaks update their cropping patterns each year. Subak *i* compares the derived harvest per hectare with every other subak *j* but updates the cropping pattern only when the condition in equation 1 is met. This means that subaks take care of adjusting inequalities with their neighbors but generally do not change their cropping patterns when distant subaks perform better. This is a more general, but similar, implementation of imitating neighbors than worked out by Lansing and Kremer, who assume a fixed set of neighbors. We also assume that there is opportunity for experimentation. When a subak *i* performs worse than the average harvest per hectare within the watershed, it is assumed that there is a probability γ that the cropping pattern will be changed to a random configuration.

We assume that agents are able to learn and adapt their strategies by changing the values of γ_p and γ_w. Each year, agents update their values by comparing these with their direct neighbors. Neighbors with high harvest will have more impact on changing the values by using the equation

$$\gamma_i = \sum_{j \in N} \frac{\gamma_j \cdot e^{\mu \cdot H_j}}{\sum_{k \in N} e^{\mu \cdot H_k}}$$

where γ is a parameter that values the sensitivity of updating γ to value differences between the harvest values among the neighbors.

Adaptive Subaks.

An alternative, plausible way subaks can make decisions on cropping patterns is to make decisions during the year about whether to leave a field fallow or to plant a crop. We assume that a subak makes this decision based on the availability of water and dispersal of pests. A crop needs 150 cubic m/day of water per hectare. If water availability is expected to be above a certain threshold, m_w, then the subak may expect to have sufficient water to make planting crops worthwhile if the pest biomass per hectare among the neighbors and within the subak is, on average, below m_p. Similar to imitative subaks, adaptive subaks update their threshold values m_p and m_w in line with their best-performing neighbors.

The Effect of Changed Network Structures

For both the imitative subaks and the adaptive subaks, we explored the consequences if the neighbors with whom they are connected by pest dispersal change. In the default network are 161 connections among the subaks that disperse pests. We define probability p_e as the probability that an existing connection is deleted. Furthermore, we define probability p_n as the probability that a new connection is created. New connections are created between subaks who share a source and/or a return dam and are assumed to be geographically in the same neighborhood.

For each experiment, we run the irrigation for one hundred years one hundred times and calculate average harvest per hectare during the last fifty years of the simulation. When p_e and p_n are equal to zero, the harvest for the original network is calculated. The resulting harvest is similar to the value we derive when optimizing the thresholds γ_w and γ_p or m_p and m_w, indicating that the agents are learning to find high-performance threshold values. In plates 17 and 18, we see that the average harvest per hectare is sensitive to varying the probabilities. For the imitative subaks, the harvest decreases when links are added that can disperse pests. With more of those links, the subaks will synchronize on a larger scale, leading to water shortages. Decreasing the number of links that disperse pests does not affect the average performance of the subaks. The results for the adaptive subaks are different (plate 18). Adaptive subaks are not as sensitive to adding links that disperse pests. They are able to find suitable threshold values m_w and m_p to adjust for high connectivity; however, they are sensitive to adding additional connections. When the number of connections declines, the performance of adaptive subaks increases significantly. Note that the effects of adding and removing links is linear only to adding or only to removing links, which suggests that the effects are sensitive to density and not to topology of the network.

When we calculate the average harvest per hectare as a function of the original density of the pest-related network within the Bali irrigation network, we see that the imitative subak leads to the highest performance of the original network but is outperformed by the adaptive subaks (figure 8.3). There is no systematic understanding of how the real subaks make their decisions. Their decision-making processes are almost certainly much more comprehensive than those of our simple agents. Nevertheless, with regard to highly optimized tolerance, we argue that imitative agents are only suitable for a very particular density of pest networks. The results of Lansing-Kremer (1993) show that the use of imitative subaks is a simple solution to generate cropping patterns as observed. Our results show that this might be an artifact of the particular ecological system.

Irrigation Infrastructure, Short-term Robustness, and Long-term Fragility

In the preceding section, our focus is on the nature of the controller as represented by a network of subaks. The measure of the controller's effectiveness is harvest per hectare of a subak. In this section, we look at the problem of irrigation from a slightly different perspective. In many situations, the system being controlled actually comprises more than one subsystem. The actual control of the system then involves decisions about how to combine varying outputs from subsystems to meet an overall objective. In this case, social-ecological systems face two issues: not only the issue associated with controlling a system via a network of individuals, but also the problem of shifting

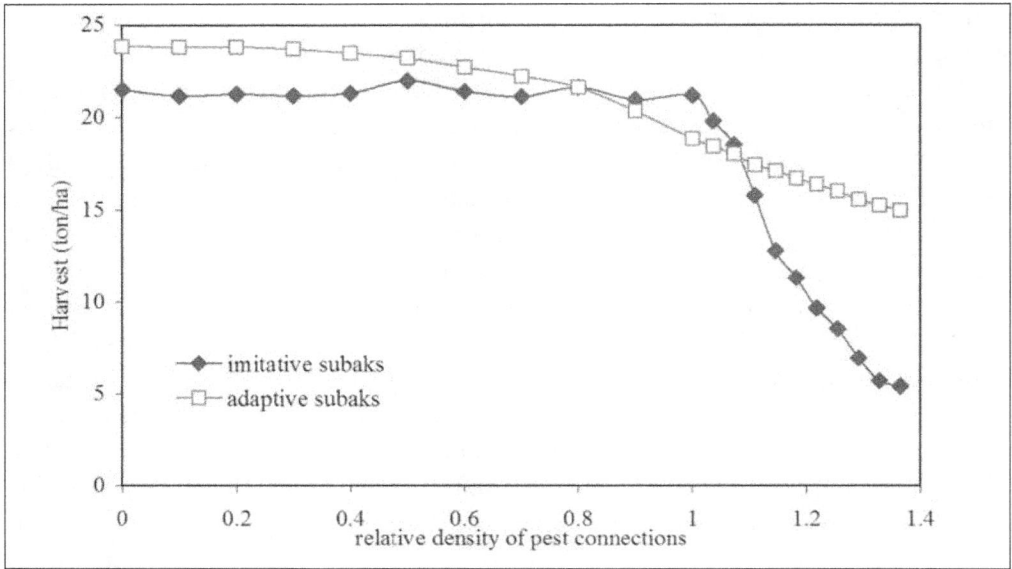

Figure 8.3. Average harvest per subak (per ha) as a function of the relation to the original pest network density (original density is equal to 1).

vulnerabilities associated with shifting emphasis from one resource type to another. Here we focus on this latter issue.

A common example of balancing a multiple resource system composed of elements with different risk characteristics is portfolio management in finance. In this case, productive resources are financial investments such as equities, options, and bonds. The problem is to design an optimal portfolio (proportion of each type of investment owned) at each time over a planning horizon, based on past performance of each investment (except in the case of options). Another example is a society that relies on a combination of irrigated agriculture and hunting and gathering of wild resources. In terms of risk, irrigated agriculture might be thought of as a bond. The yield of the irrigation-system capital stock (land, canals, and institutions) is agricultural output. The yield is less variable than the alternative of hunting and gathering, but when measured per unit of labor input, the yield is comparatively low. The high-yield activity of hunting and gathering is more subject to environmental fluctuations and is thus more variable. What is the best allocation of labor to irrigated agriculture and to hunting and gathering?

Obviously, societies typically do not make optimal investment decisions, and the time frames of interest are typically much longer than those in decision analysis problems. Nonetheless, ideas from portfolio management can provide important insights if applied in a broader context. For example, thinking in terms of asset management, we can ask the question of how the risks change as the asset mix between wild (hunting and gathering) and highly managed (irrigated agriculture) changes over time. Our focus is how the changing risk may feed back into the system and influence the co-evolution of the social-ecological system.

Motivation: The Hohokam Cultural Sequence

The model developed below is based on the archaeological record from the American Southwest, specifically the Hohokam cultural sequence. The model is not intended to capture specific characteristics of the Hohokam experience but rather attempts to capture key structuring processes most likely at play. As such, the model could be equally well applied to any situation characterized by the use of wild and irrigated resources.

The context for the Hohokam cultural sequence is extremely rich and detailed, filling the pages of books (for example, Abbott 2003) and articles (for example, Bayman 2001). Only a very rough outline of major events is presented here, based on these sources and personal communication with archaeologists specializing in the American Southwest. The Hohokam occupied Arizona and northern Mexico from around AD 1 to 1450. Table 8.1 summarizes the key periods and events. This chronology tells of the expansion of irrigated agriculture and the development of pottery production, along with a regional trading system in exotic items associated with ball court settlements. Early in the sequence (the Pioneer period), houses were built in pits, settlements were small and dispersed, and populations probably relied most heavily on wild resources. During the Colonial period that followed, the archaeological record reflects a time of continued expansion, but with elements of the solidification of Hohokam culture as a regional system. Ball courts appear, possibly signifying the increased formalization of a regional trading network. More stable settlement patterns emerge in the form of courtyard groups. This period was probably associated with the continued heavy reliance on wild resources at a larger spatial scale, as evidenced by the regional trading networks. However, reliance on irrigated agriculture was probably also intensifying, and there may have been extensive trade between the wild and irrigated resource sectors.

During the subsequent Sedentary period, major aspects of Hohokam culture remain stable yet expand in scale, as evidenced by what was perhaps the mass production of pottery for an expanding, regional trading network associated with the ball court system. The signatures of this period give a sense of success; the culture enjoyed material abundance and ideological expansion. The areal extent of this cultural signature, which probably reached its maximum during the Sedentary period, covered approximately a third of present-day Arizona. Within the core area in the Phoenix Basin, an impressive irrigation infrastructure developed. However, this period of relative stability and success gave way to the period termed the "Classic," which saw "unprecedented changes in patterns of settlement, technology, material culture, and ideology" (Bayman 2001:281).

The abandonment of the ball court system and a contraction of the regional system marked this change. Platform mounds replaced ball courts, and aboveground residential areas with compound walls replaced the open-courtyard pithouse settlements. Community centers became more nucleated. Later in the Classic period, the platform mounds were walled off. Finally, toward the end of the Classic, just before the Hohokam cultural collapse, massive structures now called "great houses" were built.

Table 8.1 Summary of the Hohokam Cultural Sequence

Period	General Characteristics
Classic (AD 1150–1450)	Aboveground residential areas with compound walls emerge. Hohokam interaction outside Gila-Salt river valleys declines as the overall regional system shrinks. Rectangular platform mounds with compound walls dominate villages. Ball court system is abandoned. Platform mounds have similar spacing to ball courts, but community centers become more nucleated. Highly stylized crafts associated with ancestor worship disappear. Population declines, and Hohokam culture collapses around AD 1450.
Sedentary (AD 900–1150)	Expansion from the Colonial period continues. Mass production of pottery. Use of ball courts continues. Maximum extent of regional system reached.
Colonial (AD 750–900)	Period of expansion. First ball courts appear, and increased trade in exotic items is evident. Artistic florescence, accompanied by elaborate cremation rituals. Colonial Courtyard groups with shared ovens emerge. Ball court system expands, related to regional exchange networks.
Pioneer (AD 1–750)	Irrigation system begins to develop; first canals built. Bow and arrow begins to be used in the Southwest. Irrigation systems continue to expand, and large canal systems appear on the north and south sides of the Salt River.
1500 BC–AD 1	Hunter-gatherers with limited agriculture. Small pithouse settlements and seasonally occupied hamlets were typical.

This historical progression can be seen as a shift in resource portfolio from one dominated by an extensive, highly productive (per unit of labor) but highly variable resource to one dominated by a less productive (labor-intensive) resource. As the resource portfolio shifted, the system became exposed to different risks. In terms of the schematic shown in figure 8.1, the system can be pictured as a control system with two subsystems and two controllers (figure 8.4). The objective of the controller is to produce a sufficient food supply with minimum effort, given environmental variation.

The top subsystem consists of uncultivated land and a small amount of land in riparian areas cultivated with flood irrigation—that is, with little built infrastructure.

On the left, the various vulnerabilities associated with each resource base are listed. Food output from wild resources is vulnerable to local drought. Food output from riparian agriculture is less susceptible to drought but more susceptible to flooding. Food output based on a portfolio composed of these two resources would be robust to short-term fluctuations in rainfall. This robustness is due to their being "orthogonal" in risk space—that is, they are robust against types of shocks that typically do not occur simultaneously. The bottom system—irrigated agriculture—is very robust against short-term fluctuations but is vulnerable to infrequent, large floods. Furthermore, the irrigation system becomes vulnerable to new types of internal shocks associated with the collective action required to maintain infrastructure.

The shift to irrigated agriculture from a portfolio dominated by wild resources and small-scale riparian agriculture is related not only to managing environmental risks but also to population growth. Success of the top system in figure 8.4 may generate population growth and, with it, a rise in food demand. As food demand surpasses the maximum possible return from wild resources and riparian agriculture, intensification of production is required, and movement to irrigated agriculture becomes necessary. The Hohokam cultural sequence can be mapped onto this asset reallocation process. The pre-Pioneer period is characterized mainly by wild resource use. The Pioneer period probably saw a gradual increase in riparian agriculture. Toward the end of this period, some irrigated agriculture began to augment the wild resource/riparian agriculture portfolio. The Colonial period, with the expansion of the ball court system, probably saw an increase in the areal extent of the wild resource base, with concentration and intensification of riparian and irrigated agriculture in the most suitable areas. The ball court system may have played an important role in mediating the exchange of outputs from the various resource types as they became more spatially distinct.

Throughout this period, food production from both agriculture and wild resources may have increased, with a slow shift in dominance toward irrigation. It seems that in the Sedentary period the maximal extent of food production from wild resources may have been reached, so the use of both types of resources was no longer expanding. Thus, intensification of irrigated agriculture increased at the expense of wild resource use. Crossing this threshold may have induced some of the social changes seen in the archaeological record—that is, the shift from the extensive ball court system to the intensive platform mound system in the Colonial period.

This shift in the resource portfolio, driven by population growth, changed the risks faced by the Hohokam. It is now clear why this situation is different from optimal portfolio management. The Hohokam did not optimally manage output from different resource classes. Rather, at each point in time they responded to a wide range of pressures that forced them into a certain development trajectory. Along this trajectory, vulnerabilities changed. An interesting question to explore is whether and how these shifting vulnerabilities may have played a role in the Hohokam cultural collapse. The model in the next section focuses on this question.

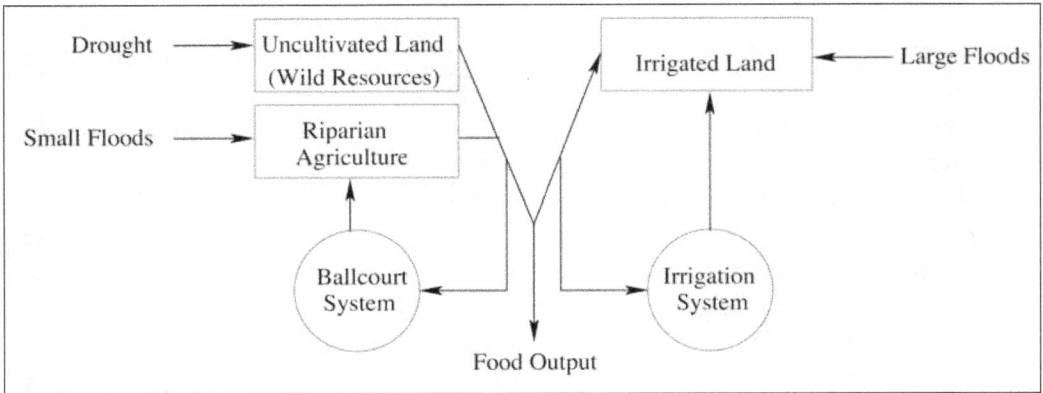

Figure 8.4. Control system consisting of three resource types (see text for explanation).

A Simple Model of Extensive and Intensive Food Production

This model, a formal representation of the system shown in figure 8.4, is motivated by several simple, representative, agent bioeconomic models of renewable resource use (Anderies 1998, 2003; Brander and Taylor 1998; Janssen and Scheffer 2004). We do not make a sharp distinction between riparian and irrigated agriculture but instead represent them on a continuum from low to high physical-infrastructure systems. Thus, we have two resource types: extensive (type 1) and intensive (type 2). The resources naturally self-regenerate and are degraded by exploitation. For the extensive resource, this regeneration is in terms of biomass that can be harvested, as in fishery models (Clark 1990). For the intensive resource, the regeneration is in terms of soil fertility—that is, soil microorganisms generate nutrients for plant uptake over time (Anderies 1998, 2003).

The society utilizes these resources to produce two types of output: protein-rich (type 1) and carbohydrate-rich (type 2). Both types of output can be produced from both resource types. The wild resource base, however, has potentially higher productivity of type 1 resources, whereas irrigated agriculture has potentially higher productivity of type 2 resources. To model the society's choices regarding the mix of resources to produce, we assume that it attempts to meet its basic needs with as little labor as possible. This is equivalent to assuming that individuals prefer leisure to additional food when their basic needs are being met. Note that "basic needs" are not equivalent to subsistence needs: what an individual defines as basic needs may be well above subsistence, including food for gifts, rituals, and so forth.

The simplest mathematical representation for this system comprises a description of the resource bases' dynamics over time, as well as the allocation of labor to gathering wild resources and conducting irrigated agriculture. The former is given by two differential equations:

$$\frac{dx_1}{dt} = r_1(R)(1-x_1) - \alpha_{11}Y_{11} - \alpha_{12}Y_{12} \qquad \text{Eq. 2}$$

$$\frac{dx_2}{dt} = r_2(S)(1-x_2) - \alpha_{21}Y_{21} - \alpha_{22}Y_{22} \qquad \text{Eq. 3}$$

where $r_1(R)$ is the intrinsic regeneration rate of the wild resource stock, x_1, which depends on rainfall, R. When left alone, the wild resource will increase to its maximum level (which has been rescaled to 1). Y_{ij} is the quantity of output of type j from resource i, and α_{ij} is the impact of producing output type j from resource type i. The regeneration rate of irrigated agricultural soil productivity, x_2, depends on the stream flow, S. For this analysis, aimed at characterizing the possible dynamics, we assume "average" conditions—that is, R and S are constant, so r_1 and r_2 are constant.

For clarity and simplicity, we assume a linear production structure. Note that lower- and uppercase letters represent per capita and total quantities, respectively ($Y_{11} = hy_{11}$, where h is the total population size). Thus, $y_{1j} = A_{1j}x_1l_{1j}$, where l_{1j} is the labor devoted to harvesting output of type j from resource 1 by a single representative agent. This is a simple mass-action production function commonly used in natural resource economics (Clark 1990). Similarly, $y_{2j} = A_{2j}x_2l_2K$. We do not make a distinction between labor directed at producing different types of output from resource 2—these come in a fixed ratio determined by A_{2j}. Output from irrigated agricultural activity depends not only on labor but also on capital, K. We refrain from defining this stock of capital precisely at this moment, but it certainly includes irrigation infrastructure. Given these definitions, each individual (all identical) chooses l_{ij} to meet her needs and minimize her total labor. This problem can be stated as follows:

$$\text{Min } l_{11} + l_{12} + l_2 \qquad \text{Eq. 4}$$

Subject to

$$y_{11} + y_{21} \geq y_{1min} \qquad \text{Eq. 5}$$
$$y_{12} + y_{22} \geq y_{2min} \qquad \text{Eq. 6}$$
$$l_{11} + l_{12} + l_2 \geq l_{max} \qquad \text{Eq. 7}$$

where y_{imin} is the minimum requirement for each resource type. Because the objective is to minimize labor in meeting basic requirements, equations 5 and 6 become equalities, and by rescaling, the right-hand sides can be replaced with 1s. The solution to this optimization problem yields the following rule: Define

$$\overline{l}_2 = \min\{1/A_{21}x_2K, \ 1/A_{22}x_2K\}.$$

Then, if

$$1 - \frac{x_2 K}{x_1} \left(\frac{A_{21}}{A_{11}} + \frac{A_{22}}{A_{12}} \right) > 0 \qquad\qquad \text{Eq. 8}$$

then $l_2 = 0$. Otherwise, $l_2 = \bar{l}_2$. When l_2 is known, y_2 can be computed, and y_{11} and y_{12} can be computed from equations 5 and 6. When these are known, multiplying each y_{ij} by the total population size, h, yields Y_{ij}, which determines the ecological dynamics via equations 2 and 3.

Several points emerge from this simple model. First, equation 8 makes the conditions favoring a switch to irrigated agriculture clear: as the left side of equation 7 becomes negative, $l_2 = \bar{l}_2 \neq 0$ so that society devotes some labor to irrigation. This becomes more likely as K increases (obviously), because the wild resource becomes degraded relative to irrigated agriculture (the ratio x_2 / x_1 increases) or the productivity of labor in irrigation is higher than that of labor devoted to wild resources. Condition 8 is sensible and intuitive. What is not intuitive and requires further analysis is the effect of population and capital stocks on the system dynamics. Simple phase-plane analysis illustrates the point (figure 8.5).

Conceptually, the model provides a preliminary mathematical formalization of the relationships among capitalization, population, shifts in resource utilization (wild resource versus irrigated crops), and associated changes in the loci of critical vulnerability (rainfall versus stream flow versus capital stocks). Here we treat population and capital stocks as parameters and explore their effect on resource use decisions. When population density is zero, the dynamical system (equations 2–8) exhibits a single stable equilibrium such that, given any initial condition, the system will move to pristine conditions of full soil fertility and high levels of wild resource biomass (the basin of attraction is the entire light gray region in figure 8.5a). Because any initial condition will return to the steady state, the system is very robust to external perturbations (resets system to new initial condition) that may reduce wild resource biomass. Figure 8.5a characterizes the Hohokam in the pre-Pioneer and early Pioneer periods.

A second stable attractor emerges (the solid circle in the dark gray region of figure 8.5b) when a critical population size is reached. These two new attractors correspond to a situation in which either the wild resource base is in good condition and able to support the population (the light gray region) or the wild resource base has become degraded and the society has introduced irrigated agriculture to complement the wild resource. Equation 8 shows that the threshold between these basins of attraction depends on the amount of investment in agricultural infrastructure (for example, canals) and the relative productivities of the two resources. There is the interesting possibility that the society may move between states. In the steady state in the light gray region (figure 8.5b), wild resources dominate the society's resource portfolio, and irrigation plays a small role. For stable population levels, the only way the system could be moved to the equilibrium in the dark gray region is by a drought (for example, wild resource biomass is reduced from .6 to .3). Only in severe drought conditions

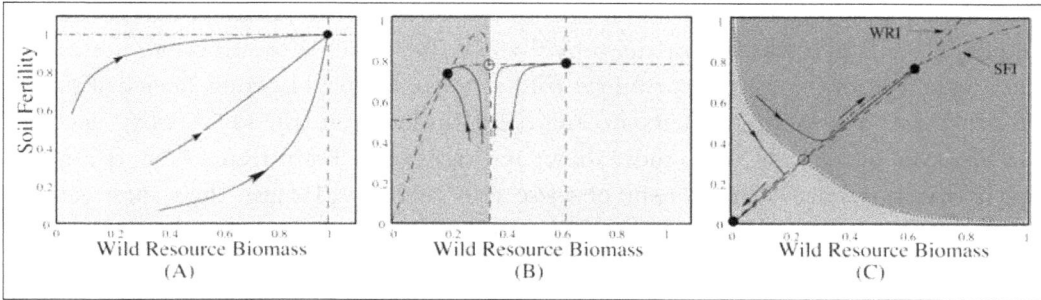

Figure 8.5. Phase plane analysis of the Hohokam subsistence agriculture model presented in equations 2–8. The curves with arrows show possible trajectories for various initial conditions. The arrows show the direction of flow over time. The population increases from (A) to (C).

does it pay for this society to move into more intensive irrigation. Note that the decision to intensify irrigation locks this society into the degraded wild-resource state. Now a large perturbation (that is, a very wet phase that increases wild resource biomass from the equilibrium level of around .2 to .33) is required to push the system back into the alternate basin of attraction. In this way, the longer-term effects of social responses to immediate problems limit future options. This dynamic may characterize patterns of Hohokam development in the Colonial and early Sedentary periods. It is interesting to speculate whether an exceptionally dry period was associated with the shift away from the ball court system to the irrigation system.

As the population increases, the relative size of the wild resource basin shrinks (that is, the boundary moves to the right) (figure 8.5b, light gray), reducing the size of a perturbation (for example, drought) required to push the system from reliance on wild resources into the irrigation basin (figure 8.5b, darker gray). This illustrates how increasing population makes the system more vulnerable to ever-smaller drought events. Moreover, higher population decreases the likelihood that the system will return to the wild resource state after it is in the irrigation basin. At even higher population and capitalization levels, the wild resource basin vanishes (figure 8.5c), and two different basins emerge, including an undesirable one (lighter gray) in which the society cannot sustainably meet its minimum needs. The dynamics illustrated in figure 8.5c are fundamentally different than in figures 8.5a and 8.5b. In figures 8.5a and 8.5b, the stable equilibria are always positive—that is, neither resource base is destroyed, and the society can always meet its basic needs. In figure 8.5c, one equilibrium is positive (in the dark gray region), and the other is at zero. When the state enters the basin of attraction corresponding to the zero equilibrium, the resource base will inevitably be destroyed, and the human population reduced. Furthermore, the social response of additional intensification cannot correct this problem, and new vulnerabilities emerge, as described below.

Increasing population and capital stocks causes the boundary between basins to move away from the origin, decreasing the distance between the undesirable basin and the desirable attractor (the black dots in figure 8.5). In this situation, all else being equal, a small perturbation in the capital stock (for example, destruction of a canal headgate) causes the dashed curve (the wild-resource biomass isocline labeled *WRI* in figure 8.5c) to move up and leftward and the dash-dot curve (the soil fertility isocline labeled *SFI* in figure 8.5c) to move down and rightward. From figure 8.5c, it can be seen that this relative movement of these two curves will cause their intersection points (the open and solid circles) to move closer together. Eventually, the two curves will no longer intersect, and the desirable basin will vanish. This situation, depicted in figure 8.5c, may correspond to events during the Hohokam Classic period.

The Dynamic Interplay between Social Change and Shifting Vulnerabilities

The simple model and analysis presented here provide a caricature of the leapfrog process of shifting vulnerability and social change. A society's success (in feeding itself) may cause it to move from figure 8.5a to 8.5b. In so doing, it becomes more vulnerable to droughts. If a sufficiently large drought occurs, then the society must respond by intensification (move from light to dark gray regions in figure 8.5b). If society does reorganize around the new irrigation equilibrium, then it becomes more robust to drought (the system will always return to the equilibrium if perturbed to the left of the equilibrium point in the dark gray region of figure 8.5b). However, as the notion of "conservation of fragility" suggests, the society has traded off one kind of vulnerability for another. Worse yet, the movement from the high wild-resource, low intensive-irrigation equilibrium (in the light gray region of figure 8.5b) to the low wild-resource, high intensive-irrigation equilibrium (in the dark gray region of figure 8.5b) is difficult to reverse and becomes more so as population increases. Put another way, the society typically has no option of doing intensive irrigation for a while until things get better and it can return to an easier lifestyle. Finally, again because of its success in coping with vulnerability, society moves from figure 8.5b to 8.5c. Now the situation is more unforgiving, and the system becomes vulnerable to any shock that reduces the capital stock (flood, social unrest, and the like). The process is one of social change in response to particular vulnerabilities, leading to new vulnerabilities, leading to further social change, and all the while leading to fewer and fewer options for society.

Discussion

Irrespective of the efforts to increase the robustness of an irrigation system, fragility always remains in the system. Because of the temporal and spatial heterogeneity of disturbances, adaptation to some disturbances may make the system more vulnerable to others. Our Hohokam analysis shows that an increasing population invests in irrigation systems to feed itself. However, this makes the system more vulnerable to large floods that destroy the infrastructure. Although irrigation systems lead to a higher production by controlling high-frequency variability such as small droughts and floods, they cannot rapidly recover from a low-frequency, high-impact perturbation. In the Bali case study, we saw that different assumptions on decision making of the subaks lead to different vulnerabilities. Although imitation of best-performing neighbors maximizes production in the original pest-related network, it does not do so when the density of the links changes. In some sense, the system performance is enhanced by particular behavior in a given network but becomes vulnerable to changes in the network.

The results reported in this study are initial results of a longer-term effort to develop computational models capable of simulating the evolution of irrigation systems. How do various assumptions affect the structure of the network? How do robust irrigation systems emerge? Do irrigation systems evolve to a HOT situation, being robust for high-frequency events but not for low-frequency events? In the longer term, we aim to "grow" irrigation systems and understand which assumptions about human behavior, institutions, ecology, and biophysical structure affect a system's development and, in turn, its robustness.

Acknowledgments

This research was funded by National Science Foundation grants BCS-0601320 and BCS-0527744.

Notes

1. Feedback control systems are used for real-time irrigation and drainage-canal control (Malaterre, Rogers, and Schuurmans 1998; Reddy and Jacquot 1999). However, we do not include these modern feedback systems in our analysis but focus solely on feedback control as a broad class of decisions irrigators had to make to control their irrigation systems.

2. For a visual representation of the Bali irrigation system, see Steve Lansing's homepage: http://www.ic.arizona.edu/~lansing/home.htm.

CHAPTER 9

Modeling Settlement Systems in a Dynamic Environment
Case Studies from Mesopotamia

Tony J. Wilkinson, McGuire Gibson,

John H. Christiansen, Magnus Widell, David Schloen,

Nicholas Kouchoukos, Christopher Woods,

John Sanders, Kathy-Lee Simunich, Mark Altaweel,

Jason A. Ur, Carrie Hritz, Jacob Lauinger,

Tate Paulette, and Jonathan Tenney

The development of early states and civilizations continues to occupy the attention of archaeologists and anthropologists. Despite the use of words like *complexity*, few have made real progress in dealing with the full range of variables involved in the development of complex societies. One trend recently observed is a shift away from the testing of explanatory models of the early state and towards an emphasis on "state dynamics," in other words, how these states actually functioned (Stein 2001:355). If early state societies were truly complex, then it is necessary to tackle the full range of complexity that exists. To do this with any degree of analytical rigor, we must build up large, complex models that incorporate a wide array of data sources and incorporate a range of interacting processes: social, economic, environmental, and political. Here we outline the early results of a program employing techniques of agent-based modeling to model the early stages of state-level society in the Near East.

Fundamental questions being addressed include (1) how and why did third- and fourth-millennium-BC cities of southern Mesopotamia grow to a greater size and complexity than those in the rain-fed north? (2) what was the dynamic trajectory of such settlements through time? and (3) how did the resultant cities respond to a capricious natural environment, and were they able to grow, survive, or decline under a range of social, environmental, and economic stresses?

In an article published in 2001, Guillermo Algaze argued that "the primacy of southern Mesopotamia was in part due to the fact that southern societies had several important material advantages over polities in neighboring areas." The factors contributing to this so-called Mesopotamian Advantage were a denser and more varied concentration of exploitable subsistence resources, higher and more reliable agricultural yields, and a more efficient distribution system based on water transport. Algaze (2001:200) suggested that "these advantages promoted the creation of inherently asymmetrical exchange patterns among independent polities in the Mesopotamian alluvium and between those polities and societies in neighboring regions which, over time, produced important organizational asymmetries between southern societies and contemporary polities."

An underlying assumption of our modeling approach is that the urban centers in northern and southern Mesopotamia were, in part, emergent phenomena resulting from positive feedback processes that promoted growth, nucleation, and population concentration and negative feedback processes that constrained such growth to within certain limits. In the northern Mesopotamian cities, which attained a size of little more than 130 ha (Stein 2004:66–7; Wilkinson 1994), the negative feedback processes—provided by, for example, the frictional effect of overland transport of staple products—constrained growth to populations of little more than ten to twenty thousand people. In contrast, for cities in the south, the higher agricultural yields, as well as the existence of an efficient system of channels for transporting staple crops products, lifted the constraining effects of negative feedback processes, thereby allowing settlements to grow to 400 ha or more in area.

Nevertheless, it would be overly simplistic to pretend that urban growth resulted simply from the operation of so-called bottom-up factors. The cuneiform literature is replete with examples of kings exerting their power by razing cities to the ground, founding new ones, and shifting river channels. Also, the contribution of the deliberate and self-conscious establishment of archaeological sites is important to understand. Possibly, the tension between bottom-up and top-down processes resulted in the pattern of urbanization we see in the archaeological record of the Bronze Age. Here we focus on the bottom-up processes that resulted in the growth of early settlements and their ultimate transformation into hierarchical systems of settlement.

Factors such as interregional exchange and networks of information flow must also have contributed to the differential patterns of growth between the south and the north. We feel, however, that by starting with the basic subsistence economy instead of the fully developed political economy, agent-based models can successfully capture the development of the latter, as well as show patterns of interregional exchange as emergent properties of the settlement systems.

At the present state of modeling, our settlements are still at the transition between

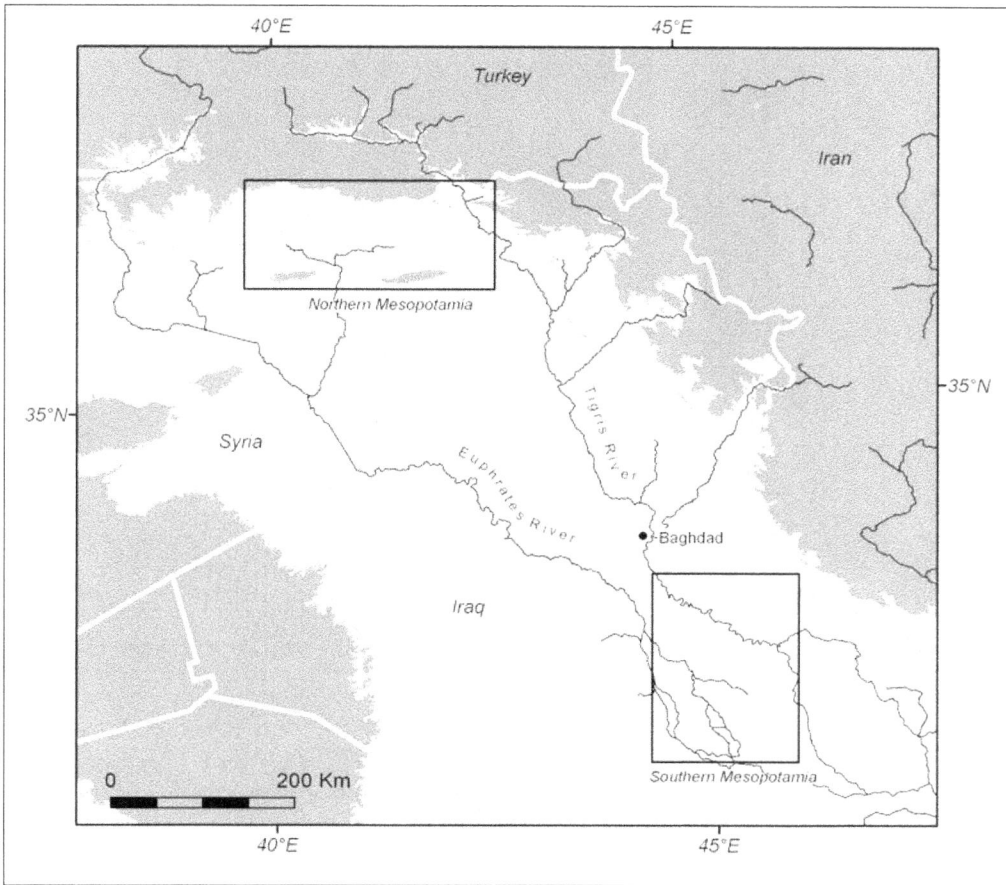

Figure 9.1. The location of main study areas in northern and southern Mesopotamia.

a subsistence economy and a political economy, but the examples discussed demonstrate how such models can supply rich insights into the development of early states.

Owing to the vast scale of the Mesopotamian region, no modeling program can successfully capture the fine granularity of the landscape, broad patterns of agricultural production and interregional exchange systems, and movements of pastoral nomads. Nevertheless, remote sensing and new technologies of 3D mapping enable archaeologists to deal with the spatial scales necessary to build up models of expansive settlement systems. Recent use of remote sensing and Digital Terrain Elevation Data (DTED) can now demonstrate the remarkable contrast between the transport networks of northern and southern Mesopotamia. For rain-fed northern Mesopotamia, Corona satellite imagery provides a sensitive rendering of the route systems (hollow ways) within part of the third-millennium polity of Nagar (Tell Brak) (figures 9.1 and 9.2). These have been mapped in a "window of landscape preservation" in the upper Khabur Valley (Ur 2003) to show a dramatic series of radial route systems around Early Bronze Age sites; the phases of occupation date from approximately the fourth millennium to

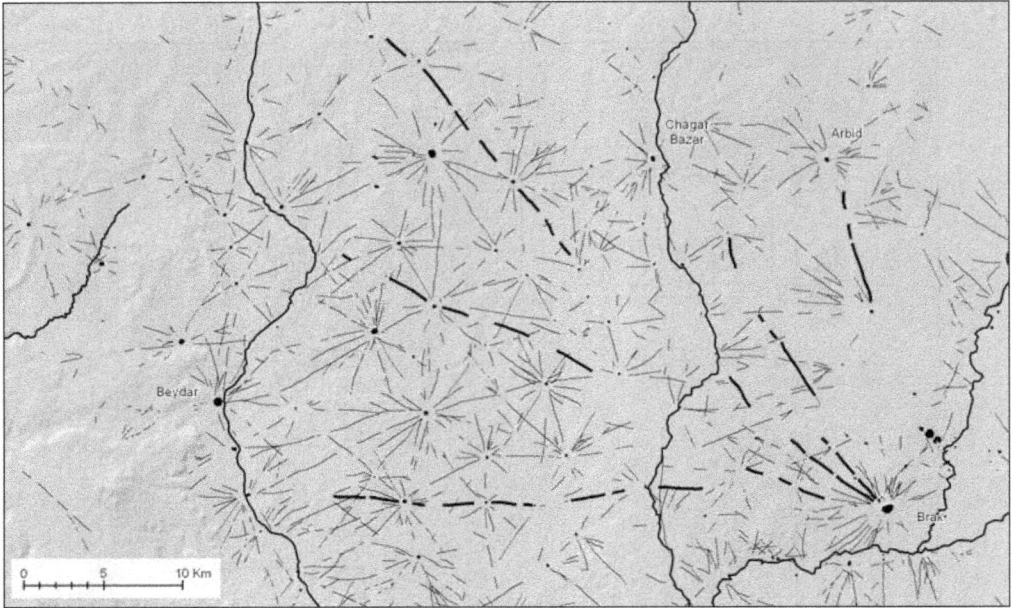

Figure 9.2. The network of communications represented by hollow way systems in the Khabur Basin, Syria.

the late third or second millennium BC. In addition to radial routes around local centers, a number of interregional routes provided evidence for the existence of cross-country networks. Viewed subjectively, it would appear that most transport was effectively local in nature and focused on the movement of people and produce from settlement to fields or the pastures just beyond (Wilkinson 1993). Nevertheless, cross-country routes were also in operation and may represent the well-known itineraries of the cuneiform sources.

In contrast, recently released Shuttle Radar Topography Mission (SRTM) (digital terrain) imagery provides a remarkable picture of the anastomosing channel patterns that provided the basic transport network of southern Mesopotamia (figure 9.3). As yet, only certain elements of this complex palimpsest of low topographic levees can be dated (although see Cole and Gasche 1998), and the pattern illustrated must be regarded as being of a multiperiod date. Nevertheless, this data is sufficient to demonstrate that the network of channels, forming "low friction" anastomosing rivers, their branches, and excavated canals, supplied a well-integrated transportation system network ideal for shifting bulk materials from place to place, thereby making up for regional disparities of production or supply. Although the existence of such a network has been known since the early days of Mesopotamian archaeology (Adams 1981; Jacobsen 1960), the new technology renders this in all its remarkable complexity.

In addition to transport systems that served either to constrain or to expedite the movement of staple products, environmental fluctuations must be incorporated into models of regional economy. High floods in the Zagros Mountains would contribute

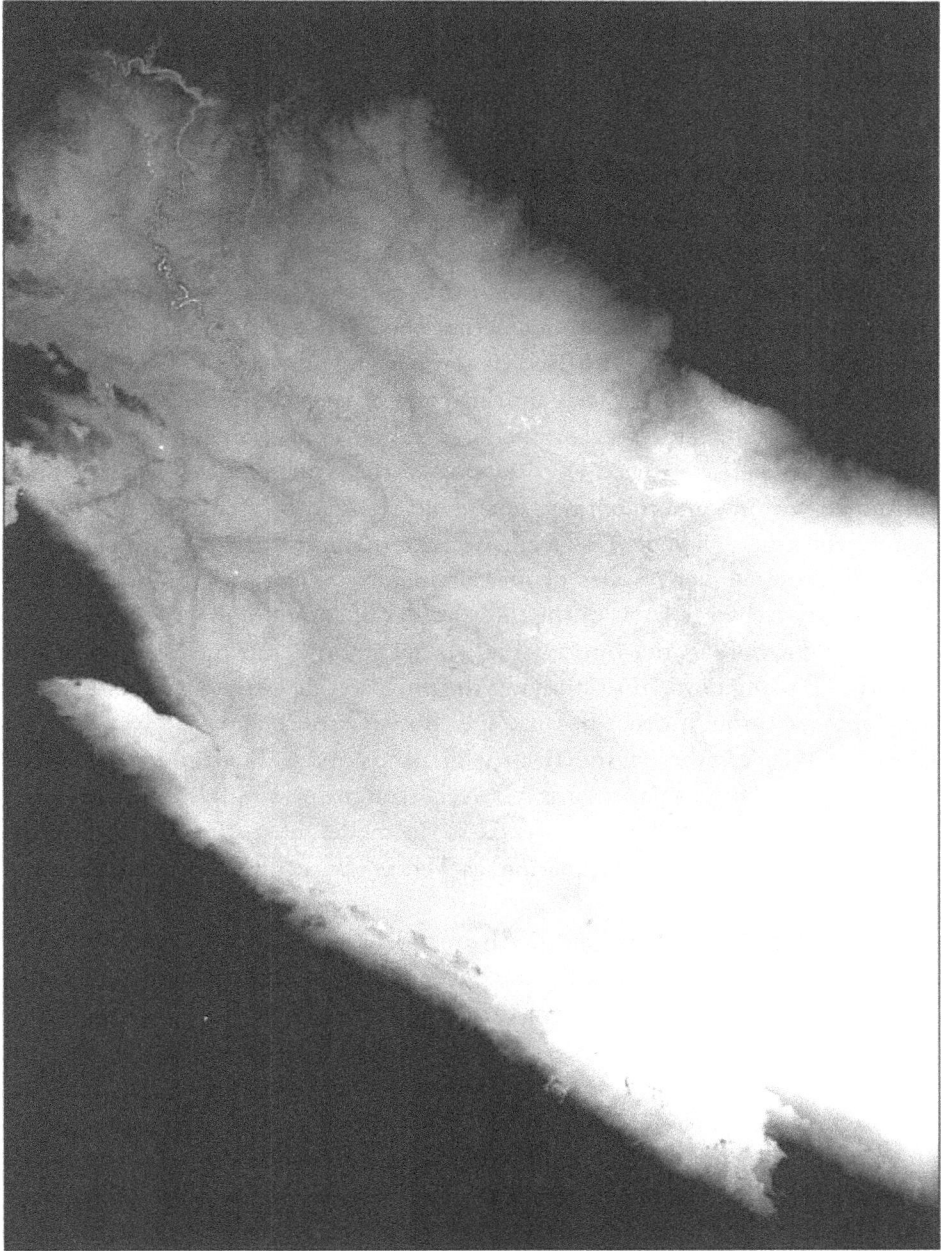

Figure 9.3. The pattern of levee systems in southern Mesopotamia, as recorded by SRTM imagery (courtesy of US Geological Survey).

to overbank flooding in the main Tigris and Euphrates rivers, thereby promoting avulsion (Gibson 1973). Runs of dry years would constrain production in the dry farming north, perhaps contributing to production failure and demographic collapse (Weiss et al. 1993), or result in stresses that would impact pastoral nomads throughout the region.

Approaches to Modeling

The basic "agent" employed in the present model is the individual as a member of a patriarchal household. This type of household is well attested as the fundamental social and economic unit in the ancient Near East (Schloen 2001). Textual evidence shows that many kinds of common action and shared interests on the part of suprahousehold groups were symbolized in terms of membership in the same patriarchal household. It is possible to scale up this concept to encompass various political, economic, and religious groups, because larger social groups (including entire kingdoms and empires) were perceived as consisting of many hierarchically nested households subsumed within an overarching "household" headed by a "master" or "father" (ultimately, the king or a god). This recursive pattern, replicating the same familiar household structure at many scales of measurement, conforms to the notion of "fractal" self-similarity characteristic of the global order of complex adaptive systems.

The household is the fundamental social group being modeled, so considerable attention is being devoted to studying the provisioning of the household, as well as its development through time. Because the subsistence economy is ultimately based on relatively simple, everyday nutritional demands and agricultural production of the household, modeling this sector is relatively straightforward. However, Mesopotamian cities depend on more than subsistence, so the model must allow for trade or exchange and the dissemination of information, as well as the accumulation and distribution of wealth.

A variation on the Earle and D'Altroy model of staple and wealth economies provides a conceptual framework for the development of economies in the ancient Near East (Earle 2002). One must be wary, though, of projecting such models back in time uncritically (see Schloen 2001:199–200). In Upper Mesopotamia, three basic components of the economy can be recognized: The staple economy (1) is easy to model because it is rooted close to the site and a significant part of production is dependent on rainfall. The flow of wealth (2) and the pastoral economy (3) are more difficult because they entail increasing the modeling framework to cover much larger areas. This is particularly acute in trade and exchange: if the modeling framework is to be expanded, then scaling up the entire model to encompass innumerable additional settlement systems becomes a potential necessity. Similar problems of increasing system scale arise when dealing with pastoral economies that range over large areas of desert or steppe. In both cases, though, adopting certain simplifying mechanisms can sidestep the problems.

The increased flow of information through time is also significant because the "urban revolution" straddles the invention or introduction of writing. Although the genesis of many settlements (in both the north and south) takes place before writing was developed, urbanization itself logically was a process that co-evolved with the development of writing. Not only did writing permit the expansion of bureaucratic processes (Gibson and Biggs 1991), but also the growth of writing and bureaucracy probably allowed the further expansion of urban institutions and cities themselves. Because of their sheer scale and complexity, the modeling of the later stages of such complex entities is not dealt with in this chapter. At present, we are still wrestling with the problem of bridging the conceptual gap between subsistence or relatively simple political economies and the complex state bureaucracies that grew up, especially in southern Mesopotamia.

Although the complexities of later Mesopotamian civilizations have yet to be incorporated, by introducing the individual as agent we can deal with more slippery concepts, such as rhetorical skill, physical strength, and charisma, all factors that can underpin political authority (Schloen 2001:200) and without which urbanization could not take place.

Input Data and the Data Manual

Constructing a computer model of an ancient community from the "ground up" requires a wide range of input data relating specifically to the basic processes of everyday life and to the behaviors of the individual agents. Factors such as the size range of the households and component families, the agricultural calendar that regulated much of everyday life, additional requirements for feast days, weddings, and the like, the components of the pastoral economy, sources of fuel, and so on all need to be represented, ideally in a quantitative way. This information must come from a wide range of sources such as archaeological excavations, ethnoarchaeology, and technical consultants' reports, as well as cuneiform texts and other historical documents.

Because most of these types of sources are common to other modeling projects, they can be summarized in tabular form (table 9.1; see also Hunt 1991). The Middle East provides a wide range of data sources because of the extensive ethnographies (for example, Russell 1988; Sweet 1974) and the rich source of consultants' reports produced for various development projects. Limited demographic data are available for the site of Kish in modern Iraq, as well as Dinka Tepe, and Hasanlu in Iran (Rathbun 1982, 1984). More extensive mortality data from the Roman period have enabled life tables to be constructed (Saller 1991), thereby providing a crucial source for the demographic profile of the community.

The Mesopotamian cuneiform record provides a unique source of evidence for the model and has played an extremely important role in the formulation of our agent-based and household-based model on a general theoretical level (see Schloen 2001). Moreover, the texts contribute in many important ways to our empirically based

Table 9.1 Source and Class of Input Data to the Model

Class	Subclass	Cuneiform Texts	Other Historical Texts	Ethnographic Data	Consultants' Reports	Archaeology	Environmental and Landscape Data
Consumption	Cereals	—			—		
	Caloric needs				—		
	Feasts		—		—		
	Building materials (chaff, wood)	—		—	—	—	
	Fuel needs		—	—	—		
Demography	Family size		—	—	—		
	Mortality		—	—			
	Marriage and inheritance		—	—			
Agricultural production	Crops grown	—		—	—	—	
	Agricultural area	—	—	—	—	—	—
	Fallow	—	—	—	—		
	Plough animals		—	—	—		
	Seeding rates		—	—	—		
	Agricultural calendar		—	—	—		
	Field shape and size		—	—	—	—	
	Land ownership	—	—	—	—		
	Labor input	—	—	—	—		—
	Soils data					—	—
Pastoral economy	Flock size		—	—	—		
	Livestock density		—	—	—		
	Fodder needs		—	—	—		
	Pastoral lands		—	—	—		—
Secondary products							
External factors	Trade exchange, tribute	—	—	—	—		
	Pestilence, locusts		—		—	—	
	Climate data		—			—	—
	Droughts					—	—
Control	Crop yields		—	—	—	—	—

modeling of Mesopotamian society and provide a wide range of specific ancient data that would be difficult to obtain with an equivalent level of detail and/or reliability through studies of solely archaeological or ethnographic material. Ideally, such sources should derive specifically from the site and area being modeled. Although we are fortunate to have some valuable texts from the site of Tell Beydar (see below), in order to extract the maximum utility from the available sources, it is necessary to extrapolate from a wider geographical region, as well as from a broader time range than the third millennium BC.

A significant part of the Mesopotamian economy was based on agriculture, and the textual evidence provides detailed information on practically every aspect of agricultural production. Whereas the late third millennium BC in southern Mesopotamia has produced a substantial corpus of textual data on agriculture, the contemporary textual evidence from Upper Mesopotamia and the dry-farming regions of the Near East remains scarce. Nevertheless, private and royal archives exist for the city of Nuzi of the kingdom of Arraphe near modern Kirkuk; these archives can be dated to the middle of the second millennium BC (Pedersén 1998:15–29). The approximately five thousand tablets offer an exceptional wealth of information concerning real estate, fields, and agricultural matters for a concise period of nearly eighty-five years. In addition, a small, earlier archive of some two hundred tablets from the Akkadian period (ca. 2350–2150 BC) has been found at the same site (Gasur).

The farmers in Nuzi appear to have relied only on broadcast sowing and the regular plow *majāru* without the seeding funnel (Widell 2005). Consequently, we have to assume that seeding rates were significantly higher than in the south (see below). In the Akkadian period, the standard seeding rate is recorded to have been 60 northern SILÀ barley per IKU of field, or approximately 87 kg per hectare (Zaccagnini 1979a: 854–855).[1] This rate is roughly twice as high as that for irrigated fields in southern Mesopotamia during the Ur III period, and Zaccagnini has argued that the Akkadian IKU in Gasur, in all likelihood, was significantly larger than the IKU in southern Mesopotamia (1979a:856). However, all other data on seeding rates come from fields where the seeder plow was employed. If we assume that the region of Gasur received similar annual rainfall in the Akkadian period as it does today (ca. 400 mm), then 87 kg per hectare appears realistic for broadcast sowing. A single text from Gasur lists the unitary barley yields from different fields (see Zaccagnini 1979a:855) as ranging from 592 to 666 kg per hectare, indicating a seed:yield ratio of 1:6.8–7.7. The system of measuring surface areas used in later texts from Nuzi is less clear (Zaccagnini 1979a), and any absolute numbers of seed rates and/or yields remain uncertain. Nevertheless, the relative proportions between seeding rates and the yields recorded in Nuzi, ranging from 1:8 to 1:1, with the majority of the attestations in the order of 1:5–7 (Zaccagnini 1975), seem to fit the ratio recorded in Gasur.

Some fields in the texts from Nuzi also were irrigated (*šaqû*), but it is generally accepted that 80 to 90 percent of the fields relied exclusively on rainfall (Zaccagnini 1979b:107–13). The shapes and sizes of the fields in Nuzi are uncertain, but the majority of them were significantly smaller than the fields in the province of Lagash in southern Mesopotamia (Zaccagnini 1979b:77). Moreover, some 98 percent of the Ur III Lagash fields were devoted to barley (Maekawa 1974:41), but only 80 percent of the Nuzi fields were used for this cereal, the remaining fields being used for emmer and wheat (Zaccagnini 1975:192–93, 217).

For southern Mesopotamia, the most comprehensive description of agricultural procedures from ancient Mesopotamia is the "Farmer's Instructions" (Civil 1994). The 111-line text, tentatively dated to the eighteenth century BC or slightly earlier, can be seen as a manual of the fundamental rules of cereal cultivation for an entire year. It has provided an overall framework for our modeling of agricultural tasks, specifically irrigation, plowing, harrowing, sowing, harvesting, threshing, and winnowing. This outline for our model of the agricultural calendar has been complemented and revised using other textual sources. In particular, the tens of thousands of published administrative and economic tablets from the second half of the third millennium provide detailed information on specific issues crucial for our modeling work. When these economic texts, which predominantly concern agricultural matters, are studied together in homogeneous series, they offer details on most aspects of ancient Mesopotamian agriculture.

As an example of such a homogeneous series, a group of about seventy cadastral texts from the province of Lagash in southern Mesopotamia, dated to the Ur III period (ca. 2112–2004 BC), provide evidence on land measurements and boundaries (Liverani 1990:155).[2] These so-called round tablets describe the agricultural landscape of the alluvial plain and provide the orientation, size, and shape of the individual fields cultivated in the province (Liverani 1990, 1996; Maekawa 1992). Moreover, many of the round tablets also provide significant data on the expected yields of the fields in question. According to Maekawa (1974:26), the average yield in the Ur III king Amar-Suen's seventh year was 31 GUR and 244 SILÀ barley per BÙR land (932 kg/ha) and 25 GUR and 11 SILÀ per BÙR (733 kg/ha) in the following year, Amar-Suen 8.[3] Such high yields compare with the average barley yields of 1,396 kg ± 67.5 per hectare on irrigated fields cultivated with primarily primitive agricultural technologies in the Diyala region in the 1950s (Adams 1965:17). Depending on the seeding rates, the Ur III yield rates would equal an average productivity of some fifteen to twenty times the seed volume used on the fields (Liverani 1990–91:365; Maekawa 1974:27). Such impressive productivity rates are easier to accept if we take into account that the farmers in southern Mesopotamia were drilling seeds into the furrows with a so-called seeder plow (APIN) pulled by oxen, a technique that reduces the amount of seed grain by half, compared with broadcast sowing (Halstead 1995:14). Naturally, this technique left its mark on the agricultural landscape of the south. The fields in the round tablets were very large; the majority were in the range of 100 to 125 IKU, or around 35 to 44 ha (Liverani 1996:figure 2). The standard seemingly was 6 BÙR (108 IKU), which would equal roughly 38 ha (Maekawa 1992:408). These fields, which were organized in a regular pattern of extremely narrow, elongated strips, constitute a clear indication of the institutional character of the cereal production in southern Mesopotamia (Liverani 1996:8–10; Maekawa 1992:407).[4] Long and narrow fields are more suitable for plowing with oxen and the seeder plow, because elongated fields would reduce the number of turns for the plowing teams (Liverani 1990:171). The main reason, however, for the shape and size of these fields can be found in the specific irrigation system (so-called furrow irrigation) that prevailed in the extremely flat alluvial plain of southern Mesopotamia. Farther to the north but well within the zone of irrigated agriculture, the fields of Mesopotamia take a more irregular and less elongated form (see Liverani 1996, 1997).

Overall, data from cuneiform texts, although skewed towards the official economy rather than everyday, village-based agricultural production, provide a valuable source of information that enables a sensitive and often quantitative comparison between the irrigated south and the rain-fed north. However, not all of these data can be harnessed as input for the model; some, instead, must act as a control for model output. The copious records of crop yields can be employed as a cross-check on the output generated from the US Department of Agriculture's Soil and Water Assessment Tool (SWAT) model (see below), thereby enabling us to determine the realism of the modeling.

The Construction of a Landscape Framework

Here we summarize the main features of the landscapes of northern and southern Mesopotamia that provide a framework for the simulations. Further details of the northern Mesopotamian landscape are found in the section on Tell Beydar.

Rain-Fed Northern Mesopotamia

Today the rain-fed lands of northern Mesopotamia are a breadbasket for agricultural production, with a history extending back to the origins of agriculture in the prepottery Neolithic (ninth millennium BC). As a result of this extended history, the landscape is peppered with multiperiod occupation mounds (tells), which occur every few kilometers along temporary and permanent watercourses and form a network of relict settlements across the landscape. The hierarchy of Early Bronze Age (third millennium BC) tells ranges in size from small, usually fortified settlements of 1–5 ha, up to towns of 100 ha or a little more. Overall, the extensive areas of cultivable land available for northern communities enabled such polities to grow because these large areas compensated for the relatively modest yields (Weiss 1986). In addition, a significant amount of land was under intensive cultivation, as is indicated by the presence of low-density scatters of ceramics across the ground surface around major settlements. Such "field scatters" are inferred to be a by-product of the spreading of household waste (including ash and burned dung from hearths and kilns) on fields as fertilizer to counteract nutrient loss and allow for increased intensity of cropping (Wilkinson 1982).

The Irrigated South

Agriculture in southern Mesopotamia is wholly reliant on irrigation systems that derive their water from a complex network of natural and dug channels developed over some seven thousand or more years. Not only did such channels allow the distribution of water, but also (perhaps more important) they enabled staple products to be transported from place to place more efficiently than was the case with the overland transport systems of the rain-fed north.

Many soils of the alluvial lowlands have decreased agricultural potential because of high salt levels, a problem that is traditionally ameliorated by the practice of fallowing (Gibson 1974). When viewed as a whole, the complex alluvial landscape of the Mesopotamian plain suggests that modeling land use patterns and settlement in southern Mesopotamia will require a different emphasis and structure than that of the rain-fed north.

The channel systems and their deposits, which crisscross the expanse of the alluvium, result in a mosaic of landscapes of different time periods. The scant archaeological and textual evidence suggests that early agriculturalists took advantage of the network of anastomosing branches of the Euphrates River, using simple techniques such as levee breaks or sluices to control the water flow to fields or settlements. A gradual shift from the reliance on natural anastomosing branches to increasingly artificially created and manipulated channels appears to have fully developed by the late third or second millennium BC. This shift from the natural branches, which constrained settlement and agriculture to narrow bands of cultivation along the main branch, to feeder channels farther away from the main branch meant that settlement could then extend along the newly created channels.

Natural processes include the abrupt splitting of river channels (avulsions), which can result in catastrophic channel shifts and the abandonment of channels and their associated settlements (Gibson 1973). Alternatively, if a new channel developed but both channels continued to flow to form a partial avulsion (Stouthamer and Berendsen 2000), the resultant increase in channel length within an otherwise desertic area would have increased the opportunity for settlement and therefore settlement system growth.

Similarly, the excavation of canals may have contributed to demographic growth. Because indigenous communities may have been fully occupied maintaining existing canals and undertaking routine agricultural tasks, the excavation of new canals would require additional labor, perhaps in the form of corvée. The introduction of massive labor forces, along with their camp followers, would necessarily increase food demand and would entail additional increases in the food production systems, further increasing the scale and complexity of irrigation systems (Wilkinson 2003:87–99). Overall, both the natural process of channel splitting and the deliberate act of cutting large canals could have fueled positive feedback processes and the consequent growth of population and urban settlements.

Key datasets used for this preliminary model are Corona images from the late 1960s, Spot images of the 1990s, and ASTER images from 2001 (used to create a

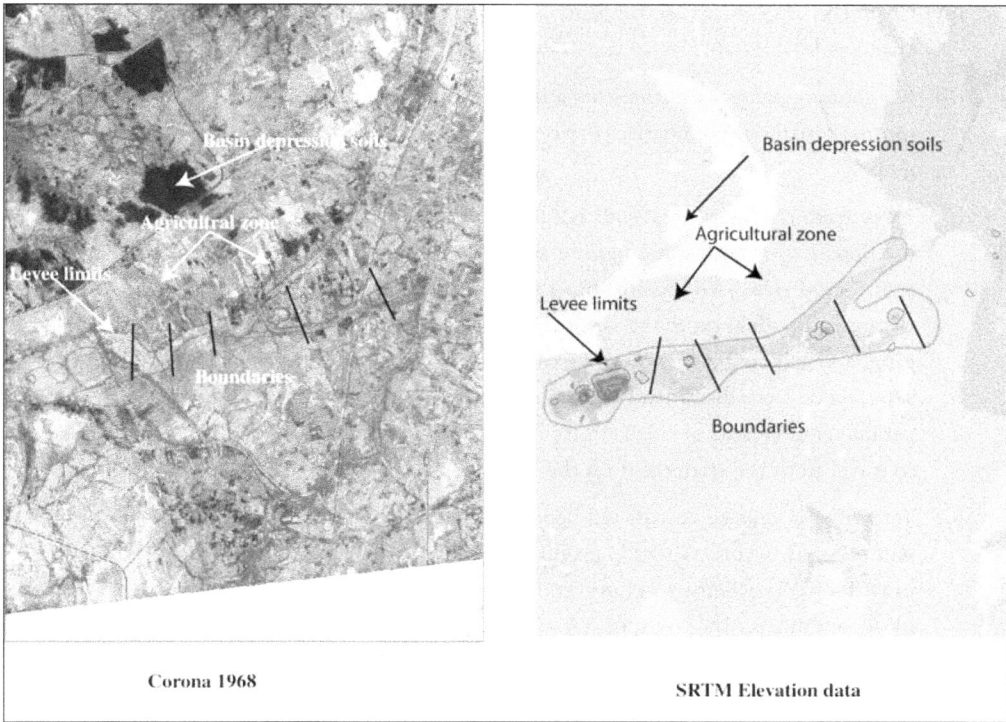

Figure 9.4. Settlements distributed along the line of a levee system near Borsippa, southern Iraq.

Digital Elevation Model [DEM]), as well as archaeological ground survey information and ground soil data. Integration of these datasets into a GIS format allows us to determine the basic layout of settlements of a known date and their relationship to irrigation canals.

The basic settlement module that forms the core of the present model can be distinguished on satellite images and DTED models as a series of settlement mounds recognizable at regular intervals along low, sinuous levees (figure 9.4). The populations of these settlements would be supported by the products of palm gardens along the levee crest and cultivated fields on the slope that led down to flood basins beyond (Postgate 1992). Such flood basins, evident on images and terrain models as enclosed hollows, provided sumps for excess irrigation water, as well as seasonal pastureland. Beyond the agricultural land, desert steppe, often saline, supplied intermittent pasture for larger flocks of sheep and goats, as well as refuges for wild animals. Marshlands were also important (Cole 1994), and the procurement of marshland and riverine resources must have formed a significant component of the local economy, especially in the far south of the plains (Pournelle 2003).

A basic model of settlement and agricultural territory uses the module described above and makes a limited number of assumptions (figure 9.5):

(a) Channels bifurcate and settlements are arranged at intervals along the component channels.

(b) For contemporaneous settlements aligned along the crest of a channel levee, the mutual territorial boundaries between settlements are estimated using Thiessen polygons.

(c) Away from the levee, crest soils become more clay-rich and fine grained, and towards the flood basins both waterlogging and the likelihood of salinization increase. As a result, crop yields will decline until it becomes counterproductive to grow crops. Because crop yield on the levee slope will be a function of soil properties, waterlogging, and salt content, this can be modeled by means of our crop model (SWAT) to supply a de facto distal land-use boundary. In addition to being a function of the soil parameters, the area of cultivation may be constrained by the amount of time it takes to travel from the settlement on the levee crest.

(d) Territorial boundaries estimated between settlements and parallel to the levee crest will necessarily constrain crop production, which, in turn, could limit the overall growth of the settlement. However, because the riverine channels or canals provide ideal conduits for the transport of staple goods, any shortfalls in production can be alleviated by importing grain by boat, that is, as long as areas upstream or downstream are providing a sufficient surplus.

Overall, if social or economic conditions in any given settlement are propitious for growth, there are fewer reasons for such growth to be constrained in southern Mesopotamia than in the north. Because irrigation systems produce both higher and more reliable yields than rain-fed farming areas, we anticipate that shortfalls in supply from any one center could be counteracted by imports from elsewhere, provided that the political and social conditions are appropriate. In fact, conditions of production constraint may encourage and even suck surplus production from other areas along the same channel system. The irrigated landscape therefore differs significantly from landscape in the rain-fed farming zone, where the efficient import of bulk products from reliable surplus products along the channel cannot override the constraints arising from the limited size of cultivated territories.

Modeling a Northern Settlement Enclave in the Tell Beydar Area

The current model focuses on a single settlement system localized around Tell Beydar in the Khabur Basin of northern Syria. Rainfall there, at approximately 300 mm per year, is just sufficient for rain-fed cultivation. Surveyed by a team from the Oriental Institute in 1997 and 1998, in collaboration with the Syrian-Belgian team based at Tell Beydar (Lebeau and Suleiman 1997), this area has yielded the remains of some eighty-two sites (Wilkinson 2000). The twenty Bronze Age sites, which are aligned

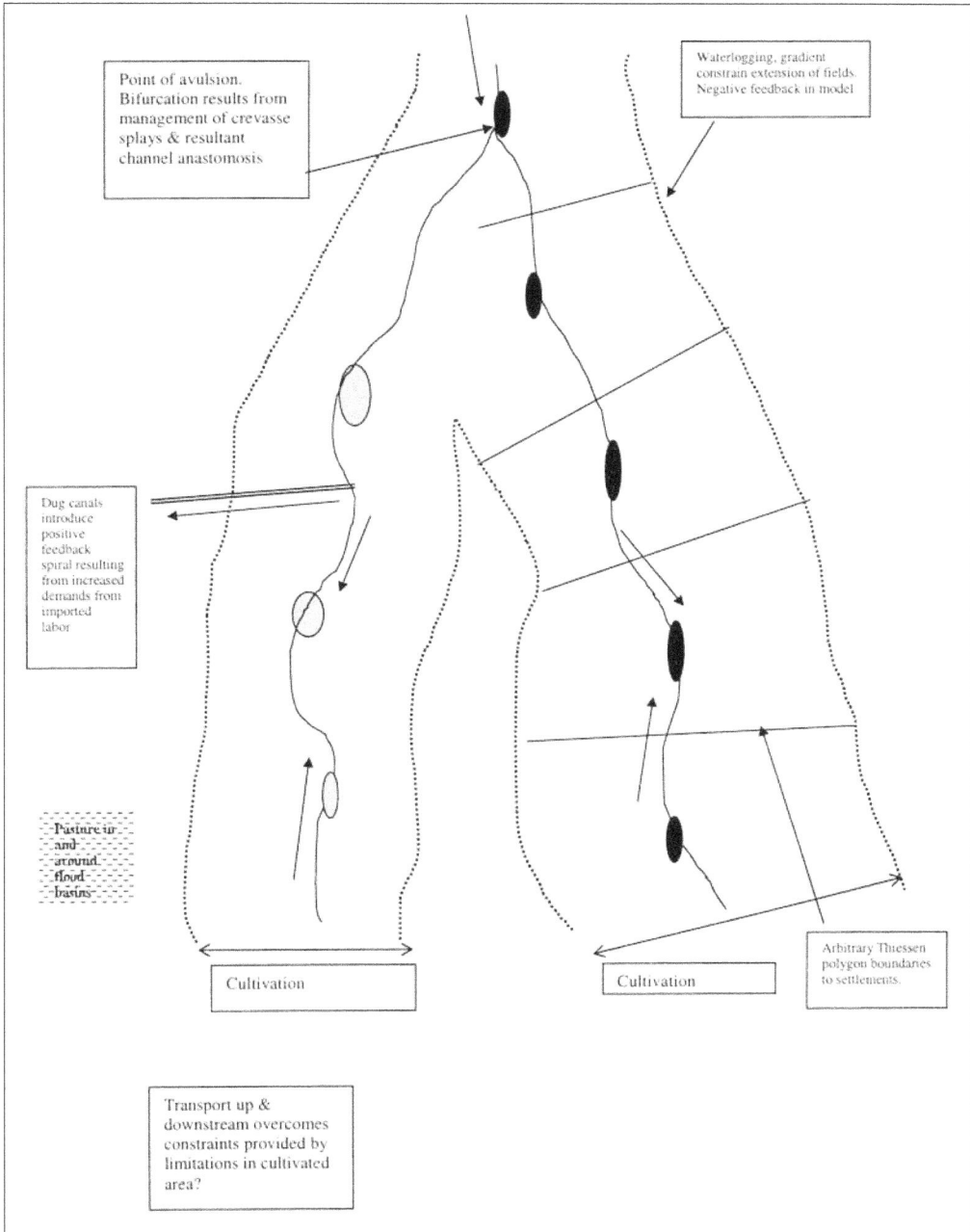

Figure 9.5. A model illustrating structural features and constraints operating along a typical levee system in southern Mesopotamia.

mainly along the seasonal watercourses (wadis) or natural route systems, form a hierarchical distribution, with Tell Beydar (at 17–22 ha) at the apex (table 9.2). An extensive basalt plateau extending to the west of Tell Beydar and the main Wadi Awaidj

Table 9.2 Settlement Hierarchy in the Vicinity of Tell Beydar

Rank in Settlement Hierarchy	Number of Sites
Provincial capital (Tell Beydar) ca. 22.5 ha (17 ha)	1
"Towns" (7–9 ha)	3
Village (2.5–4.0 ha)	5
Small village (<2 ha)	8

shows only sporadic evidence for settlement, of which a negligible amount dates to the Bronze Age (van Berg et al. 2003). The basalt plateau provided a long-term pastoral resource for the inhabitants of the nearby communities. To the east, this must have been supplemented by more limited areas of open space that extended between the reconstructed cultivation zones (figure 9.6).

The spatial layout of the subsistence economy can be reconstructed (1) from the estimation of site-sustaining areas derived from site areas, (2) from the area of cultivated land inferred from the fade-out point of hollow ways, and (3) by the evidence for plow teams derived from cuneiform texts (Widell 2004; Wilkinson et al. in press). The site areas provide a coarse estimate of site population, assuming that on-site population falls within a specified range, conventionally one to two hundred persons per hectare (Adams 1981; Stein and Wattenmaker 1990). The so-called fade-out points of the radial hollow ways, by providing estimates of long-term cultivation (see figure 9.6), indicate how much land was available to support the population of the contained settlement. Beyond this cultivation territory, areas of nonfarmed land can be inferred. By default, these presumably comprised pasture, fuel-gathering areas, or waste that extended to the next settlement land-use module.

Because cuneiform texts from Tell Beydar provide evidence for the number of plow teams in use for a specified season, the landscape evidence for cultivated areas can be cross-checked. The cuneiform texts, written in a form of Old Akkadian (Ismail et al. 1996), specify the number of plow animals used around Tell Beydar, as well as around six neighboring satellite communities. Assuming that each team was capable of plowing .3–.4 ha per day (.2–.3 for asses; Palmer and Russell 1993) and allowing for biennial fallow and an appropriate amount of waste (25 percent; Van Driel 1999/2000:85 n. 30), we can estimate the total area of cultivated land for Beydar and its neighbors (table 9.3).

The landscape approach coupled with the textual data provides estimates of settlement populations, as well as the capacity of the agricultural area to support that population. Although coarse, these estimates suggest that Beydar's population exceeded the agricultural production of its fields and that surplus product was required and indeed produced from its neighbors. In a similar manner, discrepancies between the

Figure 9.6. Reconstructed land use zones of the Tell Beydar area (Syria), with the basalt plateau in gray and areas of cultivated land estimated from the fade-out point of hollow ways in diagonal hatching.

estimated cultivation catchment and the on-site population demonstrate that, for a more extensive area encompassing Tell Brak (Nagar, the regional capital), the larger settlements were net importers of food whereas the smaller tells were net exporters (Wilkinson et al. in press). Although necessarily coarse, such techniques enable us to perceive the rough structure of the political economy.

Table 9.3 Estimated Cultivated Areas for Tell Beydar and Its Satellite Sites

Beydar with Satellites

	Area Required to Sustain the Estimated Site Population (100–150 persons/ha)	Area Estimated from All Plow Animals Administrated by Beydar
Total land allocated (demand?)	2,267–3,400 ha	1,683–3,132 ha

Beydar Only

	Area Estimated from Hollow Way Catchment around Beydar	Area Estimated from Plow Animals Working Beydar Fields
Arable land around Beydar (supply?)	1,503 ha	1,131–2,097 ha

The Simulation Framework

The model of landscape outlined for northern Mesopotamia provides a "static" view of settlement and land use. Here agent-based models are introduced to capture the dynamics of population change as it occurs within a system of land use and settlement that experiences a series of stress situations or alternative scenarios imposed during the simulations.

Overview of the Simulation Engine

To provide insights into the complex process dynamics of ancient Mesopotamian settlement systems, we have developed "Enkimdu," a new, holistic, agent-based simulation engine. This simulator is a multidisciplinary, dynamic software object model of the social and natural world of ancient Mesopotamia, capable of representing diverse natural and social processes and their interactions at variable scales and scopes.

Enkimdu differs from most agent-based simulation systems that have been used in archaeological/anthropological modeling investigations: its explicit, fine-scale representation of the dynamics of key natural processes operates concurrently with the dynamics of the social processes carried out by the social agents. This approach has made it possible to model important fine-scale interactions and feedbacks between social and natural processes.

The simulations for the Tell Beydar pilot studies described below address natural processes (weather, crop growth, hydrology, soil evolution, population dynamics) and societal processes (farming and herding practices, kinship-driven behaviors, trade) interacting daily across simulation runs that span decades to centuries. Software objects representing the key components of the simulation domain are resolved and modeled at the level of individual persons and households, individual agricultural fields, and individual herd animals. Each of the decision-making "agents" in the simulation domain—each person, each household or other organization—governs its own behavior in the simulations, based on its own local rules and in response to its own perceptions, preferences, capabilities, and goals.

Close coupling of heterogeneous dynamic processes can be represented by taking advantage of some of the advanced simulation technologies developed over the past decade at Argonne National Laboratory. One of these technologies is the Dynamic Information Architecture System (DIAS) (Christiansen 2000a), a generic, object-based computer simulation framework. The DIAS infrastructure has made it feasible to build and manipulate complex simulation scenarios in which many thousands of objects can interact via simulation models that represent dozens to hundreds of concurrent dynamic processes. In the DIAS object-based modeling paradigm, the domain objects (for example, household objects and field crop objects) drive the simulation. These domain objects express their own dynamic behaviors by invoking simulation models that can address specific aspects of these objects' behaviors. Essentially every domain object, social or natural, that possesses dynamic behaviors can act as its own software agent. The simulation models, which can include proven, existing models and new, purpose-built codes, are not embedded directly in the software objects. Instead, they are selected for execution by their "owner" objects as they are needed, as a function of simulation context. Each such model converses with the simulation in the language of the relevant domain object attributes; models interact with the objects that their owner objects "know," but models never need to interact directly with other models. This approach pays major dividends in simulation scalability as more and more process models are added to a simulation framework: there is no need to maintain an exponentially growing set of model-to-model linkages and data protocols as models are added.

In developing Enkimdu, we are also making extensive use of Argonne's Framework for Addressing Cooperative Extended Transactions (FACET) (Christiansen 2000b), a facility for constructing flexible and expressive agent-based object models of social behavior patterns. By using FACET models to implement social behaviors of individuals and organizations within the context of larger DIAS-based natural systems simulations, it has become possible for us to conveniently address a broad range of issues involving interaction and feedback among natural and social processes.

Dynamic Software Object Representation of the Simulation Domain

A simplified schematic representation of many of the classes of software object that make up our ancient Mesopotamian simulation domain appears in figure 9.7. The major classes of domain entity (Field, Household, and the like) are shown as the large

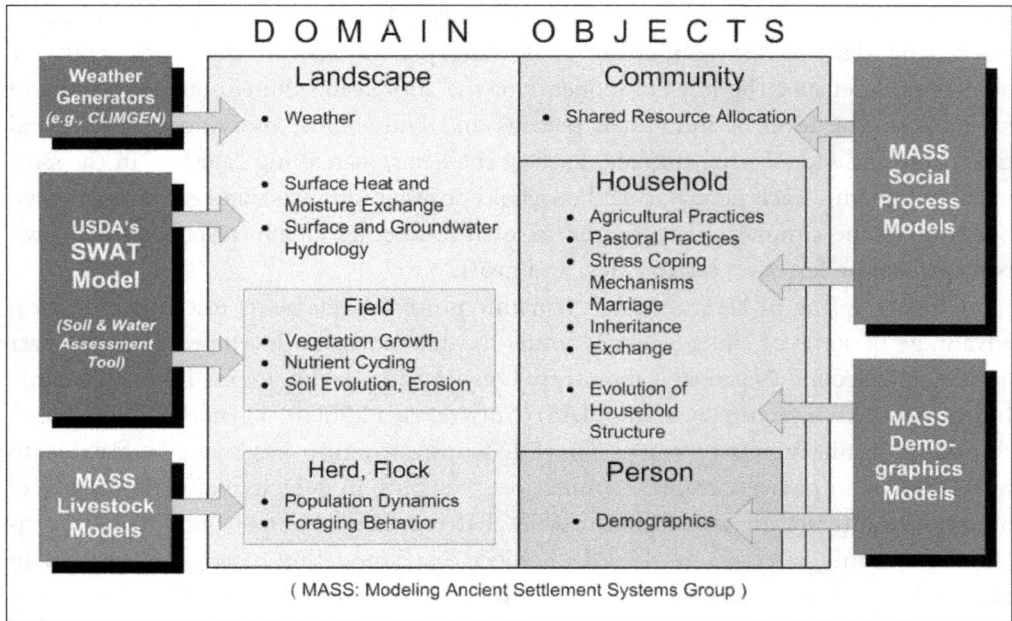

DOMAIN OBJECTS

Weather Generators (e.g., CLIMGEN)

USDA's SWAT Model (Soil & Water Assessment Tool)

MASS Livestock Models

Landscape
- Weather
- Surface Heat and Moisture Exchange
- Surface and Groundwater Hydrology

Field
- Vegetation Growth
- Nutrient Cycling
- Soil Evolution, Erosion

Herd, Flock
- Population Dynamics
- Foraging Behavior

Community
- Shared Resource Allocation

Household
- Agricultural Practices
- Pastoral Practices
- Stress Coping Mechanisms
- Marriage
- Inheritance
- Exchange
- Evolution of Household Structure

Person
- Demographics

MASS Social Process Models

MASS Demo-graphics Models

(MASS: Modeling Ancient Settlement Systems Group)

Figure 9.7. Simulation entities and dynamic behavior models.

blocks occupying the center of the figure. The bulleted lists within each entity block call out modeled dynamic behaviors of these simulation entities. The entity behaviors are implemented by the ensemble of simulation models depicted as shadowed blocks at the left and right margins of the figure.

The simulation software includes both custom-built models created by the MASS team and existing, off-the-shelf models well suited to represent some of the key behaviors needed to support our model settlement system dynamics. One such off-the-shelf model is the US Department of Agriculture's SWAT simulator (Arnold et al. 1998; Arnold and Allen 1992). The list of processes addressed by the SWAT system includes hydrology at individual field to watershed scale, daily agricultural weather, soil evolution and erosion, nutrient cycling dynamics, vegetation growth, grazing and browsing by livestock, and various effects of human intervention, such as tillage (plowing, planting, harvesting) and irrigation.

At present, we use the ClimGen Markov chain weather generator (Stöckle, Cambell, and Nelson 1999), as well as the SWAT model's internal weather generator, to synthesize representative daily agricultural weather, based on climatological summaries. As we expand our modeling scenarios to encompass whole regions, we intend to use mesoscale numerical weather models, such as the National Center for Atmospheric Research's mesoscale model MM5 (Anthes and Warner 1978), with initial and boundary conditions drawn from long-run paleoclimate global circulation model simulations, to provide a spatially varying regional weather signal for our simulations. Regional-scale hydrological processes that are beyond the scope of applicability of the SWAT model's hydrological submodels will be addressed by the US Geological Survey's coupled ground- and surface-water model (MODBRANCH; Swain and Wexler 1993) or other comparable modeling codes.

Modeling Representation of Social Agents

Thus far, the principal categories of social-agent behavior pattern addressed within the Enkimdu framework are demographic and kinship-based behaviors, subsistence-based behaviors, and simple reciprocal exchanges of labor and commodities. The model incorporates a population generator that can produce initial populations of simulated persons, grouped into households. These are demographically sound, with appropriate proportions of each type of household structure represented, and have a plausible initial density of cross-household kinship ties. The reference demographic model is Coale and Demeny's (1966) Model West Level 2 (for males) and Level 4 (for females). Distribution of household types is based on census data for Roman Egypt (Bagnall and Frier 1994). Modeled demographic and kinship-based social agent behaviors, driven by these data sources and by results derived from investigation of ancient textual sources and ethnographic evidence, include

(a) Reproductive rates, and death probabilities by age and gender

(b) Age- and gender-dependent person role changes

(c) Marriage

(d) Inheritance

(e) Household restructuring and evolution (for example, fission and aggregation)

(f) Kin gifts of food and labor

Modeled subsistence behaviors are mainly related to agriculture or pastoralism. Modeled households with the capacity to plant a grain crop will generally do so because producing a grain harvest represents the principal means of coping with long-term food stress problems. Agricultural behavior patterns are among the elements of social agent behavior that have been incorporated into Enkimdu with the aid of the FACET modeling framework, using FACET's extensive built-in facilities for modeling and tracking resource management and conflict resolution dynamics. Examples of the layout of some of the FACET models for households' agricultural behavior patterns are shown in figure 9.8.

Each step in these FACET-based models is a submodel, with a required (though often variable) cast of participants who must provide the appropriate resources (labor, use of equipment, supplies) necessary to perform the task. The flow from step to step is generally deterministic yet can be mutable, with action sequences diverted or pre-empted by outside events. Work crew requirements are generally different for each step, tailored to the needs of the task.

Pastoralism was important to many ancient Near Eastern economies and was significant in Bronze Age Tell Beydar (van Lerberghe 1996). Our representation of the

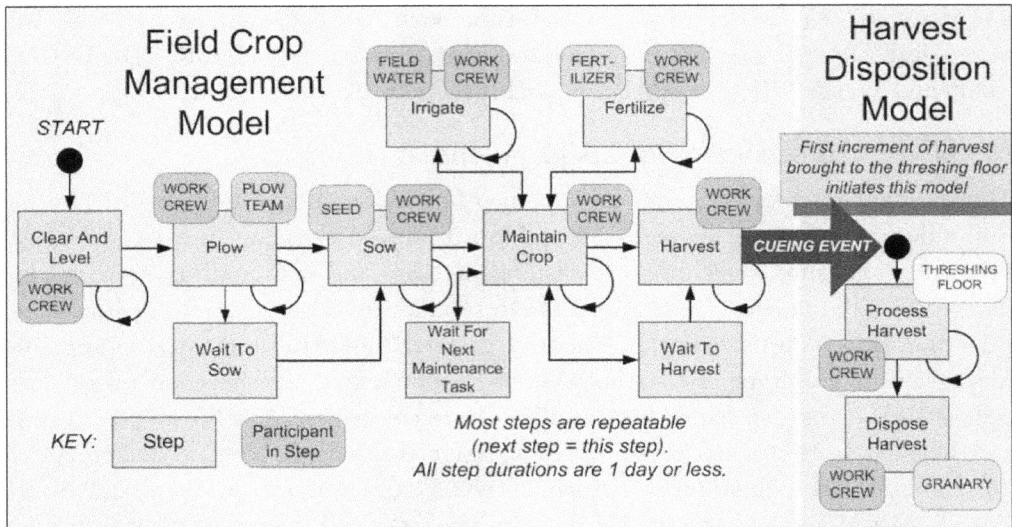

Figure 9.8. Examples of FACET models for agricultural practices.

pastoral component includes custom-built models of sheep and goat physiology and population dynamics (Blaxter 1967; Redding 1981) and new FACET-based models of the societal behavior patterns, at household and community levels, that relate to pastoral activities.

Among the main driving forces behind our present modeling representation of adaptive societal processes at the household level are social and environmental stresses and other stimuli perceived by agents representing individual households. The most prominent relate to food stress, which would have been a constant problem in the Mediterranean region (Gallant 1991). To combat food stress, household agents can choose from a spectrum of coping behaviors (figure 9.9).

Households must evaluate their stresses with respect to several time horizons because the coping mechanisms appropriate to each time frame are not generally the same. For example, if a household perceives a potential food shortage two years ahead, an appropriate response might be a plan to plant a barley crop. If the shortage is projected for two days ahead, however, then the barley crop response is not sufficiently timely; a better adaptation might be to seek a grain loan from a close kin household or to sell off some livestock for grain. The household's food stress assessments take into account resources on hand (for example, stored grain) and perceived effects of planned and ongoing household initiatives, both positive (such as anticipated future dairy products from a household's livestock holdings) and negative (such as repayment of a grain loan). Household agents periodically recheck their food stress at intervals that depend on their current, perceived stress levels (checking more frequently at higher stress). They also recheck stress levels after any occurrence that could change the household sustainability balance, such as a new bride moving into a household and a crop being harvested. As figure 9.9 indicates, for any given time horizon a household

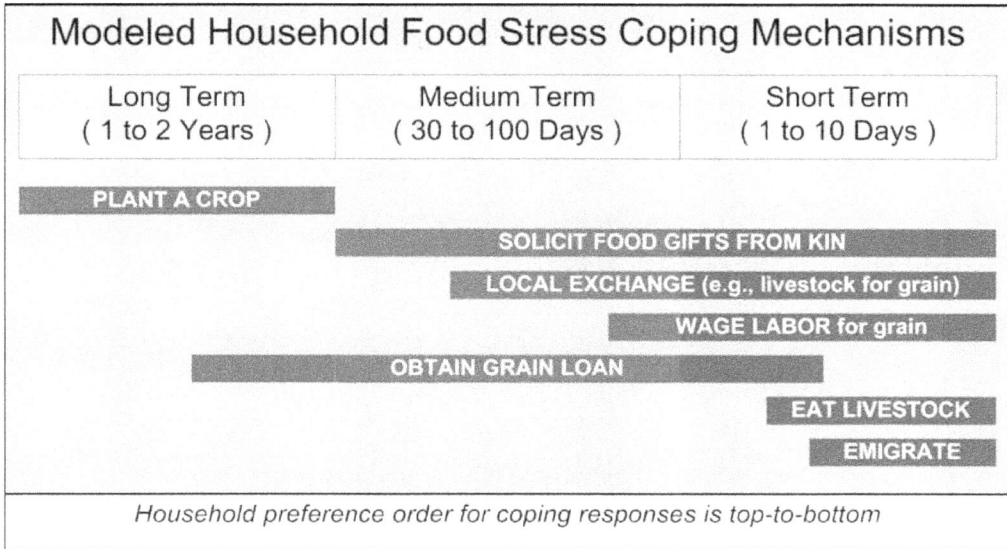

Modeled Household Food Stress Coping Mechanisms

Long Term (1 to 2 Years)	Medium Term (30 to 100 Days)	Short Term (1 to 10 Days)

PLANT A CROP

SOLICIT FOOD GIFTS FROM KIN

LOCAL EXCHANGE (e.g., livestock for grain)

WAGE LABOR for grain

OBTAIN GRAIN LOAN

EAT LIVESTOCK

EMIGRATE

Household preference order for coping responses is top-to-bottom

Figure 9.9. A household agent's food-stress coping mechanisms.

will attempt to apply coping adaptations in preference order, choosing the least disruptive means to mitigate its stress. An acutely stressed household always attempts first to utilize its kinship networks to solicit nonreciprocal gifts of food or labor. If kin households are unable to assist (because they themselves are too stressed) or the household simply has no close kin households to ask, then it tries to utilize its network of established, non-kin, trading-partner households for reciprocal exchange. Failing that, it seeks beneficial reciprocal exchanges with any other household in the community.

Another form of household stress is deficiency of labor for agricultural production. This form of stress, like food stress, can be alleviated through the use of kin networks. However, if kin are unavailable for assistance and households cannot find sufficient non-kin workforces for food production activities, this labor stress can exacerbate the food stress. Labor shortages for agricultural activity may not be a near-term problem for households, but household agents seek to address such deficiencies in the long term, before the onset of acute food stress.

Simulated Process Interactions and Feedbacks

Figure 9.10 illustrates the tempo and "temporal texture" of dynamic process model execution in a simulation. The triggering of models representing the dynamic processes for each class of domain entity shown in the figure are identified in a stylized way by vertical tick marks on a one-year time line that runs from left to right for each process. The tightest spacing of tick marks depicts *daily* process updates, though updates for some processes may occur more frequently. As figure 9.10 indicates, the characteristic time scale varies substantially by process type. Enkimdu operates as a discrete event simulation, rather than on a fixed time step basis, so modeled processes

ENTITY	PROCESS	AUG	SEP	OCT	NOV	DEC	JAN	FEB	MAR	APR	MAY	JUN	JUL
Atmosphere	Weather	‖‖										
Landscape	Hydrology	‖‖										
Field (340)	Heat, Moisture Exchange	‖‖										
	Soil Evolution, Erosion	‖‖										
	Vegetation Growth	‖‖										
Fauna (2000)	Foraging	‖‖										
	Lambing, Lactation, etc.				|			|	|				
Person (600)	Marriage, Role Change, etc.			|			*TIME →*		|				
	Childbirth, Death, etc.					|							
Household (120)	Agricultural Tasks		‖‖‖‖‖ ‖‖‖‖‖‖‖ ‖‖‖		|		|	|	|	| ‖‖‖‖‖‖‖‖‖‖‖		‖‖‖	
	Pastoral Tasks	‖‖										
	Stress Checks	|			||| |	|		|		|	||| |	|
	Coping Adaptations				|			|			| |	
	Granary Spoilage		|		|		|		|		|	|
Community	Assign Fields	|											
	Assign Pastures	‖‖										
	Update Exchange Rates	|	|	|	|	|	|	|	|	|	|	|	|

TICK MARKS INDICATE MODELED INVOCATION OF THE PROCESS BEHAVIOR

(N) *Approximate number of instances of this type in the Beydar settlement simulations*

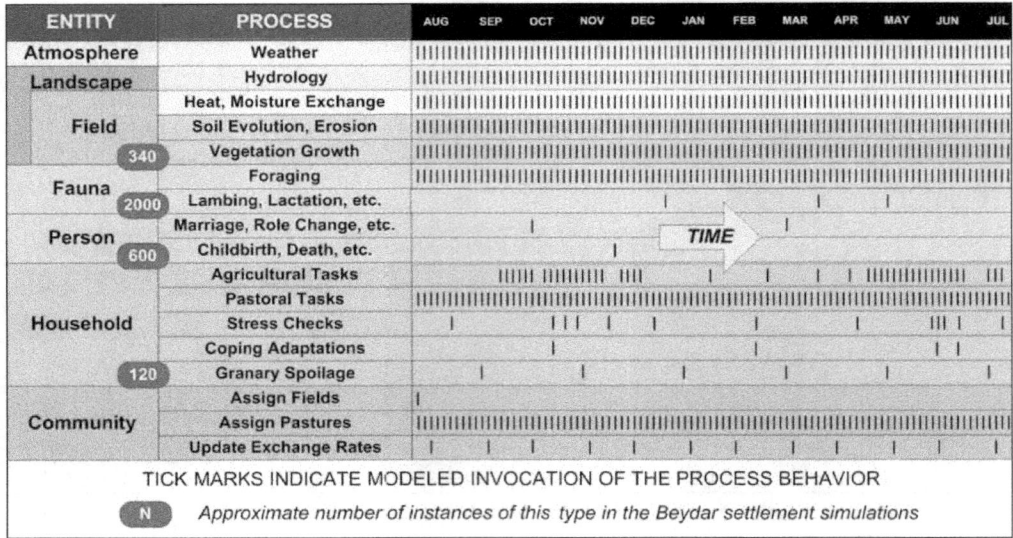

Figure 9.10. The temporal texture of modeled concurrent social and natural processes.

can be triggered to start and end at whatever times and intervals are appropriate for them. The models implementing the dynamic processes active in each Enkimdu domain object acquire the context needed as input for each increment of their execution by sampling this continually changing, natural and societal environment. Process interaction and potential feedback occur whenever one process requires a domain object attribute that may have been modified by a different process. Fine-scale, cross-discipline process interaction is a natural consequence of the way the simulation framework is structured.

The numbers in ovals in the leftmost (ENTITY) column of figure 9.10 denote the approximate number of individual objects of each type that are actively performing their specified processes in the Tell Beydar modeling scenarios discussed below. For example, in the model scenarios roughly 120 Household objects are independently performing subsistence tasks, rechecking their sustainability (via "stress checks," as discussed above) and formulating and applying adaptations to cope with stress when needed.

Simulations for Tell Beydar

The layout for the Tell Beydar simulation is depicted in figure 9.11. In developing the Tell Beydar simulation scenarios, we have used ancient textual information and modern survey data specific to the site, reinforced by substantial additional information from a wide range of applicable ancient and modern sources throughout the Near Eastern and Mediterranean world, as discussed above. Our modeling representation can best be considered as roughly representative of Bronze Age settlements *like* Tell Beydar, but it is also applicable to a broader range of pre-industrial, agropastoral settlement systems.

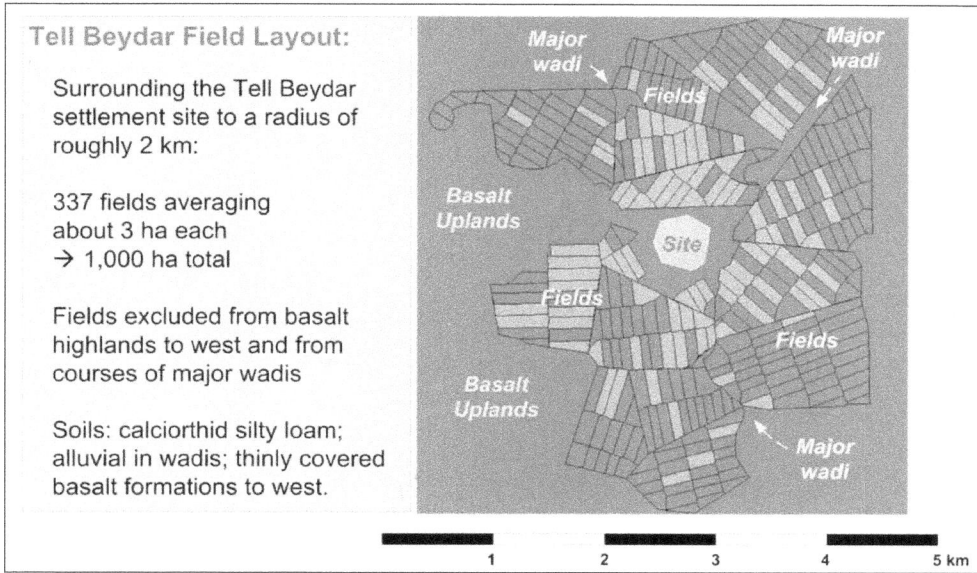

Tell Beydar Field Layout:

Surrounding the Tell Beydar settlement site to a radius of roughly 2 km:

337 fields averaging about 3 ha each
→ 1,000 ha total

Fields excluded from basalt highlands to west and from courses of major wadis

Soils: calciorthid silty loam; alluvial in wadis; thinly covered basalt formations to west.

Figure 9.11. The study area and initial conditions for the Tell Beydar simulation.

Baseline One-Hundred-Year Simulation

The initial baseline case begins with a small settlement of 501 individuals in 105 households occupying the Beydar site. Initially, each household was given twelve live-stock (eight sheep and four goats) and one inheritable field share for each male in a communally shared, agricultural-field redistribution system. All households attempted to engage in agriculture, growing an archaic strain of barley using Bronze Age farm implements and techniques and strictly observing biennial fallowing. Daily weather data were derived based on monthly climatological summaries of observations from Mosul, Iraq, using a Markov process weather generator. We did not impose any major climate trends significantly deviating from the mean value. The precipitation amounts averaged 328 mm per year but ranged from 173 to 649 mm per year over the one-hundred-year run because of normal climate variability. For the baseline run, we did not impose any external stresses on the model settlement. Such special stress cases are dealt with in separate, variant simulation scenarios.

During the span of the baseline simulation, the total settlement population rose about 41 percent, from 501 initially to 708 at the end of one hundred years. Over that same period, the number of households increased 46 percent, from 105 to 154, with a peak of 158 households in Year 89. The settlement's one-hundred-year total numbers of births and deaths were 3,521 and 2,951, respectively. The modeled population was also affected by episodes of emigration, a last-ditch option available to households that proved unable to sustain themselves. A total of 363 individuals emigrated during the entire run, or about 12 percent of the population losses due to deaths. Immigration into the settlement from the outside was not represented.

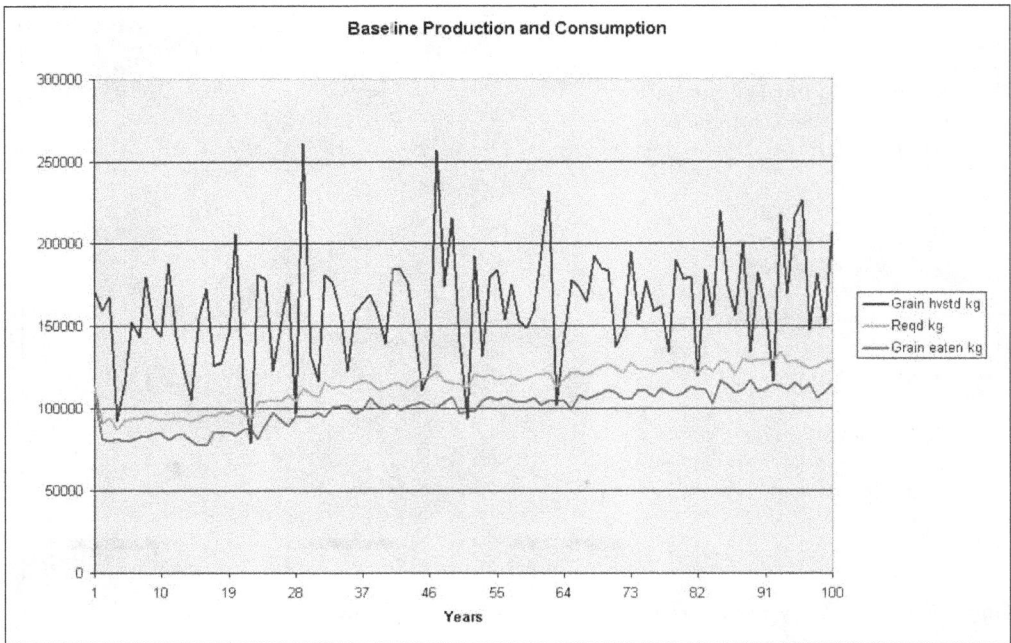

Figure 9.12. The one-hundred-year baseline simulation: food production and consumption.

It should be noted that emigrations do not necessarily indicate sustainability failure of the model settlement as a whole. Rather, they reflect specific, individual households that had become nonviable because of their inability to cope with food stress or, in some cases, social stress. An example of the latter case is a household that experiences the death of a member and is then left with no adults to manage its affairs. That household will dissolve, and members who cannot find a household willing and able to take them in are forced to emigrate.

Figure 9.12, showing the production and consumption of Tell Beydar throughout the one-hundred-year baseline period, indicates that in most years the settlement had more than a sufficient supply of food. Not only does this figure show how much grain was consumed by individuals, but also the required kilograms line indicates how much food had to be supplied by other items, such as dairy products, wild plants and game, and garden vegetables. From the figure, it is apparent that in most years the settlement had a more than adequate supply of grain to be sustainable.

In the baseline run, the settlement was not subjected to any external environmental or social stresses beyond the normal run of climate variability, soil variability, and demographic mischance. This "paradise scenario" was unlikely to prevail over long intervals. We therefore executed a series of variant scenarios to see how the model Tell Beydar settlement responds to various forms of unusual stress. We have begun to investigate the impacts of *environmental* stress factors, such as prolonged droughts and chronic crop blights (see Wilkinson et al. in press). In contrast, the results for the three

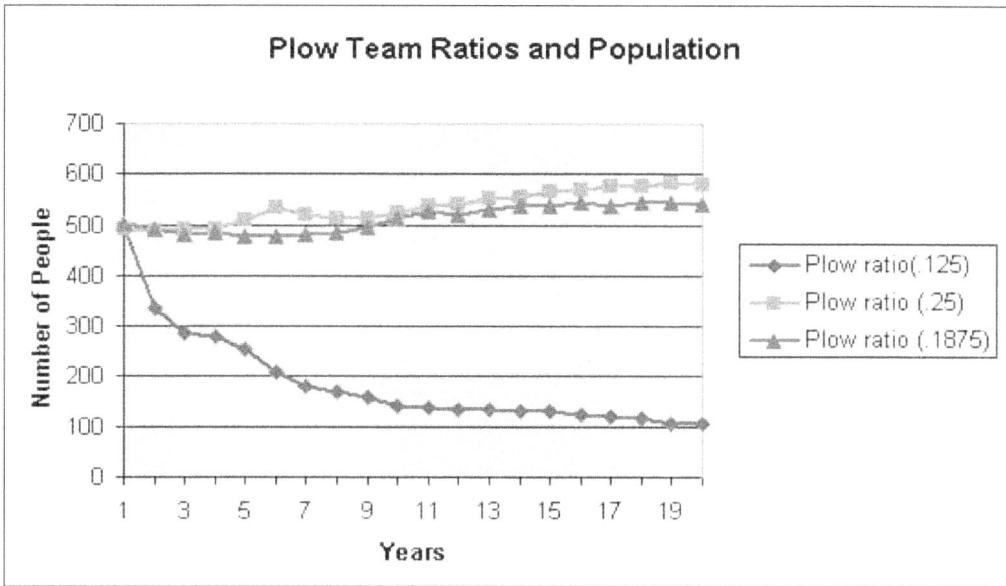

Figure 9.13. The effects of plow team availability on settlement population.

simulation scenario variants described below explore some of the effects of acute and chronic *societal* stresses.

Stress Scenario: Chronic Shortage of Plow Teams

Variations in a major component in the agricultural process—households' access to plow teams—tested the resiliency of the simulated settlement. The idea for this scenario was drawn from Tell Beydar's ancient textual sources that record the number of plow teams available for the settlement and surrounding area (Widell 2004). Ten-year simulations were run for three variants that differed from the first ten years of the baseline case only in the settlement's overall number of plow teams per household. The base case value was .5 (half as many plow teams as households). We also examined cases in which the plow team ratio was .25, .1875, and .125. For these variant cases (as well as in the baseline case), the plow teams were assumed to be community resources for which households would have to queue up for access.

Simulation results (figure 9.13) illustrate a behavior not infrequently seen in complex systems: an abrupt and vivid change in aggregated system behavior as a hidden resource threshold is reached. The population traces in figure 9.13 indicate that the .25 and .1875 plow-team-per-household ratio cases appear to be sustainable, differing little from the base case. This implies that plow team availability is not a serious constraint to successful agriculture at those resource levels. However, the simulated community in the .125 case (one plow team for every eight households) experienced an aggregate system catastrophe, with a precipitous decline in settlement population over ten years.

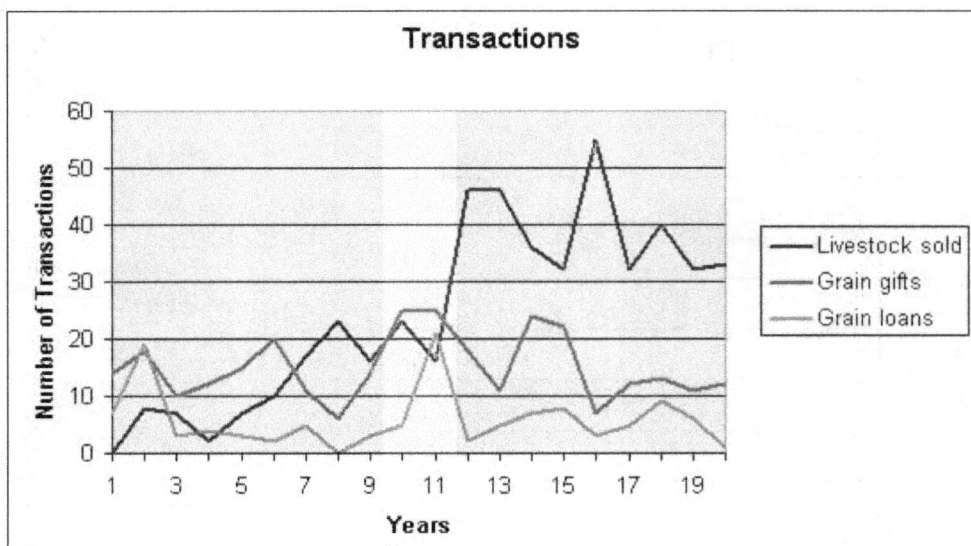

Figure 9.14. The volume of exchanges for the corvée episode scenario.

In our highly complex, multilayered simulations, a great number of possible reasons, natural and/or societal, can account for crop failure. However, in these controlled scenarios we have isolated as a critical factor the inability of some households to obtain access to a key resource—plow teams—in sufficient time to get fields plowed and crops planted before the winter rains begin. Because we made the simplifying assumption of a constant plow-team ratio, the number of plow teams dropped along with the settlement population, so the situation did not stabilize as the settlement began to empty of people. Presumably, adaptive farming households would have learned to adjust the number of plow teams to the need well before the crisis depicted in figure 9.13 had unfolded in full. Nevertheless, the "hidden" plow team constraint is genuine and constitutes a serious potential vulnerability.

Stress Scenario: Acute Labor Shortage at Harvest

Without prior warning, 90 percent of the settlement's adult male population was withdrawn for a six-month period, from March to September, in the tenth year of a twenty-year simulation (highlighted for Year 10 and Year 11; figure 9.14). Afterward, they returned to the settlement. This hypothetical episode required that the simulated community bring in its grain harvest with a drastically reduced labor force, perhaps reflecting a demand for corvée labor by a local political power. Much of the harvest could not be saved, and households unable to obtain grain gifts were compelled to seek food through alternative coping strategies such as selling livestock and borrowing grain. Figure 9.14 shows how the volume of grain gifts and grain loans peaked temporarily during and immediately after the labor crisis. However, the most noticeable change is a much higher level of livestock trading activity that began with the corvée

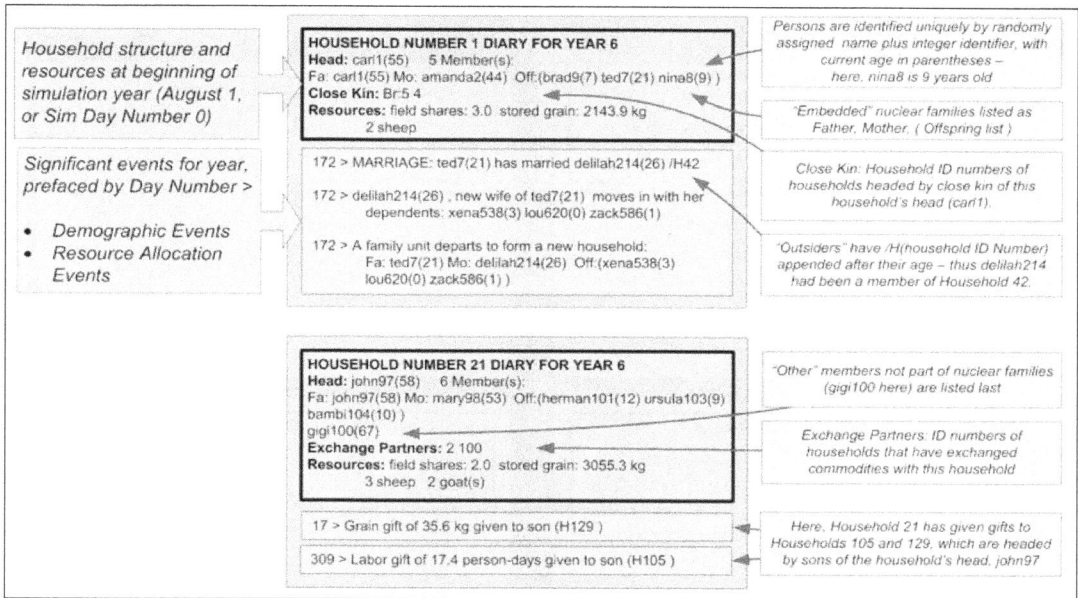

Household structure and resources at beginning of simulation year (August 1, or Sim Day Number 0)

HOUSEHOLD NUMBER 1 DIARY FOR YEAR 6
Head: carl1(55)   5 Member(s):
Fa: carl1(55) Mo: amanda2(44) Off:(brad9(7) ted7(21) nina8(9))
Close Kin: Br:5 4
Resources: field shares: 3.0 stored grain: 2143.9 kg
                  2 sheep

Persons are identified uniquely by randomly assigned name plus integer identifier, with current age in parentheses – here, nina8 is 9 years old

"Embedded" nuclear families listed as Father, Mother, (Offspring list)

Significant events for year, prefaced by Day Number >

- **Demographic Events**
- **Resource Allocation Events**

172 > MARRIAGE: ted7(21) has married delilah214(26) /H42

172 > delilah214(26) , new wife of ted7(21) moves in with her dependents: xena538(3) lou620(0) zack586(1)

172 > A family unit departs to form a new household:
          Fa: ted7(21) Mo: delilah214(26) Off:(xena538(3)
          lou620(0) zack586(1))

Close Kin: Household ID numbers of households headed by close kin of this household's head (carl1).

"Outsiders" have /H(household ID Number) appended after their age – thus delilah214 had been a member of Household 42.

HOUSEHOLD NUMBER 21 DIARY FOR YEAR 6
Head: john97(58)   6 Member(s):
Fa: john97(58) Mo: mary98(53) Off:(herman101(12) ursula103(9)
bambi104(10))
gigi100(67)
Exchange Partners: 2 100
Resources: field shares: 2.0 stored grain: 3055.3 kg
                  3 sheep 2 goat(s)

"Other" members not part of nuclear families (gigi100 here) are listed last

Exchange Partners: ID numbers of households that have exchanged commodities with this household

17 > Grain gift of 35.6 kg given to son (H129)

309 > Labor gift of 17.4 person-days given to son (H105)

Here, Household 21 has given gifts to Households 105 and 129, which are headed by sons of the household's head, john97

Figure 9.15. Sample Household Diaries for the corvée episode scenario: Year 6.

episode but persisted to the end of the scenario. This more energetic adaptation effort might be an indication that the crisis had destabilized the settlement to some degree.

The settlement appears to have weathered the crisis well. Except for a small net population loss due to emigration in Year 11 (twelve emigrants), the settlement population trajectory is comparable to the baseline case for Years 12–20. Though annual population losses due to emigration remained low, they were systematically higher after the crisis, increasing to roughly four persons per year from a pre-crisis average of 1.7 persons per year.

For deeper insights into the effects of the corvée episode on the model settlement's sustainability, it is useful to look at the scenario from the standpoint of the individual household agents, rather than at the aggregate properties of the settlement. To accomplish this, we can examine the "Household Diary" output stream from the simulations. Household Diaries record all significant demographic events (birth, deaths, marriages) and resource-related events (gifts and loans, reciprocal exchanges) for each household for each year in a simulation.

Figure 9.15 illustrates the format of the Household Diary output for two representative and comparable agent households, Household 1 and Household 21, for Year 6 of the acute harvest labor crisis scenario simulation. Household 1 consists of a five-member nuclear family. Household 21 contains a five-member nuclear family and another relative, the surprisingly durable gigi100, who at age sixty-seven is a statistical anomaly, given the brutal death rates built into the model population demographics. Both households begin Year 6 with field shares, livestock, and a substantial grain reserve. Household 1's only apparent advantage is that it can call for aid on two close-kin

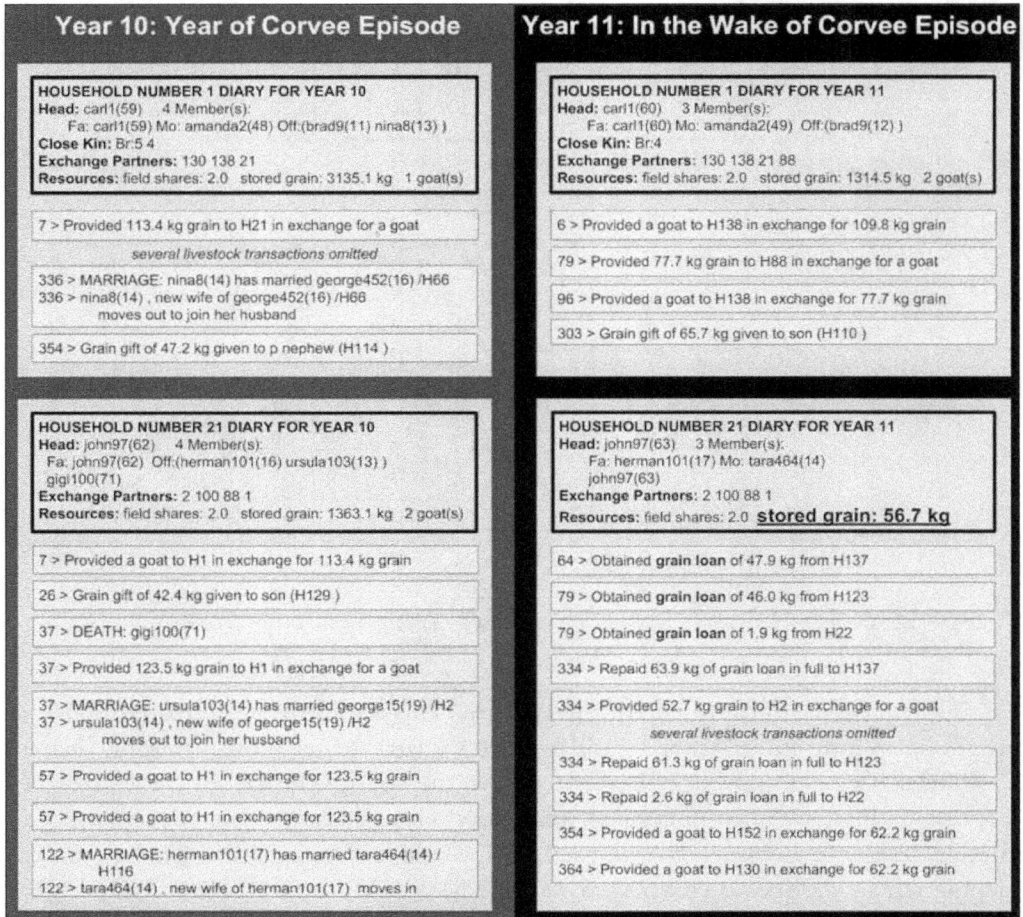

Year 10: Year of Corvée Episode	Year 11: In the Wake of Corvée Episode

HOUSEHOLD NUMBER 1 DIARY FOR YEAR 10
Head: carl1(59)   4 Member(s):
  Fa: carl1(59) Mo: amanda2(48) Off:(brad9(11) nina8(13))
Close Kin: Br:5 4
Exchange Partners: 130 138 21
Resources: field shares: 2.0 stored grain: 3135.1 kg   1 goat(s)
	HOUSEHOLD NUMBER 1 DIARY FOR YEAR 11
	Head: carl1(60) 3 Member(s):
	  Fa: carl1(60) Mo: amanda2(49) Off:(brad9(12))
	Close Kin: Br:4
	Exchange Partners: 130 138 21 88
	Resources: field shares: 2.0 stored grain: 1314.5 kg 2 goat(s)

7 > Provided 113.4 kg grain to H21 in exchange for a goat	6 > Provided a goat to H138 in exchange for 109.8 kg grain
several livestock transactions omitted	79 > Provided 77.7 kg grain to H88 in exchange for a goat
336 > MARRIAGE: nina8(14) has married george452(16) /H66 336 > nina8(14) , new wife of george452(16) /H66 moves out to join her husband	96 > Provided a goat to H138 in exchange for 77.7 kg grain
354 > Grain gift of 47.2 kg given to p nephew (H114)	303 > Grain gift of 65.7 kg given to son (H110)

HOUSEHOLD NUMBER 21 DIARY FOR YEAR 10
Head: john97(62)   4 Member(s):
  Fa: john97(62) Off:(herman101(16) ursula103(13))
  gigi100(71)
Exchange Partners: 2 100 88 1
Resources: field shares: 2.0 stored grain: 1363.1 kg   2 goat(s)
	HOUSEHOLD NUMBER 21 DIARY FOR YEAR 11
	Head: john97(63) 3 Member(s):
	  Fa: herman101(17) Mo: tara464(14)
	  john97(63)
	Exchange Partners: 2 100 88 1
	Resources: field shares: 2.0 **stored grain: 56.7 kg**

7 > Provided a goat to H1 in exchange for 113.4 kg grain	64 > Obtained **grain loan** of 47.9 kg from H137
26 > Grain gift of 42.4 kg given to son (H129)	79 > Obtained **grain loan** of 46.0 kg from H123
37 > DEATH: gigi100(71)	79 > Obtained **grain loan** of 1.9 kg from H22
37 > Provided 123.5 kg grain to H1 in exchange for a goat	334 > Repaid 63.9 kg of grain loan in full to H137
37 > MARRIAGE: ursula103(14) has married george15(19) /H2 37 > ursula103(14) , new wife of george15(19) /H2 moves out to join her husband	334 > Provided 52.7 kg grain to H2 in exchange for a goat
	several livestock transactions omitted
57 > Provided a goat to H1 in exchange for 123.5 kg grain	334 > Repaid 61.3 kg of grain loan in full to H123
57 > Provided a goat to H1 in exchange for 123.5 kg grain	334 > Repaid 2.6 kg of grain loan in full to H22
122 > MARRIAGE: herman101(17) has married tara464(14) / H116 122 > tara464(14) , new wife of herman101(17) moves in	354 > Provided a goat to H152 in exchange for 62.2 kg grain
	364 > Provided a goat to H130 in exchange for 62.2 kg grain

Figure 9.16. Sample Household Diaries for the corvée episode scenario: crisis years.

households, Households 4 and 5, each of which is headed up by a brother of carl1, the head of Household 1. The diaries for Year 6 also indicate that Household 1 celebrated the wedding of the eldest son of the house and saw his departure to form a new household with his new bride and her prior dependent children; Household 21 was sufficiently well-off to be able to provide gifts of food and labor to other close-kin households.

The Household Diaries for simulation Years 10 and 11 (figure 9.16), the years of the labor crisis, tell a different story. Household 1 enters this critical interval with a substantially deeper grain reserve than Household 21. In Year 10, both households still appear stable and capable of providing gifts to other households. However, even though Household 21 could afford to buy a goat to slaughter for ursula103's wedding feast, shortly thereafter it had to begin selling off livestock to obtain needed grain.

The temporary removal of nearly all the adult males at harvesttime in Year 10 led to serious grain losses due to insufficient harvest labor. As figure 9.16 shows, both households' grain reserves at the start of Year 11 were well below the preceding year's starting levels. Household 21 began that year with virtually no grain and consequently began to obtain grain loans. It was able to repay these loans but had to sell all its livestock, indicating that it was experiencing considerable food stress. At this point, grain loans became Household 21's primary option for obtaining food until the next harvest was in. This option, however, became less viable as the household defaulted or struggled to repay its loans and other households began denying its loan requests.

In Year 14, Household 21 gave up the fight and emigrated. When it needed kin support the most, the lack of close kin who can provide frictionless assistance (that is, grain gifts) sealed its fate. Household 1 continued to thrive. Its kinship connections to other households in the settlement improved its ability to sustain itself.

These household-level examples demonstrate that the fine-scale details do matter: the specific circumstances in which each household finds itself can have a greater influence on the household's sustainability than do the aggregate properties of the community. This scenario example underlines the desirability of analyzing communities at agent household and person levels and highlights some of the diverse social behavior and natural factors represented in the Enkimdu framework that are key in understanding household dynamics.

Stress Scenario: Diphtheria Epidemic

We imposed an acute stress on the Tell Beydar model settlement in the form of a severe epidemic, perhaps an outbreak of diphtheria, that specifically targeted the children. Diphtheria can cause rapid and widespread death among populations, particularly among very young individuals. For years, in fact, diphtheria was a leading cause of death for children under fourteen years of age in many countries, with death often occurring within one week of contraction (Hardy 1998). It is well known that disease can have devastating impacts on human populations; however, it can be difficult to determine how acute fatal diseases such as diphtheria affect long-term population dynamics under given cultural norms of marriage and household structure.

The modeled epidemic occurred in Year 20 and caused the deaths of approximately 80 percent of children and infants under age twelve. We selected a severe death rate for illustrative purposes; 20 percent death rates for a total population have been recorded for outbreaks in the past century (Kleinman 1992). The epidemic was modeled as a purely demographic event; we did not attempt physiological simulation of the onset and progression of diphtheria.

In the scenario population results (figure 9.17), the settlement population growth rate recovered in the first few years after the epidemic. However, the settlement population declined in the long term because the age cohort struck by the disease was not available for reproduction under our given social rules of marriage. Initially, the high attrition of that age cohort did not negatively affect household sustainability. In fact, it was a moderate positive factor because young children are a drain on households in terms of their resource utilization relative to the amount of food they help to produce.

Within fifteen years of the epidemic, at about the age most of the young victims would have been productive adults, the losses for that age group began to exert a more severe effect on the settlement. Labor shortages and overall decline in births relative to deaths (from a ratio of 1.2 births to deaths in the baseline case, to 1.1 in the diphtheria case) substantially compromised some households' resilience to stress. With greater food stress caused by declining labor resources, the overall volume of economic exchanges among households increased, as can be seen in figure 9.18.

The missing children left gaps in family continuity across generations, reducing the average number of close-kin households that a household could call upon for non-reciprocal assistance by about 20 percent with respect to the pre-epidemic levels. By Year 95 in the diphtheria case, no household had more than four kin household connections; in the same period for the baseline case, some households had seven kin-related households. The emigration of many households due to failure to cope with food stress further eroded the interhousehold kinship network.

What the diphtheria scenario shows is that short-term population shocks can have significant impacts on long-term population trends. Certainly, cultural behaviors could have changed this dynamic, specifically if immigration was an option to help replenish the population. The point this example makes is that we cannot easily predict population trends without looking at concurrent interactions of social and natural systems.

Discussion

The Tell Beydar reconstructions show that the more traditional landscape model (summarized previously) provides a plausible model in which the various data sources, in general, converge on a similar outcome. However, it results in a static equilibrium model that relates to a situation in which agricultural production had seemingly stabilized at its maximum extent. In contrast, the simulations capture more dynamics of the community, so one can discern detailed, agent-level social evolutionary trends. The example of the two households in the labor shortage scenario effectively shows the different forms of evolutionary trends that households can follow. Throughout the interval, simulated fine-scale dynamics of social and natural processes profoundly affected both households' abilities to function and survive. The fine-scale outcome of the corvée episode was particularly instructive because one household collapsed while a very similar household was able to sustain itself. In addition, by looking at the aggregate behaviors of the agent households, we can discern how our "Tell Beydar–like" settlement evolves through time. This makes Enkimdu a valuable tool for studying long-term socioevolutionary trends at both the individual/household and settlement levels.

Certain households also show signs of accumulating more pastoral animals as a result of favorable conditions of exchange. In contrast, other households lose resources and in certain cases become impoverished, thereby leaving the simulation. Such processes hint that, over time scales in excess of the present century-long simulation runs, we may discern the development of elites and impoverished clients. Overall, such

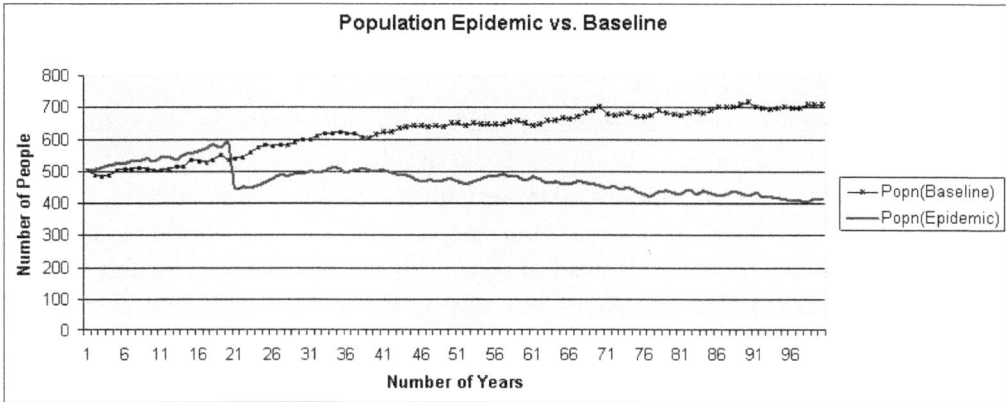

Figure 9.17. Settlement population trends in the epidemic case and the baseline case.

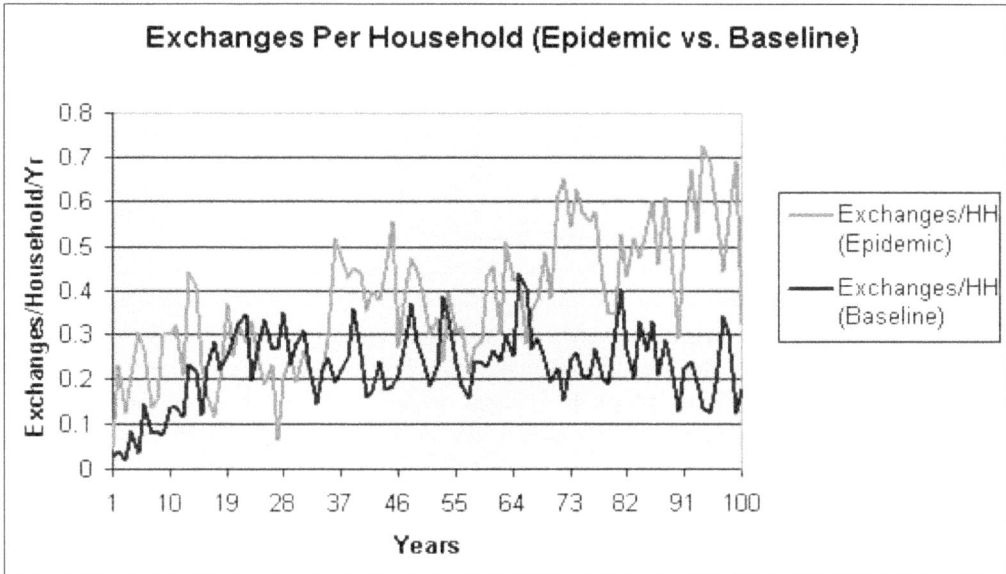

Figure 9.18. The volume of exchanges for the epidemic case and the baseline case.

dynamics will change not simply the consumption patterns but also, in theory, the social dynamics of the entire community. In the near future, as the simulation incorporates additional social dynamics and simulation functionality, we can expand this engine to look at regional dynamics and interactions among multiple settlements and nonsettled populations.

When we compare input data (such as trends in annual rainfall) with "output" in the form of number of households or community population, it becomes apparent, for the parameters we have chosen to model, that high amplitude and variable inputs result in low amplitude outputs (Wilkinson et al. in press). This may suggest that system complexity and the number of opportunities offered for exchange or modifying production may suppress the fluctuation of what appears to be a key driving variable in the form of climate. This has significant implications for the understanding of human-environment interactions.

The plow team scenario demonstrates how modeling efforts can be valuable in testing data derived from texts. In this case, the simulation framework provided a test for a text-derived range of values of a key agricultural production parameter, namely, plow teams per household. This simulation suggests that the assumption of one plow team per household is too rigid. Instead, it apparently would have been feasible to allocate plows to more than one household, but only up to the given threshold after which the community suffered critical losses of agricultural production.

The overall outcome of the simulations, although preliminary, shows how complex datasets can be analyzed to produce plausible, nonlinear, and frequently unexpected results. Our understanding of Mesopotamian social mechanisms is far from complete, but the ability to test our hypotheses makes the simulation effort valuable in answering questions concerning socioecological dynamics. Ultimately, we aim to run multiple scenarios in order to produce sensitivity studies, as well as sets of trajectories for each community or set of communities.

Acknowledgments

The project "Modeling Bronze Age Settlement Systems in a Dynamic Environment," discussed in this chapter, is a collaborative effort of the Oriental Institute and the Department of Anthropology at the University of Chicago, the University of Durham, and Argonne National Laboratory. We are particularly grateful to the National Science Foundation Program: Dynamics of Coupled Natural and Human Systems (Grant No. 0216548) for providing major funding for this project. Earlier exploratory work was funded by the University of Chicago/Argonne National Laboratory Collaborative Grants Program in 1998 and 1999, as well as by the University of Chicago, Advanced Technology Initiative (2000). We must also thank Steven Cole, Colleen Coyle, Jesse Casana, and Jayne Dolphe, all of whom contributed significantly to the earlier stages of the project. Satellite remote sensing was undertaken in the Oriental Institute's Center for the Archaeology of Middle Eastern Landscape (CAMEL) laboratory, and thanks must go to the Oriental Institute and its director, Professor Gil Stein, for providing facilities for the research. The area of Tell Beydar in Syria provides a model landscape for the simulation, but this simulation is not using the actual field data supplied by the survey. Nevertheless, we are very much indebted to the Tell Beydar Project, especially Marc Lebeau, Karel Vanlerberghe, and Antoine Suleiman, for providing the opportunity for TJW and JAU to undertake fieldwork around that site.

Notes

1. Note that this measurement corresponded to .842 liters in northern Mesopotamia.

2. Most of the tablets can be dated to the seventh and eighth years of King Amar-Suen's reign.

3. All calculations assume that 1 IKU (1/18 BÙR) equals 3,528 sq m, 1 SILÀ in southern Mesopotamia (1/300 GUR) equals 1 liter, and 1 liter barley equals .62 kg.

4. Obviously, the round tablets were drawn up within the "public sector" of the society, so it is not surprising that the fields in these texts belonged to the same public or official part of the economy. The organization of private fields—if they existed—remains uncertain.

CHAPTER 10

Evolution toward Complexity in a Coastal Desert Environment

The Early Bronze Age in the Ja'alan, Sultanate of Oman

Serge Cleuziou

This chapter is an initial contribution toward modeling long-term culture change in a region where Neolithic and Early Bronze Age (EBA) societies differ considerably from those of the major cultural areas of the Middle East. Our purpose is to understand why, beyond the obvious limitations of climate and geography, the area never reached the same level of social complexity as the early states that developed around it and with which it was in continual contact.

The Oman Peninsula (figure 10.1) is a region in which archaeological research started late but has grown considerably in the past thirty years.[1] Yet our knowledge is far from complete; some areas and topics have been studied in more depth than others. At the easternmost tip of the Arabian Peninsula and the Arab world, the Ja'alan has been the subject of more than twenty years of in-depth research. Intensive surveys, as well as extensive excavations of selected sites and sampling of many others, have been carried out together with paleoenvironmental studies. These allow us to reconstruct the evolution of the population and the transformations of its environment since the Early Holocene. In spite of the fact that we are still lacking data, and in order to detect what remains to be done, we are currently working on a model of at least part of the social trajectory of this region during the third millennium BC.

Late Prehistoric Roots

For the sake of discussion, we can divide the late prehistory of the Oman Peninsula into several periods. By the end of the Holocene wet phase, around 4000 BC, the region

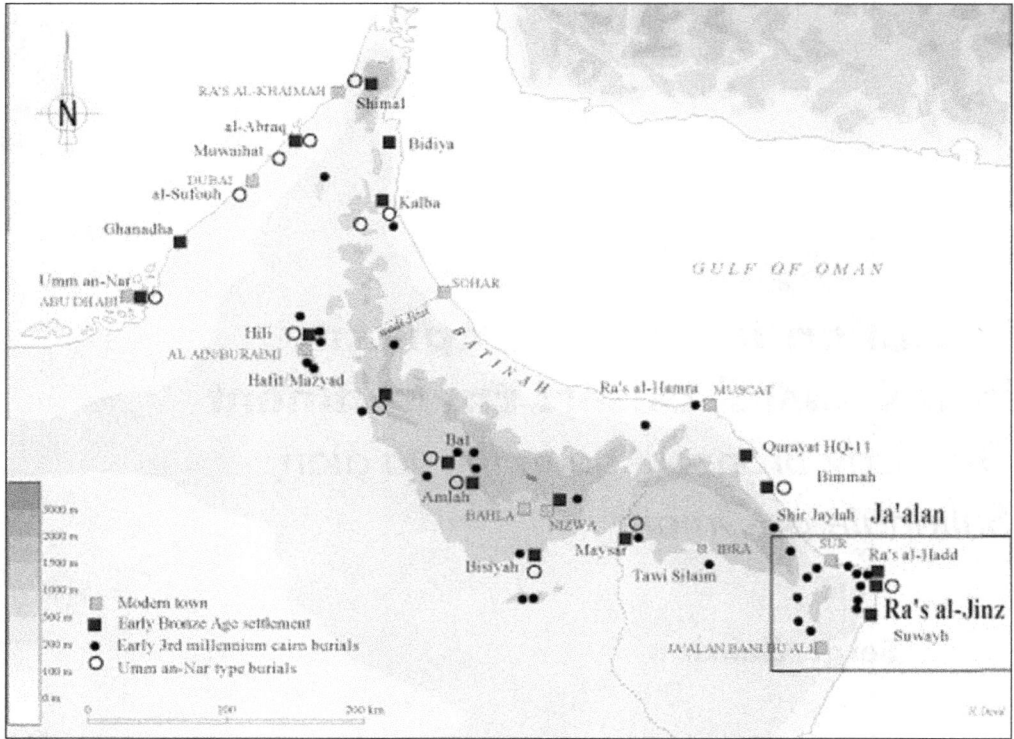

Figure 10.1. The Oman Peninsula during the third millennium BC.

appears to have been populated for several millennia by small communities that for-
aged seasonally across its various environments (Cleuziou 2005). Typically, these
groups would spend winters in the coastal areas, mainly exploiting lagoons and mangroves, or on the shores of the lakes that were present in areas now covered by the sand
dunes of the Ru'b al-Khali Desert. Typical seaside winter stations are found at Ra's al-
Hamra near Muscat or as-Suwayh in the Ja'alan. Their seasonal occupation is demonstrated by an increasing number of bioarchaeological studies (for example, Martin
2005). We assume that scatters of flint on the surface of Holocene deposits between
the desert dunes correspond to winter stations; these were the only known sites in the
desert until the discovery of circular stone structures at Karimat al-Manahil, deep in
the Ru'b al-Khali. At present, the only known spring station is site BH-18 at al-
Buhais on the western piedmont of the Omani Mountains in the Emirate of Sharjah,
utilized in April or May (Uerpmann, Uerpmann, and Jasim 2000). Many roasting pits
were found on a large area along a hillslope, just north of a large cemetery that yielded
a huge number of burials .5 m below the surface in an area of 160 sq m. Three hundred and forty-six skulls were recovered, but according to the excavators, probably
twice as many burials are present (Kiesewetter 2003:36–7). The site was likely one of
those gathering places where some communities met after spending the winter on the

coast, before they split into smaller groups to evade the worst of the summer heat in the deep mountain valleys.

According to the very rich zooarchaeological record, the people gathering at BH-18 were herders. Their meat diet consisted mainly of beef, mutton, and goat; smaller numbers of cattle, sheep, and goat bones are also found on all documented coastal sites. Hunting at these locations was marginal. Except for a few clearly imported date stones in a fifth-millennium site on Dalma Island, we have almost no information about the use of vegetal resources. The possibility that these "fishing-herder-gatherers" occasionally also practiced a kind of opportunistic agriculture cannot be excluded but remains unproven.

With the desiccation of the climate, this pattern of seasonal use of the desert may have decreased, but it was still in place, notably in the Ja'alan, during the fourth millennium BC. Seven sites there have been tested, and some twenty more mapped, along about 80 km of the Arabian Sea coast. Because of slightly higher sea levels, large lagoons and mangrove swamps could be exploited by small communities (Berger et al. 2005), which also turned to fishing in the open sea, concentrating on a few species such as tuna. Fish exploitation and fish export to the interior probably increased the importance of processed fish in the diet at various times of the year. The coast may have provided a buffer to balance growing shortages of food in the interior.

The "Great Transformation"

By the end of the fourth millennium BC, the communities of the Oman Peninsula underwent deep transformations that affected all aspects of society: economy, demography, and material culture. By that time, exploitation of the rich copper belt in the Omani Mountains had begun, for export to Mesopotamia (Berthoud and Cleuziou 1984) and for local use; copper hooks, knives, needles, and pins replaced shell, flint, and bone assemblages within a few generations. Agriculture, in the form of palm oases, developed wherever possible in the piedmont and in the valleys, such as at Hili and Bat (Cleuziou 1999). Fishing with a significant focus on fish processing for exchange is well attested on site HD-6 at Ra's al-Hadd on the Ja'alan coast, but the most obvious indicator of the new society is probably the development of single-chambered tomb towers.[2] These appear wherever the necessary resources (herding areas, fishing grounds) were available or had been developed (oases), overlooking them from rocky ridges or terraces. The towers are collective burials and contain anywhere from a few to three dozen individuals of both sexes and all ages: the ancestors who created these resources or had rights to use them were now watching the newly defined territories (Cleuziou 2002b).

Our assumption is that the tomb towers represent lineage burials that appear to have been used for two to three centuries before being condemned or destroyed. (This remains to be fully demonstrated, but many indications converge to this assumption [Cleuziou 2002b; Salvatori 2001].) As a rough estimate, there are more than 100,000 such graves all around the Oman Peninsula. More than 2,500 have already been entered in a GIS that is currently under construction for the eastern Ja'alan. Beyond a reorganization of territories, these graves indicate a rapid increase in the population over a few generations, resembling Bocquet-Appel's (2002) "Neolithic demographic transition." According to him, the number of immature individuals buried in a rapidly growing population is higher than in a stable or decreasing population, and this seems precisely the case in the single-chambered burials of Oman. We consider it indicative of a new attitude encouraging higher birth rates and communities that were obviously larger than before.

Interpretative hypotheses about this "great transformation" include climate change, foreign contacts, and social dynamics. Climate change cannot be directly correlated with this transformation because the trend toward drier conditions that started around 5500 BC (Lézine et al. in press) was already in full swing by the time it occurred (Von Rad et al. 1999). Foreign contacts are likely to have been involved. They are well documented through imported objects (pottery) and raw materials (bitumen) from Mesopotamia. This is the time when large parts of the Middle East experienced a major makeover, witnessing the rise of the early Egyptian dynasties, the spread of writing, and the earliest towns in Mesopotamia, the Iranian Plateau, and beyond. The soaring demand for minerals in the early urban centers of Mesopotamia may have been the stimulus for the exploitation of the rich copper belt in the Omani Mountains, through technologies imported from southeastern Iran. This triggered some destabilization in the area, which, in turn, led to a new type of society.

We suspect, however, that local factors were key in shaping the new society. The intensification of resource exploitation in some areas may be seen as a response to their general scarcity in space and time. This induced more intensive exchange and more territorial control. The domestic donkey came into use, providing a new means of land transport. Large towers, as well as tombs, in the oasis settlements constituted landmarks of the social and political structure. These matters are not discussed further here. For now, the great transformation appears as a "black-box problem": we know what comes before and what comes after, what was the input and what was the outcome, but we still do not understand the process in its full complexity. In our attempt to model the transformation in more detail, however, we should remember that part of the input is deeply embedded in the preceding situation.

This chapter explores ways in which we can model the evolution of the newly created society during the period of almost a millennium before it was completely transformed yet again, around 2000 BC. The EBA society of the Oman Peninsula—the "Land of Magan," as it is known from Mesopotamian texts dating to the time of its upheaval—was characterized by a remarkable continuity throughout the third millennium BC, displaying high resilience in overcoming changing conditions and historical events. These include environmental perturbations (including human-induced changes), contacts with new foreign powers such as the Indus civilization, the adoption of new technologies, and even outside invasions documented in the archaeological record and in historical sources. As usual, many authors consider these events as the

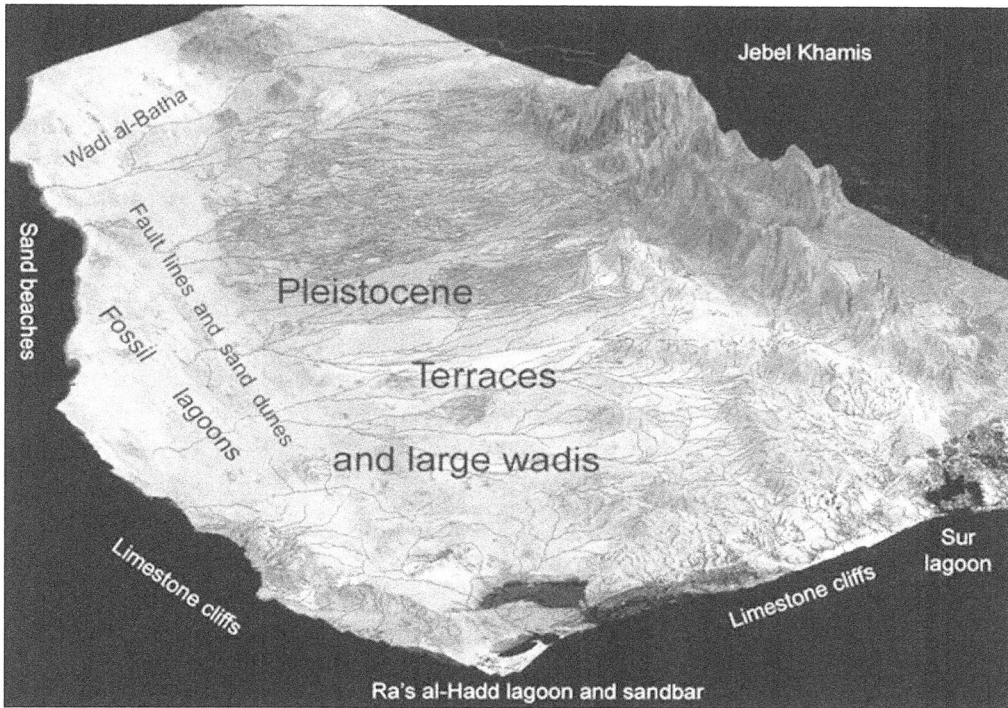

Figure 10.2. The Ja'alan, with its main economic environments.

main reasons for cultural change. We would, however, like to explore an alternative hypothesis, which accords the social dynamics a predominant role in the shift of the society toward greater complexity and in its abrupt collapse around 2000 BC—just after reaching its apogee in the last centuries of the third millennium BC.

The Northeastern Ja'alan

The study area (figure 10.2) encompasses some 3,000 sq km at the easternmost end of the Oman Peninsula. To the west, it is limited by the Jebel Khamis, a north-south oriented range reaching an altitude of 1,200 m that constitutes the easternmost edge of the Omani Mountains; to the north and to the east, it is bounded by the sea, and to the south, by the lowermost course of the Wadi al-Batha. This large seasonal river drains all the occasional water flows created by the winter rains along the southern edge of the mountains.[3]

The Wadi al-Batha is the location of large oases in constant interaction with the eastern Ja'alan in the recent past, belonging to the same social and economic system (Lancaster and Lancaster 1996). Its rich agricultural potential and the presence of thousands of third-millennium graves lead us to assume that a similar association between the two areas already existed in the Early Bronze Age. Unfortunately, because of a lack of survey and also the intensive urban and agricultural developments of the past thirty years, it is very poorly known archaeologically and cannot be included in the area of study. We will assume that similar interactions between the two areas already existed during the third millennium BC and that both followed the same evolutionary trends. Therefore, exchange of products between them, as well as a certain degree of interdependence, will be a part of the model.

In the northern part of the Ja'alan, the relief consists of a large limestone terrace of Miocene age that was eroded by high sea levels during the late Pleistocene wet phase, some 120,000 years ago. It towers over the ocean in a continuous vertical cliff about 30 m high, interrupted only by a few deep wadis ending on small beaches. The one exception is the Ra's al-Hadd, where a mid-Holocene sandbar delimits a large lagoon (Khor al-Hajar) at the point where the Sea of Oman meets the Arabian Sea. South of the abrasion terrace, several wadis feed into a large, still active lagoon (Khawr al-Jaramah) that communicates with the sea through a deep, narrow canyon cut across the terrace. We know that this lagoon was much larger at the time of higher sea levels and that the residual mangroves still visible along its southern shore were more extensive than they are today. These constituted a very rich environment for human communities. To the south, the coast takes the form of a series of large lagoons, now dry, that were active between approximately 5000 and 2000 BC because of slightly higher sea levels.

The changes occurring in these lagoons over time, which may have caused important changes in resource availability, have been studied in some detail. By the end of the Holocene wet phase, large mangrove swamps and reed belts populated the lagoons; by the EBA, they appear to have been more open and brackish (Berger et al. 2005; Lézine et al. 2002).

Between the mountains and the coast, the eastern Ja'alan plain consists of gravel terraces of quaternary age, cut by the wide, flat beds of the wadis that once fed the mangroves. A mid-Holocene, north-south fault system lifted the eastern coast and the lagoons by a few meters, inducing significant changes at the junction of the wadis and the lagoons. Nowadays, the plain is covered by small sand dunes that not only make survey difficult but also obscure a number of archaeological sites along the inner edge of the lagoons. The terraces that were covered with soil and grassy vegetation before the wet phase at the end of the Holocene are now barren, cut by wide wadi beds, where the level of freshwater is never very deep. They remain good grazing areas for a small population of camels, goats, and even some cows. Near the mountains are a few small oases, fed by permanent springs and wells. According to our surveys, these were much more numerous during the third millennium BC.

Compared with the piedmont belt of the Oman Peninsula, however, vegetal and land-mammal resources in the Ja'alan are quite scarce, and the carrying capacity of the terrestrial area cannot have exceeded a few hundred to one thousand people. By far, the main resource is the sea. Along the coast of the Arabian Sea, between Ra's al-Hadd and the Dhofar, the monsoon creates a cold upwelling during summer. The deep, cold waters bring a large quantity of nutrients to the surface, which attract an exceptional wealth of small fish (sardines and anchovies) and their predators, notably tuna and dolphin. These come very close to the coast during winter and are easy prey. It is, in fact, the only area along the entire eastern Arabian coast where such a wealth of fish approaches the agricultural wealth of the oasis belt. In addition, the beaches at Ra's al-Hadd and Ra's al-Jinz are the nesting ground of large green sea turtles (*Chelonia mydas*). They nest mainly during fall and early winter and are exploited for their eggs, meat, and fat. The settlement pattern and the economy of the Ja'alan are determined by this seasonal complementarity among oases, grazing, and fishing, and this is key in any attempt to model past cultural processes.

Another factor that became paramount during the EBA is maritime trade, mainly concentrated at Ra's al-Hadd. Despite its barren hinterland, this is an inevitable port of call when sailing across the Arabian Sea, using the alternate winds and currents of the summer and winter monsoons. For medieval Arab navigators, the lagoon of Khor al-Hajar was a mooring point to wait for proper winds and currents.[4] The discovery of abundant material from the Indus civilization at HD-1, on the sandbar that separates the lagoon from the sea, indicates that this was already the case in the second part of the third millennium BC (see Cleuziou and Tosi 2000 for a more complete description of the EBA sites). This trade began around 2500 BC, when the process we would like to model had already been under way for half a millennium. Studying the changing impact of this trade is one of our goals.

Some Elements of Method

The data we are assembling result from some twenty years of research by a multidisciplinary team that has tried to understand all facets of Neolithic and EBA occupation in the northeastern Ja'alan. This includes extensive excavation of two settlement sites (Ra's al-Hadd [HD-6] and Ra's al-Jinz [RJ-2]) and three related cemeteries (Ra's al-Hadd [HD-10], Ra's al-Jinz [RJ-1], and Ra's al-Jinz [RJ-6]), as well as test trenching in many other settlement and burial sites. Systematic surveys across most of the study area have allowed us to plot more than 2,500 burials, mostly from the EBA, and several hundred other sites of various types and periods (figure 10.3).

Paleoenvironmental and geomorphological studies enabled us to reconstruct the vegetation, landscapes, and sea levels between 7000 and 2000 BC, although we readily admit that we have not yet attained the centennial precision we seek. Combined with a Digital Elevation Model and its various derivative products, these data would allow diversified spatial studies, especially a spatial model for the evolution of available resources throughout the third millennium BC. Eventually, paleodemographic models (now under construction), which use the spatial distribution of skeletal materials and tombs, will allow us to compare the archaeological data with our social interpretations. Population pressure and the carrying capacity of the area are key issues in our work, although we do not consider them directly linked but, on the contrary, related through cultural factors. In what follows, we consider the possibility that the

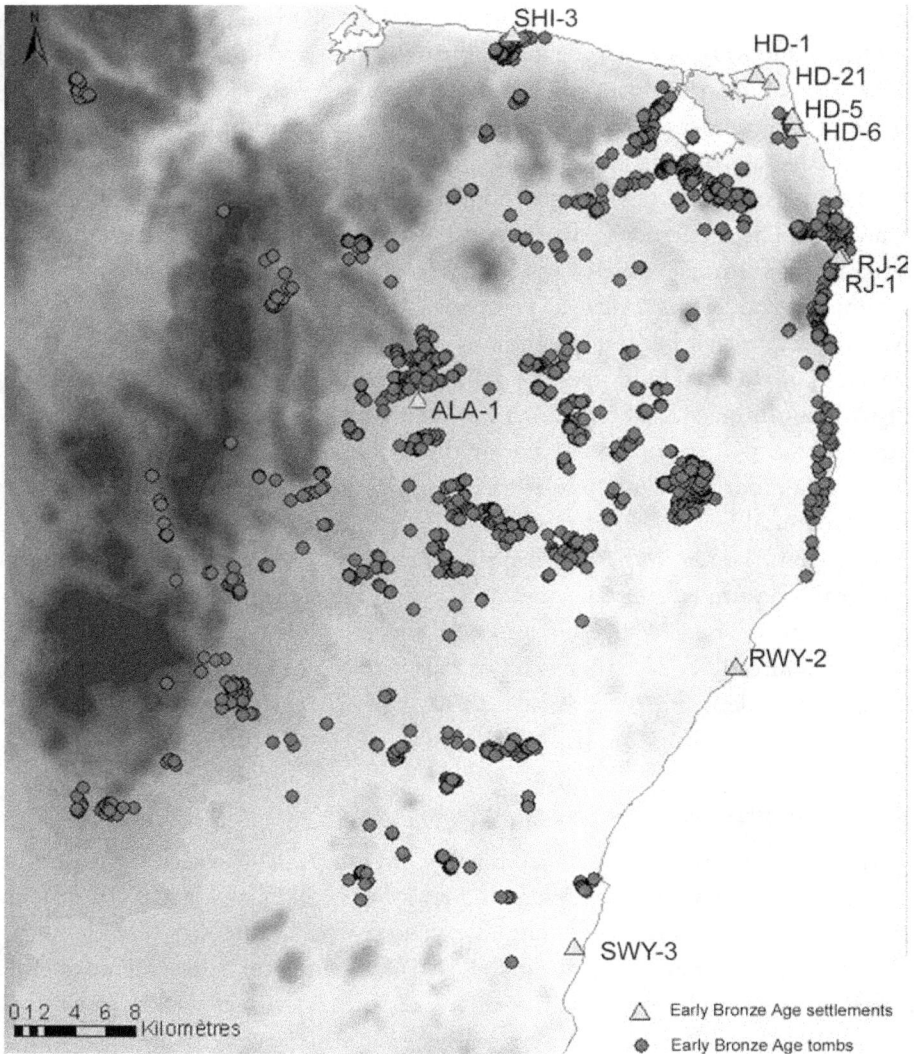

Figure 10.3. The distribution of EBA graves and sites in the Ja'alan, as presently plotted.

economic and social dynamics may have been allowed to exceed environmental limitations, making the system more and more exposed to any type of crisis. In that context, we would like to explore the idea that the late-third-millennium collapse was mainly the result of a social crisis.

A Scenario for Cultural Evolution

The starting point for the social trajectory we intend to model is the society that emerged from the "great transformation." By 3000 BC, the new cultural system encompassed the whole of the Oman Peninsula, and even the most remote areas were included in a complex web of internal and foreign exchanges. We may hypothesize that the demographic transition was already producing its effects and that population growth had returned to a more moderate pace, although on a different scale.

The landscape was marked by thousands of tower graves. Their distribution around the ecological niches previously used by mid-Holocene communities indicates that, with the exception of the most xeric areas, the newly defined territories included all these niches and their productive capacities had been maximized—to a point that greatly exceeded local needs. Conservation techniques for fish and dates, and production of cereals in the oases, allowed delayed consumption and exchange of resources that are otherwise seasonal.

Other authors have used a few events to advocate discontinuity; we assume that all developments occurred inside the same social system. One of these events is obviously the appearance, around 2700 BC, of a new type of collective burial, usually known as "Umm an-Nar graves" from the place where they were first discovered.[5] The size and monumentality of these round, multichambered monuments grew continuously with time, as did the complexity of the burial rituals associated with them and the number of bodies contained (reaching several hundred over two to three centuries). The place of these new graves in the social landscape was different, in very close proximity to settlements and sometimes even within them. We take this as an indication of a consolidation, not a transformation, of the system. In the kinship organization, they represent a higher level of lineage units, which can be matched, to some extent, to the residence patterns (see below). The tendency toward monumentality, itself, can be interpreted as indicating a strengthening of these lineages and of their structure, possibly even as the result of competition among them. However, no exceptional grave indicates higher status in death for any individual, whatever his or her position during life. We assume that the society remained strongly kinship-oriented during the whole third millennium BC.

Other events include a generalization of pottery use in daily life by 2500 BC and the rise of the Indus civilization as a trade partner around the same time. The first historical events are documented by 2300 BC, such as the victorious campaigns against the Land of Magan by two Akkadian kings of Mesopotamia, Manishtushu and Naram Sin, during the twenty-fourth and twenty-third centuries BC. But these left no traces in the archaeological record and appear to have had little impact on a society that was moving toward upheaval on its own. This does not mean that we deny any influence from foreign contacts; rather, we think that such influences should be considered in the context of local developments.

Let us just take one example. We have already emphasized the importance of food and food processing in internal exchanges. We also know from Mesopotamian texts that food was sent from Mesopotamia in the form of barley or "good sesame oil," and the archaeological record supports this. Umm an-Nar near Abu Dhabi has yielded an abundance of large Mesopotamian vessels that were obviously used for food transport from Mesopotamia, and Ra's al-Jinz and Ra's al-Hadd yielded many Indus pottery vessels with the same function. It has been convincingly argued that cheese and ghee (clarified butter) were among the imported products (Gouin 1997). Apart from transport jars, few types of foreign pottery reached the interior of Oman, and even fewer were imitated in local wares.[6] In fact, the only imitations were strainers and a special variety of pedestal cups possibly used in making and consuming cheese. We do not know whether the appearance of cheese-linked items indicates a new type of processed food or merely new ways of making it, with more fashionable or efficient tools, but this is certainly one way to consider those kinds of foreign or foreign-related items.

The system abruptly collapsed by 2000 BC, replaced by a new archaeological culture in the "Wadi Sûq" period. Whatever the interpretation of the collapse, this culture corresponds to less intensive land use, fewer people, and a major change in funerary practices. Most of the dead were buried in individual stone-cist graves. Collective burials were a minority and have different shapes; they contained fewer individuals and no longer displayed evidence of complex postmortem rituals. We take this as an indication that a sharp social transformation marked the end of EBA society in Oman. The Wadi Sûq period has often been described as the "dark ages," explained by environmental or foreign factors such as drought or collapse of international trade (both undemonstrated).

We would like to use our model as a tool to investigate another scenario, that the EBA civilization of the Land of Magan ended because it failed to make (or rejected) a further step in political organization. The constant increase in the level of regional and foreign exchange was necessary to sustain an economic system and a population that were exhausting the locally available resources. Such an increase would have favored the strengthening of the elites, who were in competition with the egalitarian ideology at the basis of the tribal system. The growing monumentality and rituality of the collective burials evidence the increasing strength of the elites. In other words, the scenario to be modeled can be summarized as follows:

a.   Continuous growth after the complete reorganization of the "great transformation"

b.   During this growth, enough resilience to overcome various environmental changes and historical events, as well as the ability to incorporate new techniques and products from the outside

c.   At some time, a conflict between trends toward more complex social hierarchies (that is, "primitive states") and the society's deeply rooted values

d.   No resolution of this conflict and therefore a quick collapse of the society, in which the economy was no longer sustainable

Some Additional Elements for the Ja'alan

The northeastern Ja'alan is fully part of the system, although it presents some particularities due to the environment and extensive research in the area. Environmental factors are, of course, linked to the sea and notably to variations in sea level throughout the third millennium BC. These may have changed the location of the sites along the coast but probably did not affect the general trend toward intensified fishing for processing and export. The wealth of the sea in the area is such that only (modern) industrial fishing in deep sea could have depleted it to a significant level, so we will consider this factor as negligible.

Another important factor is that freshwater may have been much more easily available during this period. This has been demonstrated in the interior, at Hili, for instance, where a drop of 4.5 m in the water table is documented during the third millennium BC. There, people made up for this by permanently improving the irrigation system (Cleuziou 1999). Geomorphological investigations have shown that the water table in the Ja'alan is never very far below the surface (rarely more than 1.5 m along the sea or in the wadi beds), but wells may quickly have been depleted or become brackish. The area could never have supported such large oases as the piedmont areas. Today, only a few small palm-tree gardens exist, usually close to the foothills and feeding on permanent water springs such as those of al-Ayn and an-Nakheel or on wells in some wadis. The largest one is at Wadi Sal. These never exceed a few hundred trees.

According to our surveys, however, the situation was better around 3000 BC. Only three settlements have been securely identified, but we can assume the existence of many more, in view of the hundreds of graves surrounding them. One of these, at al-Ayn, was tested; it yielded rectangular stone structures on a low sedimentary terrace. The first use of this settlement can be dated to the beginning of the third millennium BC. More than one hundred early-third-millennium, single-chambered graves perch above it; multichambered graves scattered among the houses indicate that it continued to exist throughout the Early Bronze Age.[7] This probably represents a previously unknown class in the EBA settlement hierarchy in Oman; we will call them "garden settlements" by analogy with the large "oases settlements" such as Hili, Bat, or those that were probably present in the Wadi al-Batha. In contrast to the latter, though, garden settlements have no large towers, which might also indicate their position in the social organization.

One aspect of our project is, of course, a reconstruction of the demographic trajectory over the course of the third millennium BC. According to early-twentieth-century British surveys, the population of the Ja'alan was then about three thousand people, who moved between the Wadi al-Batha oases and the sea. We can take this as an indication of the area's carrying capacity under the economic system of the time, and a broad calculation according to the number of single-chambered graves indicates that such a figure is a minimum for our period. Paleodemographic evidence from eighty individuals, studied by Olivia Munoz in grave 1 at Ra's al-Jinz (RJ-1), suggests that around 2500–2400 BC the population was still growing. Although we do not advocate a simple direct link, we do assume, because internal exchange was so important, that demographic pressure became very high by 2000 BC, before the system collapsed. Despite much more intensive survey than anywhere else in the country, we know of only two settlements (on the coast) and a few re-uses of previous graves by the beginning of the second millennium BC, clearly indicating that the area became depopulated.

Identifying the Agents

The archaeological record allows us to identify, to some extent, the nature of the agents and the structure of their interaction. A basic assumption is that the political and economic organization remained kinship-based during the whole EBA and that changing alliances among tribal segments constituted the main arena of power and politics.

The EBA site RJ-2 at Ra's al-Jinz comprises several compounds of mud-brick houses along the edge of a former Holocene beach. Following a fourth-millennium BC occupation (Period I), three main periods have been identified for the second half of the third millennium BC, broadly dated at 2500–2300 BC (Period II), 2300–2100 BC (Period III), and 2100–2000 BC (Period IV). The southern compound was built at the beginning of Period II and continued to be in use for some time during Period III. The northern compound was built at the beginning of Period III and lasted for some two centuries, with many changes and refurbishments. Period IV, after the northern compound was abandoned, is too poorly preserved to be interpreted here.

These compounds combine several basic units, each composed of three to four rooms, often including two small storerooms (figure 10.4), covering an average surface of 50–60 sq m. An isolated unit to the south, building III, made up of one large room and three smaller rooms, had a surface area of 53 sq m. Such units were probably designed to accommodate basic social units, what we could call nuclear families. The northern compound had a different organization, centered on an eight-room unit, by far the largest on the site, with a surface area of approximately 100 sq m and a courtyard used for domestic purposes. The various extensions surrounding the courtyard all appear as single units with some autonomy. From such a pattern, we can assume a grouping of nuclear family units into larger residential compounds. Considering the importance of kinship, each compound likely corresponds to an extended family.

Some form of economic and domestic cooperation must have existed inside these compounds. The latter is supported, for instance, by a long sequence of domestic ovens in the courtyard of the northern compound. One might also expect economic cooperation in fishing or fish processing. Fishing equipment is present in every house, as one would expect on a site where basically everyone engaged in fishing, but activities linked to fish processing were performed outside the houses and their remains yield nothing interpretable in terms of social organization.

There are two indications, however, of relative autonomy at the nuclear family level. One is the presence in each unit of the remains of the production of *Conus* sp. and *Pinctada margaritifera* shell rings. Each unit was engaged in this "cottage industry" and produced goods that could be channeled into internal exchange circuits, along with the main fish products, and even occasionally into overseas trade. Moreover, in each unit of the southern compound, bitumen slabs scraped from hulls of seagoing boats were found stored in a room, waiting for re-use. It seems that everyone shared in

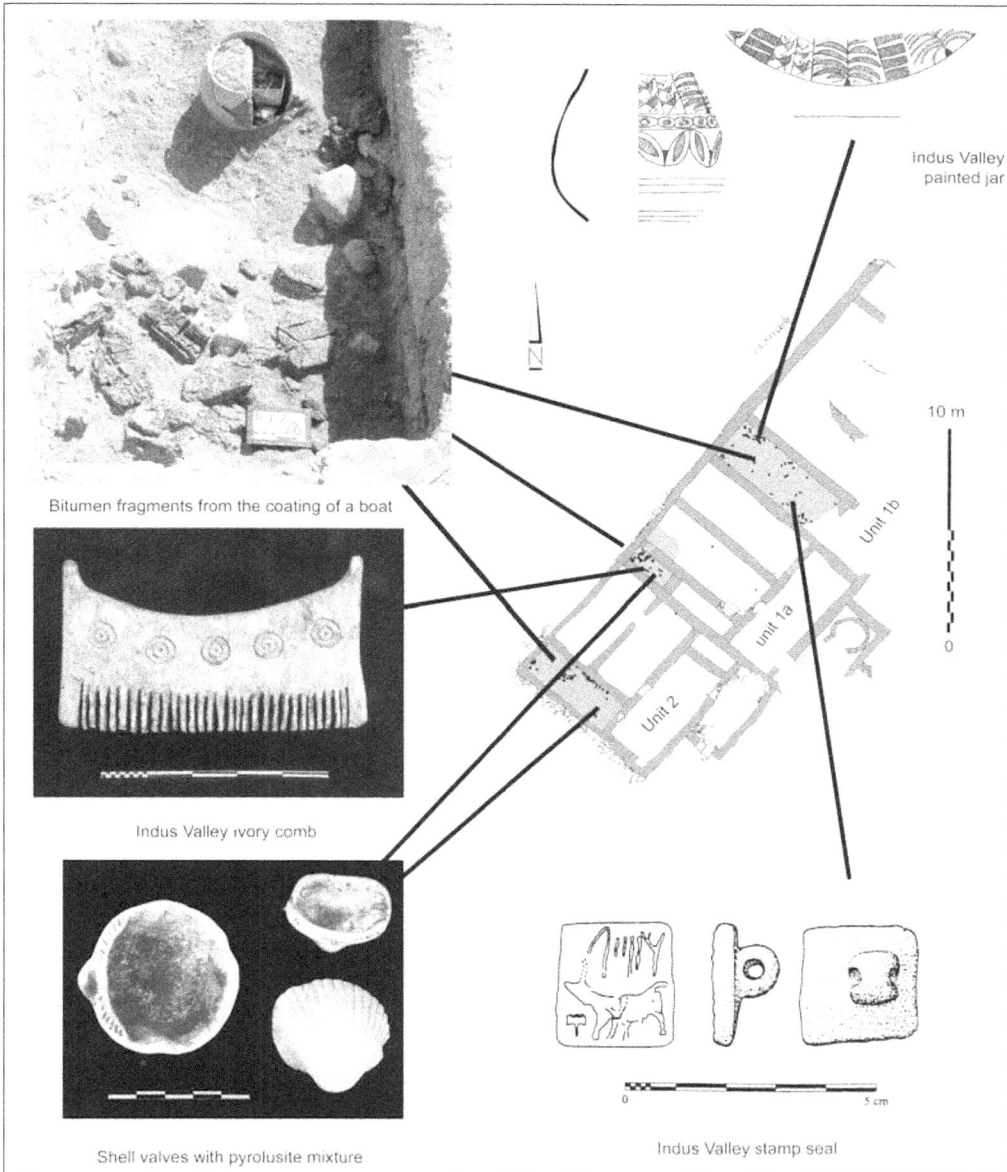

Figure 10.4. Ra's al-Jinz, the evidence for the agents.

this resource but that the use of the product was left up to decisions at the individual household level. Considering the importance of bitumen for making boats, this is a significant indication.[8] That other materials originating from imports or waiting for export were found in the same rooms strengthens the idea that each unit had some economic autonomy.[9] This leads to a definition of nuclear families (whatever their actual composition) as independent agents. While staying at Ra's al-Jinz for the fishing and fish-processing season, these agents are archaeologically represented by architectural units of some 50–60 sq m, cooperating together through the larger structure of the extended family.

At the top of the settlement hierarchy are the large oasis sites with towers. There are a few towers in each main oasis (five to six at Bat, Bisiya, and Hili), whose diameter and possibly height may vary, but there are no other, different monuments that could be considered significant at the community level. In the absence of any other monument, we consider the large oases to be aggregations of several lineages of the "tower community type," cooperating (and, to some extent, competing) through alliance-based political links. We assume that these tower communities represent the largest kinship group and the nuclear family, the smallest. In between, we will find extended families and possibly "garden communities," that is, small oases with no towers. But the important thing for us is that basic units can be considered as moving with some degree of freedom and decision autonomy within this framework.

The funerary record strengthens this broad classification. We may consider the single-chambered graves in the beginning of the third millennium BC as extended-family burials and the multichambered graves in the second part of the third millennium BC as tower-community burials. We do not assume, however, that the bodies of all members of an extended family, nor all those linked to a tower community during their lifetime, went into the same tomb. There may have been other criteria, such as ancestry, for tomb recruitment. In addition, we know from Ra's al-Jinz that some newborns, at least, were buried below house floors. The full argument for this has been developed elsewhere (Cleuziou 2002b, 2003). Broadly, the number of multichambered graves at Hili, for instance, is about three times the number of towers. Because we know from excavations that each grave was used for no more than two to three centuries before being voluntarily condemned and replaced, the figure appears coherent with a sequence of three graves for each tower during a time span of seven or eight centuries—acknowledging, of course, that human social rules are bound to be transgressed with regularity. This has important implications for our model, for we will mostly use the location of burial grounds and their number to identify the territories and assess their size.

Some scant outside historical data suggest, however, that there may have been higher levels in society. Cuneiform texts indicate that the Akkadian emperor Manishtushu conquered the thirty-two fortresses of Magan sometime around 2300 BC and that his grandson Narâm Sîn defeated Mannium (or Mannu Danu), the putative "king" or "lord" of Magan. Two centuries later, Wedum appears as an envoy of Nadub-'El, Ensi2 of Magan, to the royal court of the Sumerian king Amar Su'en. These titles have to be interpreted with some caution. Mannium may have been the temporary head of a coalition of tribes, appointed to face the threat from outside. He was defeated "in the middle of the sea," in one of the first naval battles recorded in history. Ensi2 is a title commonly given to foreign rulers by the Mesopotamian administration, and Nadub-'El might have been any kind of local potentate engaged in Gulf trade and politics, important enough that his messenger is allowed to participate in a ritual. It is impossible to elaborate further on the status of these individuals, but the existence of temporarily appointed rulers, or even the occasional emergence of powerful individuals, does not contradict the picture presented above. *Federation*, whatever it actually covers or conceals, remains a key word in the South Arabian kingdoms in the first millennium BC, as is evident from the title of the first Sabean king, *Mukarrib*, "the one who federates." The inscriptions in which he celebrates his victories leave little doubt about how he accomplished this task.[10]

For the time being, we are left with a four-level hierarchy and some possible temporary higher functions:

1. Basic house units, representing the nuclear family.

2. House compounds, representing the extended family.

3. "Palm tree garden" settlements (al-Ayn) and non-tower fishing settlements (Ra's al-Jinz).

4. Large oases with towers, which seem, however, to be absent in the Ja'alan.

5. Temporary war leaders or individuals who play a buffer role with foreign powers. By the end of the third millennium, at the upheaval of the Land of Magan, their rising power comes in conflict with the deeply rooted traditional values of the kinship-based society.

At this point, it must be recognized that the kind of hierarchy presented above does not work socially like a simple pyramid. It does not mean that all dwellers in a lower-level settlement (garden communities such as al-Ayn or fisherman villages such as Ra's al-Jinz) belong to the same higher-level entity (a tower community or even an oasis settlement as a whole). Such is not the case at present (Lancaster and Lancaster 1996) and was probably not the case in the past. Looking at such complicated webs through archaeological data is obviously a desperate task, but it may explain why Umm an-Nar–type burials near the small garden communities in the Ja'alan are more numerous than near the large oasis settlements in the piedmonts. Whether a strategy can be defined to monitor this possible effect of alliance patterns is an interesting question.

We must also take into account that, at least during the second part of the third millennium BC, the site of Ra's al-Hadd occupied a special position in the system. Because of its pivotal role in ocean navigation and Indus trade, it channeled wealth into the area that was not produced there. To some extent, the northern Ja'alan evolved between the port of Ra's al-Hadd and the large oases of the Wadi al-Batha, both of which interacted with it but were not directly part of it. Thus, we have solid data about the first three levels of the society, but the fourth, although present, is less well documented. This will have some consequences for the way we mobilize our data.

Most archaeologists working in this area may complain that in the foregoing we have oversimplified the data, and possibly extended our interpretations too far! But anyone with some experience in modeling knows that we are trying to test ideas about ancient societies, not to describe as closely as possible an ancient reality that will probably always escape us, whichever way we approach it. As a matter of fact, they may also tell us that what we are trying to do is already too complicated. We are fully aware of that.

Implementing the Model

Having determined what we consider to be our agents and their social structure, we have to define their rules of interaction. This can be characterized as building inferences from our databases—a job that is still in progress. Because we are mainly investigating tendencies toward the concentration of power, a patron-client (for example, see chapter 5, this volume) or similar strategy appears to be a good approximation at present. We also have to identify the factors that characterize the actions of our agents. These include the economic reliability of their territories, their production and exchange capacities, and their demographic dynamics. We start from the assumption that wealth was almost equitably distributed by 3000 BC. Clearly, this is not fully true for our real society but seems an acceptable working hypothesis.

By combining soil surveys and grave locations, we are able to assess the size of agricultural areas and their potential productivity and to identify the grazing areas. Elements for an evaluation of oasis productivity have been developed in various agronomic surveys, such as that of Dollé and Toutain (1990). Our control of climatic conditions is poor, although centennial-scale data are available and may be used to monitor shorter-scale change and to model vegetation variability. According to varve thickness in deep sea core SO 90-39KG/56KA (Von Rad et al. 1999), the Ja'alan—where rainfall was comparable to the present (or even slightly lower)—experienced several periods of drought (2975–2925 BC, 2800–2600 BC, 2525–2475 BC, 2250–2175 BC). These are not directly related to the collapse of the Magan society by 2000 BC but can be implemented in the model in order to evaluate its resilience. As already mentioned, we may exclude human-induced depletion of deep-sea resources, but there are limiting factors such as seasonality and labor force, which may have assumed importance as the lagoons along the eastern coastline dried up.

Our model of the demography will use what we know about the region's paleodemography based on study of four assemblages, dated to 3500–3300 BC (before the "great transformation"), 3000–2800 BC (immediately after it), 2600–2400 BC (at the time of contact with the Indus civilization), and 2250–2100 BC (just before the collapse).

Evaluating the importance of exchange with the interior and across the ocean will admittedly be complex, especially if we consider that by the end of the period, imports from outside were part of the subsistence base and essential to its sustainability. We may, however, consider factors such as the mobilization of human and material resources to build boats and the number of crew members, at least as limiting factors, because we have some insight in such issues through our ongoing experimental work (Vosmer 2003, Vosmer in press).

Table 10.1 represents a first attempt to list some of the parameters linked to exchange processes, according to their direction, geographical range, and control level

Table 10.1. Exchange Resources by Scale of Exchange and Level of the Hierarchy Participating in the Exchanges

	Resources	Geography					Hierarchy		
		Local			Regional (Oman)	International	1	2	3
		A	B	C					
I	Processed fish		■	■				■	■
	Turtle and dolphin fat, fish oil		■	■				■	■
	Marine salt	■	■	■			■	■	
II	Dried sardines (animal consumption)						■		■
	Flint and other flaking materials			■				■	
	Reeds	■	■	■			■	■	■
E / III	Conus and Pinctada rings			■			■	■	
X	Shell beads			■			■		
P	Steatite beads	■		■			■		
O	Other marine products	■	■	■	■	■	■	■	■
R / T	Pyrolusite			■				■	■
I	Dates			■	■			■	■
	Milk products			■	■			■	
	Cereals and leguminous			■	■			■	■
	Ghee			■				■	
	Other food products			■	■			■	■
	Domestic animals			■	■			■	■
	Land salt			■	■			■	
II	Copper			■	■	■	■	■	■
	Fibers and ropes			■			■	■	■
	Pottery			■	■		■		
	Firewood	■					■		
	Wood for boat building					■			■
	Bitumen					■		■	■
	Leather and hides			■		■			■
I / III	Textiles					■		■	■
M	Ivory and luxuries					■		■	■
P	Frankincense					■		■	■
O / R	Calcite vessels					■		■	■
T	Chlorite vessels					■		■	■

in our artificial society. It will probably be too complicated to study the simultaneous interaction of all these parameters; we certainly have to restrict their number. We are looking for relations between the population and its territory, assuming that by the end of the third millennium BC, the only way to sustain population growth was to (again) increase the volume of exchange, mainly to obtain more food through wider regional or even long-distance trade and thus strengthen elite control at every opportunity. From such a perspective, most commodities in the exchange network were contributing to this development in one way or another, rather than impeding it. We have to define some of the rules that will enforce the egalitarian dynamics of the tribal society, however. Compulsory redistribution to maintain the wealth of all agents at a minimal level may fulfill this role because it prevents, at least to some degree, the extinction of individual agents. The complexities of the seasonal habitation pattern may be another factor buffering local depletion of resources.

The distinction between this scheme and earlier, crudely deterministic, environment-based models may appear slight. What we advocate here is not that population growth or climatic change led to resource depletion and system collapse. On the contrary, we assume that a system that had relied since its inception on exchange in order to overcome environmental limits stimulated the development of a powerful attractor: the concentration of power and the creation of a state-level hierarchy. Meanwhile, the cooperatively oriented kinship ideology was constantly fighting against this tendency, as we know from, for instance, the multichambered graves.[11] This opposition eventually drove the social trajectory away from the attractor, causing what archaeologists usually consider to be a collapse.

In other words, referring to a dichotomy proposed by Stuart Kauffman (1995: 49–51) in a stimulating essay on complex systems, we will try to test the idea that the infracritical behavior of our agents successfully challenged the system's autocatalytic tendency toward more hierarchy. A model such as the "blue loop" applied by Harry Erwin (1997:70–5) to Minoan peer polities may be of interest in this context, but that decision is still under consideration.

We may or may not succeed. But if we can test the likelihood of this idea and if, conversely, we can check the system's resilience in the face of environmental or historical events, this can surely be considered progress in our understanding of past cultural processes. Obviously, the road is long, but as Tim Kohler once wrote, this is fun!

Acknowledgments

The surveys were carried out by the author and Maurizio Tosi, as well as many team members, notably Alberto Monti, Vincent Charpentier, and Agnese Cavallari. Survey data are included in a GIS coordinated by Jessica Giraud. Geomorphologic studies were done by Jean-François Berger, Mauro Cremaschi, and Jean-Claude Plaziat. Satellite maps and geographically referenced information were managed by Gourgen Davtian. Paleoclimatological studies were carried out under the direction of Anne-Marie Lézine. Paleoanthropology has been conducted by many specialists, including Hervé Guy, Matthieu Gaulthier, Alfredo Coppa, and Olivia Munoz.

This study is part of the Joint Hadd Project, directed by the author and Maurizio Tosi (University of Bologna). I thank the Ministry of Heritage and Culture of the Sultanate of Oman for its constant support. Grants came from the French and Italian ministries of foreign affairs, the French CNRS programs Paléoenvironnement et évolution des hominidés and ECLIPSE, the Italian CNR, and the French Ministry of Research (ACI TTT). Since January 2006, the work has benefited from a grant from the Agence Nationale de la Recherche (ANR-05-BLAN-0352-01). I would like to thank Sander E. van der Leeuw for encouraging me to enter the path of modeling and also for his improvements of this text (and of my English).

Notes

1. At present, the Oman Peninsula comprises the United Arab Emirates and the northern part of the Sultanate of Oman.

2. Often called "cairns," "Hafit graves" (from the place they were first recognized), or "beehive graves" in the archaeological literature. Other single-chambered, aboveground tombs are known from the Iron Age, but their remains are usually easy to distinguish from those of the EBA.

3. At present, average rainfall on the Omani Mountains is approximately 200–300 mm a year. In the piedmont areas, the mean annual rainfall is less than 100 mm. In the Ja'alan itself, years of complete drought are not rare, although heavy showers usually occur three to four times a year between November and February.

4. A large medieval site (HD-4) is present on the sandbar, close to the third-millennium site at HD-1. Ahmad ibn Majid's *Book of Profitable Things*, written in 1490, vividly depicts the area's importance.

5. The previous tower graves are, for the same reason, called "Hafit"-type graves. Most archaeological literature used to distinguish a "Hafit period" followed by an "Umm an-Nar period." For a refutation of this argument and archaeological arguments in favor of continuity, see Cleuziou 2002a and 2003.

6. The only other exception is the occurrence of small painted jars of Mesopotamian origin that were almost exclusively used as funerary deposits in the single-chamber burials of the early third millennium BC (Cleuziou and Méry 2002).

7. The work at al-Ayn, carried out under the direction of Olivier Blin, concerns one of these rectangular houses, approximately 10 by 15 m. It yielded several EBA layers. These overlay an earlier horizon with postholes that is provisionally dated to the fourth millennium BC.

8. Bitumen was not available in the region. Its Mesopotamian origin has been demonstrated through isotope analysis by Jacques Connan, and fragments of about thirty Mesopotamian jars once containing bitumen were found on the site.

9. Among imported objects are Indus Valley pots and an Indus Valley stamp seal. Objects linked to export are large conch shells (*Fasciolaria trapezium*) and small bivalve shells (*Anadara* sp. and *Glycymeris* sp.), the latter containing a mixture of pyrolusite, a manganese ore of local provenience (less than 5 km away), that makes a "ready to use" makeup. Both types of shells are found in the contemporaneous Royal Graves at Ur in Mesopotamia, where the *Fasciolaria trapezium* are cut into drinking vessels and the small shells still contained a makeup mixture.

10. These inferences are broadly based on ethnographic descriptions of the power structure in Arabic tribes. According to Dresch (1989) and Lancaster and Lancaster (1992), entrepreneurs like Nadub'El act outside the tribal territory as buffers between the tribal society and the state, the state being either foreign or locally established, such as in modern Yemen.

11. We interpret the increasing monumentality and rituality in Umm an-Nar–type burials as a way to conceal a more and more powerful tendency towards hierarchy.

CHAPTER 11

Progress in Cultural Modeling

Henry T. Wright

Approaches to the modeling of human communities are rapidly evolving. This volume is a key contribution in a chain of seminar and workshop volumes that are pushing the development of a useful approach in the historical and anthropological study of ancient communities. Every chapter presents new and otherwise unavailable contributions. Most of these chapters put forth novel arguments or innovative approaches to the representation of cultural systems in formal terms. Indeed, there is an exceptional number of breakthrough papers in this study, and all of them are of interest to scholars concerned with the complexities of cultural change. If several tendencies are represented, this has the value of motivating the readers to think about work they otherwise might not.

The introduction by Kohler and van der Leeuw clearly defines concepts such as "model," "theory," and "concept" with reference to a few seminal readings. Intellectual ancestors are honored. In addition, I think that it is important to place the workshop in the context of an emerging relationship between two Santa Fe institutions—the School for Advanced Research (SAR) and the Santa Fe Institute (SFI). The School was established almost one hundred years ago to sustain documentation of Native American peoples, particularly in the North American Southwest. Under the dynamic direction of Douglas Schwartz for almost forty years, the School has also supported advanced seminars with a broader theoretical focus on development of complex cultural systems.

The Santa Fe Institute was established more than twenty years ago in a founding workshop held at the School. Its aim was to seek universal principles governing the development of all forms of complex systems. Several of its founders, ranging in diversity of perspective from anthropologist Robert McCormick Adams to physicist Murray Gell-Mann, argued that cultural systems, in particular, should be an important focus for the Institute. That many of the Institute's early participants were interested in the accomplishments of southwestern native peoples over the millennia, an area long studied at the School, is also certainly significant.

While the chapter by Kohler and van der Leeuw identifies some of the differences between North American and European conceptualizations of culture change, some will still perplex readers and merit further comment here. For example, the Europeans (excluding the British contributors) use the concept of "evolution" in the pre-Darwinian sense exemplified by Auguste Comte to characterize any kind of system change. The North Americans, in contrast, use "evolution" to denote change engendered by selection, in a way similar but not identical to the "natural selection" of biologists. This European usage is not stubborn archaizing, but a deliberate choice arising from their perception that intentionality and learning give cultural change a different dynamic. Their position should be respected, whether or not one agrees with it.

Because this collection captures different lines of research at different stages of development, the reader may perhaps find it most enlightening to consider the papers in four groups.

First are the chapters by Smith and Choi (chapter 5) and Shennan (chapter 7), which are general discussions about how developing complex cultural systems might be approached. As it happens, both use a Darwinian perspective, signaling the level of sophistication and abstraction to which such arguments have been taken.

Second are the chapters by Jordan (chapter 2), Cleuziou (chapter 10), Kirch and colleagues (chapter 6), and Berger and colleagues (chapter 3). These deal with the basic steps in modeling such systems. Jordan (chapter 2) presents an analysis of data on style variation among native communities in northern California. It underlines the axiom of the Santa Fe Institute's Geoff West that we have to know something about a system before we can usefully model it. It also illustrates the analytical advantages of having both the long perspective of archaeology and the precise chronological and cultural controls afforded by ethnographic collections and linguistic data. Cleuziou (chapter 10) lucidly uses exciting recent field research in Oman, which has been stimulated by the immigration of some of the Near East's most brilliant archaeologists from more conflicted parts of the region. After summarizing the evidence of cultural change, Cleuziou illustrates the beginnings of model building, defining the parameters, agents, and interaction rules that will be used in future attempts at formalization. Kirch and his team (chapter 6) present a progress report on similar work on the island of Maui in the Hawaiian archipelago, summarizing the research undertaken on various subsystems driven by the perceived requirements of a future formalization of the whole cultural system. Included are completely new materials on natural environments, agriculture, population, and control hierarchies—heretofore presented only in specialized reports or not at all. Particularly notable, and driven by the need for more precise dating if we are to evaluate such models with archaeological data, is the development of a novel, precise dating technique using coral. Berger and colleagues (chapter 3) use the mature results of the European community–funded "Archaeomedes" project in the lower Rhône Valley of France, originally designed as part of a project to elucidate issues of long-term desertification around the Mediterranean. Various programs of different kinds of research and modeling, presented in earlier publications, targeted many subsystems of the socionatural system of the lower Rhône. In chapter 3, these analyses are used to evaluate ideas developed from general theories of system "resilience." As I understand it, there is no immediate intent to produce a total model of the evolving cultural system on the lower Rhône, but this is clearly research in the complexity perspective informed by the use of formal models.

Third are the chapters by Kohler and colleagues (chapter 4) and Wilkinson and colleagues (chapter 9), which present some of the results of established operating models. The model of the Kohler team (chapter 4)—like a parallel effort by George Gumerman's team—focuses on the American Southwest ancestral Pueblo peoples of the sixth to thirteenth centuries AD and profits from three well-established areas of knowledge. These are (1) a precise archaeological record with both regional surveys and excavated sites often dated to the year by tree-ring dating, (2) the rich cultural testimony of the Pueblo descendants, and (3) a precise climatic record provided by tree-rings. The model has a relatively long history, with a continuous series of papers published since 1994. It focuses broadly on the co-evolution of environments and human communities. Its agents—individual households—initially make decisions about their members, their residences, and subsistence economies, in a modeled environment closely patterned after the actual environments of what is today southwestern Colorado as they varied from year to year, based on tree-ring evidence. In its first years, this model's subsistence choices were focused on maize, and agent behavior was rather mechanical. Nonetheless, it yielded demographic patterning broadly comparable to that actually recorded by archaeology. In recent years, the agents have been given much more diverse subsistence strategies and structures for social learning, the "cultural algorithms" devised by Robert Reynolds. The model of the Wilkinson team (chapter 9) focuses on the third millennium BC, the Early Bronze Age, in irrigated lower Mesopotamia and rain-fed upper Mesopotamia. The model profits from regional surveys and excavations by archaeologists; a record of recent traditional production, labor, and social organization from development studies and anthropologists; and a record of third-millennium cuneiform texts. Its agents are individuals and their households. Because the model is relatively new, it has so far investigated families and food production around a dry-farming town in upper Mesopotamia in an elementary way. Nonetheless, the results challenge traditional ideas about labor, production, and health and point to new areas of research that archaeologists must pursue. Both chapters 4 and 9 are particularly clear and well illustrated, and both refer to more detailed papers the reader may consult. Neither is yet a total system model, for critical sectors and connections are not yet represented, but both are moving toward this goal.

Fourth and finally is chapter 8, by Janssen and Anderies, which presents critiques of and proposed improvements on previous efforts to model a much discussed and relatively well-understood system, that of irrigation agriculture. It begins with the well-known model of recent Balinese rice irrigators developed by Lansing and Kremer and compares the results of this modeling of Balinese irrigation with two alternative models. The authors use the expertise acquired from this comparison to propose a model for the subsistence and social systems of central Arizona Hohokam irrigators between AD 200 and 1450. This is the only model in this volume that does not have an explicit spatial structure, and some of its implications would be hard for archaeologists to evaluate. Because it represents the major elements of feedback in such a system, however, it is effective in the assessment of system robustness in the face of various kinds of shocks. In the future, we can expect to see more and more of such "second-generation" papers, comparing the results of alternative modelings and proposing new formalizations of greater generality and utility.

All these chapters are reports on works in progress. They manifest substantial advancement, not only from the first use of agent-based models in archaeology two decades ago but also from workshops published only a few years ago. We can expect to see more such publications pushing forward the frontiers of model-based archaeology, from these authors and others. Let us hope that future volumes marking this progress will be as diverse, well written, and clearly illustrated as this one.

Appendices

Appendix 1. Raw Data for Chapter Two

Table A1. Built Structures (from Driver 1939)*

Selected Culture Elements	Tolowa	Chimariko	UKarok	LKarok	MFYurok	RYurok	Wiyot	Hupa1	Hupa2	Chilula	Nongatl	Mattole	ERSinkyone	MRSinkyone	Cahto
Rectangular floor plan	1	0	1	1	1	1	1	1	1	1	0	1	0	0	0
Circular ground plan	0	1	0	0	0	0	0	0	0	0	1	1	1	1	1
Single ridge pole	1	1	1	1	1	1	1	1	1	1	1	1	1	1	1
Double ridge pole at single ridge	1	1	1	1	1	1	1	1	1	1	1	1	1	1	1
2 ridge poles, 2 ridges	0	0	1	1	1	1	1	1	1	0	0	0	0	0	0
3-pitch roof	0	0	1	1	1	1	1	1	1	0	0	0	0	0	0
2-pitch roof	1	0	0	1	1	1	1	1	1	1	0	0	0	0	0
Hip-roofed	0	1	0	0	0	0	0	0	0	0	1	1	1	1	1
Conical shape	0	1	0	0	0	0	0	0	0	0	1	1	1	1	1
Vertical walls all around	1	0	1	1	1	1	1	1	1	1	1	0	0	0	0
Center post	1	0	1	1	1	1	0	1	1	1	0	0	0	0	1
4 corner posts	1	0	1	1	1	1	1	1	1	1	0	0	0	0	0
Side posts	0	0	1	0	0	0	0	1	1	1	0	0	0	0	0
Entire floor excavated	1	1	1	1	1	1	1	1	1	1	1	0	0	0	1
Central excavated pit floor	1	0	1	1	1	1	1	1	1	0	0	0	0	0	0
Central pit with 5 sides	1	0	1	1	1	1	0	1	0	0	0	0	0	0	0
Central pit with 4 sides	0	0	0	0	0	0	1	0	0	0	0	0	0	0	0

Feature												
Earth walls of excavation lined in planks	1	0	1	1	1	1	1	1	1	1	1	0
Paved stone floor	0	0	0	1	0	0	0	1	0	0	0	0
Plank-covered floor	1	0	1	1	1	1	1	1	1	1	1	0
Plank-covered	1	0	1	1	1	1	1	1	1	1	1	0
Planks vertical in walls	1	0	1	1	1	1	1	1	1	1	1	0
Only one horizontal plank in side walls	0	0	0	0	0	0	1	0	0	0	0	0
Roof planks, slabs, bark perpendicular to ridge	1	0	1	1	1	1	1	1	1	1	0	1
Bark or slabs	1	1	1	1	1	1	1	1	1	1	1	1
Earth-covered	0	1	0	0	0	0	0	0	0	0	0	0
Entrance projecting	0	0	0	1	0	0	0	1	1	1	1	1
Entrance flush	1	1	1	1	1	1	1	1	1	1	1	1
Faces east	0	1	0	0	0	0	0	1	0	0	0	0
Faces south	0	0	0	0	0	0	0	0	0	0	0	1
Shape, looking into, round	1	0	1	1	1	1	1	1	1	1	0	0
Shape, looking into, rectangular	1	1	1	1	1	1	1	1	0	1	1	1
Shapes converges at top when looked into	0	0	0	0	0	0	0	0	1	0	0	1
Entrance in middle of side of house	1	1	1	1	1	1	1	1	1	1	1	1

Selected Culture Elements	Tolowa	Chimariko	UKarok	LKarok	MFYurok	RYurok	Wiyot	Hupa1	Hupa2	Chilula	Nongatl	Mattole	ERSinkyone	MRSinkyone	Cabto
Entrance in middle of end of house	1	0	1	1	1	1	1	1	1	1	0	1	0	0	0
Entrance in right side of end of house	1	0	1	1	1	1	0	1	1	0	0	0	0	0	0
Cut out of a single plank	1	0	1	1	1	1	1	1	1	1	0	0	0	0	0
Ground level	1	1	1	1	1	1	1	1	1	1	1	1	1	1	1
Below surface	1	0	1	1	1	1	0	1	1	1	0	0	0	0	0
Sliding wood door	1	0	1	1	1	1	1	1	1	0	0	0	0	0	0
Swinging or lifting wood door	1	0	1	1	1	1	1	1	1	1	0	0	0	0	0
Swinging or lifting mat, bark, or bough door	1	1	1	1	1	1	1	1	1	0	1	1	1	1	1
Stone hand holds outside	0	0	1	1	1	1	0	1	1	0	0	0	0	0	0
Smoke hole main entrance	1	0	1	1	1	1	1	1	1	1	0	0	0	0	0
Trench or tunnel draft exit	1	0	1	1	1	1	1	1	1	1	0	0	0	0	0
Cobble-lined outside house	0	0	1	1	1	1	0	1	1	1	0	0	0	0	0
Open, trench	1	0	1	1	1	1	0	1	1	0	0	0	0	0	0
Boarded over, tunnel	0	0	0	1	1	0	1	0	0	0	0	0	0	0	0
Carved in single plank	1	0	1	1	1	1	1	1	1	1	0	0	0	0	0

Plug stop of wood	1	0	1	1	1	1	1	1	1	1	0	0	0	0
Carved in handle	0	0	0	1	1	1	1	1	0	1	0	0	0	0
Trench inside house from fireplace to exit	1	0	0	0	0	1	0	0	1	1	0	0	0	0
Stone paving in front	1	0	0	0	0	0	0	0	0	0	0	0	0	0
Fire on surface or in shallow depression	1	0	1	1	1	1	0	1	1	1	1	1	1	1
Fire in definite pit	1	1	1	1	1	1	1	0	0	1	0	0	0	1
Round pit fireplace	1	0	1	0	0	1	1	0	1	0	0	0	0	1
Square fire pit, four stones	0	0	1	1	1	0	1	1	1	1	0	0	0	0
Pentagonal fire pit, five stones	0	0	0	0	0	1	0	1	1	1	0	0	0	0
Pit clay-lined	1	0	1	0	0	0	1	0	0	0	0	0	0	0
Pit stone-lined	1	1	1	1	1	1	1	1	1	1	0	0	0	0
Fire in center of house or between center and door	1	1	1	1	1	1	1	1	1	1	1	1	1	1
Notched plank or log ladder	1	0	1	1	1	1	1	1	1	0	0	0	0	0

*These elements relate to shared elements amongst: 3-pitch-roof plank dwelling; 2-pitch-roof plank dwelling; circular ground plan, conical or hip-roofed dwelling; 2-pitch roof rectangular plank sweat house; circular ground plan, conical or hip-roofed, earth-covered pole sweat house. Note: definite presences from original CED list recorded here as 1, all else as 0.

Table A2. Basketry (from Driver 1939)*

	Tolowa	Chimariko	UKarok	LKarok	MFYurok	RYurok	Wiyot	Hupa1	Hupa2	Chilula	Nomgatl	Mattole	ERSinkyone	MRSinkyone	Cahto
Coiling Technique	0	0	0	0	0	0	0	0	0	0	0	0	0	1	1
Clockwise (looking into basket)	0	0	0	0	0	0	0	0	0	0	0	0	0	1	0
Counterclockwise	0	0	0	0	0	0	0	0	0	0	0	0	0	1	1
To left of worker	0	0	0	0	0	0	0	0	0	0	0	0	0	0	0
To right of worker	0	0	0	0	0	0	0	0	0	0	0	0	0	1	1
Awl enters outside of basket	0	0	0	0	0	0	0	0	0	0	0	0	0	1	1
Single rod in foundation	0	0	0	0	0	0	0	0	0	0	0	0	0	1	1
Rod and splint	0	0	0	0	0	0	0	0	0	0	0	0	0	0	1
Twining Technique	1	1	1	1	1	1	1	1	1	1	1	1	1	1	1
Counterclockwise	1	1	1	1	1	1	1	1	1	1	1	1	1	1	1
To right of worker	1	1	1	1	1	1	1	1	1	1	1	1	1	1	1
Upward lean of outer weft, basket upright	1	1	1	1	1	1	1	1	1	1	1	1	1	1	1
Plain, 2-strand	1	1	1	1	1	1	1	1	1	1	1	1	1	1	1
Close work	1	1	1	1	1	1	1	1	1	1	1	1	1	1	1
Open work	1	1	1	1	1	1	1	1	1	1	1	1	1	1	1
Diagonal, start or partial	0	0	0	1	1	1	1	1	0	0	0	0	1	0	0
3-strand, start or partial	1	0	1	1	1	1	0	0	1	0	0	1	1	0	0
Cross-warp	1	0	0	1	0	0	1	0	0	0	0	0	0	0	0
Seed Beater: plain twine	0	1	1	1	1	0	1	1	1	1	1	1	0	1	1
Seed Beater: circular shape	0	1	1	1	1	0	1	1	1	1	1	1	0	1	1

Type												
Seed Beater: radiating warp	0	1	1	0	1	0	1	1	1	1	1	1
Seed Beater: parallel warp	0	0	0	0	0	0	0	0	0	0	0	0
Deep sifter or winnower: pointed bottom	1	0	0	0	1	0	1	1	1	1	0	0
Deep sifter or winnower: plain twine, circular	1	0	0	0	1	0	1	1	1	1	0	0
Circular flat tray: twined	1	1	1	1	1	1	1	1	1	1	1	1
Circular flat tray: radiating warp	1	1	1	1	1	1	1	1	1	1	1	1
Circular flat tray: close work, sifting or winnowing	1	1	1	1	1	1	1	1	1	1	1	1
Circular flat tray: tapped by hand	1	1	1	1	1	1	1	1	1	1	1	1
Circular flat tray: tapped by bone	0	0	1	1	0	0	0	0	0	0	0	0
Circular flat tray: tapped by stick	0	0	0	0	0	0	0	0	0	1	0	0
Circular flat tray: open work, general receptacle	1	1	1	1	1	1	1	1	1	1	1	1
Boiling basket: twined	1	1	1	1	1	1	1	1	1	1	1	1
Boiling basket: coiled	0	0	0	0	0	0	0	0	1	0	0	0
Twined basketry hopper	1	1	1	1	1	1	1	1	1	1	1	1
Twined carrying basket	1	1	1	1	1	1	1	1	1	1	1	1
Close work	0	1	1	1	1	1	1	1	1	1	1	1
Open work	1	1	1	1	1	0	0	0	1	1	0	1
True cone, pointed bottom	1	0	0	0	1	1	0	0	1	0	1	1

	Tolowa	Chimariko	UKarok	LKarok	MFYurok	RYurok	Wiyot	Hupa1	Hupa2	Chilula	Nongatl	Mattole	ERSinkyome	MRSinkyome	Cahto
Truncated cone, flat bottom	1	1	1	1	1	1	1	1	1	1	1	1	1	1	1
Cylindrical or barrel-shaped	1	0	1	1	0	0	0	1	0	0	0	1	0	0	0
Circular storage basket: twined	1	1	1	1	1	1	1	1	1	1	1	1	1	1	0
Maximum diameter near bottom	1	1	1	1	1	1	1	1	1	1	1	1	1	1	0
Maximum diameter near middle	0	0	0	0	0	0	0	0	0	0	0	1	0	0	0
Maximum diameter near top	0	0	0	0	0	0	0	0	0	0	0	0	0	0	1
Circular storage basket: coiled	0	0	0	0	0	0	0	0	0	0	0	0	0	0	1
Maximum diameter near top	0	0	0	0	0	0	0	0	0	0	0	0	0	0	1
Small globular basket: twined	1	1	1	1	1	1	1	1	1	1	1	0	1	0	0
Small globular basket: coiled	0	0	0	0	0	0	0	0	0	0	0	0	0	1	1
Purse Basket	0	0	0	1	1	1	0	1	1	0	0	0	0	0	0
Banded woven ornament	1	1	1	1	1	1	1	1	1	1	1	0	1	1	1
Break in	0	0	0	0	0	0	0	0	0	0	0	0	0	0	1
3 colors, besides background	1	1	1	1	1	1	0	1	1	1	0	0	0	0	0
Feather ornamentation	0	0	0	0	0	0	1	0	0	0	0	0	1	1	1
Solid	0	0	0	0	0	0	0	0	0	0	0	0	0	0	1
Overlay twining	1	1	1	1	1	1	1	1	1	1	1	0	1	1	1
Porcupine quill overlay	0	0	1	1	1	0	0	1	1	1	0	0	0	0	0

*Both coiled and twined basketry. Note: definite presences from original CED list recorded here as 1, all else as 0.

Appendix 2. Parameters for Chapter 5

Parameter Specification and Calibration

As noted in the introduction to chapter 5, the models are not intended to reflect the characteristics of any particular society realistically, but rather to be as simple and general as possible so as to provide insights into a few important causal variables that might be significant in many transegalitarian societies. Nevertheless, the choice of parameter values deserves some justification. (Note that *PC* and *MM* below refer to Patron-Client and Managerial Mutualism models, respectively.)

Demographic Parameters

Demographic parameters determine the size of local groups, basic demographic rates of agent replication and mortality, and the probability of strategy mutation. No attempt is made here to model real demographic phenomena, and the model populations have no sexual reproduction, no age structure, and no households.

Run length: Our simulations utilized runs of 2,000 periods, with each period characterized by some probability of reproduction and mortality (as a function of payoffs in the preceding period), as well as by social and economic processes that determine agent payoffs. For both MM and PC, 2,000 periods seemed long enough to allow full dynamical behavior (in cases where parameter settings led to cycling) or equilibrium (in other cases). However, this was judged by inspection rather than by systematic experiment.

Agents in a patch or group (n): In the PC model, the size of local groups co-residing in patches is limited by (1) agent strategy (some types are territorial and are therefore the sole inhabitants of their patches) and (2) patch richness (nonterritorial types proliferate on or migrate into patches until they reach local carrying capacity). In the MM model, groups of size n share collective goods and engage in other interactions. In both cases, n is kept deliberately small (5 to 15 individuals) in order to minimize complexity and (in the case of MM) make collective production more feasible.

Total population size (N): No global population limit is imposed, but an equilibrium population emerges from constraints on local group size (n), as just described. The resulting values of N range from about 100 to 300 for the PC model, which is quite realistic for a regional population in small-scale societies of foragers and horticulturalists. For the MM model, N is typically around 1,000, but all interaction is local (that is, in groups of size $n = 8$ to 15 agents), although newly born agents can and do migrate outside their natal group.

Reproductive rate: The default rate was set to .025 in both models and varied over a range from .01 to .05. Because our simulated populations have no sex or age structure, comparing this rate to demographic measures in real populations is difficult. Perhaps the least problematic comparison is our net reproductive rate (reproduction minus mortality) with population growth rates. With model mortality rates generally set below reproductive rates, this net rate was typically about .01 or less, equivalent to ≤1 percent population growth rate per period, a demographically reasonable amount if we think of a simulation period as equal to one year. Note that this net growth rate was highest when habitats were unsaturated (that is, at the start of a simulation run) and declined to near zero at equilibrium, which is again a realistic pattern.

Mortality rate: As with reproductive rate, mortality rate was a function of an agent's payoff in the preceding period (an inverse function in the case of mortality). We constrained this to cover a moderate range of rates, typically from .01 (highest payoff) to .05 (lowest payoff). Although real populations have higher rates than this in the youngest and oldest age classes, given the lack of age structure and that reproduction was allowed for all agents, the rates utilized here appear reasonable.

Mutation rate (μ): The default probability (per period) of randomly changing one's strategy to another strategy was .01 for both models. This value is much higher than what we might expect for genetically transmitted variants, but probably lower than is typical for culturally transmitted ones. Varying mutation rate from .001 to .05 had little or no effect on simulation outcomes.

Proportion of Cooperators in local group (p): This parameter indicates the proportion of agents in local group who are Cooperators (MM model) and is a multiplier for several other parameters that enter into the payoffs for each agent type. The default initial value of p was set at .33 (that is, a uniform distribution of the three strategy types) in most runs.

Income Variables

Patch productivity (P_j): Productivity of the jth patch type is set exogenously in the PC model. For most simulations, there were five discrete types with five possible values (1, 2, 3, 4, 5), assigned randomly but with equal probability. Environmental heterogeneity is widespread in nature, and many scenarios of the emergence of inequality give it some role; we therefore examined a variant with no heterogeneity (that is, setting all patches to a single type [$P_j = 2$ or $P_j = 5$]) and another variant with a spatial pattern of increasing productivity from one corner of the lattice to the opposite corner. We intend to investigate a future variant where P_j will fluctuate stochastically over various ranges during runs.

Net income (π_i): Net income of the Ith agent is a function of the payoff equations for each strategy, as specified in the text. It is calculated for each period and then fed to routines calculating demographic parameters (reproduction and mortality), as noted above.

Base income (B): Base income is the portion of net income that each agent obtains exclusive of gains from collective action or managerial role (MM model). Because we assume that it is equal for all types in any given run, it has no effect on relative payoffs, but avoiding mechanical problems that might otherwise ensue from negative payoffs is convenient. We set the default value equal to the gain from collective production if all agents in the local group were Cooperators; we varied it to ensure that it had no effect on strategy proliferation.

Interaction Variables for the Patron-Client Model

Territory defense cost (d): Territorial strategies (Solo and Patron) are assessed cost d (per period) for maintaining exclusive control over the resources of their patch, which means that agents playing territorial strategies can inhabit only patches with productivity $\geq 1 + d$. This seems reasonable because such exclusive control provides benefits (patch resources) that would otherwise go to other agents and, in real social systems (human or nonhuman), such resource defense is contested and therefore costly. In our model, however, we do not explicitly model contests over resources, so one can consider d a display cost that advertises the residents' willingness to fight to repel intruders. We assume, in effect, that territorial residents always win such contests and that nonterritorial strategies (Dove and Client) share the resources of their home patch equally without transaction costs. We have rather arbitrarily set the default value of d at .1; varying this from zero to four times the default value had almost no effect on the emergence and stability of the PC regime.

Client's labor cost for services to Patron (λ): This measures the cost to a Client of providing services to a Patron (per period). We have assigned λ a default value of .2; doubling this has a pronounced negative effect on the emergence of the PC regime; halving it has a clear positive effect.

Patron's return from a Client's labor (τ): In our model, a Patron hires one or more Clients in order to obtain some net benefit from each exchange. Each Client's labor provides a gross benefit τ to the Patron, who pays the Client a wage κ and thus receives a net benefit of $\tau - \kappa$. The default value of τ is .3, meeting the requirement that $\tau >$ κ (that is, that the exchange is profitable for the Patron). Because τ enters into the payoff equations of both Patrons (directly) and Clients (indirectly, via its contribution to a Client's wages κ, as discussed below), τ has a strong effect on the PC equilibrium. At the default value of $\tau = .3$, 24 percent of runs end with a clear PC equilibrium; at $\tau = .1$, none do, and at $\tau = .6$, virtually all (98 percent) do.

Patron's payment for Client services (κ): Without coercion or deception, we should not expect an agent to engage in an exchange without profit. In the present case, this means that a Client will not provide services to a Patron unless wages exceed labor costs ($\kappa > \lambda$). Because profitability for the Patron requires that $\tau > \kappa$, these dual constraints allow κ to lie anywhere between τ and λ, which at the default values means .2 $< \kappa < .3$. Although future analysis should allow κ to be set by either evolutionary dynamics or agent bargaining power, here we have assumed the most neutral option of an equal division of the surplus by setting $\kappa = (\tau + \lambda)/2$.

Interaction Variables for Managerial Mutualism Model

Maximum aggregate gains from collective action (G): In the MM model, Cooperators engage in collective action to produce a collective good, which is divided equally among the n agents in the group (except the Manager). The amount of collective good produced is a function of the number of Cooperators, with a maximum value of G. Thus, any Cooperator or Defector's share of the collective good is pG/n. The default value of G is 50, so in a group of all Cooperators the per capita share is 5, equal to the default value of base income (B).

Cost of producing collective good (c): The labor cost of producing the collective good, per Cooperator. The assigned default value is 1; a high value depresses the equilibrium frequency of Cooperators and Managers, and a low value increases this.

Cooperator's cost of monitoring (m): We assume that monitoring to detect instances of defection is independent of the number of Defectors in the group but is proportional to group size (n). The default value is set at $.1n$, unless a Manager is present, in which case it falls to zero.

Manager's cost of monitoring (M): We set this at .1 as well, ignoring possible efficiency gains to specialization. As with monitoring by Cooperators, this is proportional to group size.

Cooperator's cost of punishing (e): With no Manager present, a Cooperator pays .5 for each Defector in the group. The total costs of enforcement per Cooperator are $(1 - p)e$ and therefore go down as p (the frequency of Cooperators in the group) goes up; conversely, the cost of being punished per Defector is ps and therefore goes up with Cooperator frequency. With a Manager present, Cooperators pay no enforcement cost, and Defectors are punished only by the Manager.

Manager's cost of punishing (E): A Manager pays .5 for each Defector, and the total enforcement cost to a Manager goes down with p (simply because there are fewer Defectors to punish).

Cost to Defector of being punished (S or s): In groups without a Manager, punishment is done by each Cooperator in the group, and the realized cost to each Defector of being punished (ps) increases with number of Cooperators in the group. In groups with a Manager, this cost does not vary, and Defectors are punished by the resident Manager.

Punishment cost ratio: The ratio of a Defector's cost of being punished to cost of punishing a Defector is widely assumed to be >>1, on the grounds that punishers can choose circumstances to their advantage (for example, employ surprise) and utilize technology to punish at a distance (Bingham 1999). In our model, this ratio differs, depending on whether it is a Cooperator or a Manager who is doing the punishing. With no Manager present, the punishment cost ratio is a function of the number of Cooperators present, reaching 6:1 when Cooperators and Defectors are equally frequent. When a group has a Manager, the ratio is 3/.5, or 6:1. Thus, we assume that a Manager is both more efficient and more effective than a single Cooperator in punishing each Defector, on the basis of role specialization (and possibly self-selection, as per the signaling model in Gintis, Smith, and Bowles 2001). Note that Boyd and others (2003) assume a punishment cost ratio of 4:1, which is similar to our ratio for Manager-Defector interactions. Even if we allow the punishment efficiency to be as high for Cooperators as for Managers, it has no effect on the emergence of the MM system.

Managerial fee (γ): Fee paid to the Manager by each Cooperator in the local group. The default value is 1, and the MM equilibrium is quite sensitive to this value (see table 5.5). If γ is too low, Managers cannot survive; if it is too high, Cooperators suffer depressed payoffs and therefore lower success.

References

Abad, C. K. C.

2000   The Evolution of Hawaiian Socio-Political Complexity: An Analysis of Hawaiian Oral Traditions. Ph.D. dissertation, Department of Anthropology, University of Hawaii.

Abbott, D. R.

2003   Centuries of Decline during the Hohokam Classic Period at Pueblo Grande. Tucson: University of Arizona Press.

Adams, K. R., D. A. Muenchrath, and D. M. Schwindt

1999   Moisture Effects on the Morphology of Ears, Cobs, and Kernels of a Southwestern US Maize (*Zea mays* L.) Cultivar, and Implications for the Interpretation of Archaeological Maize. Journal of Archaeological Science 26:483–496.

Adams, R. McC.

1965   Land behind Baghdad. A History of Settlement on the Diyala Plains. Chicago: University of Chicago Press.

1981   Heartland of Cities. Chicago: University of Chicago Press.

Adler, M. A.

1990   Communities of Soil and Stone: An Archaeological Investigation of Population Aggregation among the Mesa Verde Region Anasazi, AD 900–1300. Ph.D. dissertation, University of Michigan, University Microfilms, Ann Arbor.

Adler, M. A., and M. D. Varien

1994   The Changing Face of Community in the Mesa Verde Region, AD 1000–1300. *In* Proceedings of the Anasazi Symposium, 1991. A. Hutchinson and J. E. Smith, compilers. Pp. 83–97. Cortez, CO: Mesa Verde Museum Association, Mesa Verde National Park.

Algaze, G.

2001   Initial Social Complexity in Southwestern Asia: The Mesopotamian Advantage. Current Anthropology 42:199–233.

Allen, J.

1991   The Role of Agriculture in the Evolution of the Pre-contact Hawaiian State. Asian Perspectives 30:117–132.

1992   Farming in Hawai'i from Colonization to Contact: Radiocarbon Chronology and Implications for Cultural Change. New Zealand Journal of Archaeology 14:45–66.

Allen, T. F. H., and T. W. Hoekstra

1992   Toward a Unified Ecology. New York: Columbia University Press.

Allen, T. F. H., and T. B. Starr
1982   Hierarchy: Perspectives for Ecological Complexity. Chicago: University of Chicago Press.

Allen, T. F. H., J. A. Tainter, and T. W. Hoekstra
2003   Supply-side Sustainability. New York: Columbia University Press.

Ammerman, A. J., and L. L. Cavalli-Sforza
1973   A Population Model for the Diffusion of Early Farming in Europe. *In* The Explanation of Culture Change. C. Renfrew, ed. Pp. 343–357. London: Duckworth.

Anderies, J. M.
1998   Culture and Human Agro-ecosystem Dynamics: The Tsembaga of New Guinea. Journal of Theoretical Biology 192:515–530.
2003   Economic Development, Demographics, and Renewable Resources: A Dynamical Systems Approach. Environment and Development Economics 8:219–246.

Anthes, R. A., and T. T. Warner
1978   Development of Hydrodynamic Models Suitable for Air Pollution and Other Mesometeorological Studies. Monthly Weather Review 106:1045–1078.

Arbogast, R.-M., M. Magny, and P. Pétrequin
1995   Expansions et déprises agricoles au Néolithique: population, cultures céréalières et climat dans la Combe d'Ain (Jura, France) de 3700 à 2500 av. J.-C. *In* L'homme et la dégradation de l'environnement, Actes des XVe Rencontres d'archéologie et d'histoire d'Antibes, 20–22 octobre 1994. S. E. van der Leeuw, ed. Pp. 19–42. Sophia Antipolis: Éditions APDCA.

Arnold, J. G., and P. M. Allen
1992   A Comprehensive Surface-Groundwater Flow Model. Journal of Hydrology 142:47–69.

Arnold, J. G., R. Srinivasin, R. S. Muttiah, and J. R. Williams
1998   Large-Area Hydrologic Modeling and Assessment, Part I: Model Development. JAWRA 34(1):73–89.

Arthur, W. B.
2005   Cognition: The Black Box of Economics. *In* Perspectives on Adaptation in Natural and Artificial Systems. L. Booker, S. Forrest, M. Mitchell, and R. Riolo, eds. Pp. 291–301. Santa Fe Institute Studies in the Sciences of Complexity. New York: Oxford University Press.

Athens, J. S.
1997   Hawaiian Native Lowland Vegetation in Prehistory. *In* Historical Ecology in the Pacific Islands: Prehistoric Environmental and Landscape Change. P. V. Kirch and T. L. Hunt, eds. Pp. 248–270. New Haven, CT: Yale University Press.

Athens, J. S., and J. V. Ward
1993   Environmental Change and Prehistoric Polynesian Settlement in Hawai'i. Asian Perspectives 32:205–223.

Athens, J. S., J. V. Ward, and S. Wickler
1992   Late Holocene Lowland Vegetation, O'ahu, Hawai'i. New Zealand Journal of Archaeology 14:9–34.

Auyang, S. Y.
1998   Foundations of Complex-Systems Theories in Economics, Evolutionary Biology, and Statistical Physics. Cambridge: Cambridge University Press.

Bagnall, R. S., and B. W. Frier
1994   The Demography of Roman Egypt. Cambridge: Cambridge University Press.

Bak, P.
1996   How Nature Works: The Science of Self-Organized Criticality. New York: Springer (Copernicus).

Baldwin, B. G., and M. J. Sanderson
1998   Age and Rate of Diversification of the Hawaiian Silversword Alliance (Compositae). Proceedings of the National Academy of Sciences 95:9402–9406.

Barbier, D.
1999   Histoire de la végétation du nord-mayennais de la fin du Weichsélien à l'aube du XXème siècle: mise en évidence d'un Tardiglaciaire armoricain; interactions homme-milieu. Ph.D. dissertation, Department of Palynology, University of Nantes.

Barbujani, G.
1995   Reply to Roberts, Moore and Romney. Current Anthropology 36:769–788.

Barth, F.
1971   Tribes and Intertribal Relations in the Fly Headwaters. Oceania 41:171–191.

Bateson, G. A.
1973   Steps to an Ecology of Mind. New York: Ballantine Books.

Baumhoff, M. A.
1978   Environmental Background. *In* California. R. F. Heizer, ed. Pp. 16–24. Handbook of North American Indians, vol. 8, W. C. Sturtevant, general ed. Washington DC: Smithsonian Institution.

Bayman, J.
2001   The Hohokam of Southwest North America. Journal of World Prehistory 15:257–311.

Beer, S.
1959   Cybernetics and Management. New York: John Wiley.

Bellwood, P., and C. Renfrew, eds.
2003   Examining the Farming/Language Dispersal Hypothesis. Oxford: Oxbow.

Bentley, R. A., M. W. Hahn, and S. J. Shennan
2004   Random Drift and Culture Change. Proceedings of the Royal Society of London 271:1443–1450.

Bentley, R. A., T. D. Price, J. Lüning, D. Gronenborn, J. Wahl, and P. D. Fullagar
2002   Human Migration in Early Neolithic Europe. Current Anthropology 43:799–804.

Benzecri, J.-P.
1979   L'Analyse des Données, vol 1: La Taxinomie, vol 2: L'analyse des correspondences. Paris: Editions Dunod.

Berger, J.-F.
1995   Facteurs anthropiques et naturels sur l'évolution des paysages holocènes dans le bassin valdainais (Drôme). *In* L'homme et la dégradation de l'environnement. Actes des XVe Rencontres d'archéologie et d'histoire d'Antibes, 20–22 octobre 1994. S. E. van der Leeuw, ed. Pp. 79–114. Sophia Antipolis: Éditions APDCA.
1996   Climat et dynamique des agrosystèmes dans la moyenne vallée du Rhône. *In* Le IIIe siècle en Gaule Narbonnaise. Données régionales sur la crise de l'Empire. Actes de la table ronde du GDR 954 "Archéologie de l'espace rural méditerranéen dans l'Antiquité et le haut Moyen-Age," Aix-en-Provence, 15–16 septembre 1995. J.-L. Fiches, ed. Pp. 299–332. Sophia Antipolis: Éditions APDCA.
2001   Évolution des agro- et des hydrosystèmes dans la région médio-rhodanienne. *In* Les campagnes de la gaule durant l'Antiquité tardive, Actes du colloque AGER IV, Montpellier, 11–14 mars 1998. P. Ouzoulias, C. Pellecuer, C. Raynaud, P. Van Ossel, et P. Garmy, eds. Pp. 369–404. Éditions APDCA, Sophia Antipolis.
2003a   Activités humaines, dynamiques ecologiques et fluctuations climatiques: une co-évolution complexe perceptible par l'etude des archives sédimentaires des géosystèmes nord-méditerranéens. *In* Quelles natures voulons-nous? Quelles natures aurons-nous? Actes du colloque PEVS, Lille Octobre 2001. C. Lévèque and S. E. van der Leeuw, eds. Pp. 161–173. Paris: Elsevier.

2003b   La dégradation des sols à l'Holocène dans la moyenne vallée du Rhône: contextes morpho-cli-matique, paléobotanique et culturel. *In* Archéologie et systèmes socio-environnementaux. Etudes multiscalaires sur la vallée du Rhône dans le programme Archaeomedes. S. E. van der Leeuw, F. Favory, and J. L. Fiches, eds. Pp. 43–161. Paris: Éditions CNRS.

Berger, J.-F., and J. L. Brochier, eds.
2006   Histoire des paysages et du climat de la fin des temps glaciaires à nos jours en moyenne val-lée du Rhône d'après les données des travaux archéologiques du TGV-Méditerranée. Paris: CNRS Éditions.

Berger, J.-F., J.-L. Brochier, J. Vital, C. Delhon, and S. Thiébault
In press Nouveau regard sur la dynamique des paysages et l'occupation humaine à l'âge du Bronze en moyenne vallée du Rhône, Actes du 129e Congrès national des sociétés historiques et scien-tifiques (Besançon, 2004). H. Richard, M. Magny, and C. Mordant, eds. Paris: Éditions du CTHS (Documents préhistoriques).

Berger, J.-F., M. Cremaschi, M. Cattani, F. Cavulli, V. Charpentier, G. Davtian, J. Giraud, P. Marquis, C. Martin, S. Méry, J.-C. Plaziat, J.-F. Saliège, and S. Cleuziou
2005   Evolution paléogéographique du Ja'alan (Oman) à l'Holocène moyen: impact sur l'évolution des paléomilieux littoraux et les stratégies d'adaptation des communautés humaines. Paléorient 31(1):46–63.

Berger, J.-F., and C. Jung
1996   Fonction, evolution et taphonomie des parcellaires en moyenne vallée du Rhône. Un exemple intégré en archéomorphologie et en géoarchéologie. *In* Les formes des paysages, II. Archéologie des parcellaires, Actes du colloque AGER-ARCHEA, Orléans, Mars 1996. G. Chouquer, ed. Pp. 95–112. Paris: Errance.

Berger, J.-F., and C. Jung, eds.
1999   Rapport "Fossés et voirie," lots 11-12-13-21 du TGV-Méditerranée, SRA Rhône-Alpes et PACA. Mimeographed document available in the Sous-Direction de l'Archéologie of the region Rhône-Alpes (part of the French Culture Ministry).

Berger, J.-F., and R. Royet
2003   Rapport annuel de fouille programmée de la villa du Vernai à Saint Romain-de-Jalionas (Isère). Partie étude géoarchéologique de la zone nord du marais du Grand Plan. Mimeographed document available in the Sous-Direction de l'Archéologie of the region Rhône-Alpes (part of the French Culture Ministry).

Berger, J.-F., R. Royet, J. Argant, and V. Forest
2003   Une Villa Gallo-Romaine en Milieu Humide: Le Vernai à Saint Romain-de-Jalionas (Isère). Actualité de la recherche en Histoire et Archéologie agraires, Actes du colloque international AGER 5. F. Favory and A. Vignot, eds. Pp. 157–172. Besançon: Presses Universitaires Franc-Comtoises.

Berthoud, T., and S. Cleuziou
1984   Farming Communities of the Oman Peninsula and the Copper of Magan. Journal of Oman Studies 6(2):239–244.

Bertoncello, F., and L. Nuninger
In press From Archaeological Sherds to Qualitative Information for Settlement Pattern Studies. *In* Beyond the Artifact: Proceedings of CAA2004, Prato, April 13–17, 2004. F. Niccolucci, ed. Budapest: Archaeolingua.

Binford, L. R.
1963   Red Ochre Caches from the Michigan Area: A Possible Case of Cultural Drift. Southwestern Journal of Anthropology 19:89–108.
1981   Bones: Ancient Men and Modern Myths. New York: Academic Press.

Bingham, P. M.
1999   Human Uniqueness: A General Theory. The Quarterly Review of Biology 74:133–169.

Blaxter, K. L.
1967   The Energy Metabolism of Ruminants. London: Hutchinson.

Bliege Bird, R., and E. A. Smith
2005   Signaling Theory, Strategic Interaction, and Symbolic Capital. Current Anthropology 46:221–248.

Boccara, N.
2004   Modeling Complex Systems. New York: Springer-Verlag.

Bocquet-Appel, J.-P.
2002   Paleoanthropological Traces of a Neolithic Demographic Transition. Current Anthropology 43:637–650.

Bode, H. W.
1945   Network Analysis and Feedback Amplifier Design. Melbourne: Krieger.

Bodley, J. H.
2003   The Power of Scale: A Global History Approach. Armonk, NY: M. E. Sharpe.

Bogaard, A.
2004   Neolithic Farming in Central Europe. London: Routledge.

Bond, G., W. Broecker, S. Johnsen, J. McManus, L. Labeyrie, J. Jouzel, and G. Bonani
1993   Correlations between Climate Records from North Atlantic Sediments and Greenland Ice. Nature 365:143–147.

Boone, J. L.
1992   Competition, Conflict, and the Development of Hierarchies. In Evolutionary Ecology and Human Behavior. E. A. Smith and B. Winterhalder, eds. Pp. 301–337. New York: Aldine de Gruyter, Hawthorne.

Boserup, E.
1965   The Conditions of Agricultural Growth: The Economics of Agrarian Change under Population Pressure. Chicago: Aldine.
1981   Population and Technological Change. Chicago: University of Chicago Press.

Boulding, K. E.
1978   Ecodynamics: A New Theory of Societal Evolution. Beverly Hills, CA: Sage Publications.

Bourdieu, P.
1990   The Logic of Practice. R. Nice, trans. Palo Alto, CA: Stanford University Press.

Boyd, R., M. Borgerhoff Mulder, W. H. Durham, and P. J. Richerson
1997   Are Cultural Phylogenies Possible? In Human by Nature: Between Biology and the Social Sciences. P. Weingart, S. D. Mitchell, P. J. Richerson, and S. Maasen, eds. Pp. 355–386. London: Erlbaum.

Boyd, R., H. Gintis, S. L. Bowles, and P. J. Richerson
2003   The Evolution of Altruistic Punishment. Proceedings of the National Academy of Sciences USA 100:3531–3535.

Boyd, R., and P. J. Richerson
1985   Culture and the Evolutionary Process. Chicago: University of Chicago Press.

Brander, J. A., and M. S. Taylor
1998   The Simple Economics of Easter Island: A Ricardo-Malthus Model of Renewable Resource Use. American Economic Review 88:119–138.

Bravard, J.-P., A. Verrot-Bourrely, and P.-G. Salvador
1992   Le climat d'après les informations fournies par les enregistrements sédimentaires fluviatiles
        étudiés sur des sites archéologiques. Les Nouvelles de l'Archéologie 50:7–13.

Bright, W.
1978   Karok. *In* California. R. F. Heizer, ed. Pp. 180–189. Handbook of North American Indians,
        vol. 8, W. C. Sturtevant, general ed. Washington DC: Smithsonian Institute.

Brookfield, H. C.
1972   Intensification and Disintensification in Pacific Agriculture: A Theoretical Approach. Pacific
        Viewpoint 13:30–48.
1984   Intensification Revisited. Pacific Viewpoint 25:15–44.

Brown, J. L.
1964   The Evolution of Diversity in Avian Territorial Systems. Wilson Bulletin 76:160–169.

Bruneton, H., G. Arnaud-Fassetta, M. Provansal, and D. Sistach
2001   Geomorphological Evidence for Fluvial Change during the Roman Period in the Lower
        Rhône Valley (Southern France). Catena 45:287–312.

Bryant, D., F. Filimon, and R. D. Gray
2005   Untangling Our Past: Languages, Trees, Splits, and Networks. *In* The Evolution of Cultural
        Diversity: A Phylogenetic Approach, Ruth Mace, Clare Holden, and Stephen Shennan. Pp.
        67-86. London: University College London Press.

Bryant, D., and V. Moulton
2002   NeighborNet: An Agglomerative Method for the Construction of Planar Phylogenetic
        Networks. *In* The Proceedings of WABI (Workshop in Algorithms for Bioinformatics) 2002.
        R. Guigó and D. Gusfield, eds. Pp. 375–391. Springer Verlag Lecture Notes in Computer
        Science, 2452.

Buck, C. E., W. G. Cavanaugh, and C. D. Litton
1996   Bayesian Approach to Interpreting Archaeological Data. Chichester, UK: John Wiley and
        Sons.

Buffat, L., and C. Pellecuer
2001   La viticulture antique en Languedoc-Roussillon. *In* La viticulture antique. J. P. Brun and F.
        Laubenheimer, eds. Pp. 91–111. Hors série GALLIA, 58. Paris: Éditions CNRS.

Bulirsch, R., and J. Stoer
1993   Introduction to Numerical Analysis. 2nd edition. New York: Springer-Verlag.

Burch, T. K.
2006   The Model-Based View of Science: An Encouragement to Interdisciplinary Work. 21st
        Century Society 1:39–58.

Burke, I. C., W. K. Lauenroth, and W. J. Parton
1997   Regional and Temporal Variation in Net Primary Production and Nitrogen Mineralization in
        Grasslands. Ecology 78:1330–1340.

Burns, B. T.
1983   Simulated Anasazi Storage Behavior Using Crop Yields Reconstructed from Tree-Rings: AD
        652–1968. 2 vols. Ph.D. dissertation, University of Arizona, Tucson, University Microfilms,
        Ann Arbor, MI.

Butzer, K.
1982   Archaeology as Human Ecology: Method and Theory for a Contextual Approach. Cambridge:
        Cambridge University Press.
1996   Ecology in the Long View: Settlement, Agrosystem Strategies, and Ecological Performance.
        Journal of Field Archaeology 23:141–150.

Byrne, D.
1998   Complexity Theory and the Social Sciences: An Introduction. London: Routledge.

Carlson, J. M., and J. Doyle
2002   Complexity and Robustness. Proceedings of the National Academy of Sciences 99:2538–2545.

Carpenter, S. R., B. H. Walker, J. M. Anderies, and N. Abel
2001   From Metaphor to Measurement: Resilience of What to What? Ecosystems 4:765–781.

Castillo, E. D.
1978   The Impact of Euro-American Exploration and Settlement. In California. R. F. Heizer, ed. Pp. 99–127. Handbook of North American Indians, vol. 8, W. C. Sturtevant, general ed. Washington DC: Smithsonian Institution.

Cater, J. D., and M. L. Chenault
1988   Kiva Use Reinterpreted. Southwestern Lore 54:19–32.

Cavalli-Sforza, L. L., and M. Feldman
1981   Cultural Transmission and Evolution: A Quantitative Approach. Princeton, NJ: Princeton University Press.

Chabal, L.
1997   Forêts et sociétés en Languedoc (Néolithique final, Antiquité tardive). L'anthracologie, méthode et paléoécologie. Collection DAF, 63. Paris: Éditions de la Maison des Sciences de l'Homme.

Chadwick, O. A., L. Derry, P. M. Vitousek, B. J. Huebert, and L. O. Hedin
1999   Changing Sources of Nutrients during Four Million Years of Ecosystem Development. Nature 397:491–497.

Chadwick, O. A., R. T. Gavenda, E. F. Kelly, K. Ziegler, C. G. Olson, W. C. Elliott, and
D. M. Hendrick
2003   The Impact of Climate on the Biogeochemical Functioning of Volcanic Soils. Chemical Geology 202:195–223.

Charnov, E. L.
1976   Optimal Foraging Theory: The Marginal Value Theorem. Journal of Theoretical Population Biology 9:129–136.

Chojnacky, D. C.
1984   Volume and Biomass for Curlleaf Cercocarpus in Nevada. Ogden, UT: USDA Forest Service Intermountain Forest and Range Experiment Station.

Chouquer, G.
1995   Aux origines antiques et médiévales du parcellaire. Histoire et Sociétés Rurales 4:11–46.

Christiansen, J. H.
2000a   A Flexible Object-Based Software Framework for Modeling Complex Systems with Interacting Natural and Societal Processes. Paper presented at the 4th International Conference on Integrating GIS and Environmental Modeling, Banff, Alberta, Canada, September 2–8.
2000b   FACET: A Simulation Software Framework for Modeling Complex Societal Processes and Interactions. Paper presented at the 2000 Summer Computer Simulation Conference of the Society for Computer Simulation International, Vancouver, British Columbia, Canada, July 16–20.

Chung, C.-J., and R. G. Reynolds
1996   Function Optimization Using Evolutionary Programming with Self-Adaptive Cultural Algorithms. In Simulated Evolution and Learning: Selected Papers. X. Yao and J.-H. Kim, eds. Pp. 17–26. Lecture Notes on Artificial Intelligence. New York: Springer-Verlag.

Civil, M.

1994   The Farmer's Instructions. A Sumerian Agricultural Manual. Aula Orientalis Supplementa, 5. Barcelona: Editorial AUSA.

Cladders, M.

2001   Die Tonware der Ältesten Bandkeramik: Untersuchung zur Zeitlichen und Räumlichen Gliederung. Bonn: Habelt.

Clark, C. W.

1990   Mathematical Bioeconomics: The Optimal Management of Renewable Resources. New York: J. Wiley.

Clark, J. E., and M. Blake

1994   The Power of Prestige: Competitive Generosity and the Emergence of Rank Societies in Lowland Mesoamerica. *In* Factional Competition and Political Development in the New World. E. M. Brumfiel and J. W. Fox, eds. Pp. 17–30. Cambridge: Cambridge University Press.

Clark, J. T.

1988   Paleodemography in Leeward Hawai'i. Archaeology in Oceania 23:22–30.

Cleuziou, S.

1999   Espace habité, espace utilisé, espace vécu dans les communautés d'Arabie orientale à l'âge du Bronze. *In* Habitat et société, XIXèmes rencontres d'histoire et d'archéologie d'Antibes. F. Braemer, S. Cleuziou, and A. Coudart, eds. Pp. 83–108. Antibes: APDCA.

2002a   The Early Bronze Age of the Oman Peninsula: From Chronology to the Dialectics of Trade and State Formation. *In* Essays on the Late Prehistory of the Arabian Peninsula. S. Cleuziou, M. Tosi, and J. Zarins, eds. Pp. 181–227. Serie Orientale Roma. Rome: IsIAO.

2002b   Présence et mise en scène des morts à l'usage des vivants dans les communautés protohistoriques: L'exemple de la péninsule d'Oman à l'âge du bronze ancien. *In* I primi popoli d'Europa. M. Molinos and A. Zifferero, eds. Pp. 17–31. Florence: Insegna dell Gioglio.

2003   Early Bronze Age Trade in the Gulf and the Arabian Sea: The Society behind the Boats. *In* Archaeology of the United Arab Emirates. D. T. Potts, H. al-Nabooda, and P. Hellyer, eds. Pp. 134–149. London: Trident Press.

2005   Pourquoi si tard? Nous avons pris un autre chemin. L'Arabie des chasseurs-cueilleurs de l'Holocène au début de l'Age du Bronze. *In* Aux marges des grands foyers du Néolithique: périphéries débitrices ou créatrices? Jean Guilaine, ed. Pp. 123–148. Paris: Errance.

Cleuziou, S., and S. Méry

2002   In between the Great Powers: Bronze Age Oman Peninsula. *In* Essays on the Late Prehistory of the Arabian Peninsula. S. Cleuziou, M. Tosi, and J. Zarins, eds. Pp. 265–308. Serie Orientale Roma. Rome: IsIAO.

Cleuziou, S., and M. Tosi

2000   Ra's al-Jinz and the Prehistoric Coastal Cultures of the Ja'lan. Journal of Oman Studies 11:19–73.

Coale, A. J., and P. Demeny

1966   Regional Model Life Tables and Stable Populations. Princeton, NJ: Princeton University Press.

Coil, J.

2004   The Beauty That Was. Ph.D. dissertation, Department of Anthropology, University of California, Berkeley.

Coil, J., and P. V. Kirch

2005   Ipomoean Landscapes: Archaeology and the Sweet Potato in Kahikinui, Maui, Hawaiian Islands. *In* Sweet Potato in the Pacific: A Reappraisal. C. Ballard, P. Brown, M. Bourke, and

T. Harwood, eds. Pp. 71–84. Ethnology Monograph 19, University of Pittsburgh; Oceania Monograph 56, University of Sydney.

Cole, S. M.

2006   Population Dynamics and Sociopolitical Instability in the Central Mesa Verde Region, AD 600–1280. M.A. thesis, Department of Anthropology, Washington State University.

Cole, S. W.

1994   Marsh Formation in the Borsippa Region and the Course of the Lower Euphrates. Journal of Near Eastern Studies 53:81–109.

Cole, S. W., and H. Gasche

1998   Second and First Millennium BC Rivers in Northern Babylonia. *In* Changing Watercourses in Babylonia. Towards a Reconstruction of the Ancient Environment in Lower Mesopotamia. H. Gasche and M. Tanret, eds. Pp. 1–64. Chicago: Oriental Institute, University of Ghent and University of Chicago.

Collard, M., and J. Tehrani

2005   Phylogenesis versus Ethnogenesis in Turkmen Cultural Evolution. *In* The Evolution of Cultural Diversity: A Phylogenetic Approach. R. Mace, C. J. Holden, and S. J. Shennan, eds. Pp. 109–131. London: University College London Press.

Cordy, R.

1974   Complex Rank Cultural Systems in the Hawaiian Islands: Suggested Explanations for Their Origin. Archaeology and Physical Anthropology in Oceania 9:89–109.

1981   A Study of Prehistoric Social Change: The Development of Complex Societies in the Hawaiian Islands. New York: Academic Press.

2000   Exalted Sits the Chief: The Ancient History of Hawai'i Island. Honolulu: Mutual Publishing.

Cordy, R. H., and M. W. Kaschko

1980   Prehistoric Archaeology in the Hawaiian Islands: Land Units Associated with Social Groups. Journal of Field Archaeology 7:403–416.

Coudart, A.

1998   Architecture et Société Néolithique. Paris: Éditions de la Maison des Sciences de l'Homme.

Cowan, G. S., and R. G. Reynolds

2003   Acquisition of Software Engineering Knowledge. SWEEP: An Automatic Programming System Based on Genetic Programming and Cultural Algorithms. Hackensack, NJ: World Scientific Press.

Cowan, J. A., T. A. Kohler, C. D. Johnson, and K. D. Cooper

N.d.   Supply, Demand, Return Rates, and Resource Depression: Hunting in the Village Ecodynamics World. *In* Archaeological Simulation: Into the 21st Century. A. Costopoulos, ed. Unpublished MS, University of Utah Press, Salt Lake City.

Csete, M. E., and J. Doyle

2002   Reverse Engineering of Biological Complexity. Science 295:1664–1669.

Currat, M., and L. Excoffier

2005   The Effect of the Neolithic Expansion on European Molecular Diversity. Proceedings of the Royal Society of London B272:679–688.

Cuthill, I. C., and A. I. Houston

1997   Managing Time and Energy. *In* Behavioral Ecology: An Evolutionary Approach. 4th edition. J. R. Krebs and N. B. Davies, eds. Pp. 97–120. Oxford: Blackwell.

Danchin, E., L.-A. Giraldeau, T. J. Valone, and R. H. Wagner

2004   Public Information: From Nosy Neighbors to Cultural Evolution. Science 305:487–491.

Dansgaard, W., S. J. Johnsen, H. B. Clausen, D. Dahl-Jensen, N. Gundestrup,
C. U. Hammer, and H. Oeschger
1984   North Atlantic Climate Oscillations Revealed by Deep Greenland Ice Cores. *In* Climate
        Processes and Climate Sensitivity. J. E. Hansen and T. Takahashi, eds. Pp. 288–298.
        Geophysical Monographs, 29, Maurice Ewing Series. Washington DC: American Geophysical
        Union.

Davis, E. L.
1965   Small Pressures and Cultural Drift as Explanations for Abandonment of the San Juan Area,
        New Mexico and Arizona. American Antiquity 30:353–354.

de Vries, B. J. M., M. S. Thompson, and K. W. Wirtz
2002   Understanding: Fragments of a Unifying Perspective. *In* Mappae Mundi: Humans and Their
        Habitats in a Long-term Socio-ecological Perspective. B. J. M. de Vries and
        J. Goudsblom, eds. Pp. 257–300. Amsterdam: Amsterdam University Press.

Dean, J. S., and C. R. Van West
2002   Environment-Behavior Relationships in Southwestern Colorado. *In* Seeking the Center Place:
        Archaeology and Ancient Communities in the Mesa Verde Region. M. D. Varien and R. H.
        Wilshusen, eds. Pp. 81–99. Salt Lake City: University of Utah Press.

Delhon, C.
2005   Anthropisation et paléoclimats du Tardiglaciaire à l'Holocène en moyenne vallée du Rhône:
        études pluridisciplinaires des spectres phytolithiques et pédo-anthracologiques de séquences
        naturelles et de sites archéologiques. Ph.D. dissertation, University of Paris I (Panthéon-
        Sorbonne).

Denton, G. H., and W. Karlen
1973   Holocene Climatic Variations—Their Pattern and Possible Cause. Quaternary Research
        3:155–205.

Dixon, B., P. J. Conte, V. Nagahara, and W. K. Hodgins
1997   Upland Forest Periphery Subsistence and Settlement in the Ahupua'a of Kipapa, Nakaohu,
        and Nakaaha: A Preliminary Assessment. *In* Na Mea Kahiko o Kahikinui: Studies in the
        Archaeology of Kahikinui, Maui. P. V. Kirch, ed. Pp. 28–44. Oceanic Archaeology
        Laboratory, special publication, 1. Berkeley: Archaeological Research Facility, University of
        California.
1999   Risk Minimization and the Traditional Ahupua'a in Kahikinui, Island of Maui, Hawai'i.
        Asian Perspectives 38:229–255.

Dollé, V., and G. Toutain
1990   Les systèmes agricoles oasiens. IIe, Séminaire sur les Systèmes Agricoles Oasiens, Tozeur,
        Tunisia, November 19–21, 1988. Montpellier: CIHEAM-IAMM.

Dominguez, S.
2002   Optimal Gardening Strategies: Maximizing the Input and Retention of Water in Prehistoric
        Gridded Fields in North Central New Mexico. World Archaeology 34:131–163.

Dresch, P.
1989   Tribes, Government, and History in Yemen. Oxford: Clarendon Press.

Driver, H.
1939   Culture Element Distributions: X Northwest California. Anthropological Records 1:6.

Driver, J. C.
1996   Social Complexity and Hunting Systems in Southwestern Colorado. *In* Debating Complexity:
        Proceedings of the Twenty-Sixth Annual Chacmool Conference.
        D. A. Meyer, P. C. Dawson, and D. T. Hanna, eds. Pp. 364–374. Calgary, Alberta, Canada:
        Archaeological Association of the University of Calgary.

Duff, A. I., and R. H. Wilshusen

2000   Prehistoric Population Dynamics in the Northern San Juan Region, AD 950–1300. The Kiva 66:167–190.

Dugatkin, L. A., ed.

2001   Model Systems in Behavioral Ecology: Integrating Conceptual, Theoretical, and Empirical Approaches. Princeton, NJ: Princeton University Press.

Dunnell, R.

1978   Style and Function: A Fundamental Dichotomy. American Antiquity 43:192–202.

Durand, E.

2002   Un habitat des basses plaines rhodaniennes du milieu de l'âge du Fer à Bollène (Pont-de-Pierre 2 Nord, Vaucluse). *In* Archéologie du TGV-Méditerranée, Fiches de synthèse, Tome 2, La Protohistoire. Monographies d'Archéologie Méditerranéenne 9:479–488.

Durham, W.

1991   Coevolution: Genes, Culture, and Human Diversity. Palo Alto, CA: Stanford University Press.

Durham, W. H.

1979   Towards a Coevolutionary Theory of Human Biology and Culture. *In* Evolutionary Biology and Human Social Behaviour. W. Chagnon and W. Irons, eds. Pp. 39–59. North Scituate, MA: Duxbury Press.

1992   Applications of Evolutionary Culture Theory. Annual Review of Anthropology 21:331–355.

Dye, T., and E. Komori

1992a   Computer Programs for Creating Cumulative Probability Curves and Annual Frequency Distribution Diagrams with Radiocarbon Dates. New Zealand Journal of Archaeology 14:35–43.

1992b   A Pre-censal Population History of Hawai'i. New Zealand Journal of Archaeology 14:113–128.

Dyson-Hudson, R., and E. A. Smith

1978   Human Territoriality: An Ecological Reassessment. American Anthropologist 80:21–41.

Earle, T. K.

1977   A Reappraisal of Redistribution: Complex Hawaiian Chiefdoms. *In* Exchange Systems in Prehistory. T. Earle and J. Erikson, eds. Pp. 213–229. New York: Academic Press.

1978   Economic and Social Organization of a Complex Chiefdom: The Halelea District, Kaua'i, Hawaii. Anthropological Papers, 63, Museum of Anthropology. Ann Arbor: University of Michigan.

1987   Specialization and the Production of Wealth: Hawaiian Chiefdoms and the Inka Empire. *In* Specialization, Exchange, and Complex Societies. T. K. Earle and E. M. Brumfiel, eds. Pp. 64–75. Cambridge: Cambridge University Press.

1997   How Chiefs Come to Power: The Political Economy in Prehistory. Palo Alto, CA: Stanford University Press.

2002   Bronze Age Economics: The Beginnings of Political Economies. Boulder, CO: Westview Press.

Earle, T. K., ed.

1991   Chiefdoms: Power, Economy and Ideology. Cambridge: Cambridge University Press.

Ekren, E. B., and R. N. Houser

1965   Geology and Petrology of the Ute Mountains Area, Colorado. US Geological Survey Professional Paper 481. Washington DC: United States Geological Survey.

Elsasser, A. B.

1978a   Basketry. *In* California. R. F. Heizer, ed. Pp. 626–641. Handbook of North American Indians, vol. 8, W. C. Sturtevant, general ed. Washington DC: Smithsonian Institution.

1978b   Mattole, Nongatl, Sinkyone, Lassik and Wailaki. *In* California. R. F. Heizer, ed. Pp.
         190–204. Handbook of North American Indians, vol. 8, W. C. Sturtevant, general ed.
         Washington DC: Smithsonian Institution.
1978c   Wiyot. *In* California. R. F. Heizer, ed. Pp. 155–163. Handbook of North American Indians,
         vol. 8, W. C. Sturtevant, general ed. Washington DC: Smithsonian Institution.

Erwin, H. R.
1997   The Dynamics of Peer Polities. *In* Time, Process and Structured Transformation in
         Archaeology. S. E. van der Leeuw and J. McGlade, eds. Pp. 57–96. One World Archaeology,
         26. London: Routledge.

Evans, J. G.
2003   Environmental Archaeology and the Social Order. London: Routledge.

Favory, F., J.-J. Girardot, L. Nuninger, and F.-P. Tourneux
1999   Archaeomedes II: une étude de la dynamique de l'habitat rural en France méridionale, dans la
         longue durée (800 av. J.-C.-1600 ap. J.-C.). AGER 9:15–35.

Favory, F., and S. E. van der Leeuw
1998   Archaeomedes, une recherche collective sur la dynamique spatio-temporelle de l'habitat
         antique dans la vallée du Rhône: Bilan et Perspectives. Revue Archéologique de Narbonnaise
         31:257–298.

Feinman, G. M., and J. Marcus, eds.
1998   Archaic States. School of American Research. Santa Fe, NM: SAR Press.

Ferguson, T. J., and E. R. Hart
1985   A Zuni Atlas. Norman: University of Oklahoma Press.

Fetterman, J., and L. Honeycutt
1987   The Mockingbird Mesa Survey. Cultural Resource, 22. Denver, CO: Bureau of Land
         Management.

Flannery, K. V.
1968   Archeological Systems Theory and Early Mesoamerica. *In* Anthropological Archeology in the
         Americas. B. J. Meggers, ed. Pp. 68–87. Washington DC: Anthropological Society of
         Washington.
1972   The Cultural Evolution of Civilizations. Annual Review of Ecology and Systematics
         3:399–426.
1995   Prehistoric Social Evolution. *In* Research Frontiers in Anthropology. C. R. Ember and M.
         Ember, eds. Pp. 1–26. Englewood Cliffs, NJ: Prentice-Hall.

Flannery, K. V., J. Marcus, and R. G. Reynolds
1989   Flocks of the Wamani. San Diego: Academic Press.

Foley, R.
1985   Optimality Theory in Anthropology. Man 20:222–242.

**Forey, P. L., C. J. Humphries, I. L. Kitching, R. W. Scotland, D. J. Siebert, and
D. M. Williams**
1992   Cladistics: A Practical Course in Systematics. Oxford: Clarendon Press.

Freethey, G. W.
1988a   Lithologic and Hydrologic Properties of Mesozoic Rocks in the Upper Colorado River Basin.
         In Regional Aquifer Systems of the United States: Aquifers of the Western Mountain Area. J.
         S. McLean and A. I. Johnson, eds. Pp. 81–99. American Water Resources Association
         Monograph 14. Bethesda, MD: The Association.
1988b   Upper Colorado River Basin Regional Aquifer Systems Analysis: Mesozoic Rocks in
         Colorado, Utah, Wyoming, Arizona, and New Mexico. *In* Regional Aquifer Systems of the
         United States: Aquifers of the Western Mountain Area. J. S. McLean and A. I. Johnson, eds.

Pp. 57–70. American Water Resources Association Monograph 14. Bethesda, MD: The Association.

Fretwell, S. D., and H. L. Lucas
1970   On Territorial Behavior and Other Factors Influencing Habitat Distribution in Birds. Acta Biotheoretica 19:16–36.

Fried, M.
1967   The Evolution of Political Society. New York: Random House.

Friedman, J.
1982   Catastrophe and Continuity in Social Evolution. In Theory and Explanation in Archaeology. C. Renfrew, M. Rowlands, and B. Seagraves, eds. Pp. 175–196. New York: Academic Press.

Gallant, T. W.
1991   Risk and Survival in Ancient Greece. Palo Alto, CA: Stanford University Press.

Geertz, C.
1963   Agricultural Involution: The Processes of Ecological Change in Indonesia. Berkeley: University of California Press.

Giambelluca, T. W., and T. A. Schroeder
1986   Climate. In Atlas of Hawaii. J. O. Juvik, S. P. Juvik, and T. R. Paradise, eds. Pp. 49–59. Honolulu: University of Hawaii Press.

Gibson, McG.
1973   Population Shift and the Rise of Mesopotamian Civilization. In The Explanation of Cultural Change: Models in Prehistory. C. Renfrew, ed. Pp. 447–463. London: Duckworth.
1974   Violation of Fallow and Engineered Disaster in Mesopotamian Civilization. In Irrigation's Impact on Society. T. E. Downing and McG. Gibson, eds. Pp. 7–19. Tucson: The University of Arizona Press.

Gibson, McG., and R. D. Biggs
1991   The Organization of Power: Aspects of Bureaucracy in the Ancient Near East. 2nd edition. Chicago: Oriental Institute of the University of Chicago.

Giere, R. N.
1999   Science without Laws. Chicago: University of Chicago Press.

Gintis, H., E. A. Smith, and S. L. Bowles
2001   Cooperation and Costly Signaling. Journal of Theoretical Biology 213:103–119.

Gleick, P. H.
2000   The World's Water 2000-2001. The Biennial Report on Freshwater Resources. Washington DC: Island Press.

Goddard, I.
1996   Introduction. In Languages. I. Goddard, ed. Pp. 1–16. Handbook of North American Indians, vol. 17, W. C. Sturtevant, general ed. Washington DC: Smithsonian Institution.

Godfrey-Smith, P.
2003   Theory and Reality: An Introduction to the Philosophy of Science. Chicago: University of Chicago Press.

Goldman, I.
1970   Ancient Polynesian Society. Chicago: University of Chicago Press.

Gouin, P.
1997   Ancient Dairy Techniques Based on Archaeological Evidence. Food and Foodways 7:1–33.

Gould, R. A.
1978   Tolowa. In California. R. F. Heizer, ed. Pp. 128–136. Handbook of North American Indians, vol. 8, W. C. Sturtevant, general ed. Washington DC: Smithsonian Institution.

Gray, R., and F. Jordan

2000   Language Trees Support the Express-Train Sequence of Austronesian Expansion. Nature 405:1052–1055.

Guglielmino, C. R., C. Vignotti, B. Hewlett, and L. L. Cavalli-Sforza

1995   Cultural Variation in Africa: Role of Mechanisms of Transmission and Adaptation. Proceedings of the National Academy of Sciences 92:7585–7589.

Guichard, V.

2000   Autoroute A710: archéologie préventive. Archéologie en Grande Limagne d'Auvergne sur le tracé de l'autoroute A710: contribution à l'histoire de l'exploitation d'un milieu palustre. Unpublished report, available from the Service Régional de l'Archéologie, Clermont Ferrand (in collaboration with the AFAN and the ARAFA).

Gumerman, G. J.

1988   A Historical Perspective on Environment and Culture in Anasazi Country. In The Anasazi in a Changing Environment. G. Gumerman, ed. Pp. 1–24. Cambridge: Cambridge University Press.

Gunderson, L. H.

2000   Resilience in Theory and Practice. Annual Review of Ecology and Systematics 31:425–439.

Gunderson, L. H., and C. S. Holling

2002   Panarchy: Understanding Transformations in Human and Natural Systems. Washington DC: Island Press.

Hachem, L.

2000   New Observations on the Bandkeramik House and Social Organisation. Antiquity 74:308–312.

Hahn, M. W., and R. A. Bentley

2003   Drift as a Mechanism for Cultural Change: An Example from Baby Names. Proceedings of the Royal Society of London B270 (suppl. 1):S120–S123.

Halstead, P.

1995   Plough and Power: The Economic and Social Significance of Cultivation with the Ox-Drawn Ard in the Mediterranean. In Domestic Animals of Mesopotamia, Part II. J. N. Postgate and M. A. Powell, eds. Pp. 11–22. Bulletin on Sumerian Agriculture, 8. Cambridge: Aris and Phillips.

Hardy, I. R. B.

1998   Diphtheria. In Bacterial Infections of Humans: Epidemiology and Control. 3rd edition. A. S. Evans and P. S. Brachman, eds. Pp. 253–268. New York and London: Plenum Press.

Hayden, B.

1995   Pathways to Power: Principles for Creating Socioeconomic Inequalities. In Foundations of Social Inequality. T. D. Price and G. M. Feinman, eds. Pp. 15–86. New York: Plenum Press.

Haynes, D. D., J. D. Vogel, and D. G. Wyant

1972   Geology, Structure, and Uranium Deposits of the Cortez Quadrangle, Colorado—Utah. US Geological Survey Miscellaneous Geologic Investigations Map 1-629.

Heizer, R. F., ed.

1978   California. Handbook of North American Indians, vol. 8. W. C. Sturtevant, general ed. Washington DC: Smithsonian Institution.

Hennig, W.

1966   Phylogenetic Systematics. D. D. Davis and R. Zangerl, trans. Urbana: University of Illinois Press.

Hodder, I.

2001   Introduction: A Review of Contemporary Theoretical Debates in Archaeology. In

Archaeological Theory Today. I. Hodder, ed. Pp. 1–13. Cambridge, UK: Polity.

Holden, C., and R. Mace
2003   Spread of Cattle Led to the Loss of Matriliny in Africa. A Co-evolutionary Analysis. Proceedings of the Royal Society of London B270:2425–2433.

Holden, C. J.
2002   Bantu Language Trees Reflect the Spread of Farming across Sub-Saharan Africa: A Maximum-Parsimony Analysis. Proceedings of the Royal Society of London B269:793–799.

Holling, C. S.
1973   Resilience and Stability of Ecological Systems. Annual Review of Ecology and Systematics 4:1–23.
1986   The Resilience of Terrestrial Ecosystems: Local Surprise and Global Change. *In* Sustainable Development of the Biosphere. W. C. Clark and R. E. Munn, eds. Pp. 292–317. Cambridge: Cambridge University Press.

Hommon, R. J.
1986   Social Evolution in Ancient Hawai'i. *In* Island Societies; Archaeological Approaches to Evolution and Transformation. P. V. Kirch, ed. Pp. 55–68. Cambridge: Cambridge University Press.

Hooper, D. U., and L. Johnson
1999   Nitrogen Limitation in Dryland Ecosystems: Responses to Geographical and Temporal Variation in Precipitation. Biogeochemistry 46:247–293.

Howell, J., Jr.
1941   Piñon and Juniper Woodlands of the Southwest. Journal of Forestry 39:542–545.

Hunt, C. B.
1956   Cenozoic Geology of the Colorado Plateau. US Geological Survey Professional Paper 279. Washington DC: United States Geological Survey.

Hunt, R. C.
1991   The Role of Bureaucracy in the Provisioning of Cities: A Framework for Analysis of the Ancient Near East. *In* The Organization of Power: Aspects of Bureaucracy in the Ancient Near East. 2nd edition. McG. Gibson and R. D. Biggs, eds. Pp. 141–168. Chicago: Oriental Institute of the University of Chicago.

Husan, D. H., and D. Bryant
2006   Application of Phylogenetic Networks in Evolutionary Studies. Molecular Biology and Evolution 23(2):254–267.

Ismail, F., W. Sallaberger, P. Talon, and K. Van Lerberghe
1996   Administrative Documents from Tell Beydar (Seasons 1993–95). Subartu 2. Turnhout, Belgium: Brepols.

Iversen, G. R.
1984   Bayesian Statistical Inference. Sage University Paper Series on Quantitative Applications in the Social Sciences, 07-043. Newbury Park, CA: Sage Publications.

Jablonka, E., and M. J. Lamb
2005   Evolution in Four Dimensions: Genetic, Epigenetic, Behavioral, and Symbolic Variation in the History of Life. Cambridge, MA: Bradford Books.

Jacobsen, T.
1960   The Waters of Ur. Iraq 22:174–185.

Jaillette, P.
1996   Les dispositions du code Théodosien sur les terres abandonnées. *In* Le IIIe siècle en Gaule Narbonnaise. Données régionales sur la crise de l'Empire. Actes de la Table-Ronde d'Aix-en-Provence. J. L. Fiches, ed. Pp. 333–404. Sophia Antipolis: Éditions APDCA.

Janssen, M. A.
In press Coordination in Irrigation Systems: An Analysis of the Lansing-Kremer Model of Bali. Agricultural Systems.

Janssen, M. A., and M. Scheffer
2004 Overexploitation of Renewable Resources by Ancient Societies: Sunk Cost Effects as Explanation for Their Collapse. Ecology and Society 9:6. Electronic document, http://www.ecologyandsociety.org/vol9/iss1/art6.

Jeunesse, C.
1997 Pratiques Funéraires au Néolithique Ancien: Sépultures et Nécropoles Danubiennes 5500–4900 av. Paris: J.-C. Errance.

Johnson, C. D.
2006 Critical Natural Resources in the Mesa Verde Region, AD 600–1300: Distribution, Use, and Influence on Puebloan Settlement. Ph.D. dissertation, Department of Anthropology, Washington State University.

Johnson, C. D., T. A. Kohler, and J. Cowan
2005 Modeling Historical Ecology, Thinking about Contemporary Systems. American Anthropologist 107:96–108.

Johnson, G. A.
1982 Organisational Structure and Scalar Stress. In Theory and Explanation in Archaeology. C. Renfrew, M. J. Rowlands, and B. A. Segraves, eds. Pp. 389–421. New York: Academic Press.

Johnston, K. J.
2003 The Intensification of Pre-industrial Cereal Agriculture in the Tropics: Boserup, Cultivation Lengthening, and the Classic Maya. Journal of Anthropological Archaeology 22:126–161.

Jordan, P., and T. Mace
2006 Tracking Culture-Historical Lineages: Can "Descent with Modification" Be Linked to "Association by Descent"? In Mapping Our Ancestors: Phylogenetic Methods in Anthropology and Prehistory. C. P. Lipo, M. J. O'Brien, S. J. Shennan, and M. Collard, eds. Pp. 149–168. New York: Aldine de Gruyter.

Jordan, P., and S. J. Shennan
2003 Cultural Transmission, Language and Basketry Traditions amongst the California Indians. Journal of Anthropological Archaeology 22:42–74.
2005 Cultural Transmission in Indigenous California. In The Evolution of Cultural Diversity: A Phylogenetic Approach. R. Mace, C. J. Holden, and S. J. Shennan, eds. Pp. 165–198. London: University College London Press.

Jorgensen, J. G.
1980 Western Indians: Comparative Environments, Languages, and Cultures of 172 Western American Indian Tribes. San Francisco: W. H. Freeman and Company.

Jung, C., T. Odiot, J.-F. Berger, and D. Seris
2001 Vigne, vin et viticulture dans le Tricastin. In La viticulture antique. J. P. Brun and F. Laubenheimer, eds. Pp. 113–128. Hors Série GALLIA, 58. Paris: Editions CNRS.

Kantner, J.
2004 Ancient Puebloan Southwest. Cambridge: Cambridge University Press.

Kauffman, S. A.
1993 The Origins of Order: Self-organization and Selection in Evolution. New York: Oxford University Press.
1995 At Home in the Universe: The Search for Laws of Self-Organization and Complexity. Oxford: Oxford University Press.

Keeley, L. H.

1988   Hunter-Gatherer Economic Complexity and "Population Pressure": A Cross-cultural Analysis. Journal of Anthropological Archaeology 7:373–411.

Kennedy, M. J., O. A. Chadwick, P. M. Vitousek, L. A. Derry, and D. M. Hendricks

1998   Replacement of Weathering with Atmospheric Sources of Base Cations during Ecosystem Development, Hawaiian Islands. Geology 26:1015–1018.

Kerig, T.

2003   Von Gräben und Stämmen: Zur Interpretation bandkeramischer Erdwerke. *In* Spuren und Botschaften: Interpretationen materieller Kultur. U. Veit, T. L. Kienlin, C. Kümmel, and S. Schmidt, eds. Pp. 225–244. Münster: Waxman.

Khan, A. Q., B. A. Wani, H. Shah, and S. Irfannulah

2001   Assessment of Rural Energy Needs in Hilkot Watershed, Pakistan. The Pakistan Journal of Forestry 51(2):1–14.

Kiesewetter, H.

2003   The Neolithic Population at Jebel Buhais 18: Remarks on Funerary Practices, Palaeodemography and Palaeopathology. *In* Archaeology of the United Arab Emirates. D. T. Potts, H. al-Nabooda, and P. Hellyer, eds. Pp. 35–44. London: Trident Press.

Kirch, P. V.

1980   The Archaeological Study of Adaptation: Theoretical and Methodological Issues. Advances in Archaeological Method and Theory 3:101–156.

1982   The Impact of the Prehistoric Polynesians on the Hawaiian Ecosystem. Pacific Science 36:1–14.

1984   The Evolution of the Polynesian Chiefdoms. Cambridge: Cambridge University Press.

1985   Feathered Gods and Fishhooks: An Introduction to Hawaiian Archaeology and Prehistory. Honolulu: University of Hawaii Press.

1990   The Evolution of Sociopolitical Complexity in Prehistoric Hawaii: An Assessment of the Archaeological Evidence. Journal of World Prehistory 4:311–345.

1994   The Wet and the Dry: Irrigation and Agricultural Intensification in Polynesia. Chicago: University of Chicago Press.

2000   On the Road of the Winds: An Archaeological History of the Pacific Islands before European Contact. Berkeley: University of California Press.

2004   Oceanic Islands: Microcosms of "Global Change." *In* The Archaeology of Global Change. C. L. Redman, S. R. James, P. R. Fish, and J. D. Rogers, eds. Pp. 13–27. Washington DC: Smithsonian Institution.

Kirch, P. V., ed.

1997   Na Mea Kahiko O Kahikinui: Studies in the Archaeology of Kahikinui, Maui. Oceanic Archaeology Laboratory, special publication, 1. Berkeley: Archaeological Research Facility, University of California.

Kirch, P. V., J. Coil, A. S. Hartshorn, M. Jeraj, P. M. Vitousek, and O. A. Chadwick

2005   Intensive Dryland Farming on the Leeward Slopes of Haleakala, Maui, Hawaiian Islands: Archaeological, Archaeobotanical, and Geochemical Perspectives. World Archaeology 37(2):240–258.

Kirch, P. V., and R. C. Green

1987   History, Phylogeny, and Evolution in Polynesia. Current Anthropology 28:431–456.

2001   Hawaiki, Ancestral Polynesia: An Essay in Historical Anthropology. Cambridge: Cambridge University Press.

Kirch, P. V., A. Hartshorn, O. Chadwick, P. Vitousek, D. Sherrod, J. Coil, L. Holm, and W. Sharp
2004   Environment, Agriculture, and Settlement Patterns in a Marginal Polynesian Landscape. Proceedings of the National Academy of Sciences USA 101:9936–9941.

Kirch, P. V., and S. Millerstrom
2004   Petroglyphs of Kahikinui, Maui, Hawaiian Islands: Rock Images within a Polynesian Settlement Landscape. Proceedings of the Prehistoric Society 70:107–128.

Kirch, P. V., and S. O'Day
2002   New Archaeological Insights into Food and Status: A Case Study from Pre-contact Hawaii. World Archaeology 34:484–497.

Kirch, P. V., and J.-L. Rallu, eds.
In press The Growth and Collapse of Pacific Island Societies: Archaeological and Demographic Perspectives. Honolulu: University of Hawaii Press.

Kirch, P. V., and M. Sahlins
1992   Anahulu: The Anthropology of History in the Kingdom of Hawaii. 2 volumes. Chicago: University of Chicago Press.

Kirch, P. V., and W. Sharp
2005   Coral 230th Dating of the Imposition of a Ritual Control Hierarchy in Precontact Hawaii. Science 307:102–104.

Kishino, H., and M. Hasegawa
1989   Evaluation of the Maximum Likelihood Estimate of the Evolutionary Tree Topologies from DNA Sequence Data, and the Branching Order in Hominoidea. Journal of Molecular Evolution 29:170–179.

Kitching, I. J., P. L. Forey, C. J. Humphries, and D. M. Williams
1998   Cladistics: The Theory and Practice of Parsimony Analysis. Oxford: Oxford University Press.

Kleinman, L. C.
1992   To End an Epidemic: Lessons from the History of Diphtheria. New England Journal of Medicine 326:773–777.

Kneipp, J.
1998   Bandkeramik zwischen Rhein, Weser und Main. Studien zu Stil und Chronologie der Keramik. Bonn: Habelt.

Kobti, Z., and R. G. Reynolds
2005   Modeling Protein Exchange across the Social Network in the Village Multi-Agent Simulation. Proceedings of the 2005 IEEE International Conference on Systems, Man and Cybernetics 4:3197–3203.

Kobti, Z., R. G. Reynolds, and T. A. Kohler
2003   A Multi-agent Simulation Using Cultural Algorithms: The Effect of Culture on the Resilience of Social Systems. Proceedings of the 2003 Congress on Evolutionary Computation 3:1988–1995.
2004   The Effect of Kinship Cooperation Learning Strategy and Culture on the Resilience of Social Systems in the Village Multi-agent Simulation. Proceedings of the Congress on Evolutionary Computation 2:1743–1750.

Kohler, T. A.
2004   Prehistoric Human Impact on Upland North American Southwestern Environments: Evolutionary Ecological Perspectives. *In* The Archaeology of Global Change. C. Redman, S. James, P. Fish, and J. D. Rogers, eds. Pp. 224–242. Washington DC: Smithsonian Books.

Kohler, T. A., and E. Blinman
1987   Solving Mixture Problems in Archaeology: Analysis of Ceramic Materials for Dating and

Demographic Reconstruction. Journal of Anthropological Archaeology 6:1–28.

Kohler, T. A., and G. J. Gumerman, eds.

2000   Dynamics in Human and Primate Societies: Agent-Based Modeling of Social and Spatial Presses. Santa Fe Institute Studies in the Sciences of Complexity. New York: Oxford University Press.

Kohler, T. A., J. Kresl, C. R. Van West, E. Carr, and R. H. Wilshusen

2000   Be There Then: A Modeling Approach to Settlement Determinants and Spatial Efficiency among Late Ancestral Pueblo Populations of the Mesa Verde Region, US Southwest. *In* Dynamics in Human and Primate Societies: Agent-Based Modeling of Social and Spatial Processes. T. A. Kohler and G. J. Gumerman, eds. Pp. 145–178. New York: Oxford University Press.

Kohler, T. A., and M. H. Matthews

1988   Long-term Anasazi Land-Use Patterns and Forest Reduction: A Case Study from Southwest Colorado. American Antiquity 53:537–564.

Kohler, T. A., M. Van Pelt, and L. Yap

2000   Reciprocity and Its Limits: Considerations for a Study of the Pre-Hispanic Pueblo World. *In* Alternative Leadership Strategies in the Pueblo World. B. J. Mills, ed. Pp. 180–206. Tucson: University of Arizona Press.

Kohler, T. A., and C. R. Van West

1996   The Calculus of Self-Interest in the Development of Cooperation: Sociopolitical Development and Risk among the Northern Anasazi. *In* Evolving Complexity and Environmental Risk in the Prehistoric Southwest. J. Tainter and B. Tainter, eds. Pp. 169–196. Santa Fe Institute Studies in the Sciences of Complexity, 24. Reading, MA: Addison-Wesley.

Kohler, T. A., C. R. Van West, E. P. Carr, and C. G. Langton

1996   Agent-Based Modeling of Prehistoric Settlement Systems in the Northern American Southwest. *In* Proceedings of the Third International Conference Integrating GIS and Environmental Modeling, Santa Fe, New Mexico, January. Pp. 1–9. Santa Barbara, CA: National Center for Geographic Information and Analysis.

Kolb, M. J.

1992   Diachronic Design Changes in Heiau Temple Architecture on the Island of Maui, Hawaii. Asian Perspectives 31:9–38.

1994a   Monumentality and the Rise of Religious Authority in Precontact Hawaii. Current Anthropology 35:521–548.

1994b   Ritual Activity and Chiefly Economy at an Upland Religious Site on Maui, Hawai'i. The Journal of Field Archaeology 21:417–436.

Kolb, M. J., and B. Dixon

2002   Landscapes of War: Rules and Conventions of Conflict in Ancient Hawai'i (and Elsewhere). American Antiquity 67:514–534.

Kolb, M. J., and E. Radewagen

1997   Na Heiau o Kahikinui: The Temples of Kahikinui. *In* Na Mea Kahiko o Kahikinui: Studies in the Archaeology of Kahikinui, Maui. P. V. Kirch, ed. Pp. 61–77. Oceanic Archaeology Laboratory, special publication, 1. Berkeley, CA: Archaeological Research Facility.

Kolm, K. E.

1993   Conceptualization and Characterization of Hydrologic Systems. International Ground Water Modeling Publication GWMI 93-01, Golden, CO.

1996   Conceptualization and Characterization of Ground-water Systems Using Geographical Information Systems. *In* Remote Sensing and GIS for Site Characterization: Applications and Standards, ASTM STP 1279. V. H. Singhroy, D. D. Nebert, and A. I. Johnson, eds. Pp. 120–134. West Conshohocken, PA: American Society for Testing and Materials.

Kristiansen, K.
2004   Genes versus Agents: A Discussion of the Widening Theoretical Gap in Archaeology. Archaeological Dialogues 11:77–99.

Kroeber, A. L.
1905   Basket Designs of the Indians of Northwestern Californian. University of California Publications. American Archaeology and Ethnology 2(4):102–164.
1925   Handbook of the Indians of California. Smithsonian Institution Bureau of American Ethnology Bulletin 78. Washington DC: Government Printing Office.

Kuckelman, K. A., ed.
2000   The Archaeology of Castle Rock Pueblo: A Thirteenth Century Village in Southwestern Colorado. Electronic document, http://www.crowcanyon.org/castlerock, accessed September 16, 2001.

Kurtz, A. C., L. A. Derry, and O. A. Chadwick
2001   Accretion of Asian Dust to Hawaiian Soils: Isotopic, Elemental, and Mineral Mass Balances. Geochimica et Cosmochimica Acta 65:1971–1983.

Ladefoged, T. N.
1995   The Evolutionary Ecology of Rotuman Political Integration. Journal of Anthropological Archaeology 14:341–358.

Ladefoged, T. N., and M. W. Graves
2000   Evolutionary Theory and the Historical Development of Dry-Land Agriculture in North Kohala, Hawai'i. American Antiquity 65:423–448.
2005a   The Formation of Hawaiian Territories. In Archaeology in Oceania. I. Lilley, ed. Pp. 259–283. Oxford: Blackwell.
2005b   Human Ecodynamics of Kohala, Hawai'i. In The Reñaca Papers. VI International Conference on Rapa Nui and the Pacific. C. M. Stevenson, J. M. Ramírez Aliaga, F. J. Morin, and N. Barbacci, eds. Pp. 155–160. Los Osos, CA: The Easter Island Foundation.

Ladefoged, T. N., M. W. Graves, and R. P. Jennings
1996   Dryland Agricultural Expansion and Intensification in Kohala, Hawai'i Island. Antiquity 70:861–880.

Ladefoged, T. N., M. W. Graves, and M. D. McCoy
2003   Archaeological Evidence for Agricultural Development in Kohala, Island of Hawai'i. Journal of Archaeological Science 30:923–940.

Ladefoged, T. N., M. W. Graves, B. V. O'Connor, and R. Chapin
1998   Integration of Global Positioning Systems into Archaeological Field Research: A Case Study from North Kohala, Hawai'i Island. SAA Bulletin 16:23–27.

Laland, K. N., J. Odling-Smee, and M. W. Feldman
2000   Niche Construction, Biological Evolution, and Cultural Change. Behavioral and Brain Sciences 23:131–145.

LaMotta, V. M., and M. B. Schiffer
2001   Behavioral Archaeology: Towards a New Synthesis. In Archaeological Theory Today. I. Hodder, ed. Pp. 14–64. Cambridge, UK: Polity.

Lancaster, F., and W. Lancaster
1992   Tribal Formations in the Arabian Peninsula. Arabian Archaeology and Epigraphy 3:145–172.
1996   Reflections on the Social Organization of the Arabian Bedu in Coastal Oman. In The Prehistory of Asia and Oceania, UISPP XIII, préactes du colloque 16. G. Afanas'ev, S. Cleuziou, J. R. Lukacs, and M. Tosi, eds. Pp. 141–154. Forli, France: Abaco.

Lansing, J. S.
1991   Priests and Programmers: Technologies of Power in the Engineered Landscape of Bali. Princeton, NJ: Princeton University Press.

Lansing, J. S., and J. N. Kremer
1993   Emergent Properties of Balinese Water Temples. American Anthropologist 95:97–114.

Lebeau, M., and A. Suleiman
1997   Tell Beydar, Three Seasons of Excavations (1992–1994): A Preliminary Report. Subartu 3.
        Turnhout, Belgium: Brepols.

Lee, C., S. Tuljapurkar, and P. Vitousek
2006   Risky Business: Temporal and Spatial Variation in Preindustrial Dryland Agriculture.
        Human Ecology 34:739–763.

Leroyer, C.
1997   Homme, climat, végétation au Tardi- et Postglaciaire dans le bassin parisien: apport de l'é-
        tude palynologique des fonds de vallées. Ph.D. dissertation, University of Paris I (Panthéon-
        Sorbonne).

Leveau, P.
1998   Échelles d'anthropisation et archéologie des campagnes de Gaule du Sud à l'époque romaine.
        Méditerranée 4:17–26.

Levin, S.
1999   Fragile Dominion: Complexity and the Commons. Reading, MA: Perseus Books.

Levins, R.
1966   The Strategy of Model Building in Population Biology. American Scientist 54:421–431.

Lézine, A.-M., C. Robert, S. Cleuziou, M.-L. Inizan, F. Braemer, J.-F. Saliège, F. Sylvestre, J.-J.
Tiercelin, R. Crassard, S. Méry, V. Charpentier, and T. Steimer-Herbet
In press Climate Change and Human Occupation in the Southern Arabian Lowlands during the Last
        Deglaciation and the Holocene, Global and Planetary Change. Theme issue, Hugues Faure.

Lézine, A.-M., J.-F. Saliège, R. Mathieu, T.-L. Tagliatela, S. Méry, V. Charpentier, and
S. Cleuziou
2002   Mangroves of Oman during the Late Holocene: Climatic Implications and Impact on Human
        Settlements. Vegetation History and Archaeobotany 11:221–232.

Lightfoot, R. R.
1994   The Duckfoot Site, vol. 2: Archaeology of the House and Household. Occasional Papers, 4.
        Cortez, CO: Crow Canyon Archaeological Center.

Lipe, W. D.
1970   Anasazi Communities in the Red Rock Plateau, Southeastern Utah. In Reconstructing
        Prehistoric Pueblo Societies. W. A. Longacre, ed. Pp. 84–139. Albuquerque: University of
        New Mexico Press.
2002   Social Power in the Central Mesa Verde Region, AD 1150–1290. In Seeking the Center Place:
        Archaeology and Ancient Communities in the Mesa Verde Region. M. D. Varien and R. H.
        Wilshusen, eds. Pp. 203–232. Salt Lake City: University of Utah Press.

Lipe, W. D., and M. D. Varien
1999   Pueblo III (AD 1150–1300). In Colorado Prehistory: A Context for the Southern Colorado
        River Basin. W. D. Lipe, M. D. Varien, and R. H. Wilshusen, eds. Pp. 290–352. Denver:
        Colorado Council of Professional Archaeologists.

Liverani, M.
1990   The Shape of Neo-Sumerian Fields. In Irrigation and Cultivation in Mesopotamia, Part II. J.
        N. Postgate and M. A. Powell, eds. Pp. 147–186. Bulletin on Sumerian Agriculture, 5.
        Cambridge: Aris and Phillips.
1990–91 Il rendimento dei cereali durante la III dinastia di Ur. Contributo ad un approccio realistico.
        Origini. Preistoria e protostoria delle civiltà antiche 15:359–368.

1996   Reconstructing the Rural Landscape of the Ancient Near East. Journal of the Economic and Social History of the Orient 39(1):1–41.

1997   Lower Mesopotamian Fields: South vs. North. *In* Ana šadî Labnāni lū allik. Festschrift für Wolfgang Röllig. Alter Orient und Altes Testament, 247. B. Pongratz-Leisten, H. Kühne, and P. Xella, eds. Pp. 219–227. Neukirchen-Vluyn, Germany: Butzon & Bercker Kevelaer.

Lloyd, E. A.

1988   The Semantic Approach and Its Application to Evolutionary Theory. Proceedings of the Biennial Meeting of the Philosophy of Science Association 2:278–285.

Lyman, R. L., and M. J. O'Brien

2000   Measuring and Explaining Change in Artifact Variation with Clade-Diversity Diagrams. Journal of Anthropological Archaeology 19:39–74.

Maddison, D. R., and W. P. Maddison

2000   MacClade 4: Analysis of Phylogeny and Character Evolution. Sunderland, MA: Sinauer.

Maekawa, K.

1974   Agricultural Production in Ancient Sumer—Chiefly from Lagash Materials. Zinbun 13:1–60.

1992   The Shape and Orientation of the Domain Units in the "Round Tablets" of Ur III Girsu: A Critical Review of Liverani, "The Shape of Neo-Sumerian Fields," BSA 5 (1990), pp. 147–186, esp. pp. 155ff. Acta Sumerologica 14:407–423.

Magny, M.

1993   Solar Influences on Holocene Climatic Changes Illustrated by Correlations between Past Lake-Level Fluctuations and the Atmospheric ^{14}C Record. Quaternary Research 40: 1-9.

Malaterre, P.-O., D. C. Rogers, and J. Schuurmans

1998   Classification of Canal Control Algorithms. Journal of Irrigation and Drainage Engineering 125:3–10.

Mantel, N.

1967   The Detection of Disease Clustering and a Generalized Regression Approach. Cancer Research 27:209–220.

Marcus, J.

1992   Dynamic Cycles of Mesoamerican States: Political Fluctuations in Mesoamerica. National Geographic Research and Exploration 8:392–411.

Marcus, J., and K. V. Flannery

1996   Zapotec Civilization: How Urban Society Evolved in Mexico's Oaxaca Valley. New York: Thames and Hudson.

Markman, A. B.

1999   Knowledge Representation. Mahwah, NJ: Lawrence Erlbaum.

Marshack, A.

1985   Hierarchical Evolution of the Human Capacity: The Paleolithic Evidence. Fifty-fourth James Arthur Lecture on the Evolution of the Human Brain. New York: American Museum of Natural History.

Martin, C.

2005   Les malacofaunes marines archéologiques du Ja'alan (Sultanat d'Oman): un indicateur des modes de vie des populations dans leur environnement, du Néolithique à l'Âge du Bronze. Ph.D. dissertation, Muséum national d'histoire naturelle, Paris.

Matson, R. G., and B. Chisolm

1991   Basketmaker II Subsistence: Carbon Isotopes and Other Dietary Indicators from Cedar Mesa, Utah. American Antiquity 56:444–459.

McCullough, D. R.

1997   Irruptive Behaviour in Ungulates. *In* The Science of Overabundance. W. J. McShea, H. B. Underwood, and J. H. Rappole, eds. Pp. 69–98. Washington DC: Smithsonian Institution Press.

McDonald, M. G., and A. W. Harbaugh

1988   A Modular Three-Dimensional Finite-Difference Ground-Water Flow Model (MODFLOW). *In* Techniques of Water-Resources Investigations of the United States Geological Survey, book 6, chapter A1. Denver, CO: US Geological Survey.

McGlade, J.

1995   Archaeology and the Ecodynamics of Human-Modified Landscapes. Antiquity 69:113–132.

McGlade, J., and S. van der Leeuw

1997   Introduction: Archaeology and Non-linear Dynamics—New Approaches to Long-term Change. *In* Time, Process and Structured Transformation in Archaeology. S. E. van der Leeuw and J. McGlade, eds. Pp. 1–32. London: Routledge.

Medin, D. E., and A. E. Anderson

1979   Modeling the Dynamics of a Colorado Mule Deer Population. Wildlife Monographs 68:3–67.

Mervis, J.

1998   National Science Foundation: The Biocomplex World of Rita Colwell. Science 281:1944–1947.

Miller, H. V.

1938   Industrial Development of New Albany, Indiana. Economic Geography 14:47–54.

Moore, J. H.

1994   Putting Anthropology Back Together Again: The Ethnogenetic Critique of Cladistic Theory. American Anthropologist 96:925–948.

2001   Ethnogenetic Patterns in Native North America. *In* Archaeology, Language and History: Essays on Culture and Ethnicity. J. E. Terrell, ed. Pp. 30–56. Westport, CT: Bergin and Garvey.

Morrison, K. D.

1994   The Intensification of Production: Archaeological Approaches. Journal of Archaeological Method and Theory 1:111–160.

Muenchrath, D. A., M. Kuratomi, J. A. Sandor, and J. A. Homburg

2002   Observational Study of Maize Production Systems of Zuni Farmers in Semiarid New Mexico. Journal of Ethnobiology 22:1–33.

Mulrooney, M., and T. N. Ladefoged

2005   Hawaiian Heiau and Agricultural Production in the Kohala Dryland Field System. Journal of the Polynesian Society 114:45–67.

Murphy, R. F.

1977   Introduction: The Anthropological Theories of Julian H. Steward. *In* Evolution and Ecology: Essays on Social Transformation by Julian H. Steward. J. C. Steward and R. F. Murphy, eds. Pp. 1–39. Urbana: University of Illinois Press.

Myers, J. E.

1978   Cahto. *In* California. R. F. Heizer, ed. Pp. 244–248. Handbook of North American Indians, vol. 8, W. C. Sturtevant, general ed. Washington DC: Smithsonian Institution.

Myers, K.

1964   Influence of Density on Fecundity, Growth Rates, and Mortality in the Wild Rabbit. CSIRO Wildland Resources 9:134–137.

Nagaoka, L.

2002   Explaining Subsistence Change in Southern New Zealand Using Foraging Theory Models. World Archaeology 34:84–102.

Neiman, F. D.

1995   Stylistic Variation in Evolutionary Perspective: Inferences from Decorative Diversity and Interassemblage Distance in Illinois Woodland Ceramic Assemblages. American Antiquity 60:7–36.

1997   Conspicuous Consumption as Wasteful Advertising: A Darwinian Perspective on Spatial Patterns in Classic Maya Terminal Monument Dates. *In* Rediscovering Darwin: Evolutionary Theory in Archaeological Explanation. C. M. Barton and G. A. Clark, eds. Pp. 267–290. Arlington, VA: American Anthropological Association.

Newman, T. S.

1970   Hawaiian Fishing and Farming on the Island of Hawaii in AD 1778. Honolulu: Division of State Parks, State of Hawaii.

Nicolis, G., and I. Prigogine

1977   Self-Organisation in Non-equilibrium Systems: From Dissipative Structures to Order through Fluctuations. New York: Wiley.

Nuninger, L.

2002   Peuplement et Territoires protohistoriques du VIIIe au Ier s. avant J.-C. en Languedoc Oriental (Gard-Hérault). 2 vols. Ph.D. dissertation, University of Franche-Comté, Besançon.

Odling-Smee, F. J., K. N. Laland, and M. W. Feldman

2003   Niche Construction: The Neglected Process in Evolution. Princeton, NJ: Princeton University Press.

Oesterheld, M., J. Loreti, and O. E. Sala

2001   Inter-annual Variation in Primary Production of a Semi-arid Grassland Related to Previous-Year Production. Journal of Vegetation Science 12:137–142.

O'Neill, R. V., D. L. De Angelis, J. B. Waide, and T. H. F. Allen

1986   A Hierarchical Concept of Ecosystems. Monographs in Population Biology, 23. Princeton, NJ: Princeton University Press.

Orschiedt, J., A. Häußer, M. N. Haidle, K. W. Alt, and C. H. Buitrago-Téllez

2003   Survival of a Multiple Skull Trauma: The Case of an Early Neolithic Individual from the LBK Enclosure at Herxheim (Southwest Germany). International Journal of Osteoarchaeology 13:375–383.

Ortman, S. G.

1998   Corn Grinding and Community Organization in the Pueblo Southwest, AD 1150–1550. *In* Migration and Reorganization: The Pueblo IV Period in the American Southwest. K. A. Spielmann, ed. Pp. 165–192. Anthropological Research Papers, 51. Tempe: Arizona State University.

Ortman, S. G., D. M. Glowacki, M. J. Churchill, and K. A. Kuckelman

2000   Pattern and Variation in Northern San Juan Village Histories. Kiva 66:123–146.

Ortman, S. G., M. D. Varien, and T. L. Gripp

2007   An Empirical Bayesian Approach to Analysis of Archaeological Survey Data from Southwest Colorado. American Antiquity.

Ozenda, P.

1964   Biogéographie végétale. Paris: Douin.

Page, R.

1993   COMPONENT (version 2.0). London: Natural History Museum.

2003   Introduction. *In* Tangled Trees: Phylogeny, Cospeciation and Coevolution. R. Page, ed. Pp. 1–21. Chicago: University of Chicago Press.

Palmer, C., and K. W. Russell
1993   Traditional Ards of Jordan. Annual of the Department of Antiquities of Jordan 37:37–53.

Palmer, W. C.
1965   Meteorological Drought. Research Paper 45. Washington DC: US Department of Commerce, US Weather Bureau.

Pannell, J. P.
N.d.   Soil Survey of the Animas-Dolores Area, Colorado. Durango, CO: US Department of Agriculture, Natural Resources Conservation Service.

Parton, W. J., D. S. Schimel, C. V. Cole, and D. S. Ojima
1987   Analysis of Factors Controlling Soil Organic Matter Levels in Great Plains Grasslands. Soil Science Society of America Journal 51:1173–1179.

Parton, W. J., J. W. B. Stewart, and C. V. Cole
1988   Dynamics of C, N, P, and S in Grassland Soils: A Model. Biogeochemistry 5:109–131.

Pattee, H. H.
1973   Hierarchy Theory: The Challenge of Complex Systems. New York: Braziller.

Pearson, R., ed.
1968   Excavations at Lapakahi: Selected Papers. Hawaii State Archaeological Journal 69-2. Honolulu: Department of Land and Natural Resources.

Pedersén, O.
1998   Archives and Libraries in the Ancient Near East 1500–300 BC. Bethesda, MD: CDL.

Petrasch, J.
2001   Seid fruchtbar und mehret euch und fullet die Erde und.machet sie euch untertan. Archaeologisches Korrespondenzblatt 31:13–25.
2005   Demografischer Wandel am Beginn der Bandkeramik. Paper presented at the conference "Die Neolithisierung Mitteleuropas," June 24–26, 2005, Mainz, Germany.

Pilling, A. J.
1978   Yurok. In California. R. F. Heizer, ed. Pp. 137–154. Handbook of North American Indians, vol. 8, W. C. Sturtevant, general ed. Washington DC: Smithsonian Institute.

Pinhasi, R., J. Fort, and A. J. Ammerman
2005   Tracing the Origin and Spread of Agriculture in Europe. Public Library of Science Biology 3(12)(e410):2220–2228. Electronic document, http://biology.plosjournals.org, accessed July 19, 2006.

Postgate, J. N.
1992   Early Mesopotamia. Society and Economy at the Dawn of History. London: Routledge.

Pournelle, J. R.
2003   Marshland of Cities: Deltaic Landscapes and the Evolution of Early Mesopotamian Civilization. Ph.D. dissertation, University of California, San Diego.

Price, J. P., and D. Clague
2002   How Old Is the Hawaiian Biota? Geology and Phylogeny Suggest Recent Divergence. Proceedings of the Royal Society of London B269:2429–2435.

Provansal, M., J.-F. Berger, J.-P. Bravard, P.-G. Salvador, G. Arnaud-Fassetta,
H. Bruneton, and A. Verot-Bourrely
1999   Le régime du Rhône et les mutations des environnements fluviaux du lac de Genève à la mer. Gallia 56:13–32.

Py, M.
1993   Les Gaulois du Midi, de la fin de l'Âge du Bronze à la conquête romaine. Collection La Mémoire du Temps. Paris: Hachette.

Ramsey, D. K.

2003   Soil Survey of Cortez Area, Colorado. Cortez, CO: US Department of Agriculture, Natural Resources Conservation Service.

2006   Soil Survey of the Ute Mountain Ute Indian Reservation, Montezuma County, Colorado. Cortez, CO: US Department of Agriculture, Natural Resources Conservation Service.

Rathbun, T. A.

1982   Morphological Affinities and Demography of Metal-Age Southwest Asian Populations. American Journal of Physical Anthropology 59:47–60.

1984   Skeletal Pathology from the Paleolithic through the Metal Ages in Iran and Iraq. *In* Paleopathology at the Origins of Agriculture. M. N. Cohen and G. J. Armelagos, eds. Pp. 132–167. New York: Academic Press.

Raynaud, C.

1990   Le village gallo-romain et médiéval de Lunel-Viel (Hérault): les fouilles du quartier ouest (1981–1983). Annales Littéraires de l'Université de Besançon, 97. Paris: Les Belles Lettres.

Redding, R. W.

1981   Decision Making in Subsistence Herding of Sheep and Goats in the Middle East. Ph.D. dissertation, University of Michigan.

Reddy, J. M., and R. G. Jacquot

1999   Stochastic Optimal and Suboptimal Control of Irrigation Canals. Journal of Water Resources Planning and Management 125:369–378.

Redman, C. L.

1999   Human Impact on Ancient Environments. Tucson: The University of Arizona Press.

Redman, C. L., S. R. James, P. R. Fish, and J. D. Rogers, eds.

2004   The Archaeology of Global Change: The Impact of Humans on Their Environment. Washington DC: Smithsonian Institution.

Redman, C. L., and A. Kinzig

2002   Resilience of Past Landscapes: Resilience Theory, Society and the Longue Durée. Conservation Ecology 7(1):14–28.

Reeve, H. K., and S. T. Emlen

2000   Reproductive Skew and Group Size: An N-Person Staying Incentive Model. Behavioral Ecology 11:640–647.

Reynolds, R. G.

1979   An Adaptive Computer Model of the Evolution of Agriculture for Hunter-Gatherers in the Valley of Oaxaca, Mexico. Ph.D. dissertation, University of Michigan.

1994   Introduction to Cultural Algorithms. *In* Proceedings of the Third Annual Conference on Evolutionary Programming. A. V. Sebald and L. J. Fogel, eds. Pp. 131–139. Singapore: World Scientific Press.

1999   An Overview of Cultural Algorithms. *In* New Ideas in Optimization. D. Corne, F. Glover, and M. Dorigo, eds. Pp. 367–378. London: McGraw-Hill.

2005   Cultural Emergence. *In* Perspectives on Adaptation in Natural and Artificial Systems: Essays in Honor of John Holland. L. Booker, S. Forrest, M. Mitchell, and R. Riolo, eds. Pp. 253–280. New York: Oxford University Press.

Reynolds, R. G., Z. Kobti, T. A. Kohler, and L. Yap

2005   Unraveling Ancient Mysteries: Re-imagining the Past Using Evolutionary Computation in a Complex Gaming Environment. IEEE Transactions on Evolutionary Computation 9:707–720.

Reynolds, R. G., T. A. Kohler, and Z. Kobti

2003   The Effects of Generalized Reciprocal Exchange on the Resilience of Social Networks: An

Example from the Prehispanic Mesa Verde Region. Journal of Computational and Mathematical Organization Theory 9:227–254.

Reynolds, R. G., and D. Ostrowski

2003   Using Software Engineering Knowledge to Drive Genetic Program Design Using Cultural Algorithms: Exploiting the Synergy of Software Engineering Knowledge in Evolutionary Design. *In* Advances in Genetic Programming. R. Riolo and B. Wurzel, eds. Pp. 63–80. Boston: Kluwer Academic.

Richerson, P. J., and R. Boyd

2004   Not by Genes Alone: How Culture Transformed Human Evolution. Chicago: University of Chicago Press.

Rivers, W. H. R.

1926   Psychology and Ethnology. London: Kegan Paul, Trench, Trubner.

Robertson, I. G.

1999   Spatial and Multivariate Analysis, Random Sampling Error, and Analytical Noise: Empirical Bayesian Methods at Teotihuacan, Mexico. American Antiquity 64:137–152.

Rock, J. F.

1915   Indigenous Trees of the Hawaiian Islands. Privately published. Honolulu.

Rohn, A. H.

1977   Cultural Continuity and Change on Chapin Mesa. Lawrence: Regents' Press of Kansas.

Rosendahl, P. H.

1972   Aboriginal Agriculture and Residence Patterns in Upland Lapakahi, Island of Hawaii. Ph.D. dissertation, Department of Anthropology, University of Hawaii.

1994   Aboriginal Hawaiian Structural Remains and Settlement Patterns in the Upland Agricultural Zone at Lapakahi, Island of Hawai'i. Hawaiian Archaeology 3:14–70.

Russell, K. W.

1988   After Eden: The Behavioral Ecology of Early Food Production in the Near East and North Africa. BAR International, 391. Oxford: Archaeopress.

Sahlins, M.

1958   Social Stratification in Polynesia. Seattle, WA: American Ethnological Society.

1972   Stone Age Economics. Chicago and New York: Aldine Atherton.

Saller, R.

1991   Patriarchy, Property, and Death in the Roman Family. Cambridge: Cambridge University Press.

Salmon, M. H.

1978   What Can Systems Theory Do for Archaeology? American Antiquity 43:174–183.

Salvador, P.-G., J.-F. Berger, M. Fontugne, and E. Gauthier

2005   Etude des enregistrements sédimentaires des paléoméandres du Rhône dans le secteur des Basses Terres dauphinoises (Ain, Isère, France), colloque AFEQ-INQUA, Strasbourg, 22–23 septembre 2004: Continuité et discontinuité dans les enregistrements quaternaires. Quaternaire 16(4):315–328.

Salvatori, S.

2001   Excavations at the Funerary Structures HD 10-3.1, 3.2, 4.1, 4.2 and 2.1 at Ra's al-Hadd (Sultanate of Oman). Rivista di archeologia XXV:67–85.

Schloen, D.

2001   The House of the Father as Fact and Symbol: Patrimonialism in Ugarit and the Ancient Near East. Winona Lake, IN: Eisenbrauns.

Schmidt, B., W. Gruhle, and O. Rück

2004   Klimaextreme in Bandkeramischer Zeit (5300–5000 v. Chr.): Interpretation Dendrochronologischer und Archäologischer Befunde. Archäologisches Korrespondenzblatt 34:303–307.

Schrage, L.

1979   A More Portable FORTRAN Random Number Generator. ACM Transactions on Mathematical Software 5:132–138.

Scriver, C. R.

2001   Human Genetics: Lessons from Quebec Populations. Annual Review of Genomics and Human Genetics 2:69–101.

Service, E. R.

1975   Origins of the State and Civilization. New York: Norton.

Shanks, M., and C. Tilley

1992   Re-constructing Archaeology: Theory and Practice. 2nd edition. London: Routledge.

Shennan, S. J.

2000   Population, Culture History, and the Dynamics of Culture Change. Current Anthropology 41:811–835.

2001   Demography and Cultural Innovation: A Model and Its Implications for the Emergence of Modern Human Culture. Cambridge Archaeological Journal 11:5–16.

2002   Genes, Memes and Human History: Darwinian Archaeology and Cultural Evolution. London: Thames and Hudson.

Shipley, W.

1978   Native Languages of California. *In* California. R. F. Heizer, ed. Pp. 80–90. Handbook of North American Indians, vol. 8, W. C. Sturtevant, general ed. Washington DC: Smithsonian Institution.

Silver, S.

1978   Chimariko. *In* California. R. F. Heizer, ed. Pp. 205–210. Handbook of North American Indians, vol. 8, W. C. Sturtevant, general ed. Washington DC: Smithsonian Institution.

Simon, H. A.

1973   The Organization of Complex Systems. *In* Hierarchy Theory: The Challenge of Complex Systems. H. H. Pattee, ed. Pp. 3–27. New York: George Braziller.

1981   The Sciences of the Artificial. 2nd edition. Cambridge, MA: MIT Press.

Skyrms, B.

1996   Evolution of the Social Contract. New York and Cambridge: Cambridge University Press.

Smith, A. B.

1994   Systematics and the Fossil Record: Documenting Evolutionary Patterns. Oxford: Blackwell Science.

Smith, E. A.

2001   On the Co-evolution of Cultural, Linguistic and Biological Diversity. *In* On Biocultural Diversity: Linking Language, Knowledge, and the Environment. L. Maffi, ed. Pp. 95–117. Washington DC: Smithsonian Institution Press.

Sober, E., and S. Orzack

1993   A Critical Assessment of Levins' "The Strategy of Model Building" (1966). Quarterly Review of Biology 68:534–546.

Soltis, J., R. Boyd, and P. Richerson

1995   Can Group-Functional Behaviors Evolve by Cultural Group Selection? An Empirical Test. Current Anthropology 36:473–493.

Spencer, C. S.

1990　On the Tempo and Mode of State Formation: Neoevolutionism Reconsidered. Journal of Anthropological Archaeology 9:1–30.

1993　Human Agency, Biased Transmission, and the Cultural Evolution of Chiefly Authority. Journal of Anthropological Archaeology 12:41–74.

Spielmann, K. A., and E. A. Angstadt-Leto

1996　Hunting, Gathering, and Health in the Prehistoric Southwest. *In* Evolving Complexity and Environmental Risk in the Prehistoric Southwest. J. A. Tainter and B. Bagley Tainter, eds. Pp. 79–106. Santa Fe Institute Studies in the Sciences of Complexity Proceedings, XXIV. Reading, MA: Addison-Wesley.

Stannard, D.

1989　Before the Horror: The Population of Hawai'i on the Eve of Western Contact. Honolulu: Social Science Research Institute, University of Hawaii.

Stein, G. J.

2001　Understanding State Societies in the Old World. *In* Archaeology at the Millennium: A Sourcebook. G. M. Feinman and T. Douglas Price, eds. Pp. 353–379. New York: Kluwer.

2004　Structural Parameters and Sociocultural Factors in the Economic Organization of North Mesopotamian Urbanism in the Third Millennium BC. *In* Archaeological Perspectives on Political Economies. G. M. Feinman and L. M. Nicholas, eds. Pp. 61–78. Salt Lake City: University of Utah.

Stein, G. J., and P. Wattenmaker

1990　The 1987 Tell Leilan Regional Survey: Preliminary Report. *In* Economy and Settlement in the Near East: Analyses of Ancient Sites and Materials. MASCA Research Papers in Science and Archaeology, 7. N. Miller, ed. Pp. 8–18. Philadelphia: University of Pennsylvania Museum.

Stillings, B. R.

1973　World Supplies of Animal Protein. *In* Protein in Human Nutrition. J. W. G. Porter and B. A. Rolls, eds. Pp. 11–33. London: Academic Press.

Stiner, M. C., and N. D. Munro

2002　Approaches to Prehistoric Diet Breadth, Demography, and Prey Ranking Systems in Time and Space. Journal of Archaeological Method and Theory 9:181–214.

Stock, J., J. Coil, and P. V. Kirch

2003　Paleohydrology of Arid Southeastern Maui, Hawaiian Islands, and Its Implications for Prehistoric Human Settlement. Quaternary Research 59:12–24.

Stöckle, C. O., G. S. Cambell, and R. Nelson

1999　ClimGen Manual. Pullman: Biological Systems Engineering Department, Washington State University.

Stouthamer, E., and H. J. A. Berendsen

2000　Factors Controlling the Holocene Avulsion History of the Rhine-Meuse Delta (the Netherlands). Journal of Sedimentary Research 70:1051–1064.

Strien, C.

2000　Untersuchungen zur Bandkeramik in Württemberg. Bonn: Habelt.

Stuiver, M., and T. Braziunas

1993　Sun, Ocean, Climate and Atmospheric $^{14}CO_2$: An Evaluation of Causal and Spectral Relationship. The Holocene 3:289–305.

Suppe, F.

1977a　Afterword—1977. *In* The Structure of Scientific Theories. 2nd edition. F. Suppe, ed. Pp. 617–730. Urbana: University of Illinois Press.

1977b   The Search for Philosophical Understanding of Scientific Theories. *In* The Structure of
          Scientific Theories. 2nd edition. F. Suppe, ed. Pp. 3–241. Urbana: University of Illinois
          Press.

Sutherland, W. J.
1996   From Individual Behavior to Population Ecology. Oxford: Oxford University Press.

Swain, E. D., and E. J. Wexler
1993   A Coupled Surface-Water and Ground-Water Model for Simulation of Stream-Aquifer
          Interaction. US Geological Survey Open File Report. Pp. 92–138.

Sweet, L. E.
1974   Tell Toqaan: A Syrian Village. Anthropological Papers. Ann Arbor: Museum of
          Anthropology, University of Michigan.

Swofford, D. L.
1998   PAUP*: Phylogenetic Analysis Using Parsimony (*and Other Methods) (version 4).
          Sunderland, MA: Sinauer.

Tehrani, J., and M. Collard
2002   Investigating Cultural Evolution through Biological Phylogenetic Analyses of Turkmen
          Textiles. Journal of Anthropological Archaeology 21:443–463.

Terrell, J. E.
1987   Comment on "History, Phylogeny and Evolution in Polynesia" by P. V. Kirch and
          R. C. Green. Current Anthropology 28:447–448.
1988   History as Family Tree, History as an Entangled Bank: Constructing Images and
          Interpretations of Prehistory in the South Pacific. Antiquity 62:642–657.

Terrell, J. E., T. L. Hunt, and C. Gosden
1997   The Dimensions of Social Life in the Pacific: Human Diversity and the Myth of the
          Primitive Isolate. Current Anthropology 38:155–195.

Teschler-Nicola, M., F. Gerold, M. Bujatti-Narbeshuber, T. Prohaska, C. Latkoczy,
G. Stingeder, and M. Watkins
1999   Evidence of Genocide 7000 BP—Neolithic Paradigm and Geo-climatic Reality. Collegium
          Antropologicum 23:437–450.

Thomas, B. E.
1986   Simulation Analysis of Water-Level Changes in the Navajo Sandstone due to Changes in the
          Altitude of Lake Powell near Wahweap Bay, Utah and Arizona. US Geological Survey Water-
          Resources Investigations Report 85-4207.
1988   Simulation Analysis of the Ground Water System in Mesozoic Rocks in the Four Corners
          Area, Utah, Colorado, Arizona, and New Mexico. US Geological Survey Water Resources
          Investigations Report 88-4086.

Thompson, M., R. Ellis, and A. Wildavsky
1989   Cultural Theory. Boulder, CO: Westview Press.

Tinner, W., A. Lotter, B. Ammann, M. Conedera, P. Hubschmid, J. van Leeuwen, and
M. Wehrli
2003   Climatic Change and Contemporaneous Land-Use Phases North and South of the Alps 2300
          BC to 800 AD. Quaternary Science Reviews 22:1447–1460.

Tourneux, F. P.
2000   Modes de représentation des paysages. Ph.D. dissertation, University of Franche-Comté,
          Besançon.

Travers, J., and S. Milgram
1969   An Experimental Study of the Small-World Problem. Sociometry 32:425–443.

Trément, F., C. Ballut, B. Dousteyssier, V. Guichard, and M. Segard
2004   Des espaces et des paysages. Essai de restitution dynamique des relations habitat-milieu humide en Grande Limagne, de l'Âge du Fer au Moyen-Âge. *In* L'historien en quête d'espaces. J.-L. Fray and C. Pérol, eds. Pp. 17–37. Coll. Histoires croisées. Clermont-Ferrand: Presses Universitaires Blaise-Pascal.

Tufte, E. R.
1990   Envisioning Information. Cheshire, CT: Graphics Press.

Tuggle, H. D., and P. B. Griffin, eds.
1973   Lapakahi, Hawaii: Archaeological Studies. Asian and Pacific Archaeology, 5. Honolulu: Social Science Research Institute.

Tuzin, D.
2001   Social Complexity in the Making: A Case Study among the Arapesh of New Guinea. London: Routledge.

Uerpmann, M., H.-P. Uerpmann, and S. A. Jasim
2000   Stone Age Nomadism in SE-Arabia: Palaeo-economic Considerations on the Neolithic Site of al-Buhais 18 in the Emirate of Sharjah, UAE. Proceedings of the Seminar for Arabian Studies 30:229–234.

Ugan, A.
2005   Does Size Matter? Body Size, Mass Collecting, and Their Implications for Understanding Prehistoric Foraging Behaviors. American Antiquity 70:75–89.

Ur, J. A.
2003   CORONA Satellite Photography and Ancient Road Networks: A Northern Mesopotamian Case Study. Antiquity 77:102–115.

Valeri, V.
1985   Kingship and Sacrifice: Ritual and Society in Ancient Hawaii. Chicago: University of Chicago Press.

van Andel, T. H., and C. N. Runnels
1995   The Earliest Farmers in Europe. Antiquity 69:481–500.

van Berg, P.-L., N. Cauwe, J.-P. Hénin, S. Lemaitre, V. Picalause, and M. Vander Linden
2003   Fieldwork at the Archaeological and Rock Art Sites of the Hemma Plateau, Hasseke, Syria (Season 2002). Adumatu 7:7–20.

van der Leeuw, S. E.
2004   Why Model? Cybernetics and Systems 35(2-3):117–128.

van der Leeuw, S. E., ed.
1998   Understanding the Natural and Anthropogenic Causes of Land Degradation and Desertification in the Mediterranean Basin. Luxembourg: Office for Official Publications of the European Communities.

van der Leeuw, S. E., and J. McGlade, eds.
1997   Time, Process and Structured Transformation in Archaeology. London: Routledge.

van der Leeuw, S., and C. Redman
2002   Placing Archaeology at the Center of Socio-Natural Studies. American Antiquity 67:597–607.

van der Velde, P.
1990   Banderamik Social Inequality—A Case Study. Germania 68:19–38.
1996   Dust and Ashes: The Two Neolithic Cemeteries of Elsloo and Niedermerz Compared. Analecta Praehistorica Leidensia 25:173–188.

Van Driel, G.
1999/2000   The Size of Institutional Umma. Archiv für Orientforschung 46/47:180–191.

Van Geel, B., and M. Magny

2002   Mise en évidence d'un forçage solaire du climat à partir de données paléoécologiques et
        archéologiques: la transition Subboréal-Subatlantique. *In* Équilibres et ruptures dans les
        écosystèmes durant les 20 derniers millénaires en Europe de l'Ouest, Actes du colloque inter-
        national de Besançon, septembre 2000. H. Richard and A. Vignot, eds. Pp. 107–122.
        Annales Littéraires, 730, Série "Environnement, sociétés et archéologie," 3. Besançon: Presses
        Universitaires Franc-Comtoises.

van Lerberghe, K.

1996   The Livestock. *In* Administrative Documents from Tell Beydar (Seasons 1993–95). Subartu
        2. F. Ismail, W. Sallaberger, P. Talon, and K. van Lerberghe, eds. Pp. 107–117. Turnhout,
        Belgium: Berpols.

Van West, C. R.

1994   Modeling Prehistoric Agricultural Productivity in Southwestern Colorado: A GIS Approach.
        Reports of Investigations, 67. Pullman: Department of Anthropology, Washington State
        University; Cortez, CO: Crow Canyon Archaeological Center.

Varien, M. D.

1999   Sedentism and Mobility in a Social Landscape: Mesa Verde and Beyond. Tucson: The
        University of Arizona Press.

In press Occupation Span and the Organization of Activities at Residential Sites: A Case Study from
        the Mesa Verde Region. *In* Ancient Households of the Americas: Conceptualizing What
        Households Do. J. G. Douglass and N. Gonlin, eds. Boulder: University of Colorado Press.

Varien, M. D., ed.

1999   The Sand Canyon Archaeological Project: Site Testing. CD-ROM version 1.0. Cortez, CO:
        Crow Canyon Archaeological Center.

Varien, M. D., W. D. Lipe, M. A. Adler, I. M. Thompson, and B. A. Bradley

1996   Southwestern Colorado and Southeastern Utah Settlement Patterns: AD 1100–1300. *In* The
        Prehistoric Pueblo World, AD 1150–1350. M. A. Adler, ed. Pp. 86–113. Tucson: The
        University of Arizona Press.

Varien, M. D., and B. J. Mills

1997   Accumulations Research: Problems and Prospects for Estimating Site Occupation Span.
        Journal of Archaeological Method and Theory 4:141–191.

Varien, M. D., and S. G. Ortman

2005   Accumulations Research in the Southwest United States: Middle-Range Theory for Big-
        Picture Problems. World Archaeology 37:132–155.

Varien, M. D., S. G. Ortman, T. A. Kohler, D. M. Glowacki, and C. D. Johnson

2007   Historical Ecology in the Mesa Verde Region: Results from the Village Project. American
        Antiquity 71:?.

Vehrencamp, S. L.

1983   A Model for the Evolution of Despotic versus Egalitarian Societies. Animal Behaviour
        31:667–682.

Verhagen, P., and J.-F. Berger

2001   Predictive Modeling of Buried Archaeological Sites in the Tricastin-Valdaine Region (Middle
        Rhône Valley, France). *In* CAA 2000: Computing Archaeology for Understanding the Past,
        Proceedings of the Joint CAA/UISPP Commission IV conference, April 18–21, 2000,
        Ljubjana, Slovenia. Z. Stancic and T. Veljanovic, eds. Pp. 219–231. British Archaeological
        Reports International, 931. Oxford: Archaeopress.

Vital, J.

1990   Protohistoire dans le Défilé de Donzère. L'Âge du Bronze dans la Baume des Anges (Drôme).

Documents d'archéologie française, 28. Paris: Éditions de la Maison des Sciences de l'Homme.

Vitousek, P. M.

2002   Oceanic Islands as Model Systems for Ecological Studies. Journal of Biogeography 29:573–582.

2004   Nutrient Cycling and Limitation: Hawai'i as a Model System. Princeton, NJ: Princeton University Press.

Vitousek, P. M., T. L. Ladefoged, P. V. Kirch, A. S. Hartshorn, M. W. Graves,

S. C. Hotchkiss, S. Tuljapurkar, and O. A. Chadwick.

2004   Agriculture, Soils, and Society in Precontact Hawai'i. Science 304:1665–1669.

Voland, E.

1998   Evolutionary Ecology of Human Reproduction. Annual Review of Anthropology 27:347–374.

Von Rad, U., M. Schaaf, K. H. Michels, H. Schulz, W. H. Berger, and F. Sirocko

1999   5000-Yr Record of Climate Change in Varved Sediments from the Oxygen Minimum Zone off Pakistan, Northeastern Arabian Sea. Quaternary Research 51:39–53.

Vosmer, T.

2003   The Magan Boat Project: A Process of Discovery, a Discovery of Process. Proceedings of the Seminar for Arabian Studies 33:49–58.

In press   Riding the Crest: Lessons from the Loss of the Magan Boat. Proceedings of the Seminar for Arabian Studies 36.

Wagner, A.

1999   Causality in Complex Systems. Biology and Philosophy 14:83–101.

Wahl, J., and H. G. König

1987   Anthropologisch-traumatologische Untersuchung der menschlichen Skelettreste aus dem bandkeramischen Massengrab bei Talheim, Kreis Heilbronn. Fundberichte aus Baden-Württemberg 12:65–193.

Wallace, E.

1978   Sexual Status and Role Differences. *In* California. R. F. Heizer, ed. Pp. 683–689. Handbook of North American Indians, vol. 8, W. C. Sturtevant, general ed. Washington DC: Smithsonian Institution.

Wallace, W. J.

1978   Hupa, Chilula and Whilkut. *In* California. R. F. Heizer, ed. Pp. 164–179. Handbook of North American Indians, vol. 8, W. C. Sturtevant, general ed. Washington DC: Smithsonian Institution.

Wallmo, O. C., L. H. Carpenter, W. L. Regelin, R. B. Gill, and D. L. Baker

1977   Evaluation of Deer Habitat on a Nutritional Basis. Journal of Range Management 30:122–127.

Watson, P. J., S. A. LeBlanc, and C. L. Redman

1971   Explanation in Archaeology: An Explicitly Scientific Approach. New York: Columbia University Press.

Weigel, J. F.

1987   Selected Hydrologic and Physical Properties of Mesozoic Formations in the Upper Colorado River Basin in Arizona, Colorado, Utah, and Wyoming—Excluding the San Juan Basin. US Geological Survey Water-Resources Investigations Report 86-4170.

Weisler, M., and P. V. Kirch

1985   The Structure of Settlement Space in a Polynesian Chiefdom: Kawela, Moloka'i, Hawaiian Islands. New Zealand Journal of Archaeology 7:129–158.

Weiss, H.

1986   The Origins of Tell Leilan and the Conquest of Space in Third Millennium Mesopotamia. *In* The Origins of Cities in Dry-Farming Syria. H. Weiss, ed. Pp. 71–108. Guilford, CT: Four Quarters Press.

Weiss, H., M.-A. Courty, W. Wetterstrom, F. Guichard, L. Senior, R. A. Meadow, and A. Curnow

1993   The Genesis and Collapse of Third Millennium North Mesopotamian Civilization. Science 261:995–1004.

Welsch, R. L.

1987   Reply to Kirch and Green, History, Phylogeny and Evolution in Polynesia. Current Anthropology 28:448–450.

White, D., and M. Houseman

2003   The Navigation of Strong Ties: Small Worlds, Tie Strength, and Network Topology. Complexity 8:72–81.

White, L.

1962   The Pueblo of Sia, New Mexico. Bureau of American Ethnology Bulletin 184. Washington DC: US Government Printing Office.

Whitfield, M. S., Jr., W. Thordarson, W. J. Oatfield, E. A. Aimmerman, and B. F. Reuger

1983   Regional Hydrology of the Blanding-Durango Area, Southern Paradox Basin, Utah and Colorado. US Geological Survey Water Resources Investigations Report 83-4218.

Widell, M.

2004   Some Observations on the Administration, Agriculture and Animal Management of Tell Beydar. Ugarit-Forschungen 35:717–733.

2005   Seeding and Plowing Practices in Nuzi. Studies on the Civilization and Culture of Nuzi and the Hurrians 15:169–173.

Wilkinson, T. J.

1982   The Definition of Ancient Manured Zones by Means of Extensive Sherd-Sampling Techniques. Journal of Field Archaeology 9:323–333.

1993   Linear Hollows in the Jazira, Upper Mesopotamia. Antiquity 67:548–562.

1994   The Structure and Dynamics of Dry-Farming States in Upper Mesopotamia. Current Anthropology 35:483–520.

2000   Archaeological Survey of the Tell Beydar Region, Syria, 1997: A Preliminary Report. *In* Tell Beydar: Environmental and Technical Studies. Subartu 6. K. Van Lerberghe and G. Voet, eds. Pp. 1–37. Turnhout, Belgium: Berpols.

2003   Archaeological Landscapes of the Near East. Tucson: The University of Arizona Press.

Wilkinson, T. J., J. C. Christiansen, J. A. Ur, M. Widell, and M. Altaweel

In press   Urbanization within a Dynamic Environment: Modeling Bronze Age Communities in Upper Mesopotamia. American Anthropologist.

Witkind, I. J.

1964   Geology of the Abajo Mountains Area, San Juan County, Utah. US Geological Survey Professional Paper 453. Washington DC: United States Geological Survey.

Wittfogel, K. A.

1957   Oriental Despotism: A Comparative Study of Total Power. New Haven, CT: Yale University Press.

Wood, J. W.

1998   A Theory of Preindustrial Population Dynamics—Demography, Economy, and Well-being in Malthusian Systems. Current Anthropology 39:99–135.

Wooster, L. D.

1935   Notes on the Effects of Drought on Animal Populations in Western Kansas. Transactions of the Kansas Academy of Science 38:351–352.

Zaccagnini, C.

1975   The Yields of the Fields at Nuzi. Oriens Antiquus 14:181–225.

1979a   Notes on the Nuzi Surface Measures. *In* Festschrift für Claude F. A. Schaeffer zum 80. Geburtstag am 6. März 1979. Ugarit-Forschungen, 11. K. Bergerhof, M. Dietrich, and O. Loretz, eds. Pp. 849–856. Neukirchen-Vluyn, Germany: Butzon and Bercker Kevelaer.

1979b   The Rural Landscape of the Land of Arraphe. Rome: Università di Roma.

Zahavi, A.

1975   Mate Selection—A Selection for a Handicap. Journal of Theoretical Biology 53:205–214.

Zerjal, T., Y. Xue, G. Bertorelle, R. S. Wells, W. Bao, S. Zhu, R. Qamar, Q. Ayub, A. Mohyuddin, S. Fu, P. Li, N. Yuldasheva, R. Ruzibakiev, J. Xu, Q. Shu, R. Du, H. Yang, M. E. Hurles, E. Robinson, T. Gerelsaikhan, B. Dashnyam, S. Q. Mehdi, and C. Tyler-Smith

2003   The Genetic Legacy of the Mongols. American Journal of Human Genetics 72:717–721.

Zilhao, J.

2001   Radiocarbon Evidence for Maritime Pioneer Colonization at the Origins of Farming in West Mediterranean Europe. Proceedings of the National Academy of Sciences USA 98:14180–14185.

Zimmermann, A.

1995   Austauschsysteme von Silexartefakten in der Bandkeramik Mitteleuropas. Bonn: Habelt.

2002   Landschaftsarchäologie I Die Bandkeramik auf der Aldenhovener Platte. Bericht der Römisch-Germanischen Kommission 2002:17–38.

Index

Adams, Robert McCormick, 66, 230
agent-based models: for analysis of irrigation systems and social-ecological networks, 160–63; for emergence of inequality in small-scale societies, 105–19; for interpretation of archaeological record from Oman Peninsula, 220–24; for settlement ecodynamics in southwestern Colorado, 62–63, 96–104; for social-agent behavior patterns in Mesopotamia, 195–97. *See also* model-based archaeology; models and modeling
age-specific mortality, and demographic trends in Hawai`i, 135–36
aggregation, cycles of in community centers of central Mesa Verde region, 83, 85, 102
agriculture: and co-evolutionary interactions between society and environment in Hawai`i, 123, 124, 127, 128–34, 138, 139; and ecodynamics of settlement in southwestern Colorado, 62, 64–67, 100; evolutionary models for spread of into central Europe, 141–55; landscapes and economies of northern and southern Mesopotamia, 183–88, 195, 199–206; and settlement patterns in middle Rhône Valley, 48, 51, 52, 54–55, 56; settlement patterns and social structure in Oman Peninsula, 211. *See also* food stress; gardening; irrigation systems; maize; soils
Algaze, Guillermo, 176
Anderies, John M., 9, 232
Annales school, 9
aquifers, and hydrologic system of central Mesa Verde region, 69–70, 71, 73
archaeology, as model-based science, 2–4. *See also* agent-based models; historical archaeology; model-based archaeology; models and modeling; New Archaeology

architecture, and archaeological record for ecodynamics of settlement in southwestern Colorado, 80
Argonne National Laboratory, 193
Arthur, W. B., 11
ASTER images, 186
Auyang, S. Y., 8
al-Ayn (Oman Peninsula), 219, 227n7

balanced reciprocal network (BRN), 93, 94, 96–100
Bali, irrigated rice agriculture and temple system of, 159–64, 173
ball court system, and Hohokam culture, 165, *166*, 167
barbarian invasions, of Roman Empire, 58
Barth, F., 153
basic income, 242
basketry, and cultural diversification in northwest California, 20–22, 27, 28, 30–33, 37–38, *238–40*
Baumhoff, M. A., 19
Bayman, J., 165
Benzecri, J. –P., 59n5
Berger, Jean-François, 9, 43, 230, 231
Binford, Lewis R., 11
biocomplexity: concept of, 10–12; study of in Hawai`i, 125–39
biodiversity, and degree of language diversity, 20
biogeochemical gradients, and agricultural systems in Hawai`i, 128–30, 139
Blake, M., 118
Blanchard Plaque, 2
blending models, of cultural diversification, 16–18
Blin, Olivier, 227n7
boat building, and Oman Peninsula, 220–21, 224, 227n8

Boccara, N., 5, 7, 8
Bocquet-Appel, J.-P., 145, 212
Boone, J. L., 109, 111
bootstrap analysis, 31, 34
Boserup, E., 131
Boulding, Kenneth, 10
Bourdieu, P., 103
Boyd, R., 9, 15, 17, 143, 244
"branching" processes: and evolutionary
    metaphors for cultural descent, 16–18; and
    study of cultural and linguistic diversity in
    northwest California, 30–31, 34, 36
Bronze Age: landscape change and settlement
    systems in middle Rhône Valley, 45–48, 49;
    landscapes and settlement systems of north-
    ern and southern Mesopotamia, 176,
    185–92, 198
Bryant, D., 31
Bulirsch, R. , 75
burials: and Linear Pottery Culture in central
    Europe, 151, 152, 154; settlement patterns
    and cultural evolution in Oman Peninsula,
    210, 211–12, 215, 217, 218, 219, 222,
    226, 227n11
Burns, B. T., 64

Cahto (California), 27, 31
California, and case study of cultural and linguis-
    tic diversity in northwest, 19–39
causality, and model-based analysis of ecodynam-
    ics of settlement in southwestern Colorado,
    103–104
Cavalli-Sforza, L. L., 9
cemetery populations, and demographic trends in
    central Europe, 145, 151. See also burials;
    skeletal assemblages
Central Europe, evolutionary models for spread of
    agriculture into, 141–55
Century model, of agriculture, 131
Chadwick, Oliver A., 122
Charnov, E. L., 86
chiefdoms: in Polynesian societies, 123; and
    sociopolitical development in Hawai`i, 138,
    139
Chilula (California), 25, 26, 32, 34
Chimariko (California), 26, 30–31, 34, 35, 37
Choi, Jung-Kyoo, 7, 230
chronostratigraphical context, of settlement pat-
    terns in middle Rhône Valley, 51
cladistics: basketry and cultural diversity in
    northwest California, 30, 31, 34, 35; and
    evolutionary metaphors in culture history,
    17. See also tree diagrams
Clark, J. E., 118

Cleuziou, Serge, 9, 227n5, 230
climate: of Dark Ages in Mediterranean Europe,
    56; and environmental gradients in
    Hawaiian Islands, 122, 132; and precipita-
    tion in central Europe during Linear Pottery
    Culture, 150; and seasonal use of desert in
    Oman Peninsula, 211; simulation software
    for reconstruction of Mesopotamian,
    194–95, 199–201, 207–208; and socioenvi-
    ronmental systems of middle Rhône Valley,
    43–44, 50, 51, 57; and social transforma-
    tion in Oman Peninsula, 212, 214–15, 224,
    227n3. See also drought; monsoons
ClimGen Markov chain weather generator, 194
Coale, A. J., 195
co-evolution: and human ecodynamics in
    Hawai`i, 121–39; of socioenvironmental
    systems in Rhône Valley, 41–59
cognitive science, and views of models and mod-
    eling, 2, 4
collective action, and agent-based simulations for
    emergence of social inequality, 113
colonialism, and history of California, 38
Colorado, and study of settlement ecodynamics in
    central Mesa Verde region, 61–104
Colwell, Rita, 10–11
community centers, and ecodynamics of settle-
    ment in southwestern Colorado, 63, 81–85,
    102. See also great houses
complexity: approaches to analysis of in model-
    based archaeology, 5–10; and co-evolution-
    ary interactions between society and
    environment in Hawai`i, 122–25; evolution
    of in coast desert environment of Oman
    Peninsula, 209–26; irrigation societies and
    evolution of, 159; and state dynamics, 175.
    See also biocomplexity; social organization;
    sociopolitical structure
COMPONENT 2.0, 36, 37
computers, and development of model-based
    archaeology, 4
Comte, Auguste, 230
concepts, model-based archaeology and relation-
    ship among theories, empirical research,
    and, 7–8
conformity bias, in cultural transmission, 14, 18,
    143
Connan, Jacques, 227n8
control hierarchies, and social structure in
    Hawai`i, 137–38
coping mechanisms, and food stress in
    Mesopotamia, 196–97
coral, temple offerings in Hawai`i and growth
    rates of, 137, 138

Corona images, 186, *187*
correspondence analysis, 50, 59n5
"co-speciation," and evolutionary metaphors for cultural and linguistic diversity, 17, 35
Coudart, A., 150–51
Cowan, Jason, 63, 75
Csete, M. E., 159
cultural algorithms, patterns of exchange and ecodynamics of settlement in southwestern Colorado, 89–100, 103
culture: and categories of knowledge, 89–90; and concepts of cultural core and drift, 14–15, 17; as system of social inheritance, 13–19. *See also* complexity; cultural algorithms; culture history
culture history: and Darwinian theory, 141–44; and dual-inheritance theory, 15–19; and modeling of cultural and linguistic diversification in northwest California, 19–39
cuneiform texts, and Mesopotamia, 181, 183–85, 190, 212, 222
"cybernetic" systems, 8

Dark Ages, and sociopolitical dynamics in northern Mediterranean Basin, 56
Darwinian theory, and culture history, 141–44. *See also* evolution and evolutionary biology; neo-Darwinism
Dean, J. S., 71
"decision-making biases," and cultural transmission, 143
defense: and Linear Pottery Culture in central Europe, 153; and settlement patterns in middle Rhône Valley, 50. *See also* territoriality; warfare
Demeny, P., 195
demography: and agent-based simulations for emergence of social inequality, 106–107, 111, 113; and diphtheria epidemic in Mesopotamia, 205–206, *207*; and farming societies in central Europe, 144–55; model of for Oman Peninsula, 224; and reconstruction of settlement patterns in central Mesa Verde region, 81. *See also* population
Digital Elevation Model, 215
Digital Terrain Elevation Data (DTED), 177, 187
Dinka Tepe (Iran), 181
"directly biased" transmission, 14
dispersal opportunity, and spread of farming into central Europe, 144–45
Dollé, V., 224
Dolores River (Colorado), 69
Doyle, J., 159

Dresch, P., 227n10
Driver, H., 28, 32, 33, *234, 238*
drought, and regional settlement system in central Mesa Verde region, 83, 85. *See also* climate
dual-inheritance theory, 15–19
Dugatkin, L. A., 7
Dunnell, R., 143
Dynamic Information Architecture System (DIAS), 193
dynamic software object representation, and Mesopotamian simulation domain, 193–95

Earle, T. K., 124, 180
ecodynamics: and co-evolutionary interactions between society and environment in Hawai`i, 121–39; and settlement patterns in southwestern Colorado, 61–104; use of term, 10
ecology. *See* ecodynamics; environment; social-ecological network
economics: conceptual framework for development of in Mesopotamia, 180; exchange network and ecodynamics of settlement in southwestern Colorado, 93–94. *See also* exchange; income variables; labor; political economy; production; resource use; wealth acquisition
ecosystem. *See* environment
Eel River (California), 27, 37
egalitarian societies, archaeological and ethnographic evidence for, 105. *See also* inequality
Ekren, E. B., 68
Elsasser, A. B., 22, 27
elites: and burials in Oman Peninsula, 218; and interpretations of social inequality, 118
Enkimdu (simulation engine), 192, 193, 195, 197–98, 206
environment: and agent-based simulations for emergence of social inequality, 106–107; characteristics of in middle Rhône Valley, 43–48; and co-evolutionary interactions between society and environment in Hawai`i, 121–39; description of in northwest California, 19; development of state in northern and southern Mesopotamia and dynamics of, 175–208; and evolution of complexity in Oman Peninsula, 209–26; socionatural systems and concepts of, 10. *See also* climate; ecodynamics; landscape change; paleoenvironmental data; rivers; socioenvironmental systems; wetlands
environmental determinism, 61, 109
Environmental Modeling Systems, Inc., 69

epidemic disease, and population dynamics in Mesopotamia, 205–206, *207*

Erwin, Harry, 226

ethnohistory and ethnography: and agricultural methods of Hopi and Zuni, 66; and control hierarchies in Hawai`i, 138; and power structure in Arabic tribes, 227n10

Europe. *See* Central Europe; Rhône Valley

Euphrates River (Mesopotamia), 186

Evans, J. G., 61

evolution and evolutionary biology: and culture as system of social inheritance, 13–19; and development of complexity in coast desert environment of Oman Peninsula, 209–26; differences in cultural applications of concept, 230; and models for spread of agriculture into central Europe, 141–55. *See also* co-evolution; natural selection

exchange: and cultural algorithms for ecodynamics of settlement in southwestern Colorado, 89–100, 103; and Hohokam culture as regional system, 165; Linear Pottery Culture in central Europe and networks of, 152, 154–55; and maritime trade of Oman Peninsula, 215, 217–18, 220, 223, 224–26, 227n9

exponential growth, and demographic trends in Hawai`i, 135, 136

FACET modeling framework, 195

factor analysis, 59n5

feedback: and control systems for irrigation and drainage canals, 157, 173n1; and simulated process interactions for Mesopotamia, 197–98

Feldman, M., 9, 61

Ferguson, T. J., 101

fertility rates, and demographic trends in Hawai`i, 135. *See also* reproductive rate

feudal society, emergence of in middle Rhône Valley, 50

fire history, and agricultural systems in Hawai`i, 134

fishing: cultural and linguistic diversity in northwest California, 19, 23, 27; settlement patterns and social complexity in Oman Peninsula, 211, 215, 219, 220

Foley, Robert, 102

food stress, and coping mechanisms of households in Mesopotamia, 196–97, 205, 206

Framework for Addressing Cooperative Extended Transactions (FACET), 193

Freethey, G. W., 68

fuel. *See* wood

game theory: and agent-based simulations for emergence of social inequality, 114–15; analyses of natural selection and culture in evolutionary, 143

gardening: and agricultural systems in Hawai`i, 131; and settlement patterns in Oman Peninsula, 219, 222, 223

Gasur (Iraq), 183

Gell-Mann, Murray, 230

gender. *See* men; women

generalized reciprocal network (GRN), 92–93, 94, 96–100

genetics: cultural analogues to processes of, 14–15; and "Paleolithic" or "Neolithic" genes in modern European populations, 155n1

geography, and study of linguistic and cultural diversity in northwest California, 23–28. *See also* geomorphology; hydrologic system

Geologic Modeling System (GMS), 68–69

geomorphology, and reconstruction of environment of Oman Peninsula, 215, 219

Germany, and Linear Pottery Culture, 148

Giere, R. N., 3

Goddard, I., 35–36

Gould, R. A., 26

Graves, Michael W., 127–28

Gray, R., 16

great houses, and Hohokam culture, 165. *See also* community centers

Gripp, T. L., 78

group identity, and study of cultural and linguistic diversity in northwest California, 30

Gruhle, W., 153

Gumerman, George, 231

Haleakala Volcano (Hawai`i), 126, 130

Hana Volcanic Series (Hawai`i), 126

"handicap principle," 8

Hart, E. R., 101

Hasanu (Iran), 181

Hawai`i, and co-evolutionary interactions between society and environment, 121–39

heiau. See temples

hierarchical systems analysis (HAS), 68

highly optimized tolerance (HOT), 159, 173

Hili (Oman Peninsula), 222

historical archaeology, 9–10

Hodder, Ian, 3

Hohokam, irrigation system and social-ecological network of, 159, 165–67, 172

Holling, C. S., 59

Holocene: climate and landscape changes in middle Rhône Valley during, 43, 44, 57; and late prehistory of Oman Peninsula, 209–10, 214

homologies and homoplasies, and models of culture history, 30

Hopi, and ethnohistorical data on agriculture, 66

"house count," and estimates of specific populations, 136

households: and ecodynamics of settlement in southwestern Colorado, 62, 88–89; as fundamental social group in Mesopotamian cities, 180; and social agent behavior in Mesopotamia, 195, 196–97, 203–204, 205. *See also* housing

Houseman, M., 92

Houser, R. N., 68

housing: and Linear Pottery Culture in central Europe, 148–51; settlement patterns and social complexity in Oman Peninsula, 220; and study of cultural and linguistic diversity in northwest California, 22–23, 25, 28, 33–37, 38, *234–37. See also* households

"hub nodes," and social network in central Mesa Verde region, 92, 94, 95, 98

human ecology, 10

Hunt, C. B., 68

hunting, and ecodynamics of settlement in southwestern Colorado, 62, 73–77, 86, 87, 96, 100, 101

Hupa (California), 25, 32, 35, 37

hybridization, and study of cultural and linguistic diversity in northwest California, 33, 38

hydraulic system, and settlement patterns in middle Rhône Valley, 52, 54, 56–57

hydrologic system, and ecodynamics of settlement in southwestern Colorado, 68–73

ideal despotic distribution, and spread of farming into central Europe, 145–47

income variables, and modeling of emergence of social inequality, 242

Indus civilization, and trade with Oman Peninsula, 215, 217–18, 223, 227n9

inequality: agent-based models of emergence in small-scale societies, 105–19; and Linear Pottery Culture of central Europe, 152–54. *See also* complexity; egalitarian societies; elites; social organization

inheritance mechanism, and interpretation of culture history, 141–44

Iron Age, and study of socioenvironmental systems in middle Rhône Valley, 43, 44, 46, 49, 54, 55, 57

irrigation systems: and agriculture in southern Mesopotamia, *179,* 186–88; and settlement

patterns in Oman Peninsula, 219; stylized models for analysis of emergence, robustness, and collapse of, 157–73. *See also* agriculture

island chains: and research on evolutionary radiation and speciation, 121–22; and study of cultural diversification, 18, 19

Ja'alan (Oman Peninsula), and environmental influences on evolution toward social complexity, 209–26

Jaillette, P., 55

Janssen, Marco A., 9, 231

Jeunesse, C., 151

Johnson, C. David, 63, 102

Jordan, F., 16

Jordan, Peter, 8–9, 230

Jorgensen, J. G., 20, 26–27

Kahikinui study area (Maui Island), 126–39

Kah`olawe (Hawai`i), 138

Karimat al-Manahil (Oman Peninsula), 210

Karok (California), 25, 32

Kaua`i (Hawai`i), 124

Kauffman, Stuart A., 226

Khor al-Hajar (Oman Peninsula), 215

kinship: basketry and cultural diffusion in northwest California, 37–38; household stress and agricultural production in Mesopotamia, 197; networks of and ecodynamics of settlement in southwestern Colorado, 91–93; and social organization in Oman Peninsula, 217. *See also* marriage; social organization

Kinzig, A., 42

Kirch, Patrick V., 124, 126, 131, 230

Kish (Iraq), 181

Kishino-Hasegawa test, 35, 36

Klamath River (California), 23, 34, 37

Kneipp, J., 151

knowledge, cultural evolution model and basic categories of, 89–90

Kobti, Ziad, 63–64, 86, 91, 92, 94

Kohala study area (Hawai`i), 127–39

Kohler, Timothy A., 9, 63, 64, 85, 91, 92, 94, 226, 229, 230, 231

Kolm, Kenneth E., 63

Kremer, J. S., 160, 161, 163, 232

Kroeber, A. L., 22, 23, 25, 27, 30, 35

Kula Volcanic Series (Hawai`i), 126

Kuni Volcanic Series (Hawai`i), 126

labor: allocation of in multiple resource systems, 164; and costs of territorial defense, 243; household stress and agricultural production

in Mesopotamia, 197, 202–205, 206; and
models of extensive and intensive food production, 168–72
Ladefoged, Thegn N., 127–28
Lagash (Mesopotamia), 184
Laland, K. N., 61
Lana`i (Hawai`i), 138
Lancaster, F. & W., 227n10
landscape change: and agriculture in northern
and southern Mesopotamia, 185–88; component processes of in middle Rhône Valley,
44–45; and settlement patterns in middle
Rhône Valley, 48–49, 52, 53; and simula-
tion framework for northern Mesopotamia,
192–98, 206. See also environment
Lansing, J. S., 160, 161, 163, 173n2, 232
Late Antiquity, and climate change in middle
Rhône Valley, 43
LeBlanc, S. A., 2–3
Levins, Richard, 7
Linear Pottery Culture (central Europe), 145,
147–55
linguistics: and cultural diversification in northwest California, 19–39; and evolutionary
metaphors for diversification of languages,
15–16, 17
Little Ice Age, and middle Rhône Valley, 43, 44,
58
Lloyd, E. A., 3
Lowry Ruin (Colorado), 71, 72–73

MacClade 4.03, 35
Maekawa, K., 184
maize, and ecodynamics of settlement in southwestern Colorado, 64–67, 86, 94–95, 101
Managerial Mutualism (MM), and emergence of
social inequality, 105, 106, *108*, 111–16,
117, 118, 241, 242, 243–44
Mantel Matrix tests, 32–33, *36*, 37
Marginal Value Theorem, 86, 87
marriage, and study of cultural and linguistic
diversity in northwest California, 25, 26,
27–28, 33
material culture, and patterns of linguistic diversity in northwest California, 30
mathematical model, of hydrologic system of
central Mesa Verde region, 70–73
Mattole (California), 27, 32
Maui (Hawai`i), 124, 125, 126, 137, 138, 139
McGlade, J., 5, 10, 42
Mediterranean morpho- and bioclimatic systems,
43
men, and housing construction in northwest
California, 23, 38

Mervis, J., 11
Mesa Verde region, study of settlement eco-
dynamics in prehispanic, 61–104
Mesolithic era, and population densities in central Europe, 145
Mesopotamia: environmental dynamics of settlement patterns and development of state in
northern and southern, 175–208; and "Land
of Magan" (Oman Peninsula), 212, 217, 222
Middle Ages: and climate change in middle
Rhône Valley, 43; and study of landscape
change and settlement systems in middle
Rhône Valley, 45–48, 49, 50, 55, 58
Miller, Harold V., 10
Minoan peer polities, and modeling of complex
systems, 226
model-based archaeology (mba): and agent-based
simulations of inequality in small-scale
societies, 105–19; and analysis of robustness of irrigation systems, 157–73; and co-
evolutionary interactions between society
and environment in Hawai`i, 121–39; and
complexity in coastal desert environment
of Oman Peninsula, 209–26; cultural and
linguistic diversification in northwest
California, 19–39; and dealing with complexity, 5–10; and ecodynamics of settlement in southwestern Colorado, 61–104;
and environmental influences on comparative development of state in northern and
southern Mesopotamia, 175–208; evolutionary theory and spread of agriculture into
central Europe, 141–55; and relationship
among concepts, theories, and empirical
research, 7–8; and resilience in socioenvironmental co-evolution in Rhône Valley,
41–59; and use of term, 12n1. *See also*
agent-based models; models and modeling
models and modeling: advantages of formal, 6–7;
cognitive science and, 2, 4; definition of,
3–4; recent progress in cultural, 229–32.
See also agent-based models; model-based
archaeology
MODFLOW model, 70
monsoons, and Oman Peninsula, 214–15
monumentality, and burials in Oman Peninsula,
217, 227n11
mortality rates: and demographic trends in
Hawai`i, 135–36; and epidemic disease in
Mesopotamia, 205–206; and parameter
values for modeling of emergence of social
inequality, 242
Moulton, V., 31
Muenchrath, D. A., 66

multidisciplinary research, and advantages of formal models, 6–7
Munoz, Olivia, 219
Murphy, R. F., 11
mutations: cultural equivalents of genetic, 14; and parameter values for modeling of emergence of social inequality, 242

Na-Dene (Athapaskan) languages, in northwest California, 20, 25, 26–27, 28, 33, 34
Nagar (Mesopotamia), 177
National Center for Atmospheric Research, 194
National Climatic Data Center, 71
natural selection: cultural analogues for, 14; Darwinian theory and interpretation of culture history, 142–43; and population processes, 144
NeighborNet plots, 31, *32*, 33, 34, 35
neo-Darwinism, and cultural inheritance, 13
Neolithic period: and climate change in middle Rhône Valley, 43, 45; and decline of Linear Pottery Culture in central Europe, 154
Netherlands, and Linear Pottery Culture, 148, 150
net income, 242
net primary productivity (NPP), 74, 76–77
networks: agent-based models and analysis of irrigation system performance, 160–63; and biological evolutionary metaphors for culture history, 16–17, 31; and cultural algorithms for ecodynamics of settlement in southwestern Colorado, 89–100, 103. *See also* social networks
New Archaeology, and model-based archaeology, 3
New Guinea, and defense systems in Faiwolmin communities, 153
"niche construction," 61
nodes, and small-world networks in central Mesa Verde region, 92, 94, *95*, 98
Nongatl (California), 25
Northern Illinois University, 126
Nuzi (Iraq), 183–84

Oʻahu (Hawaiʻi), 124
oasis sites, and settlement patterns in Oman Peninsula, 219, 223
Odling-Smee, F. J., 61
Oman Peninsula, and environmental influences on evolution of social complexity, 209–26
oral traditions, and control hierarchies in Hawaiʻi, 138
organic systems, and complexity in model-based archaeology, 8

Oriental Institute, 188
Ortman, Scott G., 63, 78, 79–80

Page, R., 36
paleobotany, and settlement patterns in middle Rhône Valley, 51–52. *See also* pollen analysis; vegetation
paleoenvironmental data, for Dark Ages in Mediterranean Europe, 56
Paleolithic, and genetics of modern European populations, 155n1
Palmer Drought Severity Index (PDSI), 64, 65
parameter values, for modeling of emergence of social inequality, 241–44
pastoral societies: and climatic changes in middle Rhône Valley, 57; and social agent behavior patterns in Mesopotamia, 195–96
patch defense, and resource control, 109
Patron-Client (PC) scenario, for emergence of social inequality, 106, *107*, 109–11, *112*, 118, 241, 243
Paup 4.0b10, 36, 37
payoffs, and agent-based models, 114
Petrasch, J., 145
phylogenetic model, of long-term cultural evolution, 38
physical systems, and complexity in model-based archaeology, 8
phytolith assemblages, and agricultural systems in Hawaiʻi, 134
Pilling, A. J., 25
platform mounds, and Hohokam regional system, 165, *166*
political economy, and agent-based simulations for emergence of social inequality, 109–11
political organization, and hierarchy in Oman Peninsula, 223. *See also* chiefdoms; sociopolitical structure; state
pollen analysis, and agricultural systems in Hawaiʻi, 134. *See also* paleobotany; vegetation
Polynesia: and chiefdoms, 123; and study of cultural diversification, 18, 19. *See also* Hawaiʻi
population: of community centers in central Mesa Verde region, 82, 83–85; and co-evolutionary interactions between society and environment in Hawaiʻi, 123, 135–37; and epidemic disease in Mesopotamia, 205–206, *207*; estimate of for central Mesa Verde region, 80–81, 99, 100–102, 103; ideal despotic distribution concept and ecology of, 146; and models of extensive and intensive food production, 171–72; and parameter values for modeling emergence of social

inequality, 241–42; and resource portfolio of Hohokam, 167, 172; and settlement patterns in Oman Peninsula, 212, 219, 226; and settlement patterns in southern Mesopotamia, 190–91; size of and concept of cultural drift, 15. *See also* demography

pottery, and ecodynamics of settlement in southwestern Colorado, 80. *See also* Linear Pottery Culture

precipitation. *See* climate; drought; monsoons

precision, and models of complex systems, 7

prestige-driven diffusion, in northwest California, 38

production: and basketry in northwest California, 22, 33; model of extensive and intensive for food, 168–72

property rights, and study of cultural and linguistic diversity in northwest California, 25

protein exchange, and social networks in central Mesa Verde region, 94–95, 100, 101

public goods game, and collective action, 113

Ra's al-Hadd (Oman Peninsula), 211, 214, 215, 217, 223

Ra's al-Hamra (Oman Peninsula), 210

Ra's al-Jinz (Oman Peninsula), 217, 219, 220–22

realism, and models of complex systems, 7

Redman, C. L., 2–3, 42

Redwood Creek drainage (California), 26

regional system, Hohokam culture as, 165

religion. *See* temples

reproductive rate, and parameter values for modeling emergence of social inequality, 241–42. *See also* fertility rates

"reproductive skew," dynamics in models of, 116

resilience, and co-evolution of socioenvironmental systems in Rhône Valley, 41–59

resource use: and agent-based simulations for emergence of social inequality, 109; and balancing of multiple resource systems, 164; and ecodynamics of settlement in southwestern Colorado, 64–78, 85–89; and ecodynamics of sociopolitical structure in Hawai`i, 123; intensification of in Oman Peninsula, 212; and models of extensive and intensive food production, 168–72. *See also* agriculture; fishing; food stress; hunting

Reynolds, Robert G., 63–64, 86, 91, 92, 94, 231

Rhône Valley, and role of resilience in co-evolution of socioenvironmental systems, 41–59

Richerson, P. J., 9, 15, 143

ritual. *See* monumentality; temples; tower tombs

rivers: and study of cultural and linguistic diversity in northwest California, 19, 23, 25, 27; and transport networks in Mesopotamia, 178. *See also* wetlands

Roman period: and mortality data from Mesopotamia, 181; and socioenvironmental change in middle Rhône Valley, 43, 44, 47–48, 49, 53, 54–55, 56–57, 58

route systems, and settlement patterns in Mesopotamia, 177–78

Ru'b al-Khali Desert (Oman Peninsula), 210

Rück, O., 153

Sahlins, M., 93, 126

Salmon, M. H., 4

Sand Canyon Pueblo (Colorado), 71, 72, 73

Santa Fe Institute (SFI), 229–30

Saxe-Goldstein model, 151

scale, of irrigation systems, 158–59

Schmidt, B., 153

School for Advanced Research (SAR), 229–30

Schrage, L., 36

Schwartz, Douglas, 229

seasonality, and settlement patterns in Oman Peninsula, 210–11

sedentism: and movement of households in prehispanic southwestern Colorado, 88–89; and study of cultural and linguistic diversity in northwest California, 23

settlement systems: and ecodynamics in southwestern Colorado, 61–104; and environmental change in middle Rhône Valley, 45–59; and environmental influences on comparative development of state in northern and southern Mesopotamia, 175–208. *See also* community centers; sedentism

Shanks, M., 64

Sharjah, Emirate of (Oman Peninsula), 210

Shennan, Stephen J., 8–9, 230

Shuttle Radar Topography Mission (SRTM), 178, *187*

Silver, S., 35

similarity matrix, 32–33

simulation framework, and landscape of northern Mesopotamia, 192–98

Sinkyone (California), 27, 31

skeletal assemblages, and demographic trends in Hawai`i, 135–36. *See also* burials; cemetery populations

small-world social network, 92–93

Smith, Eric Alden, 7, 20, 230

Smith River (California), 26

social-ecological network, and analysis of emergence, performance, and collapse of irrigation systems, 159, 163–67

social inheritance, culture as system of, 13–19

social networks, and ecodynamics of settlement in southwestern Colorado, 90–95

social organization: and co-evolutionary interactions between society and environment in Hawaiʻi, 137–38; dynamic interplay between shifting vulnerabilities and changes in, 172; and modeling of dynamic environments and state development in Mesopotamia, 195–97, 201–207; social differentiation and spread of farming into central Europe, 151, 152–54. *See also* complexity; elites; kinship; social networks; sociopolitical structure

social "unit of analysis," and study of cultural and linguistic diversity in northwest California, 28

socioenvironmental systems, role of resilience in co-evolution of in Rhône Valley, 41–59

"socionatural," use of term, 10

sociopolitical structure, and Hawaiʻi as model for co-evolutionary interactions between people and environment, 121–39. *See also* chiefdoms; complexity; political organization; social organization; state

soils: and agricultural systems in Hawaiian Islands, 128–30; average productivity of classes in southwestern Colorado, 65–66, 74, 76–77; and irrigation in southern Mesopotamia, 186, 188; and landscape change in middle Rhône Valley, 45, 50

Southwest (U.S.). *See* Hohokam; Hopi; Mesa Verde region; Zuni

species, as conceptual model in culture history, 16–17

"speech community," and study of cultural and linguistic diversity in northwest California, 28

Spielmann, K. A., 100

spring discharge fluctuations, and hydrologic system of central Mesa Verde region, 70–73

state: environmental dynamics and comparative development of in northern and southern Mesopotamia, 175–208; Hawaiʻi as model system for study of archaic, 123, 124, 137, 138, 139. *See also* political organization; sociopolitical structure

steady-state simulation, and mathematical model of hydrologic system of central Mesa Verde, 70–73

Steward, Julian, 11

Stoer, J., 75

stream alluvium, and hydrologic system of central Mesa Verde region, 69–70

strontium isotope analyses, and Linear Pottery Culture of central Europe, 152

subaks. See Bali

Suppe, F., 3, 4

as-Suwayh (Oman Peninsula), 210

SWAT simulator, 194

Tell Beydar (Syria), 183, 188–93, 198–208

temples: and control hierarchies in Hawaiʻi, 123, 137–38; and irrigated rice agriculture in Bali, 159–64, 173

territoriality: and ideal despotic distribution in demographic growth models, 146–47; and parameter values for modeling emergence of social inequality, 243; and settlement boundaries in southern Mesopotamia, 188. *See also* defense; warfare

theory, model-based archaeology and relationship among concepts, empirical research, and, 7–8

Thomas, B. E., 68

Thompson, M., 59

Tilley, C., 64

Tolowa (California), 25, 26, 32, 34

tomb towers, in Oman Peninsula, 211–12, 217, 222, 227n2, 227n5

Toutain, G., 224

transport networks, and settlement patterns in southern Mesopotamia, 178

tree diagrams: and evolutionary metaphors in culture history, 16; and study of cultural and linguistic diversity in northwest California, 29, 30–31, 35–37. *See also* cladistics

tribelets, and study of cultural and linguistic diversity in northwest California, 27, 28

Tricastin Plain (Rhône Valley), 43, 46–47, 48, 51

Trinity River (California), 25, 26, 32

Umm an-Nar (Oman Peninsula), 217

United Arab Emirates. *See* Oman Peninsula

University of California at Berkeley, 126

urbanization, in Bronze Age Mesopotamia, 176, 181

Valdaine Basin (Rhône Valley), 43, 46–47, 48

van der Leeuw, Sander E., 5, 42, 229, 230

van der Velde, P., 148, 149–50, 151, 152, 154

Van West, C. R., 64, 67, 71, 85

Varien, Mark D., 63, 78, 81, 99

vegetation, agricultural effects on natural in Hawaiʻi, 134. *See also* paleobotany; pollen analysis

Village Ecodynamics Project (Colorado), 78–85, 103

viticulture, in middle Rhône Valley, 48, 51

Vitousek, Peter M., 122

Wadi al-Batha (Oman Peninsula), 213–14, 223
Wadi Sal (Oman Peninsula), 219
Wadi Sûq period (Oman Peninsula), 218
Wallace, E., 22
warfare: and Linear Pottery Culture in central Europe, 153; and settlement patterns in central Mesa Verde region, 85; and sociopolitical structure of Hawai`i, 123, 136, 137. *See also* defense; territoriality
water sources, and ecodynamics of settlement in southwestern Colorado, 62, 68–73, 86–88. *See also* irrigation systems; rivers; wetlands
Watson, P. J., 2–3
wealth acquisition: and modeling of economies of northern and southern Mesopotamia, 180; and study of cultural and linguistic diversity in northwest California, 25, 26, 27, 38. *See also* economics
Weigel, J. F., 68
Welsch, R. L., 19
West, Geoff, 230
wetlands: marshes and economy of southern Mesopotamia, 187; lagoons and mangrove swamps of Oman Peninsula, 214, 224. *See also* rivers
White, D., 92
White, Leslie, 11
Whitfield, M. S., 68
Wilkinson, Tony J., 7, 9, 10
Witkind, I. J., 68
Wiyot (California), 25, 26, 34
women, and production of baskets in northwest California, 22, 33
wood, and ecodynamics of settlement in southwestern Colorado, 62, 73–74, 78, 86–88. *See also* boat building; housing

Yap, Lorene, 64
Yellow Jacket Pueblo (Colorado), 72, 82
Yurok (California), 23, 25, 26, 27, 32

Zaccagnini, C., 183
Zahavi, A., 8
Zimmermann, A., 151–52
Zuni, and ethnohistorical information: on agricultural methods, 66; on traditional hunting areas, 101

www.ingramcontent.com/pod-product-compliance
Lightning Source LLC
Chambersburg PA
CBHW080130270326
41926CB00021B/4415